free alpine trails, very long days (light until after 21:00), and the busiest schedule of tourist fun. In late May, June, September, and early October, travelers enjoy fewer crowds, milder weather, and the ability to grab a room almost whenever and wherever they like.

During the *Zwischenzeit* ("between time," that is, between summer and ski seasons, roughly April, early May, late Oct, and Nov), the cities are pleasantly uncrowded—but the weather can be iffy, and resort towns such as Zermatt and Mürren are completely dead (with most hotels and restaurants closed).

During ski season (Dec–March), mountain resorts are crowded and expensive, while cities are quieter (some accommodations and sights are either closed or run on a limited schedule). The weather can be cold and dreary, and night will draw the shades on your sightseeing before dinnertime. You may find the climate chart in the appendix helpful. Pack warm clothing for the Alps, no matter when you go.

Sightseeing Priorities

Depending on the length of your trip, here are my recommended priorities. Assuming you're traveling by train, I've taken geographical proximity and transportation connections into account.

3 days:	Berner Oberland
5 days, add:	Luzern
7 days, add:	Bern and Lausanne, connecting with Golden Pass scenic rail journey
10 days, add:	Zermatt and Appenzell, linking with Glacier Express train
14 days, add:	Lugano and Pontresina area, connecting with Bernina Express and William Tell Express train rides
16 days, add:	Zürich and Murten
21 days, add:	More day trips (central Switzerland, French Swiss countryside), more hikes, and time to slow down

The map on page 7 and the two-week itinerary on page 6 include everything listed here (except Murten), plus modifications for a longer or shorter trip.

Travel Smart

Your trip is like a complex play—easier to follow and really appreciate on a second viewing. While no one does the same trip twice to gain that advantage, reading this book before your trip accomplishes much the same thing.

Design an itinerary that enables you to visit the various sights at the best possible times. As you read this book, make note of festivals, colorful market days, and the days sights are closed. Many sights are closed on Monday (head for the hills).

Switzerland's Best Two-Week Trip by Train

Day	Plan	Sleep in
1	Arrive Zürich Airport, head to Appenzell	Appenzell or Ebenalp
2	All day for Appenzell and Ebenalp	Appenzell or Ebenalp
3	Leave early for Luzern	Luzern
4	Luzern	Luzern
5	William Tell Express to Lugano	Lugano
6	Bernina Express to Pontresina area	Pontresina
7	Pontresina area (St. Moritz, Samedan, lifts and hikes)	Pontresina
8	Take Glacier Express; if good weather, head for Zermatt; if bad weather, consider going straight to Lausanne (see below)	Zermatt
9	Zermatt, Matterhorn-view lifts	Zermatt and hikes
10	If good weather, spend more time in Zermatt, go late to Lausanne; if bad weather, leave early for Lausanne	Lausanne
11	Take the Golden Pass to the Berner Oberland. If good weather, go early; if bad weather, linger in Lausanne/Lake Geneva area and leave late	Berner Oberland (Gimmelwald or Mürren)
12	All day for lifts and hikes in the Berner Oberland	Gimmelwald or Mürren
13	More time in the Berner Oberland	Gimmelwald or Mürren
14	Early to Bern, then on to Zürich	Zürich
15	More time in Zürich, or fly home	

Zermatt isn't worth the trip in bad weather. If your reservations are flexible, consider skipping that leg and going straight to Lausanne (take the Glacier Express only to Visp, then change for Lausanne). If you have extra time in Switzerland, I'd suggest spending it in (listed in order of priority): Murten and Bern, Zürich, Lausanne and the Lake Geneva area, Lugano (relaxing) or the Luzern area (day trips). For a short trip of a week or so, I'd just focus on the Berner Oberland, Luzern, and Bern. (If you're wondering whether to focus on the Berner Oberland or the more famous Zermatt/Matterhorn region, see the sidebar on page 171.)

Railpass: The best railpass for this itinerary is a 15-consecutive-day Swiss Pass ($336 second class, $504 first class, 15 percent less for 2 or more traveling together; confirm latest prices at www.ricksteves.com/rail; figure an additional $100 total in reservation fees for all the scenic rail journeys). While this pass doesn't cover mountain lifts, it does earn you a 50 percent discount on most of them.

By Car: While this itinerary is designed to be done by public transportation, it can be done by car with a few modifications. Obviously, you won't take the scenic rail trips. Instead, drive from Appenzell straight to the Pontresina area, then continue through Tirano and on to Lugano (via Lake Como in Italy). From Lugano, drive to Zermatt (crossing again through Italy) and resume the above itinerary, visiting Luzern at the very end before returning to Zürich. The French Swiss countryside and the area around Murten merit more time if you have a car.

Beyond Switzerland: Switzerland, right in the middle of Western Europe, splices neatly into a multi-country trip by car or train. For instance, the Appenzell region is a likely gateway to Germany's Bavaria or Austria's Tirol (Innsbruck). Italy's Lake Como is a stone's throw from Lugano or Ticino (in fact, the Bernina Express bus drives right alongside it)—and Milan is not much farther. If you're in Lausanne, you're literally looking at France (across Lake Geneva)—a handy train ride whisks you to Lyon or Chamonix. And big Swiss cities are efficiently connected via night trains and fast day trains to destinations in all of these countries and beyond.

Saturdays in Europe are virtually weekdays with earlier closing hours. Sundays have the same pros and cons as they do for travelers in the US: Sightseeing attractions are generally open; shops, banks, and markets are closed; public-transportation options are fewer; and city traffic is light. Popular places are even more popular on weekends—especially sunny weekends. Rowdy evenings are rare on Sundays.

To give yourself a little rootedness, minimize one-night stands. It's worth a long drive (or train ride) after dinner to be settled into a town for two nights. People renting private rooms are also more likely to give a good price to someone staying more than one night.

Be sure to mix intense and relaxed periods in your itinerary. Every trip (and every traveler) needs at least a few slack days. Pace yourself. Assume you will return.

Perhaps more than anywhere else in Europe, weather plays a huge factor in your sightseeing in Switzerland. The mountains are stunning—if it's not raining. But bad weather needn't ruin a trip. Switzerland has plenty of rainy-weather options. And it's so small and has such a slick train network that you can easily double-back later in your trip to visit the mountaintop hideaway that was clouded over your first time through.

Be flexible. For maximum spontaneity, consider traveling without room reservations (realizing that this comes with some risk). For example, you might plan on three days split between the city of Bern and the mountainous Berner Oberland region. If it's raining as you approach the area, head for Bern. If it's sunny, make a beeline for the mountains, then hit Bern on your way out of the area. To help you decide, tune into TV stations and websites that show the weather in various parts of the country. Many high-altitude observation decks come with 24-hour cameras that pan slowly back and forth, showing you exactly what you'll see when you get up top (for example, www.swisspanorama.com for the Berner Oberland, www.zermatt.ch for Zermatt).

Reread this book as you travel, and visit local tourist information offices. Upon arrival in a new town, lay the groundwork for a smooth departure; write down the schedule for the train, bus, or boat you'll take when you depart.

Plan ahead for banking, laundry, picnics, and Internet stops. Get online at Internet cafés or your hotel to research transportation connections, confirm events, check the weather, and get directions to your next hotel. Buy a phone card (or carry a mobile phone) and use it for reservations, re-confirmations, and double-checking hours—most Swiss people who work with tourists speak some English.

Connect with the culture. Enjoy the hospitality of the Swiss

Budget Tips

Switzerland is pricey, but there are ways to stretch your dollars. For example, many expensive alpine lifts offer discounted "early bird" tickets for the first trip of the day. Train trips get cheaper when you choose the right railpass (see all the deals on page 294); the Swiss Pass not only covers trains, but also many museums (see below). Cut down on restaurant costs by having scenic picnics and seeking out self-service cafeterias (often attached to department or grocery stores), which offer delicious food at a fraction of the cost of dining out.

Save on Sightseeing with the Swiss Pass

The Swiss Pass railpass—offering consecutive-day or flexi-day coverage of Switzerland's trains, boats, and buses, and a 50 percent discount on lifts—also covers admission to more than 400 Swiss museums. This is a swinging deal for most travelers.

You can use your Swiss Pass to cover museum admission only during its validity period. For a consecutive-day pass, that means from the day you activate your pass (that is, use it for the first time) until the last day it's valid for travel. If you have a flexipass, visiting a museum uses up a day of your pass—to get the most out of your pass, use it for a museum either on the same day you arrive at that destination or on the day you depart. Unlike flexipasses for most other countries, the validity of a Swiss flexipass ends with your last used-up travel day; for more information, see "Transportation" in the appendix.

The following sights, which are covered in this book, are free with the pass (for a full list of covered museums, see www.museumspass.ch):

Zürich—Swiss National Museum and Rietberg Museum.

Luzern—Rosengart Collection, Picasso Museum, Depot History Museum, Bourbaki Panorama, Glacier Garden, Alpineum, Swiss Transport Museum, Richard Wagner Museum, Museum of Art Luzern, and the Museum of Natural History, plus Fortress Fürigen Museum nearby.

Bern—Museum of Fine Arts and Paul Klee Center.

Near Murten—Roman Museum in Avenches.

Near Interlaken—Swiss Open-Air Folk Museum at Ballenberg.

Zermatt—Matterhorn Museum.

Appenzell Region—Appenzell Museum and folk museums in Stein and Urnäsch.

Lausanne—Collection de l'Art Brut, Olympic Museum, and City History Museum.

Lake Geneva Region—Château de Chillon.

French Swiss Countryside—Castle and H. R. Giger Museum in Gruyères.

people. Slow down and ask questions—most locals are eager to point you toward their idea of the right direction. Keep a notepad in your pocket for organizing your thoughts. Wear your money belt, familiarize yourself with the currency, and practice the virtue of simplicity. Those who expect to travel smart, do.

PRACTICALITIES

Red Tape: You need a passport—but no visa or shots—to travel in Switzerland. Your passport should be valid for at least six months beyond the time you leave Europe. Pack a photocopy of your passport in your luggage in case the original is lost or stolen.

Borders: While Switzerland isn't in the European Union, its citizens recently voted to join the Schengen Zone—which means border controls may be gone in time for your visit. Either way, remember that when you change countries, you must also change phone cards, stamps, and *Unterhosen.*

Time: In Switzerland—and in this book—you'll use the 24-hour clock. It's the same through 12:00 noon, then keep going—13:00, 14:00, and so on. For anything after 12, subtract 12 and add p.m. (14:00 is 2:00 p.m.)

Switzerland is generally six/nine hours ahead of the East/West Coasts of the US. The exceptions are the beginning and end of Daylight Saving Time: Europe "springs forward" the last Sunday in March (two weeks after most of North America) and "falls back" the last Sunday in October (one week before North America). For a handy online time converter, try www.timeanddate.com/worldclock.

Business Hours: Swiss shops are generally open Monday through Friday 9:00–18:30, Saturday 8:00–16:00, and closed Sunday. They are often open later on Thursdays; smaller shops often close at lunchtime.

Medical Help: If you get sick, do as the locals do and go to a pharmacist. They can help you with almost any ailment. If you need in-depth attention, ask your hotelier for the nearest hospital.

Watt's Up? Europe's electrical system is different from North America's in two ways: the shape of the plug (two round prongs) and the voltage of the current (220 volts instead of 110 volts). For your North American plug to work in Europe, you'll need an adapter, sold inexpensively at travel stores in the US. As for the voltage, most newer electronics or travel appliances (such as hair dryers, laptops, and battery chargers) automatically convert the voltage—if you see a range of voltages printed on the item or its plug (such as "110–220"), it'll work in Europe. Otherwise, you can buy a converter separately in the US (about $20).

Just the FAQs, Please

Whom do I call in case of emergency?
Dial 144 for medical emergencies and 117 for police.

What if my credit card is stolen?
Act immediately. See "Damage Control for Lost Cards," page 283, for instructions.

How do I make a phone call to, within, and from Switzerland?
For detailed dialing instructions, refer to page 290.

How can I get tourist information about my destination?
Switzerland has a national tourist information office in the US (see page 279) and branch offices in virtually every city and town covered in this book. Note that Tourist Information is abbreviated **TI** in this book.

What's the best way to pack?
Light. For a recommended packing list, see page 307.

Does Rick have other resources that could help me?
For more on Rick's guidebooks, public television series, free audiotours, public radio show, website, guided tours, travel bags, accessories, and railpasses, see page 280.

Are there any updates to this guidebook?
Check www.ricksteves.com/update for changes to the most recent edition of this book.

Can you recommend any good books or movies for my trip?
For suggestions, see pages 282–283.

Do you have information on driving, train travel, and flights?
See pages 291–300 in the appendix.

How much do I tip?
Relatively little. For tips on tipping, see page 283.

Will I get a student or senior discount?
While discounts are not listed in this book, youths (under 18) and students (with International Student Identity Cards) often get discounts—but only by asking.

How can I get a VAT refund on major purchases?
See the details on page 284.

Does Switzerland use the metric system?
Yes. A liter is about a quart, four to a gallon. A kilometer is six-tenths of a mile. I figure kilometers to miles by cutting them in half and adding back 10 percent of the original (120 km: 60 + 12 = 72 miles, 300 km: 150 + 30 = 180 miles). For more metric conversions, see page 304.

News: Americans keep in touch in Europe with the *International Herald Tribune* (published almost daily via satellite throughout Europe). Every Tuesday, the European editions of *Time* and *Newsweek* hit the stands with articles of particular interest to travelers. Sports addicts can get their fix from *USA Today*. News in English will be sold only where there's enough demand: in big cities and tourist centers. Good websites include www.europeantimes.com and http://news.bbc.co.uk. Many hotels have CNN or BBC television channels available.

MONEY

Banking

Throughout Europe, cash machines (ATMs) are the standard way for travelers to get local currency. Bring plastic—credit and debit cards—along with several hundred dollars in hard cash as an emergency backup. It's smart to bring two cards, in case one gets demagnetized or eaten by a temperamental machine. Traveler's checks are a waste of time (long waits at slow banks) and a waste of money (in fees).

Cash from ATMs

To use a cash machine to withdraw money from your account, you'll need a debit card (ideally with a Visa or MasterCard logo

---

Exchange Rates

I've priced things throughout this book in the local currency. Switzerland, which isn't a member of the European Union, has retained its traditional currency, the Swiss franc.

**1 Swiss franc (SF) = about 90 cents,
and 1.10 SF = about $1.**

One Swiss franc is broken down into 100 rappen (or centimes, in French Switzerland). To roughly convert prices from Swiss francs into dollars, subtract about one-tenth (for example, 50 SF = about $45). For the sake of simplicity, think of a Swiss franc as the same as a dollar; doing so will make getting your credit-card bill a happy (or at least less frightening) experience. There are coins for one, two, and five francs, plus several coins for very small denominations of rappen. The small coin with real value is the 50-rappen (marked with 1/2 rather than 50—worth about 45 cents). In a handful of change, it's easy to identify as the only one with ridges.

Why No Swiss Euros?

You can't help but wonder why the efficient Swiss are stubbornly hanging on to their old franc while surrounded by countries basking in the ease and convenience of the euro. The answer is simple: It's too expensive for the Swiss to change. The Swiss enjoy lower mortgage interest rates and a more stable currency than the rest of Europe. But even more importantly, a huge part of the Swiss economy is based on providing a safe and secret place for wealthy people from around the world to stash their money. When bank fees are figured in, people who "save" in Swiss banks actually earn negative interest—they *pay* the Swiss to keep their money. Compliance with European Union regulations in order to join the euro zone would mean the end of Switzerland's secret banking industry. The Swiss are not inclined to deal such a devastating blow to their economy.

But even though Switzerland hasn't officially adopted the euro, the majority of Swiss hotels, restaurants, and shops (especially in touristy areas) accept smaller euro bills. Most businesses will not take euro coins or larger bills, and you'll usually get bad rates (and your change in Swiss francs). Many coin-operated phone booths even accept euros (marked with a big yellow €). If you're just passing through the country, never fear: Your euros will work. But if you're staying a while, get some Swiss francs—you'll save money, and they're prettier.

---

for maximum usability), plus a PIN code. Know your PIN code in numbers; there are only numbers—no letters—on European keypads.

Before you go, verify with your bank that your card will work overseas, and alert them that you'll be making withdrawals in Europe; otherwise, the bank may not approve transactions if it perceives unusual spending patterns. Using your credit and debit card in Europe—whether for ATM withdrawals or purchases—can cost you additional "international transaction" fees (of up to 3 percent plus $5 per transaction), so it makes sense to ask your bank or credit-card company about these fees to avoid unpleasant surprises.

The German word for "cash machine" is *Bankomat* or *Geldautomat*. When using a cash machine, try to take out large sums of money to reduce your per-transaction bank fees: Push the "other amount" button and ask for a higher amount (though this is not always possible). If the machine refuses your request, don't take it personally. Just try again and select a smaller amount. Note that many cash machines don't issue receipts for your transactions.

Bank machines often dispense high-denomination bills, which can be difficult to break (especially at odd hours). My strategy: Request an odd amount of money from the ATM (such as 280 SF instead of 300 SF); or, if that doesn't work, go as soon as possible to a bank or a large store (such as a supermarket) to break the big bills.

In case you need a bank in Switzerland, they're generally open Monday through Friday from 8:00 to 17:00. Post offices (business hours) and train stations (long hours) usually change money if you can't get to a bank.

Keep your cash safe. Thieves target tourists, even in safe Switzerland. Use a money belt—a pouch with a strap that you buckle around your waist like a belt, and wear under your clothes. A money belt provides peace of mind, allowing you to carry lots of cash safely. Don't waste time every few days tracking down a cash machine—withdraw a week's worth of money, stuff it in your money belt, and travel!

Credit and Debit Cards

For purchases, Visa and MasterCard are more commonly accepted than American Express. Just like at home, credit or debit cards work easily at larger hotels, shops, and restaurants (though smaller businesses prefer payment in cash). Note that some receipts show your credit-card number; don't toss these thoughtlessly.

SIGHTSEEING

Sightseeing can be hard work. If you're spending time in urban Switzerland, use these tips to make your museum visits meaningful, fun, fast, and painless.

Plan Ahead: Set up an itinerary that allows you to fit in all your must-see sights. If you have your heart set on a particular sight, it's always smart to confirm the latest hours at the local TI.

Don't put off visiting a must-see sight—you never know when a place will close unexpectedly for a holiday, strike, or restoration. If you'll be visiting during a holiday, find out if a particular sight will be open by phoning ahead or visiting its website. Keep in mind, too, that opening times can change without warning.

When possible, visit key sights and museums first thing (when your energy is best) and save other activities for the afternoon. Hit the highlights first, then go back to other things if you have the stamina and time.

At the Sight: All sights have rules, and if you know about these in advance, they're no big deal.

Museums often require you to check daypacks and coats, usually for free. The checkrooms are generally safe, but if you have something you can't bear to part with, stash it in a pocket or purse. If you don't want to check a small backpack, carry it under your arm like a purse as you enter. From a guard's point of view, a backpack is generally a problem, while a purse is not.

Cameras and video cameras are normally allowed, but not flashes or tripods (without special permission). Flashes damage oil paintings and distract others in the room. Even without a flash, a handheld camera will take a decent picture (or buy postcards or posters at the museum bookstore). It's also common for a museum to generally allow photography but prohibit it for special exhibits—look for signs.

If sights have special exhibits in addition to their permanent collection, the exhibits may be included in the normal entry price or may require a separate ticket. Be aware that some museums bump up the normal entry fee when there's a special exhibit on (in that case you have to pay even if you don't want to see the exhibit).

Many sights rent audioguides, which generally offer excellent recorded descriptions of the exhibits. If you bring along your own pair of headphones and a Y-jack, two people can sometimes share one audioguide and save. Guided tours (widely ranging in quality) are most likely to occur during peak season.

Expect changes—pieces can be on tour, on loan, out sick, or shifted at the whim of the curator. To adapt, pick up any available free floor plans as you enter, and ask museum staff if you can't find a particular item.

Some sights have an on-site café or cafeteria (usually a good place to rest and have a snack or light meal). Museum WCs are generally free and clean.

If the museum has a bookshop, stop in before leaving and scan the postcards or thumb through the biggest guidebook (or skim its index) to be sure you haven't overlooked something that you'd like to see.

Most sights stop admitting people 30–60 minutes before closing time, and some rooms may close early (generally about 45 minutes before the official closing time). Guards usher people out, so don't save the best for last.

Every sight offers more than what is covered in this book. Use the information in this book as an introduction—not the final word.

SLEEPING

I favor accommodations (and restaurants) handy to your sightseeing activities. Hotels are expensive in Switzerland, so I've scoured the options and presented you with the best values, from $20 bunk beds to fancy-for-my-book $250 doubles.

Sleep Code

To help you sort easily through the listings, I've divided the rooms into three categories based on the price for a standard double room with bath:

$$$ **Higher Priced**
$$ **Moderately Priced**
$ **Lower Priced**

Prices listed in this book are per room, not per person. Hotels usually accept credit cards and include a buffet breakfast (unless otherwise noted); private accommodations rarely take plastic. Virtually all of my recommended accommodations are run by people who speak English; if they don't, I mention it in the listing.

When a range of prices is listed in one category, that means the prices fluctuate with the season; the prices and seasons are posted at or near the hotel desk. To give maximum information in a minimum of space, I use the following code to describe the accommodations.

S = Single room (or price for one person in a double).
D = Double or twin. Double beds are usually big enough for non-romantic couples.
T = Triple (often a double bed with a single).
Q = Quad (usually two double beds).
b = Private bathroom with toilet and shower or tub.
s = Private shower or tub only (the toilet is down the hall).

According to this code, a couple staying at a "Db-150 SF" hotel would pay a total of 150 Swiss francs (about $135) for a double room with a private bathroom and an included breakfast. The staff speaks English and credit cards are accepted.

Accommodations in Switzerland are normally comfortable and come with breakfast. Plan on spending $80–130 for a double room in a hotel, or $60–80 for a double (with the bathroom down the hall) in a cheap hostel-type place or a private home.

A triple is much cheaper than a double and a single. While hotel singles are expensive, rooms in private homes *(Zimmer)* often have a flat per-person rate. Hostels and dorms always charge per person. Especially in private homes, where the boss changes the sheets, people staying several nights are most desirable. One-night stays are sometimes charged extra.

I look for small, family-run places that are central, inexpensive, quiet, clean, safe, friendly, English-speaking, and not mentioned in other guidebooks. I'm more impressed by a handy location and a fun-loving philosophy than hair dryers and shoeshine machines.

I also like local character and simple facilities that don't cater to American "needs." Obviously, a place meeting every criterion is rare, and all of my recommendations fall short of perfection— sometimes miserably. But I've listed the best values for each price category, given the above criteria. The very best values are family-run places with showers down the hall and no elevator.

The price is usually posted in the room. Before accepting, confirm your understanding of the complete price. Prices can soften off-season, for stays of two nights or longer, or for payment in cash (rather than by credit card). Always mention that you found the place through this book; some of the hotels listed offer special deals to our readers.

Any room without a bathroom has access to a bathroom in the corridor. Most hotel rooms have a sink. For environmental reasons, towels are often replaced in hotels only when you leave them on the floor. In cheaper places, they aren't replaced at all, so hang them up to dry and reuse.

B&Bs

Staying in a B&B (*Gasthaus* or *Pension*) can be a great way to save money over sleeping in bigger (and more expensive) hotels. In many parts of Switzerland, people rent rooms *(Zimmer)* in their homes to travelers. Look for *Zimmer Frei* or *Privat Zimmer* signs. Booking direct saves both you and your host the cut the TI takes.

You'll get your own key to a private room that's clean, comfortable, and simple, though usually homey. Some B&Bs are like mini-hotels, with a separate entrance and several rooms, each with a private bath. Other B&Bs are family homes with spare bedrooms (the rooms sometimes lack sinks, but you have free access to the bathroom and shower in the home). Most B&Bs include a hearty continental breakfast.

Don't confuse *Zimmer* with the *Ferienwohnung*, which is a self-catering apartment rented out by the week or fortnight.

Camping, Hosteling, and Other Budget Beds

Campers can manage with *Let's Go* listings (see "Other Guidebooks," page 282) and help from the local TI (ask for a regional camping listing). Your hometown travel bookstore should also have guidebooks on camping in Europe. You'll find campgrounds just about everywhere you need them. Look for *Campingplatz*

signs. You'll meet lots of Europeans—camping is a popular, middle-class-family way to go. Campgrounds are cheap ($10 per person), friendly, safe, more central and convenient than rustic, and rarely full.

Hostelers can take advantage of the wonderful network of hostels. If you're traveling alone, hosteling is the best way to conquer hotel loneliness. Hostels are also a tremendous source of local and budget travel information. While there are no membership concerns for private hostels, International Youth Hostel Federation (IYHF) hostels require membership ($28 per year, sold at hostels in most US cities or online at www.hihostels.com, US tel. 202/783-6161). Those without cards simply buy one-night guest memberships for 6 SF.

Hostels are open to members of all ages. Hostel bunks usually cost $25–35 per night (plus $4 sheet rental if you don't have your own). Many hostels serve good, cheap meals and/or provide kitchen facilities.

If you plan to stay mainly in hostels, bring your own sheet (or pay extra at each place to rent one). While many hostels have a few doubles or family rooms available upon request for a little extra money, plan on gender-segregated dorms with 4- to 20-beds per room. Many hostel receptionists may say over the telephone that their hostel is full, but still hold a few beds for people who drop in. Follow signs marked *Jugendherberge* (with triangles; *Auberge de Jeunesse* in French) or with the logo showing a tree next to a house. If you get there and find that the hostel really is full, the staff can direct you to budget accommodations nearby.

Choose your hostel selectively. Hostels can be cozy mountain chalets, serene lakeside villas—or antiseptic spaces overrun by noisy school groups (most common on summer weekends and on school-year weekdays). While IYHF hostels are clean and predictable, they can also have an institutional feel. The independent hostels, sometimes called "backpackers," tend to be smaller than IYHF hostels, with fewer regulations and no school groups. I prefer these informal private hostels, which are usually more fun and more intimate-feeling than the IYHF variety—perfect for getting to know fellow travelers and hostel owners. Some of the hostels are even geared for special-interest guests, such as bicyclists or families traveling together. (For a list of some independent hostels, see www.swissbackpackers.ch.)

A fluffy straw bed awaits at a number of farms that have opened their haylofts to sleepy tourists. It's a fun hostel alternative and more comfortable than you'd think (see www.abenteuer-stroh .ch/en for details).

Many hotels, restaurants, and campsites provide dormitory-style accommodations. Look for the word *lager*, which indicates

Introduction

cheap dorm beds—often a loft lined with mattresses. These slumber mills may be less charming than cozy hostels, but they're cheap and convenient.

For serious hikers and climbers, mountain huts are an essential alpine experience. Don't expect ski-lodge comfort: These practical, adventurous places are simple, offering a warm place to sleep and (usually) breakfast and dinner. Most mountain-hut guests are long-distance hikers, connecting one hut to another along an extended hiking trail. You'll pay about $15 a night for your bunk and grub (see www.sac-cas.ch for more information).

Making Reservations

It's possible to travel at any time of year without reservations, but given the quality of the gems I've found for this book, I'd recommend calling for rooms in advance (especially for mountain resorts during summer weekends). Book farther in advance for holidays (see page 303).

If there's any reason to travel without reservations, it's to remain flexible, so you can modify your itinerary as you go to adapt to the weather (spending rainy days in cities and sunny days in the mountains). If tourist crowds are minimal, you might make a habit of calling between 9:00 and 10:00 on the day you plan to arrive, when the hotelier knows who'll be checking out and just which rooms will be available.

To make a reservation farther in advance, contact hotels directly by email, phone, or fax. Email is the clearest and most economical way to make a reservation. In addition, many hotel websites now have online reservation forms. To ensure you have all the information you need for your reservation, use the form in this book's appendix (also at www.ricksteves.com/reservation).

If you book your room by phone, note that I've included detailed dialing instructions (see "Telephones, Email, and Mail" on page 285). It's easy to use the telephone and convenient phone cards. Simple English is usually fine; most hotels listed are accustomed to English-only speakers. If phoning from the US, be mindful of time zones (see page 10).

When you request a room in writing for a certain time period, use the European style for writing dates: day/month/year. Hoteliers need to know your arrival and departure dates. For example, for a two-night stay in July, I would request: "2 nights, arrive 16/07/09, depart 18/07/09." Consider in advance how long you'll stay; don't just assume you can extend your reservation for extra days once you arrive.

If you don't get a reply to your email or fax, it usually means the place is already fully booked. If you get a response that gives room availability and rates, it's not a confirmation. You must tell them that you want that room at the given rate.

Whether you reserve a few hours or a few months in advance, most hoteliers will trust you and hold a room until 16:00 without a deposit, though some will ask for a credit-card number. You can email your credit-card information (I do), but some people prefer to share that personal info via phone call, fax, or secure online reservation form (if the hotel has one on its website).

If you must cancel your reservation, it's courteous to do so with as much advance notice as possible (simply make a quick phone call or send an email). Hoteliers and B&B hosts lose money if they turn away customers while holding a room for someone who doesn't show up. Understandably, some hoteliers bill no-shows for one night. Hotels sometimes have strict cancellation policies (for example, you might lose a deposit if you cancel within two weeks of your reserved stay, or you might be billed for the entire visit if you leave early); ask about cancellation policies before you book. Again, don't let these people down—I promised you'd call and cancel as early as possible if for some reason you won't show up.

Always reconfirm your room reservation a few days in advance from the road. If you'll be arriving later than 16:00, let them know.

On the small chance that a hotel loses track of your reservation, bring along a hard copy of their emailed or faxed confirmation.

EATING

The Swiss eat when we do and enjoy a straightforward, no-nonsense cuisine. Specialties include delicious fondue, rich chocolates, a melted cheese dish called raclette, *Rösti* (hash browns), fresh dairy products (try muesli with yogurt), 100 varieties of cheese, and Fendant—a good, crisp, local white wine.

Restaurants and Budget Options

When restaurant-hunting, choose a spot filled with locals, not the place with the big neon signs boasting, "We Speak English and Accept Credit Cards." Venturing even a block or two off the main drag leads to local, higher-quality food for less than half the price of the tourist-oriented places. Locals eat better at lower-rent locales.

Different kinds of restaurants offer different experiences. Hotels often serve fine food. A *Gaststätte* is a simple, less expensive restaurant. A *Weinstübli* (wine bar) or *Bierstübli* (tavern) usually serves food. Mountain huts—called *Hütte*—generally have hot chocolate and hearty meals.

If you're not too hungry, order from the *kleine Hunger* (small hunger) section of the menu. Many restaurants offer half portions, which is a great relief on your budget (although two people save even more by sharing one full portion).

Most restaurants tack a menu onto their door for browsers and have an English menu inside. Only a rude waiter will rush you. Good service is relaxed (slow to an American). To wish others "Happy eating!" offer a cheery *"En Guete!"* When you want the bill, ask for *"Rechnung, bitte."* (See the "Survival Phrases" in the appendix for more tips.)

Swiss restaurants are expensive, but there are several excellent budget alternatives. The Co-op and Migros grocery stores are the hungry hiker's best budget bet; groceries—while about 50 percent more than US prices—are a huge savings over any restaurant. These supermarkets also often come with cheap non-smoking self-service cafeterias, with good food at much lower prices than restaurants with table service. In most big cities, you'll find Manor department stores, which usually feature wonderful self-service eateries called "Manora"—with lush salad bars, tasty entrées, and fresh-squeezed juices (I've listed several specific Manora locations in this book). Bakeries are another great place for a snack or affordable light meal.

Swiss Cuisine

Here at a crossroads of Europe, the food has a wonderful diversity: heavy *Wurst*-and-kraut Germanic fare; delicate, subtle French cuisine; and pasta dishes *all'Italiana*.

Aside from clocks and banks, Switzerland is known for its cheese. Gruyère cheese is hard, with a strong flavor; Emmentaler is also hard, but milder (and looks like what we call "Swiss cheese"). Appenzeller is the incredibly pungent cheese from the northeast of Switzerland, with a smell that verges on nauseating...until you taste it. Two of Switzerland's best-known specialties are cheese-based. *Käsefondue* is usually Emmentaler and Gruyère cheese melted with white wine, garlic, nutmeg, and other seasonings. You eat it with a long fork, dipping cubes of bread into it. Raclette is cheese slowly melted by a special appliance; as it softens, scrape a mound off and eat it with potatoes, pickled onions, and gherkins. (In restaurants, raclette often comes as little slices of cheese already melted.)

Another must-try dish, most typical in the mountains of the German-speaking areas, is *Rösti:* traditional hash browns with alpine cheese, often served with an egg cracked over it...yum.

Despite all the cheese and potatoes, the Swiss tend to be

health-conscious; after all, they invented muesli. While the dry muesli served at every breakfast buffet is unremarkable, *Birchermuesli*—a yummy mixture of fresh yogurt, fresh fruit, and juice-soaked muesli—is worth seeking out in supermarket delis and on café menus. Menus often feature a *Fitnessteller* ("fitness plate")—usually a large mixed salad that comes with a steak, chicken, or fish. *Bio* means organically grown (a *Biolädeli* is a store that sells organic products).

Of course, each region has its own specialties. In French-speaking Switzerland, white wine and heavy cream are used in many dishes, and horsemeat (formerly imported from Eastern Europe, now imported from the US, New Zealand, and Australia) is common. The cuisine in eastern Switzerland (Pontresina, St. Moritz) uses chestnuts in many forms, wild mushrooms, and air-dried beef. Southwestern Switzerland (Zermatt area) specializes in all kinds of cheese, and their favorite white wine is Fendant.

Swiss wine (about two-thirds white) is good, but expensive. The dry, white Fendant is great with cheese dishes. If you're in Murten, sample the local Vully wine. Fruity St. Saphorin grows on the slopes above Lake Geneva. Menus list drink size by the tenth of a liter, or deciliter (dl). Order wine by the *Viertel* (quarter liter, or 8 oz.) or *Achtel* (eighth liter, or 4 oz.). Order it *süss* (sweet), *halb trocken* (medium), or *trocken* (dry). You can say, *"Ein Viertel Weisswein* (white wine), *bitte* (please)." *Rotwein* is red wine; a *Pfiff* is two deciliters (about 8 oz.) of red wine. *Bocalino* is a small, decorated eight-ounce ceramic jug with a light Swiss red wine called Dole.

Swiss beer is surprisingly good and inexpensive. Each pub has one brand of a local beer on tap, with others available in bottles. The standard size is a *Stange* (33 cl, or centiliters); the smaller size is called a *Herrgöttli* (20 cl). Beer mixed with lemon-flavored pop is called a *Panaché*. In summer, this light beer is refreshing.

Instead of Coke, try a local favorite: Rivella, a carbonated, vitamin-rich soft drink made with 35 percent milk serum. Its unusual (but not unpleasant) taste doesn't resemble milk at all; it's more like chewable vitamins. It comes in three colors: red is regular, blue is low-calorie, and green is mixed with green tea. Tap water—which many waiters aren't eager to bring you—is *Leitungswasser.* They would rather you buy *Mineralwasser* (*mit/ohne Gas,* with/without carbonation).

As an alternative to hot chocolate, try Ovomaltine. The Swiss have a fondness for this hot drink—a malt-derived vitamin supplement, flavored with chocolate so kids will drink it. (In the US, our Ovaltine is an Asian variation on this drink—considered by the Swiss to be a cheap copy.)

And, of course, there's chocolate. The Swiss changed the world in 1875 with their invention of milk chocolate. Nestlé, Suchard,

How Was Your Trip?

Were your travels fun, smooth, and meaningful? If you'd like to share your tips, concerns, and discoveries, please fill out the survey at www.ricksteves.com/feedback. I value your feedback. Thanks in advance—it helps a lot.

and Lindt are the major producers. Stroll the chocolate aisle of a grocery store and take your pick.

TRAVELING AS A TEMPORARY LOCAL

We travel all the way to Europe to enjoy differences—to become temporary locals. You'll experience frustrations. Certain truths that we find "God-given" or "self-evident," such as cold beer, ice in drinks, bottomless cups of coffee, and bigger being better, are suddenly not so true. One of the benefits of travel is the eye-opening realization that there are logical, civil, and even better alternatives. A willingness to go local ensures that you'll enjoy a full dose of local hospitality.

If there is a negative aspect to the image the Swiss have of Americans, it's that we are big, loud, aggressive, impolite, rich, superficially friendly, and a bit naive. Americans tend to be noisy in public places, such as restaurants and trains. Our raised voices can demolish Switzerland's reserved ambience. Talk softly.

While Europeans look bemusedly at some of our Yankee excesses—and worriedly at others—they nearly always afford us individual travelers all the warmth we deserve.

While updating my guidebooks, I hear over and over again that my readers are considerate and fun to have as guests. Thank you for traveling as temporary locals who are sensitive to the culture. It's fun to follow you in my travels.

Judging from all the happy feedback I receive from travelers who have used this book, it's safe to assume you'll enjoy a great, affordable vacation—with the finesse of an independent, experienced traveler.

Thanks, and happy travels—*gute Reise!*

BACK DOOR TRAVEL PHILOSOPHY
From *Rick Steves' Europe Through the Back Door*

Travel is intensified living—maximum thrills per minute and one of the last great sources of legal adventure. Travel is freedom. It's recess, and we need it.

Experiencing the real Europe requires catching it by surprise, going casual..."Through the Back Door."

Affording travel is a matter of priorities. (Make do with the old car.) You can travel—simply, safely, and comfortably—nearly anywhere in Europe for $100 a day plus transportation costs. In many ways, spending more money only builds a thicker wall between you and what you came to see. Europe is a cultural carnival, and, time after time, you'll find that its best acts are free and the best seats are the cheap ones.

A tight budget forces you to travel close to the ground, meeting and communicating with the people, not relying on service with a purchased smile. Never sacrifice sleep, nutrition, safety, or cleanliness in the name of budget. Simply enjoy the local-style alternatives to expensive hotels and restaurants.

Extroverts have more fun. If your trip is low on magic moments, kick yourself and make things happen. If you don't enjoy a place, maybe you don't know enough about it. Seek the truth. Recognize tourist traps. Give a culture the benefit of your open mind. See things as different but not better or worse. Any culture has much to share.

Of course, travel, like the world, is a series of hills and valleys. Be fanatically positive and militantly optimistic. If something's not to your liking, change your liking. Travel is addictive. It can make you a happier American as well as a citizen of the world. Our Earth is home to six and a half billion equally important people. It's humbling to travel and find that people don't envy Americans. Europeans like us, but, with all due respect, they wouldn't trade passports.

Globe-trotting destroys ethnocentricity. It helps you understand and appreciate different cultures. Regrettably, there are forces in our society that want you dumbed down for their convenience. Don't let it happen. Thoughtful travel engages you with the world—more important than ever these days. Travel changes people. It broadens perspectives and teaches new ways to measure quality of life. Rather than fear the diversity on this planet, travelers celebrate it. Many travelers toss aside their hometown blinders. Their prized souvenirs are the strands of different cultures they decide to knit into their own character. The world is a cultural yarn shop, and Back Door travelers are weaving the ultimate tapestry. Join in!

SWITZERLAND

Switzerland is one of Europe's richest, best organized, most expensive countries. Like the Boy Scouts, the Swiss count cleanliness, neatness, punctuality, tolerance, independence, thrift, and hard work as virtues...and they love pocketknives. Their high income, a great social security system, and the spectacular Alps give the Swiss plenty to be thankful for.

Nearly half of Switzerland, Europe's most mountainous country, consists of uninhabitable rocks, lakes, and rugged Alps. Despite the country's small size, it is unusually diverse. Its wild geography has kept people apart historically, helping its many regions maintain their distinct cultural differences. Switzerland is at a linguistic crossroads of Europe, with four official languages: German, French, Italian, and Romansh (an obscure Latin dialect spoken by a tiny group in the southeast).

Historically, Switzerland is one of Europe's oldest democracies, yet women didn't get the vote until 1971. Born when three states (cantons) united in 1291, the Swiss Confederation grew to the 26 cantons of today. The "CH" decal on cars doesn't stand for chocolate...but for "Confoederatio Helvetica," the country's official title (using the Latin name avoids linguistic controversy). The country is named for the Celtic Helvetii tribe that lived here back in Roman times. The Confederation government is decentralized, and cantonal loyalty is very strong.

Stubbornly independent (or maybe just smart), Switzerland loves its neutrality and stayed out of both World Wars. But it's far from lax when it comes to national defense. Every able-bodied man serves in the army and stays in the reserve. Each house has a gun and a fully stocked bomb shelter. (Swiss vacuum-packed emergency army bread, which lasts two years, is also said to function as a weapon.) Switzerland bristles with 600,000 rifles in homes and 12,000 heavy guns in place. Airstrips are hidden inside mountains, accessed by camouflaged doors. With the push of a button, all road, rail, and bridge entries to Swiss territory can be destroyed, sealing off the country from the outside world. Sentiments are changing, though, and Switzerland has come close to voting away its entire military.

Switzerland Almanac

Official Name: The Confoederatio Helvetica, or Switzerland, has a different name in each of its four official languages: Schweizerische Eidgenossenschaft (German), Confédération Suisse (French), Confederazione Svizzera (Italian), and Confederaziun Svizra (Romansh). Locals shorten those to "Schweiz," "Suisse," "Svizzera," and "Svizra."

Population: Switzerland has 7.5 million people (similar to the population of Virginia), many of European heritage—German, French, or Italian—though the ever-increasing immigration of foreigners concerns many natives. Three out of five Swiss speak German as their main language, one in five speaks French, seven percent speak Italian, and about half one percent speak Romansh. The populace is 42 percent Catholic, 35 percent Protestant, two percent Orthodox, four percent Muslim, and 17 percent other or unspecified.

Latitude and Longitude: 47°N and 8°E, similar latitude to Washington State or Quebec, Canada.

Area: 16,000 square miles; twice the size of New Jersey, or half the size of South Carolina.

Geography: Switzerland sits at the crossroads between northern and southern Europe. The Alps are Europe's high point and continental divide, from which the major rivers flow—Rhine, Rhône, Danube, and Po. Switzerland's highest point is the 15,200-foot Monte Rosa (specifically, the summit called Dufourspitze), along the Italian border. Though Switzerland is mostly mountainous, the center of the country consists of rolling hills and large lakes.

Biggest Cities: One in seven Swiss lives in or near Zürich (pop. 370,000 in the city; 1 million in the metropolitan area). Geneva has 185,000 people, and Basel has 166,000. The capital is Bern (pop. 128,000).

Economy: Like a fine watch, Switzerland's economy just keeps on ticking. The Gross Domestic Product is $255 billion, similar to Washington State. Its per capita GDP of $34,000 is among Europe's highest (but still 20 percent less than the US). The franc is strong, workers are highly skilled, and unemployment is half the European Union average. Blessed with hydropower and using nuclear technology, Switzerland generates 99 percent of its electricity with virtually no oil.

Though not a European Union member, Switzerland conforms to EU standards to stay competitive. Major Swiss money-makers include banking (especially secret, private accounts from around the world), insurance, watches (from top-of-the-line pieces to inexpensive Swatches), chemicals and pharmaceuticals, Nestlé chocolate, tourism, and precision instruments—Swiss-made equipment helps make everything from clothing to ballpoint-pen tips to parts for the Mars Exploration Rover.

Currency: 1 Swiss franc (SF) = 100 Rappen = about $0.90; 1.10 SF = about $1.

Government: Founded in 1291 as a confederation of cantons, the country is still a model of federalism, balancing the needs of its different linguistic/ethnic groups. No single political party (or two or even three parties) dominates the political landscape. The president, chosen by the legislature, serves for just one calendar year. The two-house Federal Assembly consists of the 46-seat Council of States and the 200-seat National Council, elected for four-year terms.

Political Issues: For the past several years, the two hot-button topics that have dominated political discussion are whether to join the European Union and how to deal with the rising tide of immigrants. Opinions are generally divided along linguistic/geographic lines: French- and Italian-speakers and urbanites tend to favor EU membership and immigrants' rights, while rural German-speakers are more likely to be opposed.

Flag: Switzerland's white cross on a distinctively square red background may have been the inspiration for the red-on-white symbol of the International Red Cross.

The Average Swiss: He or she has 1.43 children and will live to be 80. A typical Swiss man serves at least 260 days of compulsory service in the military. The average woman spends two hours a day on housework. He or she travels about 1,300 miles a year on a train, the equivalent of crossing the country six times. Sixteen percent of the average Swiss income goes to taxes, and 20 percent of the household budget is spent buying insurance. Every month, the average Swiss eats two pounds of chocolate and drinks a quart of alcohol.

Today, you can visit once-hidden military installations, now open to the public as museums (for an example, see page 77).

In 2002, Switzerland legalized marijuana use. When polls showed that more than 30 percent of the country had used marijuana, the Parliament decided to decriminalize the drug, rather than criminalize a third of its population. But, while not wanting to clog its prisons with petty pot smokers, the country doesn't want to be known as another Holland, either. So the law remains a bit ambiguous: The Swiss can possess and use pot, but they can't sell it. Each spring, there's a push for stricter control. Word gets out that Switzerland is no haven for pot, and then things ease up.

The costs of a night on the town are high. More and more locals call sitting on the pavement around a bottle of wine "going out." Hotels with double rooms for less than $100 are rare. Even dormitory beds are expensive. If your budget is tight, be sure to chase down hostels (many have family rooms) and keep your eyes peeled for *Matratzenlagers* ("mattress dorms"). Hiking is free, though major alpine lifts run around $50.

While Switzerland's booming big cities are cosmopolitan, traditional culture survives in the alpine villages. Spend most of your time getting high in the Alps. On Sunday, you're most likely to enjoy traditional music, clothing, and culture. August 1 is the festive Swiss national holiday.

A Swiss Timeline

Switzerland has a unique and impressive story—forging unity from diversity, and somehow remaining above the fray when Europe goes ballistic. Despite four languages, diverse geography, ill-defined borders, and many religious sects—and despite being surrounded by continental Europe's four big powers (France, Germany, Austria, and Italy)—the Swiss cantons banded together to form an independent federal system that still works today.

500,000,000 B.C.:	The ocean floor is rocked by earthquakes that fold the earth upward, creating the Alps.
53 B.C.:	Julius Caesar defeats the Helvetii, a Celtic tribe. The Romans' language, Latin, would eventually evolve into the French, Italian, and Romansh languages spoken in Switzerland today.
c. A.D. 300:	Germanic tribes invade and settle.
c. 600:	An Irish missionary named Columbanus arrives and converts the pagan Swiss to Christianity.
800:	Swiss lands are part of Charlemagne's empire, later called the Holy Roman Empire, under German kings.

1256–1273: During a period in which no emperor rules, the Swiss develop a measure of independence. When Austrian Hapsburgs are brought in to reign, the Swiss resent foreign control.

1291: On August 1, Swiss citizens swear the oath, "We will be a single nation of brothers..." and rise up against Hapsburg rule. The three cantons of Uri, Schwyz, and Unterwalden unite, proclaiming independence and democratic institutions. In a legend of the time, the Swiss William Tell refuses to bow to the Hapsburg hat, a symbol of their power. As punishment, he's forced to shoot an apple off his own son's head. He does so, then leads a rebellion. Although the Swiss often outbattled the more powerful Hapsburgs, they had to fight for two full centuries to drive out them out, earning a reputation as Europe's fiercest warriors. Swiss mercenaries (like the Swiss Guards that protect the Vatican today) became a major export.

1332: Luzern joins the Swiss Federation, soon followed by more cantons.

1499: A treaty makes Switzerland independent in fact, if not in name.

1500s: During the Reformation, Switzerland is bitterly divided, but offers a haven for free thinkers. Ulrich Zwingli establishes Protestantism in Zürich, John Calvin (a Frenchman) brings followers to Geneva, and Erasmus (from Holland) teaches at Basel.

1648: The Treaty of Westphalia officially makes Switzerland independent.

1798: French revolutionary forces occupy Switzerland and try to establish a strong central government. It doesn't stick, so Napoleon restores canton power (1803).

1815: The Congress of Vienna proclaims Switzerland with today's borders.

1848: Amid a Europe-wide wave of liberal reforms, Switzerland's tradition of democracy is established in a constitution. The new Confederation features a modern, bicameral parliament modeled after America's form of government, but with less power given to the executive branch.

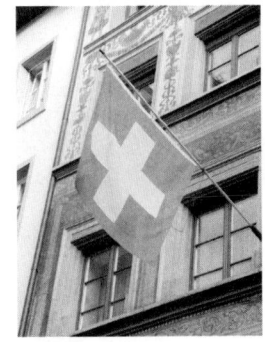

1864: The International Red Cross is founded by a Genevan.

1872–1882: The Gotthard railway is built over the Alps. A wave of breathtaking mountain engineering follows, taming much of the Alps and bringing vacationers safely and effortlessly to previously unheard-of heights.

1914–1918: In World War I, Switzerland declares neutrality, and Geneva serves as the postwar seat of the League of Nations (a forerunner to the United Nations).

1939–1945: When World War II breaks out, 850,000 Swiss men grab their rifles and mobilize to protect the borders while they declare neutrality. Critics charge that, though neutral, Switzerland's open trade policies helped supply Nazi Germany.

c. 1945: After the war, their policy of neutrality leads the Swiss to refuse membership in the UN, NATO, and the EU.

1989: The final canton (Appenzell) grants women the right to vote in regional elections (all Swiss women could vote in national elections as of 1971).

2002: Switzerland joins the United Nations, but decides to hold off on EU membership.

2003: Landlocked Switzerland wins the world's most prestigious sailboat race, the America's Cup.

Today: Switzerland's 26 cantons are autonomous, part of a loose federalist democracy. Four political parties rule in an ever-changing array of coalitions, as they have since World War II.

ZÜRICH

Zürich is one of those cities that tourists tend to skip right through. Since it's a transportation hub, people fly in or change trains here, but don't give stopping a serious thought. The local graffiti jokes: *Zürich = zu reich, zu ruhig* ("too rich, too quiet"). But even though you won't find a hint of Swiss Miss in Switzerland's leading city—and with limited time, I'd certainly spend it up in the mountains—Zürich is surprisingly comfortable and enjoyable for a quick visit.

Zürich was founded by the Romans in 58 B.C. as a customs post. Roman Turicum eventually became Zürich. It gained city status in the 10th century, and by the 19th century it was a leading European financial and economic center. Today, it's home to the world's largest gold marketplace and fourth-largest stock exchange (after New York, London, and Tokyo). Assuming you've got the money to enjoy it, Zürich is by many measures the world's most livable city. Its 370,000 people (1 million in greater Zürich) are known for their wealth and hard work. Zürich is the only place in Switzerland where you'll see men in ties running in the streets.

Planning Your Time

While Luzern and Bern provide more charming urban experiences, Zürich is worth a quick visit. With two weeks in Switzerland, I'd spend a day here. Begin by visiting the impressive Swiss National Museum, then wander along the river, using my self-guided walk (see page 33), and take a river/lake cruise. With less time, do only the self-guided walk. With more time, take your pick of the many art museums.

ORIENTATION

Zürich sprawls around the northern tip of the long, skinny Lake Zürich (Zürichsee). The grand Bahnhofstrasse cuts through Zürich's glitzy shopping center, connecting the train station and the country's top historical museum (Swiss National Museum) with the lakefront in a 15-minute walk. Running parallel to that, across the Limmat River, is the Niederdorf neighborhood—a vibrant, cobbled, Old World zone of colorful little shops, cafés, and restaurants.

Tourist Information

A helpful TI is located in the great hall of the train station (under the fat blue angel; May–Oct Mon–Sat 8:00–20:30, Sun 8:30–18:30; Nov–April Mon–Sat 8:30–19:00, Sun 9:00–18:30; tel. 044-215-4000, www.zuerich.com). Pick up their city guide and map, browse the racks of brochures, and ask about their daily walking tours.

For a whirlwind visit, consider the **ZürichCARD,** which covers transportation by train, tram, bus, and boat; admission to 43 museums; a 50 percent discount on the city walking tour; and "welcome drinks" in many restaurants (17 SF/24 hrs, 34 SF/72 hrs, sold at TI). The one-day card will pay for itself if you do the walking tour and at least one museum or boat cruise in a day.

Tours: You can tour Zürich on a **guided walk** (similar to the self-guided walk in this chapter; 2 hrs, 20 SF, 10 SF with Swiss Pass or ZürichCARD, leaves from TI mid-April–Oct daily at 15:00, Sat–Sun also at 11:00) or by **bus** (2 hrs, 32 SF, May–Oct daily at 9:45, 12:00, and 14:00). The TI has details on both tours.

Arrival in Zürich

By Train: The slick train station (with a TI and shopping mall—see beginning of self-guided walk, below) is on the north end of town; to reach most of the recommended hotels, cross the Walche-Brücke bridge in front of the station.

By Plane: From Zürich Airport (Flughafen Kloten), catch a train to the train station downtown (6 SF, 15 min, departs every 10 min 5:00–24:00) rather than take a 50-SF taxi ride. For more on the airport, see page 51.

Getting Around Zürich

A ticket good for one ride on the trams and buses costs 2.40 SF (1-hour ticket for 4 SF, 24-hour transit pass for 8 SF). All transportation is covered by the ZürichCARD, mentioned above.

Helpful Hints

Medical Help: The **Permanence** drop-in clinic at the train station offers on-the-spot medical aid (daily 7:00–22:00, Bahnhofplatz 15, tel. 044-215-4444).

Bikes: A city program called "Züri rollt" allows you to borrow a bike for free (must leave passport and 20-SF deposit, May–Oct daily 7:30–21:30, various locations including Swiss National Museum and the Opera, look for *Züri rollt* or *Velogate* signs). Popular bike paths line the lake from Zürich. For more info, ask the TI or visit www.zuerirollt.ch.

Laundry: There is no central launderette in town, but many hotels will do laundry by request.

SELF-GUIDED WALK

Welcome to Zürich

This handy walking tour is the perfect orientation for travelers blitzing Zürich from the train station. It crisscrosses the river, connecting the city center's main sights en route to the boat dock for a lazy lake-cruise finale (or a quick tram back to the station). Allow about an hour for the walk.

Train Station

Zürich's central station has great energy. This major European hub handles 2,000 trains a day, including InterCity expresses to many major capitals. Built in 1870, its vast main hall was once lined with tracks. Today, it's a farmers' market (Wed 11:00–20:00) and community hall—busy with concerts, exhibitions, and even "beach" volleyball. The station sits above a vast underground modern shopping mall (open late—until 20:00—and on Sundays).

Above you, find the fat blue angel, Zürich's "Guardian Angel" protecting all travelers. The angel has been here since 1997 to celebrate the 150th anniversary of the Swiss rail system. To the angel's right, just across the street, is the **Swiss National Museum.** It's the best museum in town, offering an essential introduction to Swiss history. To maximize your education, tour this museum before starting the walk (see page 41).

• *From the station hall, follow the six white lines that lead to Bahnhofplatz (also well-signed). The station fronts Zürich's main shopping boulevard...*

WELCOME TO ZÜRICH WALK

1. Train Station
2. Police Department
3. Schipfe Street
4. Lindenhof Park
5. St. Peter's Church
6. Rathausbrücke
7. Conditorei Schober
8. Grossmünster
9. Fraumünster
10. Paradeplatz
11. Bürkliplatz

Bahnhofstrasse

Bahnhofstrasse, stretching from here to the lake, is lined with all the big-name shops (though it's become a bit hamburgerized in recent years). Cross the street, but before heading on down, look back at the station.

The facade of the station is a huge triumphal arch, built in 1871 to symbolize the triumph of industry. In the Industrial Age, Zürich emerged as Switzerland's leading city. Presiding over all this triumph is Helvetia, the personification of Switzerland. The Helvetii were the Celtic tribe that the Romans defeated in 15 B.C. to gain control of what is now Switzerland. Romans described them as "very good warriors with an affinity for bright and shiny metal." Helvetia was adopted as a symbol of the Swiss confederation in 1848, when the diverse cantons that banded together to create Switzerland needed some symbol of unity to transcend all their linguistic and regional differences. Helvetic ethnic heritage is the one thing all Swiss cantons have in common. (The "CH" you see on Swiss bumper stickers stands for the Latin "Confoederatio Helvetica.")

Helvetia is flanked by allegories of river travel (the goddess sitting on the boat) and rail travel (another goddess sitting on a train)—reminding us that Zürich has long been a transportation hub. Zürich's river, the Limmat, eventually flows into the Rhine and then out to sea.

The statue of Alfred Escher honors the man who spearheaded the creation of the infrastructure that allowed the country to function efficiently within its mountains and connected Switzerland with the rest of Europe. Many Swiss trace their nation's strong economy and ethos of efficiency to this man.

• *Stroll down Bahnhofstrasse. In two blocks (on the right), you'll see...*

Pestalozzi Park

The only park along this pedestrian- and tram-only boulevard is dedicated to Zürich's most important teacher, Johann Heinrich Pestalozzi (1746–1827). He promoted the notion, still prevalent in today's Switzerland, that a good education should be available for everyone (not only for sons of rich families). Parks like this are rare in central Zürich because of sky-high property values—among the most expensive in the world.

In the park's far corner gurgles a copy of a Parisian **"Wallace Fountain."** If you have a big head, good luck getting a drink from this fountain. More than 1,200 fun and fresh fountains are sprinkled around town, spouting water that's as good as bottled mineral water (the city regularly checks its quality). This is a blessing in a town where restaurants charge for a glass of tap water. Tourist brochures brag that Zürich is Europe's most "fountainous" city.

Switzerland's Zwingli Reformation

Today's Evangelical Reformed Church of Switzerland was founded by Huldrych Zwingli (1484–1531), who preached in Zürich from 1519 through 1531. A follower of the humanist philosopher Erasmus of Rotterdam, Zwingli believed that the true foundation of the church was based on preaching the Holy Scriptures freely—in the people's language, rather than in Latin. In 1522, most of German-speaking Switzerland embraced Zwingli's ideas...and that required leaving the Roman Catholic Church.

Zwingli was 33 in 1517, when German church reformer Martin Luther posted his revolutionary *95 Theses* (which questioned the practice of selling forgiveness, salvation, church offices, and so on). Within two years, sellers of indulgences were refused entry to Zürich. As the Reformation swept Switzerland, things heated up. In 1523, rioters were storming churches, and authorities called for an orderly removal of all images in Zürich houses of worship (except stained-glass windows, which were destroyed).

The new, reformed Swiss church let priests marry. (Zwingli—like Luther—promptly took advantage of this freedom.) Fancy Masses were replaced by simple services. At Zürich's main church, the Grossmünster, preachers studied Latin, Greek, and Hebrew in order to translate the Bible into the people's German. In 1531, the Zwingli Bible (the first complete Bible translated into German) was published. It's still used today (like the King James Bible is in English).

Zwingli gave the Swiss church an unusual austerity: no altar, no pictures, and for a while, not even any music. Church services focused on preaching. Holy Communion was celebrated only on holidays. This puritanical simplicity permeated Swiss society in general. Zwingli was no fan of the "separation of church and

From Pestalozzi Park to Lindenhof: From the park, head left a couple of blocks to the Limmat River. Then go right onto Werdmühlestrasse, and head toward Werdmühleplatz (following signs to *Stadtpolizei*), and make a short stop at the **Police Department,** facing the river (generally open daily 9:00–11:00 & 14:00–16:00). Don't be shy—show your ID and enter for a free peek at a fine example of Swiss Jugendstil—an amazing wall painting by Swiss artist Augusto Giacometti. His famous *Hall of the Flowers* (*Blüemlihalle*, 1926), awash in bright colors, reflects the relief and joy the artist felt when World War I ended. (Augusto's nephew, Alberto, is the more famous Giacometti, much appreciated for his tall, skinny statues.)

From here, walk along the river upstream toward the church spires (without crossing the river, take the stairs down to the boardwalk below the Heimatwerk Swiss folk-crafts shop). Back state." Pushing for a theocracy, he established an ironclad city law: The government's duty was to oversee public worship, and only preaching true to the Bible was to be tolerated.

But Zwingli's reforms were by no means universally supported. Oh, it was a mess: Switzerland's Protestant movement split over baptism. Luther and Zwingli split over the Eucharist (is Christ's body really *in* the bread, or there only in a spiritual sense?). And, as old-school Catholics predicted, putting the Bible into the hands of regular people brought chaos—enabling every Tom, Dick, and Hans to "carve his own path to hell." Switzerland was embroiled in a religious civil war, as Protestant cantons fought Catholic ones. In 1531, while fighting as a "citizen soldier," Zwingli was killed in battle. His friend and partner Heinrich Bullinger succeeded him as the leader of German-speaking Swiss Protestantism.

Bullinger collaborated with John Calvin as Swiss Protestantism matured. The Protestant focus on preaching promoted the translation and interpretation of the Bible. Everyone was reading the Bible directly, which promoted literacy. The Reformation provided a basis of the autonomous community spirit, strong work ethic, and high literacy of a prosperous Switzerland for the future. The Swiss church became a place where equals would meet and worship God. Zwingli's heritage included transferring the notion of social charity from being a church phenomenon to being the social welfare responsibility of any self-respecting modern state. The foundations of Swiss democracy and its present social policies are rooted in Zwingli's teaching. And these Swiss reformers planted the seeds of what became the Presbyterian Church in the United States.

when the city's trade depended on river traffic, this small riverside street, called **Schipfe**, was Zürich's harbor. Today it retains its old river-merchant ambience. You'll pass a fun riverside eatery (Restaurant Schipfe 16—see page 50) and an arcade.

• *Twenty yards before the ugliest bridge in Switzerland, head up the stairs for two blocks, and then climb right up Pfalzgasse, to enjoy a great view from another park...*

Lindenhof

Important forts and strategic buildings stood on this hilltop square from Roman times through the Carolingian era. The statue commemorates the townswomen who cleverly defended the town in 1292. Their men were engaged in another battle. The Hapsburgs circled the city, ready to attack. The women put on armor and made like a big, rowdy army, tricking the Hapsburgs into thinking the whole city was prepared to attack.

When Zürich became a free city in the 13th century, the townspeople destroyed the fort here and established a law forbidding any new construction. The citizens realized that whoever lived on this hill would rule over the city—and they didn't want any more rulers. Today, this is a people's square, where locals relax under linden trees (for which the square is named) and enjoy the commanding city view.

Survey Zürich beyond its river. The **university** (behind the green spire) is the largest in Switzerland, with 25,000 students. Left of that is Zürich's renowned technical college, the ETH (Eidgenössische Technische Hochschule, or Federal Institute of Technology), with 15,000 students. The ETH has graduated 25 Nobel Prize winners, including Albert Einstein and Wilhelm Röntgen (who discovered X-rays). The ETH terrace offers a great city viewpoint (which you can visit later by riding the little Polybahn funicular). Lining the far side of the river, the Niederdorf is the lively restaurant, café, and bar district (see "Eating," page 48). On a clear day, you can see the Alps (behind the twin domes).

• *Take the stairs at the back of the park, just left of the chess players,*

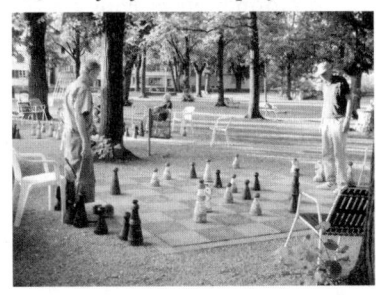

down to Strehlgasse, and follow Glockengasse, jogging left around the Golden Bell. Continue down tiny Robert-Walser-Gasse toward St. Peterhofstatt. You'll pass a characteristic eatery, Reblaube Gaststube, made famous by visits from Goethe in 1779. He'd meet here for long, wine-fueled discussions with the minister of...

St. Peter's Church (St. Peterskirche)

Founded in the seventh century, this church—Zürich's oldest—has one of Europe's largest clock faces (28 feet in diameter). The

town watchman used to live above the clock. If he spotted a fire, he would ring the alarm and hang a flag out of the window facing the blaze. This system seems to have worked—Zürich never suffered a devastating fire. In the 18th century, this church had such a well-loved preacher, Johann Kaspar Lavater (1741–1801), that people reserved their seats for Sunday Mass.

From St. Peter's Church to the Grossmünster: Continue past the

Zürich

church on Schlüsselgasse and take the first left, down the narrow Thermengasse (Bath Lane). Under your feet are excavations of a **Roman bath,** discovered by accident in 1984. A sketch on the wall at the bottom of the steps shows the bath. You're standing over studs that elevated the floor, which was heated from below.

The lane empties out on **Weinplatz,** a wine market of centuries past (notice the grape-picker on the fine little fountain). A wall mural inside the Barchetta bar shows the medieval river action circa 1570, including a mill on the bridge that raised drinking water to pipes that led to nearby buildings. (Note the dock here for the "river bus"—see page 41.)

The city's oldest bridge, the **Rathausbrücke,** goes back to Roman times. Cross the bridge, passing the 17th-century, Renaissance-style City Hall, which faces a fancy Neoclassical police station, and walk a block uphill to Marktgasse—the gateway to the bustling Niederdorf neighborhood.

To the left runs Niederdorfstrasse, which was the leading commercial street of Zürich before the old city wall was torn down to create Bahnhofstrasse. The Starbucks a block down from here faces the charming square. The **Niederdorf** continues on from here—a district of colorful streets, fun shopping, restaurants, and nightlife. You can explore this area now...or, better yet, tonight.

To continue our walk, go the opposite direction (right), heading up **Münstergasse.** Dada enthusiasts will know that in 1916, at the Cabaret Voltaire (#26), this "anti-art" art movement was born. At #19, pop into Schwarzenbach, which still advertises "merchandise from the colonies" out front and sells things the old-fashioned way inside (in loose bags, by the weight). Inhale. Pick up 100 grams of dried bananas from Togo or some Thai sticks... coconut, of course. Across the street, Zürich's popular **Conditorei Schober,** a riot of silk flowers, serves famously good (and expensive) hot chocolate and champagne truffles. Try not to look at the kinky knights on the plaque opposite #17.

• *Farther up the street is the "big cathedral" (literally)...*

Grossmünster

It was here that Huldrych Zwingli—whose angry religious fervor made Martin Luther seem mellow—sparked the Reformation in German-speaking Switzerland (see "Switzerland's Zwingli Reformation" sidebar, page 36). The domes of its towers (early examples of Neo-Gothic) are symbols of Zürich. They were rebuilt following a 1781 fire, and after much civic discussion, were left a plain stone color. Step inside and sit down. Let the strength and purity of the 12th-century Romanesque architecture have its way with you. The simple round arches seem strong, and the wide triumphal arch separating the nave from the altar makes you feel like a winner. The impact of the architecture is made stronger since it's uncluttered—Zwingli's reforms led to a clean sweep of Catholic decor in 1519.

In the front are three choir windows by Augusto Giacometti (c. 1933). Mary and the Baby Jesus (at her feet) meet two of the three kings bearing their gifts, while angels hover above with offerings of flowers. In the crypt (stairs below altar), you'll see an original 15th-century statue of Charlemagne (a copy now fills its niche on the river side of the church exterior). The church is free and open daily (9:00–18:00, pick up English story of the Swiss Reformation). For 2 SF and 200 steps, you can enjoy a fine city view from atop the tower (Mon–Sat 9:15–17:00, Sun 13:00–17:00).

Leaving the church, go right and into the corner, where a door leads to a fine Romanesque cloister ringed with fanciful 12th-century carvings (free, Mon–Fri 9:00–17:00, closed Sat–Sun). Upon entering, take eight steps to the left and meet the sculptor (self-portrait on the highest arch).

• *Cross the river to another tall-steepled church.*

Fraumünster

This was founded as an abbey church for a convent in 853, when Zürich was little more than a village. The current building,

which sits on the same footprint as its Carolingian predecessor, dates from 1250. With the Reformation of Zwingli, the church was taken by the Zürich town council in 1524 and—you know the drill—gutted to fit Zwingli's taste. Today, it's famous for its windows by Chagall, described in the "Fraumünster's Chagall Windows" sidebar on page 42.

From the Fraumünster to Lake Zürich: From the church, Poststrasse (continuing away from the river) takes you back to Bahnhofstrasse and the busy **Paradeplatz.** Survey the scene: The train station is a 10-minute walk to your right, and the lake is a few minutes to your left, down the classiest stretch of Bahnhofstrasse. You're facing Sprüngli, Zürich's top café for the past century. Its "Luxemburgerli" macaroons—little cream-filled, one-inch macaroon-meringue hamburgers—are a local favorite

Zürich

(you can buy just a couple; if you buy 100 grams, you'll get a selection of 12). The café upstairs offers elegant finger-sandwich lunches. To the right is Credit Suisse (with a luxurious ground floor full of fancy shops—worth a look). A bit farther (at #31) is the fine little Beyer watch museum (the watchmaker's personal collection, in the basement of his watch shop; 5 SF, Mon–Fri 14:00–18:00, closed Sat–Sun).

• *Turning left, follow Bahnhofstrasse to the boats and riverside terrace at Bürkliplatz. We'll finish this walk at...*

Lake Zürich (Zürichsee)

Lake Zürich is 17 miles long, 2.5 miles wide, and—because it's relatively shallow—warm enough for swimming. From here, you can enjoy the lakeside promenade (a fine strolling path 3 miles in either direction; left is sunnier and more interesting) or a short cruise (see below). Tram #11 zips you back to the station (catch it from the inland side, across the street), and so will the riverboat-bus (described next).

SIGHTS AND ACTIVITIES

Cruises on Limmat River and Lake Zürich—You have two basic boat-ride options: 1) small, low-floating buses that take local commuters and joy-riding visitors up and down the river and to points nearby on the lake; and 2) big, romantic lake ships taking tourists on longer rides around Lake Zürich. All boats leave from Bürkliplatz (lake end of Bahnhofstrasse) and are covered by rail-passes (but it costs a flexi-day—handy if you're already using that day for a train trip to or from Zürich). None of the boats come with commentary.

The riverboat-buses (very low, to squeeze under the bridges) make a 60-minute loop around the Zürich end of the lake and down the river to the train station and Swiss National Museum (2/hr, daily 10:00–22:00, schedule posted at pier 6, buy ticket on boat; 3.80 SF for any ride, short or long; free with 24-hr transit pass or ZürichCARD). These buses can be handy for connecting the lake and the Swiss National Museum.

The big, touristy, lake-only boats run daily from spring through fall (8 SF for basic 90-min version, 2/hr, 11:00–19:30). They also offer longer trips, jazz and dinner cruises, and so on. The ticket kiosk is near pier 1; boats depart from piers 1 through 6.

▲**Swiss National Museum (Schweizerisches Landes-museum)**—This massive museum, in a Neo-Gothic castle next to the train station, presents a wide range of artifacts from Swiss history. In the late 19th century, it was clear that the world was changing, and the Swiss wanted to protect their unique heritage. A

Zürich

Fraumünster's Chagall Windows

The church's claim to fame is its collection of 30-foot-tall stained-glass windows by Marc Chagall (1887–1985), the Russian-born French artist. Chagall gave an exhibit in Zürich in 1967. It was such a hit that the city offered the world-famous artist a commission. To their surprise, the 80-year-old Chagall accepted. Chagall designed the windows to stand in the church's spacious choir (zone behind the altar; underutilized in Protestant-style worship)—a space where he intuitively felt his unique mix of religious themes could flourish.

For the next three years, Chagall threw his heart and soul into the project, making the sketches at his home on the French Riviera, then working in close collaboration with a glassmaking factory in Rheims. After the colored panes were made, Chagall personally painted the figures on with black outlines, which were then baked into the glass. Chagall spent weeks in Zürich overseeing the installation and completion.

His inimitable painting style—deep colors, simple figures, and shard-like Cubism—is perfectly suited to the medium of stained glass. Blending Jewish and Christian traditions, Chagall created a work that can make people of many faiths comfortable.

The five windows (left to right) depict Bible scenes, culminating in the central image of the crucified Christ:

1. The Prophets (red): The prophet Elisha (bottom) looks up to watch a horse-drawn chariot carry his mentor Elijah off to heaven. Further up, Jeremiah (blue in color and mood) puts his hand to his head and ponders the destruction of wicked Jerusalem. Up in heaven (top), a multicolored, multifaceted God spins out his creation, sending fiery beams down to inspire his Prophets on earth. This window is artificially lit, as it's built into an interior wall.

2. Jacob (blue—Chagall's favorite color): Jacob (bottom, in deep purple amid deep blue) dreams of a ladder that snakes up to heaven, with red-tinged angels ascending and descend-

national competition was held, and Zürich (promising to provide a piece of land, pay for construction, and donate an impressive collection) won the privilege of hosting the country's National Museum. The quirky building is a mish-mash of architectural themes from around the country. The museum, while huge and entertaining, is decidedly old school, but a slick new wing may be open in time for your visit (5 SF, covered by Swiss Pass, Tue–Sun 10:00–17:00, closed Mon, Museumstrasse 2, good café in courtyard that leads into Platzspitz Park, tel. 044-218-6511, www.musee-suisse.com).

Here are a few highlights, by floor: The basement features

ing, symbolizing the connection between God above and Jacob's descendants (the Children of Israel) below.

3. Christ (green): The central, biggest window depicts the central figure in God's plan of salvation—Jesus Christ, who as the Messiah fulfills the promises of the Old Testament prophets. Mother Mary suckles baby Jesus (bottom) amid the leafy family tree of Jesus' Old Testament roots. The central area is an indistinct jumble of events from Christ's life, leading up to his crucifixion. The life-size ascendant Christ is crucified in a traditional medieval pose, but he's surrounded by a circle that seems to be bearing him, resurrected, to heaven. Chagall signed and dated the work (1970).

4. Zion (yellow): King David (bottom right) strums his harp and sings a psalm, while behind him stands his mistress Bathsheba, who gave birth to Solomon, the builder of Jerusalem's temple. At the end of history, an angel (top) blows a ram's horn, announcing the establishment of a glorious New Jerusalem, which descends (center), featuring rust-colored, yellow, and green walls, domes, and towers.

5. The Law (blue): Moses, with horns of light and the Ten Commandments (top), looks sternly down on lawbreaking warriors on horseback wreaking havoc. At the bottom, an angel (in red) embraces the prophet Isaiah (very bottom) and inspires him to foretell the coming of the Messiah (in red, above the angel).

Everyone comes away with a different interpretation of this complex work, which combines images from throughout the Bible. The tall, skinny windows seem to emphasize the vertical connection between heaven above and earth below, both bathed in the same colored light. Some think Chagall used colors symbolically: Blue and green represent the earth, while red and yellow are heavenly radiance. But all recognize that the jumble of images—evoking the complexity of God's universe—reaches its Point Omega in the central window, celebrating the idea of salvation through Christ's crucifixion.

exhibits on medieval bookmaking and winemaking, an intricate diorama of the pivotal Battle of Murten (see page 105), and a room of huge church bells with an inviting rubber mallet (unique in Europe...bang away). The ground floor has pre-Reformation church art—all the fancy stuff the Protestants gutted from the churches so they could concentrate. There's also a Zwingli room about the Reformation in Switzerland and medieval living rooms. On the first and second floors are living rooms from the Renaissance and the 18th and 19th centuries. The third floor is home to a small toy exhibit, plus traditional folk costumes from around the country.

Platzspitz Park—What used to be a riverside hangout for drug addicts has been cleaned up and—apart from a rusty needle here and there—is now a safe, friendly place for a scenic picnic (free, daily 6:00–21:00, behind train station and Swiss National Museum, clean WC). From here, you can take a riverboat-bus down the river and around the lake (included in 24-hour transit pass or ZürichCARD, departures at :05 and :35 past each hour, described above).

Switzerland has a progressive drug policy that treats addicts as people needing medical help, rather than as criminals. For

instance, on the far side of the Walche-Brücke bridge, just before the Platzspitz Park, there's a big, yellow, nondescript vending machine selling safe and government-subsidized syringes to heroin junkies. Go ahead, buy a box—it's about the cheapest souvenir you can purchase in Zürich.

Kunsthaus Zürich—Switzerland's top collection of modern art includes Swiss artists (Alberto Giacometti, Johann Heinrich Füssli, and Ferdinand Hodler) as well as international greats such as Munch, Picasso, Kokoschka, Beckmann, Corinth, Monet, and Chagall. The younger generation is also represented, with works by Rothko, Merz, Twombly, Beuys, Bacon, and Baselitz (10 SF, Tue–Thu 10:00–21:00, Fri–Sun 10:00–17:00, closed Mon; tram #3, #5, #8, or #9, or bus #31 to Kunsthaus stop, Heimplatz 1; tel. 044-253-8484, www.kunsthaus.ch).

Rietberg Museum—Filling historic villas set in a beautiful park, this museum houses art from Asia, Africa, America, and the South Pacific (12 SF, covered by Swiss Pass, Tue–Sun 10:00–17:00, Wed–Thu until 20:00, closed Mon, tram #7 to Museum Rietberg stop, Villa Wesendonck, Gablerstrasse 15, tel. 044-206-3131, www.rietberg.ch).

E. G. Bührle Collection—This collection is a must for lovers of the French Impressionists, their forerunners, and their followers. Here you'll find exceptional paintings by Manet, Degas, Cézanne, Monet, Renoir, Gauguin, van Gogh, Picasso, and Braque. You'll also see a smattering of Dutch Baroque and 18th-century Venetian works, plus religious sculptures from medieval times to the Renaissance (12 SF; open Tue–Wed, Fri, and Sun 14:00–17:00; closed Mon, Thu, and Sat; tram #2 or #4 to Wildbachstrasse stop, or bus #77 to Altenhofstrasse stop, Zollikerstrasse 172, tel. 044-422-0086, www.buehrle.ch).

Zürich Zoo—With 360 species, an impressive Madagascar rain forest hall, and a huge indoor exhibit, the city's zoo is a kid-friendly, fun place to see locals at play (22 SF, daily 9:00–18:00, less off-season, tram #6 from Bahnhofstrasse in front of the station, direction: Zoo, ride to last stop, Zürichbergstrasse 221, tel. 084-896-6983).

SLEEPING

High season in Zürich is May, June, September, and October. About 10 days a year, festivals and conventions send prices higher. Zürich is one of several Swiss and Austrian cities hosting the Euro 2008 soccer championship—it's critical to book ahead if you'll be in town on or around game days: June 9, 13, and 17.

My listings are near the train station, ideal for those passing through or leaving on an early-morning train or plane (train to airport: 6 SF, 15 min, leaves every 10 min). Your hotel may include the hotel tax in its price, or charge you an extra 2.50 SF per person per night.

Across the River from the Train Station

With this efficient, handy neighborhood as your home base, you're a quick stroll away from the train station, Swiss National Museum, riverboat dock, a huge underground mall of services and shops (under the station), and the Niederdorf restaurant and nightlife zone (down Stampfenbachstrasse). To reach these hotels, exit the train station from the huge hall with the "Guardian Angel" sculpture and the TI. Cross the river on the Walche-Brücke bridge, and use the map on page 46 to find your hotel.

$$$ Alexander Hotel is a fine, business-class hotel in a very central location offering a decent value (Sb-150–170 SF,

---

Sleep Code

(1.10 SF = about $1, country code: 41)
S = Single, **D** = Double/Twin, **T** = Triple, **Q** = Quad, **b** = bathroom, **s** = shower only. Unless otherwise noted, credit cards are accepted, English is spoken, and breakfast is included.

To help you sort easily through these listings, I've divided the rooms into three categories, based on the price for a standard double room with bath:

  $$$ Higher Priced—Most rooms 200 SF or more.
   $$ Moderately Priced—Most rooms between 140–200 SF.
    $ Lower Priced—Most rooms 140 SF or less.

ZÜRICH HOTELS AND RESTAURANTS

❶ Hotel Bristol
❷ Hotel Arlette
❸ Hotel Leoneck
❹ Alexander Hotel
❺ Hotel Krone
❻ Alexander Guesthouse
❼ Walhalla Hotel
❽ City Backpacker Hotel Biber
❾ Commihalle Restaurant
❿ Café Zähringer
⓫ Kantorei Restaurant
⓬ Wirtschaft Neumarkt
⓭ Rest. Swiss Chuchi
⓮ Rest. Bauschänzli
⓯ Zeughauskeller
⓰ Rest. Schipfe 16
⓱ To Hiltl Vegetarian Restaurant
⓲ Manora Cafeteria
⓳ Free Bikes (3)

Db-210–230 SF, 10 percent discount for readers of this book, air-con, Niederdorfstrasse 40, tel. 044-251-8203, fax 044-252-7425, www.hotel-alexander.ch, info@hotel-alexander.ch).

$$ Hotel Bristol, run by Martin Hämmerli and his friendly staff, offers 52 modern, cozy rooms an eight-minute walk from the station. This is a business-quality place with family-run warmth. The staff at the reception desk is helpful and happy to answer travel questions (Sb-140–150 SF, small Db-175, big Db-210 SF, Tb-210–250 SF, Qb-230–270 SF, 5 percent discount if you book direct and mention this book, laundry–15 SF, Stampfenbachstrasse 34, tel. 044-258-4444, fax 044-258-4400, www.hotelbristol.ch, info @hotelbristol.ch).

$$ Hotel Arlette is a bit forgettable, but comfortable, functional, and centrally located in a quiet neighborhood (Sb-135–145 SF, Db-175–195 SF, Stampfenbachstrasse 26, tel. 044-252-0032, fax 044-252-0923, hotel.arlette@bluewin.ch, family Schlotter).

$$ Hotel Leoneck offers 78 modern yet kitschy, bovine-themed rooms at a good price. The hotel—and the fine attached Crazy Cow restaurant (daily 6:30–22:30)—somehow manages to make Swiss cows seem cool; enjoy the moo-velous mural in your room (Sb-120–170 SF, Db-170–230 SF, Tb-230–280 SF, Qb-280–320 SF, ask for a 10 percent Rick Steves discount when you reserve, half are non-smoking rooms, elevator, Internet access, some street noise—ask for quieter back room, Leonhardstrasse 1, tel. 044-254-2222, fax 044-254-2200, www.leoneck.ch, info@leoneck.ch, Herr Gold). From the station, cross the Walche-Brücke bridge and walk 12 minutes uphill, or use the Bahnhofstrasse exit and find tram #6 or #10 (direction: Bahnhof Oerlikon, two stops to Haldenegg, look for Crazy Cow restaurant).

$ Hotel Krone is a big, old-school place renting 26 well-worn but sleepable rooms in a great location, next to the river in the Niederdorf old town. The rooms have ratty showers and tattered furniture, but it's safe and well-run. A third of the rooms face the river (Sb-73 SF, Db-96 SF, Tb-105 SF, breakfast-10 SF, reception closed 22:45–7:00, Limmat-Quai 88, tel. 044-251-4222, fax 044-251-4763, krone@reconline.ch, www.hotel-krone-linmmatquai.ch.

$ Alexander Guest House, a block away from the Alexander Hotel at Zähringerstrasse 16, is the Alexander's annex of 20 simple but perfectly good twin-bedded rooms. While the rooms are basic and uninspiring, they are clean and quiet (Sb-95 SF, Db-140 SF, extra bed-25 SF, ask for a 10 percent Rick Steves discount when you book, contact through Alexander Hotel—see page 45—where you'll also have breakfast).

Near the Station

$$ Walhalla Hotel, just behind the train station, has 48 modern, spacious rooms (Sb-130–160 SF, Db-175–230 SF, breakfast-16 SF, Limmatstrasse 5, tel. 044-446-5400, fax 044-446-5454, www .walhalla-hotel.ch, info@walhalla-hotel.ch). Their annex, around the corner, rents 26 simpler but still good rooms for less (Db-150–160 SF).

Hostel

$ City Backpacker Hotel Biber, buried right in the middle of the Niederdorf action three floors above a restaurant, offers the cheapest backpacker beds in the old center, with an ambience young travelers will find cool (65 bunks in 6-bed dorms for 36 SF each, includes sheets, no breakfast, lockers, kitchen, smoky lobby, street noise at night, no curfew, reception open daily 8:00–11:00 & 15:00–22:00, Niederdorfstrasse 5, tel. 044-251-9015, www.city -backpacker.ch, sleep@city-backpacker.ch).

EATING

The Niederdorf is Zürich's dining district, and the traffic-free Niederdorfstrasse is its restaurant row. While the countless eateries lining this main drag don't offer the best values, the people-watching is hard to beat. Browse the street and survey the eating options (including many colorful ethnic places). All of these recommendations are within a few minutes' walk of this spine of Zürich's people zone. They're listed clockwise, in order from the train station through the Niederdorf and back up again along the train-station side of the Limmat River. Many of the venerable guild houses—no longer economic powers—are now convivial traditional restaurants.

Commihalle Restaurant, near the recommended hotels, is part of a popular Italian chain. Their 34-SF "Tavolata" special—ideal for big eaters—gets you an antipasto buffet, pasta dish, main meat dish, and dessert-buffet finale (available only Tue–Sat 18:15–21:30). The interior is plain but dressy, and there's fine outdoor seating (filling 20-SF pastas, no pizza, always a good vegetarian option, daily 11:00–22:30, Stampfenbachstrasse 8, tel. 044-250-5960).

Café Zähringer is an artsy, bohemian co-op with a passion for serving reasonably priced healthy food to people who take time to keep life in balance. Linger in the stay-a-while interior, or enjoy the leafy seating out on the square—a block from where Lenin lived before heading back to Russia (20-SF daily specials, always good veggie and vegan plates, organic produce, salads, also meat dishes and wok dishes, famously good coffee, daily until 24:00,

Zähringerplatz 11, tel. 044-252-0500). You may also enjoy the sweet smell of an herb not on the menu.

Kantorei Restaurant serves well-presented modern Mediterranean cuisine with an Italian touch in a classy but unpretentious setting. Sit inside or out on the quiet, atmospheric square next to a fountain (30–40-SF plates, 17–20-SF lunch specials, daily 11:30–14:30 & 17:30–23:00, proud of its wine list, good vegetables, Neumarkt 2, tel. 044-252-2727).

Wirtschaft Neumarkt, tucked away in the old town, offers creative international dishes. It prides itself in using only healthy ingredients such as organic vegetables, salads, and additive-free meat, which justifies the higher prices. The interior is unremarkable—eat outdoors here. In good weather, the restaurant's long and fun-loving garden is packed with in-the-know locals eating well under chestnut trees. The upper garden is best, so it's usually filled with diners who made reservations (30-SF plates, lunch specials, Mon–Sat 11:30–14:00 & 18:00–24:00, closed Sun, extensive wine list and good beer on tap, Neumarkt 5, tel. 044-252-7939).

Restaurant Swiss Chuchi is a busy place popular with tourists and locals for traditional cheese dishes. They offer a fun selection of cheese and meat fondues. The 30-SF fondue is splittable when the restaurant isn't too busy (daily 11:30–24:00, indoor and outdoor seating, follow your nose to Rosengasse 10 on Hirschenplatz, tel. 044-266-9666).

Restaurant Bauschänzli is both a fancy riverside restaurant and a sloppy beer garden (a block inland from the boat docks at Bürkliplatz). Filling a small island in the river, its fun-loving and popular self-serve restaurant offers Zürich's best beer-garden experience—like a Munich *Biergarten* without the kraut. Help yourself to the cheap salad bar and the beer and wine from big casks (grab the glass or carafe of your choice). *Citro* (lemonade) is mixed with lager to make a shandy (known here as a *Panaché*). *Süssmost* is apple juice. The garden is open daily in good weather May through mid-September, followed in fall by a raucous Oktoberfest (40-SF plates, daily 11:00–23:00, live Bulgarian folk band plays Euro-folk music daily as locals dance—15:00–17:00 & 19:15–22:30, Stadthausquai 2, tel. 044-212-4919, reserve only for the fine-dining restaurant).

Zeughauskeller fills an atmospheric 500-year-old armory with medieval battle gear (William Tell's crossbow?) and happy eaters enjoying typically Swiss cuisine. Their fun and accessible menu offers traditional meals, including lots of soft meats (but no cheese—which the Swiss don't like to smell unless they're eating it). *Kalbsgeschnetzeltes*—calf's liver with *Rösti* (35 SF)—is a house specialty and a local fave. The outside seating is boring; the inside has all the character, and stays cool even when it's hot (15–35-SF plates, daily until 23:00, plenty of beer and wine, kid-friendly, near

Paradeplatz at Bahnhofstrasse 28, tel. 044-211-2690).

Restaurant Schipfe 16, gorgeously and peacefully situated on the river with an old-town view, is part of a city-run organization providing work for hard-to-employ people. Originally a soup kitchen, the location was just too charming to stay that way, so it's now open to the general public. Don't expect polished service... but you're contributing to a worthy cause and enjoying healthy and decent food at a very good price. The best seats are right along the river (lunch only, 20-SF two-course daily specials, Mon–Fri 10:00–16:00, closed Sat–Sun, Schipfe 16, tel. 044-211-2122).

Hiltl Vegetarian Restaurant is a treat for vegetarians. In 1898, Ambrosius Hiltl was fighting rheumatoid arthritis. His doctor said, "No more meat." So Ambrosius established the world's first vegetarian restaurant. Today his great-great-great-grandson, Rolf, carries on the family tradition. Historic photos decorate the walls, but the loyal clientele's attention is on the enticing buffet and friendly conversation. At dinner, along with the salad buffet, there's an Indian buffet (endorsed by Indian tourists). Fill your plate, which is sold by the weight—generally 22–28 SF per hearty meal. At lunch, the salad bar is cheaper, but with fewer Indian options. The à la carte menu comes with delightful salads, curries, and fancy fruit juices. Hiltl's food is legendary for its freshness and lack of preservatives (daily 7:00–23:00, non-smoking, 2 blocks off Bahnhofstrasse where it kinks at Sihlstrasse 28, tel. 044-227-7000).

Manora, a non-smoking cafeteria at the Manor department store on Bahnhofstrasse, is reliably good and fast. Choose between a fresh salad bar (big plate-10 SF) and a variety of main dishes (10–15 SF). It's popular with locals—eat early or late (Mon–Fri 9:00–20:00, Sat 9:00–17:00, closed Sun, fifth floor, Bahnhofstrasse 75).

TRANSPORTATION CONNECTIONS

From Zürich by Train to: Luzern (3/hr, 1 hr), **Interlaken** (hourly, 2 hrs, most direct but some with transfer in Bern and/or Spiez), **Bern** (2/hr, 1–1.5 hrs), **Murten** (2/hr, 1.75–2 hrs, transfer in Bern, Fribourg, or Kerzers), **Appenzell** (2/hr, 1.75 hrs with transfer in Gossau or 2.25 hrs with transfer in St. Gallen), **Lausanne** (2/hr, 2.25 hrs), **Zermatt** (hourly, 4.5 hrs, 1–2 changes), **Chur** (2/hr, 1.5 hrs), **Lugano** (hourly, 3 hrs, half with easy change in Arth-Goldau), **Munich** (nearly hourly, 3 direct in 4.25 hrs, otherwise 5–5.5 hrs with 1–3 changes), **Frankfurt** (hourly, 4 hrs, some direct but most with transfer in Basel or Stuttgart). Train info: toll tel. 0900-300-3004 or www.rail.ch.

Zürich Airport (Flughafen Kloten)

Smooth, compact, and user-friendly, Zürich Airport is an eye-opening introduction to Swiss efficiency. There are three levels: 1) train station on the bottom floor, with train info and ticket desk; 2) main level, with a top-end food court, Migros supermarket, fancy souvenir shops, Swiss Post Office (easy to mail things home—pack light), banks, ATMs, and lockers; and 3) departures, upstairs. Eateries and ATMs are plentiful before and after the customs checkpoint. For flight information, call the automated toll number: 0900-300-313 (press 2 for English).

Upon arrival by plane, pick up a free baggage cart, which you can wheel up and down the escalators. The train station underneath the airport can whisk you about anywhere you'd want to go in Europe, including downtown Zürich (6 SF, 15 min, leaves every 10 min 5:00–24:00, much cheaper than the 50-SF taxi ride). Your train ticket into Zürich is good for the following two hours on all city public transportation.

If catching an early-morning flight, don't spend a fortune to stay near the airport (**$$$ Hilton,** Db-from 250 SF, tel. 044-828-5050). Sleep near the train station downtown, then zip to the airport in the morning on the frequent and fast train.

From Zürich Airport by Train to: Luzern (2/hr, 1.25 hrs), **Interlaken** (hourly, 2.25 hrs), **Bern** (2/hr, 1.5 hrs), **Murten** (hourly, 2–2.25 hrs, change in Fribourg or Bern), **Appenzell** (2/hr, 1.5 hrs with transfer in Gossau), **Lausanne** (2/hr, 2.5 hrs, a few with change in Biel), **Zermatt** (at least hourly, 4.75 hrs, 1–2 changes), **Chur** (2/hr, 1.75 hrs, change at Zürich main station), **Lugano** (hourly, 3.25 hrs, 1–2 changes), **Munich** (4/day direct, 4 hrs, more with 2–3 changes, 4.75–5.5 hrs).

LUZERN
and CENTRAL SWITZERLAND

Luzern has long been Switzerland's tourism capital. Situated on the edge of a lake, with a striking alpine panorama as a backdrop, Luzern was a regular stop on the "Grand Tour" route of Europe during the Romantic era, entertaining visitors such as Goethe and Queen Victoria. And with a charming old town, a pair of picture-perfect wooden bridges, a gaggle of fine museums, and its famous weeping lion, there's still enough in Luzern to earn it a place on any Swiss itinerary.

Luzern also makes a fine home base for exploring the surrounding region, known as Central Switzerland (Zentralschweiz). A wide variety of boat trips, mountain lifts, and other excursions make fun day trips (described on page 72).

Planning Your Time

Many visitors home-base in Luzern for a week of side-trips. While I'd rather settle into the high country instead, Luzern is worth at least a full day and two nights. To get the most out of your day, begin with the TI's two-hour walking tour (see "Tours," page 55), or follow the self-guided walk in this chapter (see "Reuss River Stroll," page 55). Then hit the museums that interest you most: Art buffs flock to the Rosengart and Picasso museums; gearheads will have a ball at the Swiss Transport Museum; and geologists dig the Glacier Garden. In the late afternoon, take a peaceful boat trip on Lake Luzern, then wander the town's scenic bridges at sunset.

Luzern

Luzern (or "Lucerne" in English) is a charming midsize city with about 60,000 residents (and a metropolitan area sprawling to almost 200,000). It sits where the Reuss River meets Lake Luzern (Vierwaldstättersee). South of the river is the train station and bustling new town (Neustadt), and north of the river is the quaint, traffic-free old town (Altstadt). The river is spanned by a series of pedestrian bridges, including two classic wooden ones: the Chapel Bridge, with its famous stone water tower, and the Mill Bridge. Museums, restaurants, and hotels are scattered on both sides of the Reuss.

ORIENTATION

Tourist Information

Luzern's helpful, modern TI is right inside the train station (mid-June–mid-Sept daily 8:30–19:30; May–mid-June and mid-Sept–Oct Mon–Fri 8:30–18:30, Sat–Sun 9:00–18:30; Nov–April Mon–Fri 8:30–17:30, Sat–Sun 9:00–13:00; Bahnhofstrasse 3, tel. 041-227-1717, phone not answered on weekends, www.luzern.org).

At the TI, ask about their walking tour (listed under "Tours," below), and pick up the free, handy *City Guide* (loaded with info and museum discounts; see "Helpful Hints," next page) and *Cultural Guide* (with music and entertainment listings). Browse through their other literature as well. The TI also provides a free room-booking service (with some great last-minute deals) and sells tickets to various activities around town, such as boat trips. If you have kids (or are one), ask about the pedal boats.

Arrival in Luzern

Luzern's train station is refreshingly user-friendly. The TI is just off track 3. Most other important services are down the escalators at the front of the tracks, in an underground shopping mall called RailCity. There you'll find the ticket desks, WCs, ATMs, lockers, a convenient self-service cafeteria, a long-hours grocery store, and lots of other shops and restaurants. If all the other stores in town are closed (for example, on Sunday), head for RailCity.

For the quickest route into the old town, ride any escalator down into the underground RailCity and follow signs to *Altstadt* (to avoid having to cross the busy streets above).

In front of the train station is Bahnhofplatz (where buses fan out in every direction) and the pleasant lakefront.

Helpful Hints

Medical Help: Permanence is a welcoming drop-in medical clinic open 24/7 at the train station (downstairs in RailCity, near Co-op store).

Guest Card: When you check into your Luzern hotel, have them stamp your *City Guide* tourist brochure (free at TI). This stamped brochure becomes a "Visitor's Card" *(Gästekarte)* that gives you minor discounts at all of Luzern's museums. Remember to carry this brochure with you, and ask for this discount when buying entrance tickets.

Internet Access: An Internet point is inside the TI (4 SF/10 min). The cheaper **Inside** is in RailCity (3 SF/15 min, 8 SF/hr, Mon–Sat 9:00–21:00, Sun 9:00–20:00). Even cheaper is the city **library**—*Stadtbibliothek*—situated in the same building as the Bourbaki Panorama (4 SF/hr—which is also the minimum charge, 10 SF deposit for plastic card required, Mon 13:30–18:30, Tue–Fri 10:00–18:30, Thu until 20:00, Sat 10:00–16:00, closed Sun, Löwenplatz 10, tel. 041-417-0707, www.bvl.ch). You'll also see other Internet signs scattered around town.

Post Office: The main post office (Hauptpost) is kitty-corner from the train station (Mon–Fri 7:30–18:30, Sat 8:00–16:00, closed Sun).

Cinema: In Switzerland, movies are shown in their original version with subtitles. The Bourbaki Panorama building (see page 66) has several screens.

Bike Rental: You can rent bikes at the train station to enjoy Luzern's delightful lakeside bike paths (23 SF/half-day, 31 SF/day, 5 SF less with Eurailpass or Swiss Pass; at counter #21 downstairs in RailCity).

Water Fountains: Luzern is proud of its clean drinking water and its more than 200 public fountains, each with a fun design and spouting drinkable water. In the summer, you'll see locals take full advantage of these fountains—refilling their plastic water bottles again and again.

Getting Around Luzern

Except for the Swiss Transport Museum, all the sights, hotels, and restaurants recommended in this chapter are within easy walking distance from the station. The Swiss Transport Museum is a 25-minute walk around Lake Luzern. To get there without the hike, catch bus #6 or #8, or take a boat (summer only) to "Verkehrshaus." Buses and all boats depart from Bahnhofplatz, in front of the train station. The TI's *City Guide* includes a map of bus routes. On the bus, the stops for all the major sights are announced in English.

Public transportation prices in Luzern depend on which zones you travel in; a single ticket within the primary zone (Zone 1) costs 2.60 SF. Short rides, up to six stops—which would cover a trip to the Swiss Transportation Museum or the Lion Monument—cost 2 SF. A day pass is 9.50 SF, and a six-day pass costs 47.50 SF.

TOURS

Walking Tour—A two-hour tour in both English and German is offered every morning in summer (18 SF, departs from TI at 9:45, daily May–Oct, only Wed and Sat Nov–April).

Tourist Train—A tacky little train does a 40-minute circuit of the city's sights, departing from Hotel Schweizerhof (10 SF, 24-SF combo-ticket also includes walking tour and saves 4 SF, headphone commentary, daily April–Oct every hour from 11:00, less frequently off-season, tel. 041-220-1100).

Local Guide—Ursula Korner is a good guide (150 SF/2 hrs, tel. 041-248-6048, ursula.korner@ko5ive.com). The TI has a list of other guides.

SELF-GUIDED WALK

Reuss River Stroll

This self-guided orientation stroll will give you a brief overview of the town—going up along the Reuss River, then across one of Luzern's famous wooden bridges, then back through the old town. Begin at Bahnhofplatz, the busy zone between the lake and the train station. Stand in front of the big stone arch.

Bahnhofplatz: This is the transportation hub of Luzern—and all of Central Switzerland. From the area in front of the station, buses zip you anywhere in town. Along the lakefront, you can catch a boat for a lazy cruise around Lake Luzern. And underneath you is the extensive RailCity shopping mall, honeycombed with pedestrian passageways leading to different parts of town. The big stone **arch** was the entrance of the venerable old train station—built in the late 19th century when Switzerland became a top tourist spot, with Luzern as its main attraction. But it burned down in 1971 and was replaced with the modern station. Today, the arch hides vents for the huge underground parking lot below. This is a popular evening meeting spot for local teens.

• *The huge, new building with the big overhanging roof (on your right, with your back to the station) is the...*

LUZERN'S REUSS RIVER STROLL

Culture and Conference Center (Kultur-und-Kongress-zentrum): This building, finished in 1998 by Parisian architect Jean Nouvel, features a concert hall that hosts the Luzern Festival, one of Switzerland's biggest music events (mid-Aug–mid-Sept, www.lucernefestival.ch). Lake water is pumped up, into, through, and out of the building; if you wander around its far side, you'll see open channels that go right through the middle of the structure (blocked by benches, so distracted tourists don't fall in), as well as a big pond. The architect claims this design recalls earlier times, when Luzern was swamplands...but it more likely recalls his own original plans for the building. Nouvel wanted to put the center out in the middle of the lake. When he was voted down by the people of Luzern, he decided to surround it with water anyway. The plaza under the roof (which reflects the lake and weather, further incorporating the building into the surrounding environment) is a busy community space popular for open-air concerts.

• *Now walk in the opposite direction from the conference center, across the busy street. Stroll Bahnhofstrasse along the river until you have a good view of Luzern's most famous landmark, the wooden...*

Chapel Bridge (Kapellbrücke): Luzern began as a fishing village. By the 13th century, traffic streaming between northern and southern Europe went through nearby Gotthard Pass—and

Map

❶	Bahnhofplatz
❷	Culture & Conference Center
❸	Chapel Bridge
❹	Jesuit Church
❺	Reuss River Water Spikes
❻	Mill Bridge
❼	Mühlenplatz
❽	Weinmarkt Square
❾	Hirschenplatz
❿	Weggisgasse
⓫	Sternenplatz
⓬	St. Peter's Chapel & City View

To Löwenplatz sights

HALDENSTRASSE

ALTENSTR.

SCHWEIZERHOFQUAI

NATIONALQUAI

Kurplatz   To Swiss Transport Museum

Lake Luzern

To Swiss Transport Museum & other lake destinations

BOAT DOCKS (LANDUNGSBRÜCKEN)

FOUNTAIN

INSELQUAI

❶ WALK BEGINS

Bahnhofplatz

❷ CULTURE & CONFERENCE CENTER

TRAIN STATION

FROHBURGSTRASSE

POST

200 Meters
200 Yards

Luzern

Luzern became a bustling trading center. In the 14th century, this bridge was built—at an angle, to connect the town's medieval fortifications. As the bridge was part of the city defense system, the "window" openings facing the lake are smaller than the inland side, giving defenders more cover. The octagonal stone **Water Tower** (Wasserturm) predates the bridge by a century.

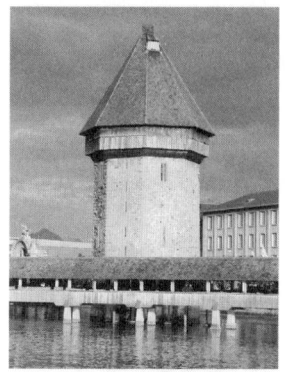

In 1993, a leisure boat moored under the bridge caught fire, and before long, Luzern's wooden landmark was in flames. (A plaque at the start of the bridge tells the story.) When you venture onto the bridge, you'll notice the wood is a lighter color—that is, newer—in the middle. Chapel Bridge was painstakingly rebuilt, but many of its famous paintings were lost (those still remaining under the wooden roof are the 17th-century originals, but are restored). Boats are no longer allowed under the bridge, it's now strictly non-smoking, and you'll notice tiny security cameras everywhere.

Wander out onto the bridge itself. Notice the colorful paintings overhead, which depict scenes from Luzern and Swiss history. The coats of arms on the paintings tell you which aristocratic families sponsored them. Painting #1 features a legendary and formidable giant, an icon of Luzern you'll see all over town. This big boy dates back to the Middle Ages, when mammoth bones discovered locally were mistakenly identified as the bones of a 15-foot-tall human giant. Painting #2 shows an angel shining a divine light on the place where the town would be born (and where, in the eighth century, a monastery was founded). The name "Luzern" is derived from the Latin word for "light." Painting #3 shows Luzern circa 1400—see how the bridge was already part of the city fortifications. Painting #6 shows a bigger city as it looked in 1630. In the middle, a painting features the town's patron saint, Mauritius (a plaque mid-bridge tells why he matters to Luzern). Paintings

#9 and #10 are left charred black as a reminder of the tragic fire.

Any swans out? Locals say they originated as a gift from the French king, Louis XIV, in appreciation for the protection his "Swiss guards" gave him. Today, local children make sure the swans get their daily bread.

• *Now head back to the train-station end of the bridge, and continue up the river. Enter the big, white...*

Jesuit Church (Jesuitenkirche): This was the first major Baroque church in Switzerland (built 1666–1677). It's dedicated to

the great missionary Francis Xavier, a co-founder of the Jesuit order, who's shown on the facade baptizing Asians (depicted looking like American Indians).

Even though Luzern was a relatively small town back then, the pope wanted to establish a strong presence in Central Switzerland to empower the local Catholics during the tense times of the Protestant Reformation. The interior of the church once dripped with Baroque stucco. It's been retouched in the lighter Rococo style (c. 1750). Rich as it looks, there's no real marble here—what you see is stucco made from ground-up marble laid smoothly and economically upon a wooden foundation.

The decorations on the ceiling celebrate the life (and afterlife) of Xavier. After the missionary dies, you see him heaven-bound (in the center). In an exuberant setting that includes both this church and Luzern's landmark Chapel Bridge, the pope's representative and townsfolk gather to wish him Godspeed. Xavier's cart is pulled by an elephant, a leopard, and a camel—commemorating his mission trips to the exotic Far East. Riding his chariot into heaven, he anticipates a hero's welcome (free, daily 6:00–18:30, www .jesuitenkirche-luzern.ch). As the local music school uses the church pipe organ for practice, you may enjoy an impromptu concert.

In the second niche up on the right, you can meet the only Swiss saint: Brother Klaus, a 15th-century hermit monk who lived in the nearby mountains. He was a great peacemaker between the cantons and is considered the original Swiss isolationist. Since Klaus' time, Switzerland has employed this ethic of avoiding pointless entanglement in foreign squabbles. The statue wears Klaus' original robe. His walking stick is at his feet.

• *Back outside, continue strolling downriver past the recommended Opus Restaurant and iron pedestrian bridge (at the narrowest crossing spot, marking the location of Luzern's first bridge in the 12th century) toward Luzern's other wooden bridge. Stop at the spiky fence partially damming up the river.*

Reuss River Water Spikes: This big river (pronounced "royce") flows out of the lake. Lake Luzern's main source of water is snowmelt, which trickles in from streams coming off the surrounding mountains. The water drains out of the lake here on its way to the Rhine. Luzern is responsible for controlling the flow of water and preventing the flooding of lakeside villages by maintaining the lake level. In the mid-19th century, the city devised and built a simple yet ingenious extendable dam (*Nadelwehr*, "water spikes"). When the water is highest (in the spring), they remove spikes to open the flow; as the summer wears on and the water level drops, they gradually broaden the dam to keep the water level up. In the winter, they close the dam entirely to keep the lake level high enough for boats. Engineers will want to study the information posted here.

• *Continuing along the river, you'll pass the Depot History Museum on your left (see "Museums," later in this chapter) before coming to the wooden...*

Mill Bridge (Spreuerbrücke): Unlike the rebuilt Chapel Bridge, this one's original—and the city is determined to keep it that way (try to find the low-profile security cameras). Cross the bridge, appreciating the fine old 17th-century paintings. Painting #1 shows Luzern's favorite giant again, with the blue-and-white city and cantonal banners under the double eagle of the Holy Roman Empire—a reminder that the German emperor granted free status to the city. The flip side shows Judgment Day, with some going to heaven and others to hell. As you cross the bridge, notice that each painting includes a skeleton. Townsfolk crossed the bridge daily, and these scenes provided vivid reminders that nobody, in any walk of life, can escape death (an especially poignant message in times of war and plague, when these were painted). Like the other wooden bridge, this bridge was part of the city fortification—its downstream defending wall is higher.

Midway across is a little 16th-century chapel, built to guard against destruction by flood. A line of family crests acknowledges the volunteers who, over the years, have kept the chapel decorated according to the season. Since 1987, this has been the work of Frau Segesser. While you're paused here, notice the serious woodwork.

The wide stretch at the end of the bridge was to accommodate wagons delivering grain or whatever to be milled. Once upon a time, 10 mills churned here—this was the medieval industrial center of Luzern. The bridge's name, "Spreu" means "chaff" (the sheath surrounding the wheat), which was separated from the wheat at the mill. You can see sketches of these mills as you leave the bridge (on the red wall on the left). A turbine that generated power in 1889 sits quiet on the left, and the tradition of harnessing water power continues here. The stream of water spurting into the air (on the right) indicates that the modern hydroelectric plant—underwater below you—is engaged. It creates enough power for 1,000 households. (From here, sometimes it's possible to walk out on the fishing pier.)

After crossing the bridge, you find yourself in **Mühlenplatz** (traffic-free each summer), the square at the entrance to the old town. The riverfront Hug bakery on your right is a good place for lunch or a snack (see "Eating," page 70). The fun facade next door to Fischer Stube (Mühlenplatz 11) tells the story of the wine god Bacchus (and marks the only down-and-dirty bar you'll see in this elegant town).

• *At the top of the square (under the Swiss Marilyn Monroe), head right on Kramgasse, then take the first left onto Weinmarktgasse, which leads to...*

Weinmarkt Square: In medieval Luzern, this square served as a marketplace for wine (as the name implies). The big mural on the decrepit green building at the top of the square looks like the Last Supper, but it's actually the Wedding Feast at Cana, where Jesus turned water into wine. On the right (as you face the mural), the facade of a now-gone pharmacy comes with a wise saying, *Amor medicabilis nvllis herbis* (roughly, "No medicine can cure a broken heart"). Across the square is a modern building with a secret message hiding in its strange zigzags. Start at the top left and read: W-E-I-N-M-A-R-K-T.

The soldiers on the fine 15th-century fountain are there to remind visitors that this town is tough and strong.

• *Leave the square on the left side of the big mural. You'll walk one block to...*

Hirschenplatz: This square hasn't always been a square—notice the footprints of two former buildings in the middle. It's named for the Hirschen ("Deer") Restaurant, with the elaborate golden sign. Across from that, try to guess who used to have a shop in the big green building. Yep—the jeweler (see all the rings?). Notice that, along with a happy cupid at the top, death is lurking again. To the right of that building, look for the painting of a famous German writer with the legend, *"Goethe logierte hier 1779."* Goethe—the "German Shakespeare"—visited Luzern and stayed in a hotel on this corner. The grand facade on the Dornach House, from 1899, celebrates the 400-year anniversary of the last battle against the Germans. Switzerland has enjoyed a durable understanding that there can be disagreements but no wars with its historically aggressive and militaristic neighbor to the north.

Continue out of the square onto the busy **Weggisgasse.** As you stroll, consider that every building in the old town—whether new or rebuilt—is required to offer residential apartments to prevent this historic zone from becoming only office space and touristy shops.

• *After a few blocks, you'll come to the Manor department store, with a tasty and convenient top-floor cafeteria (see page 71). Turn right after the Manor store and walk one block to...*

Sternenplatz: This tiny square is dominated by the colorful facade of the Restaurant Fritschi. The paintings feature symbols from Luzern's annual Mardi Gras celebration—the city's biggest event, called Fasnacht here. Pictured near the top of the building are the restaurant owners, Mr. and Mrs. Fritschi, celebrating Fasnacht by wearing masks and throwing oranges. Flanking them are their trusty servants, a nanny and a jester—who, in this case, bear a striking resemblance to the Fritschis. Below them is the story of Fasnacht: The cock calls at 5:00 in the morning the Thursday before Ash Wednesday (on the left), and the people get up to frighten winter away. Mr. and Mrs. Fritschi arrive on their wagon to kick off the festivities (on the right). Flying around the scene are oranges—traditionally tossed from the Fritschis to their adoring fans. Once rare here in winter, oranges are special to the festivities, as they mark the beginning of spring.

Continue down the street at the bottom of the square (Hans-Holbein-Gasse), and you'll stumble on a colorful fountain with masks of Herr and Frau Fritschi and their servants. Continue around to the riverfront, walking around **St. Peter's Chapel,** the namesake of Chapel Bridge—which you've arrived at once again. We finish our walk here, with *the* classic Luzern view: the Chapel Bridge and Water Tower, with Mount Pilatus hovering in the background.

• *From here you may want to take a...*

Lakefront Stroll: Consider walking from here along the lakefront, past the National Hotel toward the Swiss Transport Museum. The delightful pathway was built during the tourism boom in the 19th century, when this part of the bay was filled in and fancy resort hotels went up—giving this city the nickname "Monte Carlo of Switzerland." Simply follow the tree-lined waterfront promenade (Nationalquai) that begins near the Hofkirche (the big church with the pointy spires). Believe it or not, Luzern's wooden Chapel Bridge used to stretch all the way to that church.

SIGHTS

Museums

Luzern is charming enough that simply strolling the streets and bridges and cruising the lake would be enough for a happy day of sightseeing. But the city also offers some fine museums, especially if you're into modern art.

▲Rosengart Collection (Sammlung Rosengart Luzern)—In the 1930s and 1940s, wealthy resident Siegfried Rosengart palled around with all-star modern artists, financing and collecting their works. This museum displays the fruits of his labor, with three floors of all the big names from the late 19th and early 20th centuries (15 SF, 13 SF with Visitor's Card, 18-SF combo-ticket also includes Picasso Museum, covered by Swiss Pass, good English booklet-2.50 SF, otherwise you can borrow English info sheets, daily April–Oct 10:00–18:00, Nov–March 11:00–17:00, a few blocks from the train station in the new town at Pilatusstrasse 10, tel. 041-220-1660, www.rosengart.ch).

The ground floor features an extensive Picasso collection (mostly lesser works from the 1950s and 1960s). Several other Rosengart Picassos were donated to the city, becoming the core of the Picasso Museum across the river (next entry). Upstairs are a few early Picassos, as well as works by Braque, Monet, Renoir, Miró, Chagall, Cézanne, Matisse, Modigliani, and Pissarro. In the basement are 125 small works by Paul Klee, displayed chronologically by room number so you can follow the evolution of his career. Watch as Klee discovers colors and blossoms from a doodler and sometime watercolor artist into a mature painter.

▲▲**Picasso Museum Luzern**—In 1978, the Rosengart family donated eight Picassos to the city of Luzern. Over the years, the collection has grown to fill three floors of a creaky old building next door to the Town Hall. You'll see various Picasso ink sketches and even a ceramic pigeon. While the "Picassos" here are nothing special, Picasso himself is: More than 200 black-and-white candid photographs of the artist, by American David Douglas Duncan, make this museum a ▲▲▲ experience for Picasso fans. I've seen a pile of Picassos, but never have I gotten personal with him as I did here. Duncan's intimate photos of the artist and his family, scattered around the museum, capture the very human personality of this larger-than-life genius. The photos—taken in Picasso's later years, and many featuring his wife Jacqueline—provide insight into his artistic process, as well as his lifestyle, showing him at work and at play. As a fly on the wall of his chaotic studio, you'll see Picasso in the bathtub, getting a haircut, playing dress-up, moving to a new house, horsing around with his kids, entertaining his guest Gary Cooper, and getting a ballet lesson from Jacqueline. The excellent English descriptions—which you must borrow when you buy your ticket—are essential for getting the stories behind the photos (8 SF, 7 SF with Visitor's Card, 18-SF combo-ticket includes Rosengart Collection, covered by Swiss Pass, 5-SF English brochure, daily April–Oct 10:00–18:00, Nov–March 11:00–17:00, in the Am-Rhyn-Haus at Furrengasse 21, tel. 041-410-3533).

▲**Depot History Museum (Depot Historisches Museum Luzern)**—This cluttered old museum is a "depot" for the accumulated bric-a-brac of Luzern's past (10 SF, 8 SF with Visitor's Card, covered by Swiss Pass, Tue–Sun 10:00–17:00, closed Mon, Pfistergasse 24, tel. 041-228-5424, www.hmluzern.ch).

The museum is in one of Luzern's oldest surviving buildings, which used to house military weapons and uniforms. Their collection is just too big to display effectively, so they've come up with an innovative concept: Throw all of their archived stuff together and display it on three crowded floors. You'll wander through shelves of old weapons, stained-glass windows, sculptures, and old-fashioned tourism posters. The items are displayed without much rhyme or reason, and each is labeled with a barcode. You'll use a scanner (included with entry) to scan the items you're interested in and get the history (in English on your handheld screen).

▲**Swiss Transport Museum (Verkehrshaus)**—This enormous complex, across the lake from the train station, includes hundreds of exhibits in several different buildings, covering virtually all modes of transportation. It's a fun excursion, but it's pricey (though covered by Swiss Pass); a bit dated (the giant country map is nothing when you've Google-Earthed); and a little overwhelming, demanding at least a half-day. If you're in town for only one day, I'd skip this and enjoy the museums and ambience in the old town. But if you have a second day, have your kids in tow, and are obsessed with trains, planes, and automobiles, this can be time well spent.

Getting There: From downtown, it's a 25-minute walk to the museum, most of it along a beautiful promenade (see "Lakefront Stroll," page 62). This is a pleasant stroll, even if you're not going to the museum. To make a faster beeline to the museum, take bus #6 or #8 from the station, and get off at the Verkehrshaus stop (the stop is announced in English, plus you'll see the huge, barrel-shaped, can't-miss-it IMAX theater). For a more scenic approach, catch a boat in front of the train station (to Verkehrshaus; 9.60 SF round-trip, 10 min each way).

Cost: 24 SF, covered by Swiss Pass. In addition to the exhibits, the museum has a wide variety of shows and demonstrations (pick up a schedule—and inquire about English-speaking events—as you enter). These include a planetarium show (included in entry price) and an IMAX theater (costs 16 SF extra, www.imax.ch). Combo-tickets are also available (32 SF for museum plus IMAX).

Hours and Information: Daily April–Oct 10:00–18:00, Nov–March 10:00–17:00, IMAX shows Fri–Sat until 21:00, Lidostrasse 5, tel. 0848-852-020, www.verkehrshaus.ch).

Touring the Transport Museum: Starting in the first building, you'll come across a 30-minute show about the Gotthard Tunnel. Then you'll wander through endless halls of train engines and tram cars. As you exit, you'll be face-to-face with some Swissair jetliners, and surrounded by pavilions devoted to various vehicles (such as planes, cars, boats, motorcycles, spaceships, and high-mountain lifts). Many of the exhibits are interactive, like the parasailing simulator, where you lie down on a smoothly gliding platform and peer down at the countryside below. Upstairs in the boat and cable-car building, be sure to seek out the **Swissarena**—an enormous (more

than 2,000 square feet) aerial photograph of Switzerland (follow signs that look like a Swiss map in a CBS-style eye). This photo map, spread out on the floor like laminated linoleum, is detailed enough to show virtually every single building within Switzerland's borders. Slide on the Swiss slippers, borrow a map and magnifying glass, and glide across Switzerland, looking for the places you've visited so far.

Other Museums—Music fans may want to venture out to the **Richard Wagner Museum,** housed in a building where the composer lived (6 SF, 5 SF with Visitor's Card, covered by Swiss Pass, mid-March–Nov Tue–Sun 10:00–12:00 & 14:00–17:00, closed Mon and off-season, along the lakefront south of train station at Wagnerweg 27, tel. 041-360-2370). The **Museum of Art Luzern** (Kunstmuseum Luzern), in the lakeside cultural center, features special exhibits of contemporary art (16 SF, covered by Swiss Pass, Tue–Sun 10:00–17:00, Wed until 20:00, closed Mon, Europaplatz 1, tel. 041-226-7800, www.kunstmuseumluzern.ch). The **Museum of Natural History** (Natur-Museum), with an emphasis on interactive exhibits, is great for kids (6 SF, 5 SF with Visitor's Card, covered by Swiss Pass, Tue–Sun 10:00–17:00, closed Mon, Kasernenplatz 6, tel. 041-228-5411, www.naturmuseum.ch).

Near Löwenplatz

The following sights comprised the original 19th-century tourist center of Luzern. They're clustered around Löwenplatz, a square that's a 10-minute walk from the old town (or a short bus ride; take bus #1 three stops from the train station, direction Maihof, 2 SF). This remains the heart of touristy Luzern, with a must-see monument and a trio of tacky but fun attractions. If you're doing the two bigger attractions here (Glacier Garden and Bourbaki Panorama), you might as well buy the 17-SF **Lionpass,** which saves you 3 SF.

I've listed the museums in descending order of respectability (or ascending order on the international "tacky tourist trap" scale).

▲**Lion Monument (Löwendenkmal)**—This famous monument is an essential stop if you're visiting Luzern—if only because when

you get back home, everyone will ask you, "Did you see the lion?" The huge sculpture (33 feet long by 20 feet tall) is carved right into a cliff face, over a reflecting pool in a peaceful park (free, open sunrise to dusk). While it's often overrun with tour groups, a peaceful moment here is genuinely moving: The mighty lion rests his paws on a shield, with his head cocked to one side, tears streaming down his cheeks. In his side is the broken-off end of a spear, which is slowly killing the noble beast. This heartbreaking figure represents the Swiss mercenaries who were killed or executed defending the French king in the French Revolution. The inscription reads, *Helvetiorum fidei ac virtuti*—"To the loyalty and bravery of the Swiss."

▲**Bourbaki Panorama**—Here's your chance to get right in the middle of a great painting—literally. In the 19th century, before the dawn of cinema, modern people were hungry for visual entertainment. Uniform panorama theaters like this were built all over Europe and hosted various gigantic paintings, which were rolled up and taken on road trips. This 360-degree painting (a 33-foot-tall wraparound canvas with a circumference of 360 feet) tells the story of the culminating battle of the Franco-Prussian War. The 1.50-SF booklet explains it all and makes for a good souvenir (8 SF, 7 SF with Visitor's Card, covered by Lionpass and Swiss Pass, daily 9:00–18:00, Löwenplatz 11, tel. 041-412-3030, www.bourbakipanorama.ch).

Upon arrival, request an English playing of the 12-minute soundtrack of the battle. Spend your waiting time enjoying the fine first-floor exhibit about 19th-century entertainment. When the English narration plays, be on the second-floor viewing platform to savor all 360 degrees of the dramatic conclusion of the Franco-Prussian War. For three days in February of 1871, the 87,000-man French Army—led by the panorama's namesake, General Bourbaki—trudged through the snow across the Swiss border. Once in Switzerland, they gave up their weapons and surrendered to the Swiss—who, the story goes, took excellent care of the French, nursing them back to health before sending them home.

The Bourbaki Panorama was painted by Edouard Castres, who was actually there (as a Red Cross volunteer) on that frigid morning. The 1881 painting was thoroughly refurbished in 2000, when several life-size figures were added to the foreground. Sound effects fill the hall as you view the painting. The museum exhibit gives more background on the Franco-Prussian War and Bourbaki's army, as well as details about this and other panorama paintings.

Glacier Garden (Gletschergarten)—This complex is a strange sort of mini-theme-park with an eclectic hodgepodge of exhibits, most loosely relating to alpine geology. While it's very touristy, and the various pieces don't quite hang together (such as the fun but out-of-place Hall of Mirrors), it adds up to a pleasant if overpriced activity (12 SF, 10 SF with Visitor's Card, covered by Lionpass and Swiss Pass, daily April–Oct 9:00–18:00, Nov–March 10:00–17:00, Denkmalstrasse 4, tel. 041-410-4340, www.gletschergarten.ch).

Pick up the English info booklet as you enter, and follow the numbers on the confusing one-way path. First, you'll walk through the **glacier-grinded grounds** that give the museum its name. While geologists would get a thrill out of this, it was just a bunch of holes to me. Then you'll enter the **museum,** with exhibits about glacial processes, as well as (downstairs) huge 3-D reliefs of late-18th-century Luzern, and the Alps and lakes of Central Switzerland. Back upstairs, you'll cross directly into the **Amrein's House,** an old chalet with some original furnishings and models of traditional Swiss buildings. As you leave, you have the option of hiking up the steep **Tower Walk,** which leads to another old chalet and an observation tower.

At the end, be sure to visit the **Hall of Mirrors.** This undeniably enjoyable attraction, made in 1896 for a national exhibition in Geneva, is a delightfully low-tech fun house. You'll grope your way through twisting corridors—with mirrors on all sides—decorated like a Disneyfied Alhambra. It's confusing, dizzying, and claustrophobic, but goofy fun. As you run into yourself (literally) again and again, you'll lament the poor sap who has to clean the smudge marks off all those mirrors (walk slowly and—if you don't mind looking foolish—with arms outstretched). As you leave, giggling and nauseated, you'll ask yourself: So, what exactly did that have to do with glaciers?

Alpineum—This disappointing attraction, overshadowed by its substantial gift shop, displays a handful of paintings and reliefs of famous Swiss mountain peaks and panoramas. These are the same views you'll see if you visit the peaks in person—but in a musty, outmoded, tourist-trap environment. The exhibit also includes English explanations and miniature models of traditional houses, trains, boats, people, and cows. Visit this only if you're also doing the Glacier Garden and Bourbaki Panorama, in which case the Lionpass gets you in free (5 SF, covered by Swiss Pass, April–Oct daily 9:00–12:30 & 13:30–18:00, closed Nov–March, Denkmalstrasse 11, tel. 041-410-6266, www.alpineum.ch).

SLEEPING

Luzern accommodations are expensive. I've listed one big, classic hotel (the Waldstätterhof), a handful of small and basic hotels, and a good backpacker option. The prices here are for high season (April–Oct); you'll pay marginally less off-season. These are all centrally located (except Backpackers Luzern). As the city can be noisy at night, ask for a room on a high floor.

$$$ Hotel Waldstätterhof is a grand old hotel across the street from the train station with reasonable rates for its high level of comfort. Its 80 bright, spacious rooms come with all the amenities (Db-220–260 SF depending on size, pricier suites, Zentralstrasse 4, tel. 041-227-1271, fax 041-227-1272, www.hotel-waldstaetterhof.ch, info@hotel-waldstaetterhof.ch).

LUZERN HOTELS AND RESTAURANTS

$$$ Hotel des Alpes is a good bet if you want to sleep right on the river in the old town. Its lobby hides above a busy restaurant, but the 45 rooms are fresh and modern, with new bathrooms. Pricier riverfront rooms come with beautiful views (riverview rooms: Sb-160 SF, Db-255 SF; back-side rooms: Sb-135 SF, Db-205 SF, less in winter; some rooms have balconies for the same price, Furrengasse 3, tel. 041-417-2060, fax 041-417-2066, www.desalpes-luzern.ch, info@desalpes-luzern.ch).

$$$ Hotel Baslertor and its cheaper annex, **Hotel Pension Rösli** (6 rooms, across the street), offer well-located rooms for various budgets. The Baslertor's 30 rooms, with old, dark furnishings, are more expensive and come in three sizes (small Db-175 SF, medium Db-200 SF, large Db-225 SF, Sb-150 SF, extra bed-25 SF, family deals, elevator, atmospheric breakfast room, plush public spaces, small, solar-heated swimming pool). The Rösli pension—an older building with lower ceilings—has six rooms with even older furnishings and no elevator (Db-150 SF). Both hotels charge 20 SF per person extra for breakfast. Roland runs a tight ship (with strict cancellation policies) staffing both hotels from the Baslertor reception desk (Pfistergasse 17, tel. 041-249-2222, fax 041-249-2233, www.baslertor.ch, info@baslertor.ch).

To Löwenplatz sights

HALDENSTRASSE

ALPENSTR

SCHWEIZERHOFQUAI

NATIONALQUAI

Kurplatz — To Swiss Transport Museum

Lake Luzern

To Swiss Transport Museum & other lake destinations

BOAT DOCKS (LANDUNGSBRÜCKEN)

INSELQUAI

Bahnhofplatz

FOUNTAIN

CULTURE & CONFERENCE CENTER

TRAIN STATION

FROHBURGSTRASSE

To ❼

POST

200 Meters
200 Yards

❶ Hotel Waldstätterhof
❷ Jailhotel Löwengraben
❸ Hotel des Alpes
❹ Hotel Goldener Stern
❺ Hotel Baslertor & Hotel Pension Rösli
❻ To Hotel Alpha
❼ To Backpackers Luzern
❽ Restaurant Rathaus Brauerei
❾ Hug Bakery Café
❿ Manora Cafeteria
⓫ Opus Rest. & Wine Bar
⓬ Nix in der Laterne Rest.
⓭ Restaurant Schiff
⓮ Restaurant Taube

Luzern

$$ Hotel Goldener Stern is a good, solid value offering 16 perfectly acceptable rooms with some street noise over a restaurant (Sb-95 SF, smaller top-floor D-100 SF, Db-140–150 SF, Tb-180 SF, Qb-200 SF, prices drop for longer stays or when slow, elevator, church bells ring at night, Burgerstrasse 35, tel. 041-227-5060, fax 041-227-5061, www.goldener-stern.ch, hotel@goldener-stern.ch, Amrein family).

$$ Hotel Alpha, once a convent-run boarding house for village girls, is now popular with students and offers 60 big, bright, institutional rooms, most with toilet down the hall (S-70 SF, twin D-98 SF, twin Db-130 SF, T-135 SF, comfy TV room, Zähringerstrasse 24, at intersection with Pilatusstrasse, tel. 041-240-4280, fax 041-240-9131, www.hotelalpha.ch, info@hotelalpha .ch). Located in a pleasant residential area, it's a 10-minute walk or an easy bus ride from the train station (take bus #1, #2, or #10, get off at Pilatusplatz).

$$ Jailhotel Löwengraben is a theme hotel renting clean, functional cells in the renovated former city prison on a nondescript street a few steps from the heart of the old town. As much an experience as a place to sleep, it has 133 beds in 56 cells (3 double beds, but the vast majority—logically—are twins). Cells,

Sleep Code

(1.10 SF = about $1, country code: 41)
S = Single, **D** = Double/Twin, **T** = Triple, **Q** = Quad, **b** = bathroom, **s** = shower only. Unless otherwise noted, credit cards are accepted, English is spoken, and breakfast is included.

To help you sort easily through these listings, I've divided the rooms into three categories, based on the price for a standard double room with bath:

$$$ Higher Priced—Most rooms 150 SF or more.
  $$ Moderately Priced—Most rooms between 100–150 SF.
    $ Lower Priced—Most rooms 100 SF or less.

which can be a bit stuffy, come with cot-like beds, tiny barred windows, and reinforced doors—so (except for the mod little WCs) it indeed feels like a prison (S-69 SF, Sb-98 SF, D-98 SF, Db-128 SF, Tb-174 SF, people who actually did time here enjoy sleeping in the elaborate wardens' suites-180–240 SF, 10 percent discount if you book direct with this guidebook, non-smoking, Löwengraben 18, tel. 041-410-7830, fax 041-410-7832, www.jailhotel.ch, hotel @jailhotel.ch).

$ Backpackers Luzern is calm and well-run, sharing a modern, blocky building with student dorms (*Studentenheim*) in a peaceful residential area a 15-minute walk south of the train station. The place has 30 rooms with balconies, a pair of kitchens for guests, a welcoming lounge, no curfew, Internet access (10 SF/hr), and laundry (9 SF per load for full service). The walk to the center is mostly along the lake, through pretty parks and next to a fine beach (29 SF per person in 4-bed rooms, 34 SF per person in 2-bed rooms, includes sheets, no breakfast, reception open 7:30–10:00 & 16:00–23:00, elevator, Alpenquai 42, tel. 041-360-0420, fax 041-360-0442, www.backpackerslucerne.ch).

EATING

While eateries along the river are pricey and a bit touristy, if you have one evening in Luzern, that's where you'll make the best memories. Here's a selection of places with decent prices and great riverfront ambience (except Manora, in a department store).

Hug Bakery Café, a cuddly place overlooking the river at the old town end of the Mill Bridge, is in the middle of the sightseeing action. People come for just a drink, snack, or dessert, or to settle in for a meal. There's a selection of basic traditional Swiss dishes (such as fondue and *Rösti,* 20 SF) and 17-SF two-course lunch deals to enjoy at outdoor tables with river views or in the splendid glassed-in terrace (Mon–Sat 7:00–18:30, Sun 10:00–17:00, also open until 23:00 in summer in good weather, Mühlenplatz 6). The cheap take-away salads, pastries, and sandwiches are made to order for the inviting riverside benches just a few steps away.

Opus, next to the big Jesuit Church, is both a trendy wine bar and a good restaurant. You have several options: meat, fish, and vegetarian dishes with international flair (30–40 SF); a lush and varied salad bar ("antipasti buffet"—a small plate piled high makes a light and healthy dinner for 18 SF); or your choice of dried meats and cheeses (20–25 SF, choose and cut your own fresh bread to go with it) to complement your wine. They always have a couple dozen bottles of wine open and available by the glass. Sit in the upscale, colorful interior; in the candlelit and extremely romantic wine cellar; or out front, right on the river (open long hours daily, Bahnhofstrasse 16, tel. 041-226-4141, www.restaurant-opus.ch).

Restaurant Rathaus Brauerei is a lively microbrewery with an ideal riverfront location and a young, helpful staff. It's clearly a local favorite for its Seidel Rathausbier, brewed in such small quantities that you can only get it here. They serve their beer to ladies in a two-deciliter "elegant flute." Special seasonal brews are on the menu board, along with salads, "gourmet" pretzel sandwiches, 30-SF dishes, Swiss-style mac and cheese (20 SF), and the daily three-course 23-SF special—available until it's sold out (open long hours daily, Unter der Egg 2, tel. 041-410-5257).

Restaurant Taube is popular for serving "grandma's cooking" (great spot for a good *Rösti,* 25 SF) and for its riverside seating (18-SF 2-course business lunches, closed Sun, Burgerstrasse 3, tel. 041-210-0747).

Romantic **Nix in der Laterne** has a white-tablecloth-dressy interior and great outside seats right on the fast-rushing river. In keeping with their philosophy of using seasonal ingredients, they offer a small menu—not printed but on a roller that the waiter explains (50-SF 2-course dinners, 35-SF plates, cheaper lunch menus, daily 11:00–24:00, reservations smart in evening, Reusssteg 9, tel. 041-240-2543).

Restaurant Schiff has scenic riverfront tables in the old town with good traditional Swiss food, relatively reasonable prices, and a fun, accessible menu (plenty of salads, pizzas, most main dishes 25–35 SF, open long hours daily, music many evenings, across the river from Jesuit Church, Unter der Egg 8, tel. 041-418-5252).

Manora, a cafeteria on the fifth floor of the Manor department store in the old town, is ideal for a fast, tasty, efficient lunch. Choose between a fresh salad bar (big plate-11 SF) or a variety of main dishes (10–15 SF). In good weather, climb the stairs to the outdoor terrace, with views over the rooftops of Luzern and up to the top of Pilatus. This place is packed with locals and very crowded during peak times—eat early or late, and send your travel partner up top to claim an outdoor table while you buy the food (Mon–Wed 9:00–18:30, Thu–Fri 9:00–21:00, Sat 8:00–16:00, closed Sun, non-smoking, Weggisgasse 5).

TRANSPORTATION CONNECTIONS

Luzern is marvelously well-situated in Switzerland, with convenient connections to anywhere in the country. Note that Luzern is on both the Golden Pass and the William Tell Express scenic rail lines (see Scenic Rail Journeys chapter).

From Luzern by Train to: Zürich (3/hr, 1 hr), **Zürich Airport** (2/hr, 1.25 hrs, half change in Zürich), **Bern** (hourly, 1 hr; or 2/hr with transfer in Olten, 1.5 hrs), **Interlaken** (hourly, 2 hrs), **Lausanne** (hourly direct, 2.5 hrs; more with transfer in Olten and/or Bern), **Appenzell** (2/hr, 2.75 hrs, change in Herisau or in Zürich and Gossau), **Lugano** (hourly, 3 hrs, half with change in Arth-Goldau), **Chur** (hourly, 2.25 hrs, change in Thalwil). Train info: toll tel. 0900-300-3004 or www.rail.ch.

Central Switzerland: Day Trips from Luzern

Luzern is perched on the edge of a super-scenic lake and ringed by family-friendly mountain peaks that are easily conquerable for a price. The city is the perfect springboard for alpine excursions. The following side-trips—including a boat cruise, two different mountain lifts, and a military fortress—are all popular excursions.

If you're serious about day-tripping, consider a **Tell-Pass.** This pass includes two days of free passage on lifts, boats, and several area train lines in a seven-day period (with a 50 percent discount on the other 5 days; 148 SF, or 119 SF with a Swiss Pass, buy at TIs, train stations, and boat docks, April–Oct only, www.tellpass.ch). While this can be a good deal if you're home-basing in the region for a week, it probably won't pay for itself on a quick visit.

Note that the military fortress is open only on weekends from April through October.

Possible Do-It-All Day Trip: This plan combines most of these adventures (the fortress, a mini-lake cruise, and the Pilatus mountain lift—up one side and down the other) into one jam-packed day trip. (Note that it must be done on a Saturday or Sunday to include the fortress.) Confirm all the schedules and logistics at the TI before embarking: Take an early train or boat to Stansstad and tour Fortress Fürigen, then have lunch in Stansstad. Catch the 14:00 boat to Alpnachstad (20-min ride), where you ride up the mountain on the Pilatus cogwheel train (departing 14:30, arriving at the summit at 15:00). When you're ready to return to Luzern, catch the gondola for the seven-minute ride down to Fräkmüntegg (4/hr, last departure at 17:15, or 18:00 July–Aug), where you have a chance to do the luge ride before changing to a smaller gondola down to Kriens (they run constantly until 17:30, or 18:15 July–Aug, or 16:15 Nov–March, 30-min ride, don't get off at Krienseregg). In Kriens, walk five minutes following the white signs to *Luzern bus*. (You don't want the bus stop in front of the building.) Bus #1 gets you to Luzern's main station in 10 minutes. Whew!

Boats of Note: These boats can help you connect the excursions in this chapter: **Stansstad** (Fortress Fürigen) **to Alpnachstad** (where you catch Pilatus cogwheel train; 6 boats/day, 20–40 min, plus 2 steamboats/day July–Aug, 9.60 SF); **Stansstad to Luzern** (6 boats/day, 60–75 min, plus 2 steamboats/day July–Aug, 16 SF); **Alpnachstad to Luzern** (7 boats/day, 80–90 min, 22 SF).

Lake Cruises

Lake Luzern (or Lucerne) is the English name for the lake, but the Swiss call it the Vierwaldstättersee—"Lake of Four Forest

Cantons," since it lies at the intersection of four of Switzerland's states (or cantons, as their political units are called).

On this most-touristed lake in Switzerland, there are a variety of routes and destinations (33 stops in all). Cruises range from a one-hour sampler tour (around Luzern's "harbor") to a full-blown six-hour exploration (to Flüelen, at the far end of the lake, and back again). Some routes are round-trip; on others, you'll get out, explore, and then take the next boat back. Romantics will want to hitch a ride on one of the five old-fashioned paddleboat steamers.

The easiest and most efficient trip is to boat across from the train station to the Swiss Transport Museum (Verkehrshaus, see page 64; 9.60 SF round-trip, roughly hourly, 10 min each way). In summer, a "castle cruise" makes one-hour (14.40 SF) and two-hour (22 SF) round-trip sightseeing swings around the lake (3–5/day, from piers 3 or 4). For most, the two-hour circle is about as much of a scenic cruise as the lake deserves. Another easy two-hour excursion is to take the boat from Luzern out to Weggis or Vitznau (under Mount Rigi, across the lake; see "Mountain Lifts," next page), then back

Central Switz.

to Luzern (29 SF round-trip to Weggis, 35 SF to Vitznau). You can buy tickets and get advice on which trip best fits your schedule at the Luzern TI.

Boats leave from in front of the Luzern train station. They're operated by the Lake Lucerne Navigation Company (tel. 041-367-6767, www.lakelucerne.ch). Note that these boats are free with a Eurailpass or Swiss Pass. But remember that if you're using a flexipass, the boat trip costs a flexi-day. Doing the lake cruise on the day you arrive or depart—when you're already using a flexi-day for your train transportation—is a smart plan.

Mountain Lifts

There's no shortage of mountain lifts in Central Switzerland. I've described the two most famous and most accessible from Luzern: Mount Pilatus and Mount Rigi.

Mount Pilatus

Pilatus looms behind Luzern, offering the city a dramatic back-drop...and an enjoyable desti-nation. While legend dictates that it's named for Pontius Pilate—whose body is supposedly in one of its lakes, kicking up a fuss if disturbed—it more likely comes from a Latin word mean-ing "cloudy." It's also said to be infested with dragons.

You can ascend Pilatus (to

the overlook platform, at 7,000 feet, called "Pilatus Kulm") two different ways: by cogwheel train (the world's steepest, at 48 percent grade) or gondola (in three stages).

By Train: The cogwheel train leaves from the lakeside town of Alpnachstad—from Luzern, take the S5 train to Alpnachstad (2/hr, 20 min), or take the 90-min boat (7/day, 22 SF); cogwheel train runs mid-May–mid-Nov only, goes at least hourly, daily 8:10–17:35, 30 min up, 40 min down; for the best views going up, take a downhill-facing seat on the right side).

By Gondola: The gondola leaves from the town of Kriens, virtually a suburb of Luzern (from in front of Luzern train station, take city bus #1 for 10 min to Kriens; gondola goes continuously, daily July–Aug 8:30–17:30, April–June and Sept–Oct until 16:45, Nov–March until 15:45, closes periodically for maintenance Oct–Nov). From Kriens, you'll take a small gondola to Krienseregg (recreation area with trails and playground), then on to Fräkmüntegg (total trip 30 min).

At Fräkmüntegg, you'll have a chance to zip down Switzerland's longest luge ride, called "Dragon Speed" (8 SF, almost a mile long, good weather only, May–Oct daily 10:00–12:00 & 13:15–17:00, until 17:30 Sat–Sun, until 18:00 daily July–Aug, no midday break July–Aug or Sat–Sun, www.rodelbahn.ch). At the fun Suspension Rope Park ("Seilpark"), you can test your agility high up on seven rope courses with varying degrees of difficulty (25 SF includes material and instruction, July–Aug daily 10:00–17:30; May–June and Sept–Oct Tue–Sun 10:00–17:00, closed Mon; closed off-season).

From Fräkmüntegg, it's another seven minutes in a bigger cable car to the observation platform at Pilatus Kulm.

Costs: A one-way segment to the top, no matter how you go, costs 32 SF; a round-trip costs 64 SF (with your choice of cogwheel train or gondola for each leg; does not include your transportation between Luzern and the cogwheel train or gondola stations). Eurailpass- and Swiss Pass–holders get a 30 percent discount. When you buy your ticket, tell them which way you want to go up and down (it's most interesting to go up one way, down the other). Don't throw your ticket away, as you'll have to scan it several times until you finally exit the last station. Be warned: Buying a one-way ticket up and hiking all the way down was a fatal decision for two Americans in 2003.

The handiest way to visit Pilatus from Luzern is with the popular **Golden Round Trip** package. This includes the bus to Kriens, the cable car up to Pilatus, the cogwheel train down to Alpnachstad, and a lazy, 90-minute boat trip back to Luzern (or the same route, reversed; 89 SF, 43 SF with Eurailpass or Swiss Pass, 17 SF less to return by train instead of boat, May–mid-Oct only). Figure out the best route with the help of Luzern's TI, or check www.pilatus.ch (tel. 041-329-1111, fax 041-329-1112).

At the Summit: The summit (Pilatus Kulm) is a family fun zone with plenty of activities, including a "summer toboggan" (Switzerland's longest at more than a mile). Hotel Bellevue acts as the visitors' center, with a good information office, restaurants, a souvenir shop, and free Internet terminals. Hotel Pilatus-Kulm hosts temporary exhibits. Its three restaurants have the original furnishings from 1889; there's also a modern self-service cafeteria. Check out the fancy WC: When you open a door, a red dragon claims the stall for you. The terrace below is full of free and comfortable deck chairs.

Hikes from Pilatus: These walks lead to great viewpoints. I've listed them roughly in order of difficulty, from easiest to most strenuous. All leave from the summit, Pilatus Kulm.

Two short **Dragonpaths** lead through tunnels to various viewpoints in the rock. These paths come with signs illustrating dragon tales by the famous Swiss artist Hans Erni.

A 10-minute hike takes you up to **Esel** ("Donkey," commemorating the pre-cable-car days, when Queen Victoria came up to Pilatus on the back of a donkey). Below, Esel hides an impressive part of Switzerland's anti-aircraft defense system. Find the gray, round structures within the imitation rock. Modern missiles behind the camouflage point to the skies. The biggest radar in Switzerland towers above Hotel Pilatus-Kulm in an off-limits military zone.

Hiking to **Tomlishorn** (35 min), you'll spot more camouflaged military installations. Stop at the yellow *Echo* sign and shout your message out to the world. Somebody out there keeps yelling it back.

A 90-minute hike leads to the 6,700-foot cross-capped summit of **Matthorn** (not Matterhorn). This is moderately strenuous—generally uphill, with lots of ups and downs. A visitors' book invites you to sign and leave your impressions on this breathtaking spot.

Sleeping at the Summit: You can spend the night on the summit of Pilatus. Linger outside to enjoy the views with the marmots and mountain goats...or head inside for the hotels' free nightly entertainment: movies and a disco on alternating nights. **$$$ Hotel Bellevue** is a modern, round building with 27 rooms—clean and bright, with Nordic-style furniture (Sb-111 SF, Db-192 SF). **$ Hotel Pilatus-Kulm** is a historic building from 1900 with basic, sink-only rooms (S-77 SF, D-124 SF). Both hotels come with a big breakfast and share the same contact information (tel. 041-329-1212, fax 041-329-1213, www.pilatus.ch, hotels@pilatus.ch).

Mount Rigi

This long, shelf-like mountain, across the lake from Luzern, provides sweeping views of Central Switzerland (and, on a clear day, Germany and France, too). Even though it's at a lower altitude than Pilatus (5,900 feet), this so-called "Queen of the Mountains" claims to offer the best vistas in the area. The mountain is laced with hiking trails and other attractions to while away an afternoon.

As with Pilatus, there are two ways to approach the topmost viewpoint, Rigi Kulm: via cogwheel train (from Arth-Goldau or Vitznau) or by cable car (from Weggis).

By Train: To go by cogwheel train, you have two options: from the town of Arth-Goldau ("behind" Rigi, accessible by train from Luzern) or from Vitznau (right on Lake Luzern, accessible by boat—but not train—from Luzern). The train from Luzern to Arth-Goldau takes 30 minutes; once there, you'll take the cogwheel train up to Rigi Kulm (35 min, departs hourly, coordinated with arrival of certain trains from Luzern, daily 8:00–18:10). Or take the boat from Luzern to Vitznau (about 1 hr), then take a different cogwheel train from there up to Rigi Kulm (30 min, departs hourly, daily 8:40–22:05).

By Cable Car: To go by cable car, take the boat from Luzern to Weggis (30–45 min), then board the cable car to Rigi Kaltbad (10 min, departs 2/hr, Mon–Fri 6:50–18:45, Sat–Sun 8:15–18:45); there you'll switch to the cogwheel train that brings you the rest of the way up to Rigi Kulm.

Costs: As with Mount Pilatus, you can go up one way and down the other for maximum experience and the same price. Before ascending, figure out your complete route at the Luzern TI. No matter how you go, the price from the base of the mountain to Rigi Kulm is 35 SF one-way, 58 SF round-trip, plus the cost of getting from Luzern to the cogwheel train or cable-car stations. Figure a total of 90 SF per person for the total round-trip from Luzern (plan on 5–6 hrs). Note that cogwheel train and cable-car prices are discounted 25 percent with a Eurailpass and 50 percent with a Swiss Pass; the train trip from Luzern to Arth-Goldau and the boat trips to Vitznau and Weggis are also included in your pass (but you'll have to use one of your flexi-days). The schedules and prices listed here are for peak summer season (May–Oct); they may vary in shoulder and ski seasons (confirm at Luzern TI, or check www.rigi.ch).

Fortress Fürigen Museum of War History

The Fortress Museum of Fürigen (Festung Fürigen Museum zur Wehrgeschichte) shows you another face of the country—the reason why Switzerland was able to remain peaceful and

Swiss Military Readiness

Strolling through a peaceful Swiss village—charming pastoral greenery studded with rustic farmhouses between an Alp and a lake—my friend walked with me to the door of a nondescript barn. He said, "Stand here," and slid open the door to reveal a solitary mighty gun—pointing right at me. Crossing a field, kicking a stray soccer ball back to a group of happy grade-schoolers, we came to another barn. This time I noticed the "wooden" door was actually metal, with a clever paint job. Inside was a military canteen, now selling snacks to civilians, and a steel ladder leading down into a military-gray world that felt like a vast submarine. A network of passages, just big enough for heavily armed soldiers to race down single file, led to a series of gun barns and subterranean command rooms with charts locating other installations in the area.

Switzerland may be famous for its neutrality, but it's been anything but lax defensively. Travelers marvel at how Swiss engineers have conquered their Alps with the world's most-expensive-per-mile road system. But no one designs a Swiss bridge or tunnel without designing its destruction. Each comes with built-in explosives, so, in the event of an invasion, the entire country can be blasted into a mountain fortress.

Even today, you can't get a building permit without an expensive first-class bomb shelter worked into the plan. Old tank barriers (nicknamed "Toblerones" for their shape) stand ready to be dragged across the roads to slow any invasion. Sprawling hospitals are dug into mountains, still ventilated to be kept dry and ready for use. And halfway up alpine cliffs, Batcave-type doors can slide open, allowing fighter jets to zoom into action from hidden airstrips cut out of solid rock. If you're approaching a mountain pass by car, look for the explosive patches ominously checkering the roads near the summit.

But the end of the Cold War in 1989 brought changes even to neutral Switzerland. Western armies began cutting back on their military spending, and Switzerland followed suit, with deep cuts in its defense budget. The Swiss Army met its tighter budget in part by closing many of the 15,000 hidden fortresses that protected the country's strategic roads, train lines, and mountain passes. Some of the forts, such as Fortress Fürigen, have been turned into tourist attractions no more formidable than medieval castles.

neutral: its elaborate and secret system of bunkers and fortresses. Unfortunately, this fascinating exhibit is open only Saturday and Sunday, April through October.

Enter through an innocent-looking wooden barrack. The bunker is always chilly, but no worries: Visitors are loaned original Swiss Army coats. Put on your coat, grab the English brochure that explains each room, and you're on your way. The radio station was placed near the entrance to assure clear reception. The living quarters were gas-proof, complete with specially sealed doors and devices to monitor the air for poison. The museum is a petting zoo of 20th-century weaponry. Visitors can fiddle with and even aim guns, knowing all the ammo is now imaginary. Imagine the photo op—you, in a Swiss military uniform, manning a cannon.

Historical photographs take you back to World War II. Fortress Fürigen was built in 1941 as part of a new military strategy: to protect Switzerland with fortresses hidden in the Alps, called *Réduitfestung* (roughly "shelter fortress"—see opposite page). In case of a Nazi invasion, the Swiss government would retreat to a secret bunker in the Berner Oberland, and Swiss troops would abandon the border regions and gather around this alpine stronghold. Fortress Fürigen was meant to protect roads and rail lines that led from Luzern and Zürich along Lake Luzern into the Berner Oberland. This was one of a network of fortresses in the area. After World War II, they were retooled with a new focus: the threat of the Soviet Union and nuclear war.

Big guns in the fortress could shoot more than six miles, and machine guns protected the immediate access routes to the bunker. This fortress could house and feed 100 people for three weeks. But in 1990, with the end of the Cold War, the practical Swiss decommissioned the fortress, refit it with vintage WWII and early Cold War gear, and opened it to the curious public.

Cost and Hours: Entry costs 5 SF, covered by Swiss Pass. The museum is open only on weekends from late spring through early fall (April–Oct Sat–Sun 11:00–17:00, closed Mon–Fri and Nov–March, tel. 041-618-7522). Remember to pick up the loaner English booklet as you enter.

Getting There: Fortress Fürigen is near the lakefront town of Stansstad (on Kehrsitenstrasse), below the village of Fürigen, not far from Luzern. It's an easy trip from Luzern by **train** (hourly, :41 past each hour, train S4, direction: Engelberg, 6 SF one-way, 15-min ride) or boat (see below).

From the train station in Stansstad, walk 15 minutes, following brown signs to *Festungsmuseum* or *Kehrsiten* (down Bahnhofstrasse to Stanserstrasse, cross and follow signs, right on Achereggstrasse, left passing swimming-pool sign and tennis courts, and finally along the lake).

You can also get to Stansstad from Luzern by **boat** (7/day, 60–75 min, plus 2 steamboats/day July–Aug, 16 SF). From Stansstad's boat dock, walk 10 minutes up to the main street (Achereggstrasse) and keep left, following the brown signs for *Festungsmuseum*.

Drivers arriving in Stansstad can follow white signs to *Kehrsiten* for lakeside parking (1 SF/hr, free WC, 5-min walk along lake to museum entrance).

BERN AND MURTEN

Enjoy urban Switzerland in the charming, compact capital of Bern. Ramble the ramparts of Murten, Switzerland's best-preserved medieval town, and resurrect the ruins of an ancient Roman capital in nearby Avenches.

If you like cute, small towns (as I do), make Murten your home base. Otherwise, choose busier Bern.

Planning Your Time

On a quick trip, big Bern and little Murten—only a half-hour apart by train or car—are each worth a half-day. Either makes a fine day trip or overnight stop. Murten, while easy by train, is even better by car. With a car, I'd sleep in Murten.

Bern is a handy on-the-way stop between other destinations (such as going from the Berner Oberland to Murten or Zürich). If you're day-tripping, put your bag in a locker at the Bern station, spend a few hours taking my self-guided "Welcome to Bern" walk (page 85) and visiting some museums, then catch a late-afternoon train to your next stop. You could combine the destinations in this chapter by ending your busy Bern day in Murten—where you can spend the evening wandering the walls and savoring a lakeside dinner. In the morning, linger in Murten or move on to your next destination.

Bern

Stately but human, classy but fun, the Swiss capital gives you the most delightful look at urban Switzerland. Window-shopping and people-watching along the arcaded streets and lively market squares are Bern's top attractions, but there's more to this city: Enjoy Bern's fine museums, quaint-for-a-capital ambience, and delightful river scene.

The city, founded in 1191, has managed to avoid war damage and hasn't burned down since a great fire in 1405. After the fire, wooden buildings were no longer allowed, and Bern gained its gray-green sandstone complexion (with stones quarried from nearby). During its 12th- and 13th-century growth spurt, the frisky town grew through two walls. Looking at the map of the city contained within a bend of the Aare River, you can get a sense of how it started with a castle at the tip of the peninsula, and expanded with a series of walls—each defending an ever-bigger city from its one accessible-by-land side. The clock tower marks the first wall (1218). A generation later, another wall was built (in 1256, at today's prison tower). The final wall—where today's train station sits—was built in 1344.

In 1353, Bern became the eighth canton to join the Swiss Federation. Its power ended with the conquest by Napoleon in 1798. But in 1848, Bern rose again to become the Swiss capital.

Today, the German-speaking town has 128,000 people (one-third Protestant and two-thirds Catholic). Its pointy towers, sandstone buildings, and colorful fountains make Bern one of Europe's finest surviving medieval towns.

ORIENTATION

User-friendly Bern is packed into a peninsula bounded by the Aare River. The train station is located where the peninsula connects to the mainland. From there, a handy main drag leads gradually downhill, straight through the middle of town past most of the major sights, to the tip of the peninsula (across a bridge and finally to the bear pits).

Tourist Information

Start your visit at the TI inside the train station (June–Sept daily 9:00–20:30; Oct–May Mon–Sat 9:00–18:30, Sun 10:00–17:00; tel. 031-328-1212, www.berninfo.com). Pick up a free map of Bern (and maps for any other Swiss cities you'll be visiting), and browse through their free brochures: general information booklet, museum guide, booklet on bus and walking tours, transit map, quarterly events and exhibits listings, and informative leaflets on various sights. There's a second TI at the bear pits (June–Sept daily 9:00–18:00; March–May and Oct daily 10:00–16:00; Nov–Feb Fri–Sun 11:00–16:00, closed Mon–Thu).

Walking **tours** leave daily at 11:00 from the TI at the train station (90 min, 18 SF, June–Sept, German and English together). They also offer four-hour iPod tours.

Sightseeing Pass: If you plan to visit more than one museum in Bern, get the BernCard—unless you already have a Swiss Pass. The BernCard offers admission to all permanent collections in the city's many museums and unlimited travel on local public transportation. You can purchase it at the TI and at many Bern museums (20 SF/1 day, 31 SF/2 days, 38 SF/3 days, www.museen -bern.ch).

Arrival in Bern

By Train: Bern's bustling train station is a thriving, multistory mall. The trains almost get lost. On the upper level, you'll find a Migros grocery store (daily 8:00–21:00) and a pharmacy (daily 6:30–22:00). Near the TI are lockers (6 SF) and WCs (2 SF). From the station, it's a 30-minute downhill stroll through the heart of town to the bear pits and rose garden. My "Welcome to Bern" self-guided walk (next page) lays out the most interesting route.

By Car: Drivers approaching by freeway should follow *Bern Zentrum* signs, then *Bahnhof,* and *Bahnhof Parking.* There's a huge pay garage behind the train station (*Bahnhof*). While not the cheapest option, this is your easiest for a quick visit. The old town is essentially car-free (only service vehicles and public transit allowed).

Helpful Hints

Blue Monday: Most of Bern's museums are closed on Monday.

Internet Access: The TI has a list of centrally located Internet cafés. **Jäggi Bookstore,** in the Loeb department store on Spitalgasse, is the closest to the station (2 SF/15 min, pay at cashier, keep receipt and take it to info desk behind stairs, Mon–Fri 9:00–19:00, Thu until 21:00, Sat 8:00–17:00, closed Sun).

Bookstore: Stauffacher is a huge bookstore with an entire floor of English books, a fine travel section, and an inviting café with a terrace, good salads, and Internet access (a block below the train station at Neuengasse 34).

Laundry: Be warned that the city has no launderettes in the center.

Bike Rental: The "Bern rollt" program offers free loaner bikes during the summer at three very central locations: at the train station (on Milchgassli), near the station (on Hirschengraben), and in the old center (on Zeughausgasse near Bärenplatz). Look for a large, converted shipping container with bikes. Just leave your photo ID and a 20-SF deposit and take off with the bike of your choice (daily in summer 7:30–21:30, www .bernrollt.ch). Try the "Swiss Flyer," a clever little electric-motor-powered bike, or even a scooter or skateboard.

Private Guide: Marie-Therese Lauper is a charming and hard-working independent local guide (mobile 079-700-0880, amthlauper@dplanet.ch).

Getting Around Bern

The city is walkable, though the trams can be handy. A standard single ticket costs 3.60 SF, a shorter trip *(Kurzstrecke)* runs 1.90 SF, and a 24-hour ticket is 12 SF. The best plan for exploring the town:

Walk from the train station to the far end of town, then catch tram #12 back to the station (buy 1.90-SF *Kurzstrecke* from machine at bus stop, tram goes about every 6 min, www.bernmobil.ch).

SELF-GUIDED WALK

Welcome to Bern

This orientation walk begins at the train station and ends at the bear pits, at the far end of town. From the bear pits, you can catch bus #12 or browse your way back to your starting point, which is the...

Train Station: The station is a bright and airy shopping center, with a first-class TI (next to train information center), long-hours exchange desk, and all the shops you could need.

Stepping outside, you enter the big square called Bahnhofplatz. The old town was sealed off here with a fortified wall—replaced in the 19th century by the train station. Today all city buses and trams come and go from the station.

Bern's vision is to create a car-less city. The city was ripped up and new tram lines were put in for the big event of 2008: The Euro 2008 soccer cup. And the "Bern rollt" program provides free loaner bikes (government-subsidized and staffed by otherwise difficult-to-employ people).

Across the square stands the Heiliggeistkirche (Holy Ghost Church). Notice its gray-green Bernese sandstone, quarried nearby, used for the church and surrounding buildings. It's porous and easily eroded by water. That's why Bern's buildings have their characteristic over-sized eves. These are newer buildings, but built with the same stone as the older buildings to maintain architectural harmony (mandatory under city law).

• *From the train station TI, cross Bahnhofplatz, walk 50 yards, and turn left (around the church) onto Spitalgasse. This marks the start of one long street (with four names)—the spine of both the peninsula and this walk—that rambles downhill through the heart of town to the bridge and bear pits.*

Notice the first of Bern's 11 historical **fountains,** the Bagpiper. These colorful 16th-century fountains are Bern's trademark. The city commissioned them for many reasons: to brighten up the cityscape of gray stone buildings, to show off the town's wealth, and to remind citizens of great local heroes and events. They also gave local artists something to work on after the Reformation deprived them of their most important patron, the Catholic Church.

Shopping opportunities abound under the more than three miles of arcades that line Bern's lanes. This is my kind of shopping town: Prices are so high, there's no danger of buying anything (shops generally open Mon–Fri 9:00–18:30, Thu later, Sat

Bern

WELCOME TO BERN WALK

1. Train Station
2. Bärenplatz
3. Parliament Square
4. Terraces
5. Casino Concert Hall
6. Kornhausplatz
7. Zytglogge-Turm (Clock Tower)
8. Kramgasse Shops & Einstein's Apartment
9. Bern Cathedral
10. Münsterplattform
11. Nydegg Bridge
12. Bear Pits
13. Old Tram Depot

8:00–16:00, closed Sun). In German, the slang for the corridor under these arcades is *Rohr* (pipe). To stroll through the town is to *rohren* (go piping).

• *Continue "rohren" down Spitalgasse until you reach...*

Bärenplatz: In summer, a daily market is held on this square (busiest on Tue and Sat mornings). The street runs under the **Prison Tower** (Käfigturm)—once a part of the city wall (c. 1256). Renovated 1641–1644, the tower served as a prison until 1897 (*Käfig* means "cage"). Notice how the hand on the clock really is a hand—and how it was built in a slower-paced era, when just an hour hand told time precisely enough. The bears on the tower are from Bern's coat of arms. Live ones await you at the end of this walk.

To the left (50 yards), you'll see the **Dutch Tower** (Holländerturm). Swiss soldiers were famous mercenaries who fought all over Europe. Returning from a battle in the Netherlands, the soldiers brought back the habit of smoking. But smoking was forbidden within the city walls of Bern—so they hid in this tower to smoke secretly. (European smokers expect that, with current trends, this tower may regain its historic function within just a few years.)

Farther left at the far end of the square is a modern, controversial, and mossy **fountain** by the Swiss surrealist Meret Oppenheim. Made in 1983, it symbolizes growth and life, and is supposed to demonstrate communication between an object of art and the beholder. It worked well...too well, in fact, as most citizens immediately communicated their dislike and wanted it destroyed. But Bern's politicians proved braver than expected, and the fountain survived. Time has transformed Oppenheim's gray concrete column into a multicolored pillar decorated with moss, grass, and flowers. Locals like it only in the winter, when it's covered with ice. The grand building beyond the fountain—once the city orphanage—is the police station.

As each of the town's successive walls and moats were torn down, they provided Bern with vast, people-friendly swaths of land that function as elongated "squares"—popular today for markets and outdoor cafés. This is a top place to be seen in the evening.

• *With your back to the modern fountain, stroll to the end of Bärenplatz, filled with market stalls and lined with fun places to eat (see "Eating," page 97). The big building you'll see from the square is the...*

Parliament (Bundeshaus): You may brush elbows with some high-powered legislators, but you wouldn't know it—everything looks very casual for a national capital. The fine granite plaza in front of the parliament (built in 2004 to replace a parking lot) is a favorite spot for demonstrations. The 26-squirt fountain (one for each canton) is a real kid-pleaser (and makes for fun photos) on a hot summer day. Facing the square on the left is the Swiss National Bank—this country's Fort Knox, with half the Swiss gold stock buried under the square (the rest is in Zürich).

Standing in front of the parliament, check out the statuary. The woman on the top of the building represents political independence, the one on the left (under the "1291") stands for freedom, and the one on the right (1848) symbolizes peace.

Drop into the welcome center and pick up the generous literature on the Swiss government. Its bicameral system was inspired by the US Constitution, with one big difference: Executive power

is shared by a committee of seven, with a rotating ceremonial president and a passion for consensus. This is a mechanism to avoid power grabs by any single individual...a safeguard that the Swiss love.

Probably until mid-2008, the parliament building will be under renovation and closed to the public. When tours resume, they'll most likely be free, start around 14:00 (in English), and last an hour (tel. 031-322-8522, www.parliament.ch).

• *Continuing past the parliament info kiosk, walk around behind the parliament to the...*

Terraces: From here, you have a commanding view over the Aare River and Bern's biggest swimming pool, the **Marzilibad.** On a clear day, you can see the peaks of the Eiger, Mönch, and Jungfrau (see Gimmelwald chapter)—and the far less imposing "mountain" of Bern, the **Gurten** (with the view tower poking up above its forested summit). The Gurten is the city's favorite recreation spot, offering music festivals in summer and very modest skiing opportunities for children in winter.

Follow the tree-lined pedestrian lane left a few hundred yards to Kirchenfeld Bridge (great river views from halfway across, many museums just across). The **Casino** isn't for gamblers—it's the home of Bern's Symphony Orchestra.

• *With your back to the river, follow the tram tracks down another swath of land created by the removal of a city wall, to...*

Kornhausplatz: This square is ornamented by the colorful **Ogre** (*Chindlifresser*, "child-eater") fountain. Two legends try to explain this gruesome sight. It's either a folkloric representation of the Greek god Chronos, or a figure that was intended to scare children off the former city walls. The building behind on the left used to be the granary and now houses the modern public library and the huge **Kornhauskeller** restaurant.

Bern

If the restaurant is open, wander down the stairs and head inside. Once the vast city wine cellar, now an Italian restaurant (see page 98), this cellar was built in high Baroque style (1718) and renovated with paintings inspired by the Pre-Raphaelites in 1897. The 12 columns show traditional costumes of Bernese women.

• *Back on Kornhausplatz, step under the clock tower where Marktgasse becomes Kramgasse to see the fancy clock ornamenting its downhill side.*

Zytglogge-Turm: Bern's famous clock tower was part of the original wall marking the first gate to the city (c. 1250). The

clock, which dates back to 1530, performs four minutes before each hour: The happy jester comes to life, Father Time turns his hourglass, the rooster crows (in German, that's "kee-kee-ree-kee" rather than "cock-a-doodle-doo"), and the golden man on top hammers the bell. Apparently, this non-event was considered enter-

taining five centuries ago.

To pass the time waiting for the action, read the TI's leaflet explaining what's so interesting about the fancy old clock (the golden hour hand is an hour behind for half the year because of the modern innovation of daylight saving time). You can determine the zodiac, today's date, and the stage of the moon—look at the black-and-gold orb. Enthusiasts can tour the medieval mechanics—early Swiss engineering at its best—and see the billows that enable the old rooster to crow (12 SF, 50-min tour, May–Oct daily at 14:30, buy ticket from guide).

Under the clock are the old regional measurements (Swiss foot, the bigger Bernese foot, and the *Elle*, or "elbow," which was the distance from the elbow to the fingertip) and the official meter and double meter. It took a strong man like Napoleon to bring consistency to measurements in Europe, and he replaced the many goofy feet and elbows of medieval Europe with the metric system used today (c. 1800).

• *Continue your stroll down the main drag. At this point you enter the older part of town, where bigger department stores are replaced by quainter shops and galleries on...*

Kramgasse: Bern has wide streets like this one, but not many squares. In the Middle Ages, craftsmen exhibited their goods on the sidewalks under simple roofs. Eventually, these were formalized, buildings expanded, and arcades evolved. While the arcades are privately owned, owners must keep them clean and allow public access.

Albert Einstein (1879–1955) in Bern

The man who changed how we see our universe made his greatest discoveries during the eight years he lived in Bern (1901–1909). Raised in Germany, Albert Einstein went to college in Zürich, hoping eventually to land a job teaching math and physics. But the young grad's GPA and resume were mediocre, so he took a temp job instead in Bern's Patent Office, inspecting and registering inventions.

Twenty-three-year-old Albert and his new bride Mileva (his college sweetheart) rented a second-floor apartment at Kramgasse 49 (today's Einstein House—see page 91), where Mileva soon gave birth to little Hans Albert. Einstein punched the clock at the Patent Office and spent his spare time reading, hiking the Bern countryside, and thinking. At night, he'd join with his mates—the self-named "Olympia Academy"—to smoke, drink beer, and talk math and philosophy. Outwardly, he led an ordinary life, but his thoughts were always on science's Big Questions. At home, in pubs, or at work he'd scribble down equations and ideas, filing them in his self-described "Department of Theoretical Physics"—a desk drawer in his office.

Then one warm spring day, as Einstein walked on the outskirts of Bern, it all started coming together. So began his "annus mirabilis"—the miracle year of 1905—in which the 26-year-old unknown amateur physicist quickly wrote five papers that would shock and perplex the world. Published in a major physics journal, they touched on a variety of subjects—such as how molecules move and how light can appear as either a wave of energy or as a beam of tiny particles.

The most famous and unsettling paper, his theory of special relativity, described a world in motion. A man on a moving train and someone stationary see the world from different perspectives—that's the classic principle of relativity described by Galileo and Newton. But Einstein said there's an exception to the rule—light, whose speed always remains constant whether it's on a moving train or on the ground. So a man on a moving train and one at rest will never agree on what they observe...yet they're both right. The discrepancies only become obvious as

Bern

Most shops are underneath the arcades, but don't miss the ones in the **cellars** that you can access only from the main road. The cellars, marked by old-time hatches, were originally for storing potatoes and coal, and later, wine. People said "merry Bern" was floating on wine, just as Venice was floating on water. The merry times ended in 1798, when the French invaded (and drank all the wine). The cellars were once again used for potatoes, and the city got a new nickname: "sad Bern." Napoleon's soldiers not the train travels close to the speed of light. Then, while the man on the train thinks everything is normal, the man on the ground sees the train shrink, train clocks slow down, and the man on the train stops aging!

Einstein's papers drew little initial interest and a measure of skepticism. (Einstein did get a promotion in the Patent Office—from "technical expert third class" to "technical expert second class.") But over time, other physicists grasped the significance of Einstein's work, seeing how he took earlier findings, wove them together, and did the math that explained it. Subsequent experiments proved that, in fact, even Einstein's most bizarre assertions were correct. Time on a fast-moving jet really does slow down (hence, those interminable intercontinental flights).

Einstein was invited to lecture at the local university, though he was still working nine-to-five at the Patent Office. In his spare time, he worked on his next project, general relativity. He theorized that gravity is not a force that attracts things but a curving of space—like a bowling ball on a soft mattress—that affects the motion of nearby objects. In 1909, Einstein's growing reputation won him a job offer to teach in Zürich, and he quit the Patent Office and left Bern for good.

Einstein would never again approach the creative level of his days in Bern. In 1922, he won the Nobel Prize for work done during the 1905 "annus mirabilis." Albert and Mileva split, and he remarried. When Hitler took power in Germany (1933), Einstein—a pacifist and a Jew—left Europe for America. His curly black hair had turned white, and his aging face became a pop-culture icon of genius—pipe, moustache, basset-hound eyes, and halo of frizzy white hair.

In 1939, Einstein wrote a letter to President Roosevelt theorizing that the tiniest particle of matter could be converted into an enormous amount of energy. The principle was one he'd discovered back in 1905—that energy is equivalent to mass times the speed of light squared (a very big number). And so, $E = mc^2$ became the atomic bomb, from an idea hatched in the pubs and arcaded streets of Bern.

only liberated Bern from its wine, but also from the tremendous treasury the city was known for. Napoleon used money looted from Bern to finance his Egyptian crusade.

The apartment that **Einstein** called home between 1903 and 1905, during several of his happiest and most productive years, is 200 yards down Kramgasse from the clock tower (on the right, at Kramgasse 49). See period furniture, the original spiral staircase entrance, Einstein's Patent Office desk, photos, and manuscripts.

The museum doesn't do much for me, but I guess everything's relative (6 SF, March–Sept daily 10:00–17:00; Oct–Feb Tue–Fri 10:00–17:00, Sat 10:00–16:00, closed Sun–Mon; Kramgasse 49, tel. 031-312-0091, www.einstein-bern.ch).

• *Just below Einstein's apartment, 20 yards past the Samson Fountain, turn right and crawl through the narrow Münstergässchen to the...*

Bern Cathedral: Bern's 15th-century Münster, Catholic-turned-Protestant, is capped with a 330-foot-tall tower, the highest in Switzerland (finished only in 1893). The late-Gothic church was dedicated to St. Vincent of Zaragoza. During the Reformation, religious icons were destroyed by Protestants (an act called "iconoclasm"—see page 206). The church wasn't originally so plain. It was once adorned with 26 separate little chapels and altars dedicated to Mary and various saints. An ornate screen separated the priests from the worshippers. When the Reformation came to town in 1528, however, all this was swept away—the iconoclasts believed that images distracted worshippers from focusing on God. The new center of attention was the pulpit, where Protestant preachers shared the word of God—not in Latin, but in the people's language.

This church's main portal, with its striking gold-leaf highlights, seems pretty un-Protestant. It probably survived because its theme, the Last Judgment, showed that no matter how rich you are or what rank you have in Church hierarchy, *anyone* can end up in hell (an idea Protestants dug). Condemned people are popping in the flames like lottery balls. Notice the humorous details in the commotion of people heading to hell (especially what the little green devil is doing to the sinful monk).

Cathedral entrance is free (April–Oct Tue–Sat 10:00–17:00, Sun 11:30–17:00, closed Mon; Nov–March Tue–Fri 11:00–13:00 & 14:00–16:00, Sat until 17:00, Sun 11:30–14:00, closed Mon; tel. 031-312-0462). Climb the spiral staircase 210 feet above the town for the view and the exercise (4 SF, 344 steps). Marie-Therese Lauper works up there, watching over the church, answering questions, and giving those with a ticket a fine city view and a chance to peek at her bells.

• *Head behind the cathedral to a terrace overlooking the river, the...*

Münsterplattform: This terrace was built, starting in the 14th century, from all kinds of "recycled" stones from older buildings. Archaeologists even unearthed some heads of statues that were victims of Reformation iconoclasts. Look down on the Aare (find the bear out on the breakwater). Notice the security nets below you. The platform used to be the favorite place for suicides—to the terror of the people living below. The Pavilion Café offers a scenic spot under a chestnut tree for a bite or drink on a sunny day. The pavilion opposite is a tiny branch of the city library, providing park-goers with books, boules, and table tennis. This little park is frequented by pot smokers, and nobody seems to care. Behind the café the "vertical tram" has been carrying locals up and down since 1896 (1.20 SF).

With your back to the river, return to the main drag, Kramgasse. On the Fountain of Justice, a blindfolded figure of Justice triumphs over the mayor, pope, sultan, and emperor. A few steps above the fountain, a grate reveals a bit of the stream that used to flow open down the middle of the peninsula, providing people with a handy disposal system.

• *From here, it's a straight stretch through the oldest part of town to the bridge at the end of the old town...*

Nydegg Bridge: Look downstream from the Nydegg Bridge. To your left is the site of the original town castle (now a church). The small bridge below is the oldest in Bern (until 1844 the only bridge crossing the Aare here). Above on the ridge (just behind and to the right of the pointy spire) is the Rosengarten restaurant (see next page). And just upstream stands the site of the original Lindt chocolate factory, evoking an age when this stretch of river was lined with mills powering the industrial zone of Bern—tanneries, shipyards, lumber mills, and so on. The area is now routinely flooded when the river runs high. As you look upstream, notice the peaceful path along the left bank, a nice place for a walk.

• *Continue across the bridge to reach the...*

Bear Pits (Bärengraben): The symbol of Bern is the bear, and some lively ones frolic in these big, barren, concrete pits, to

the delight of locals and tourists alike (daily 9:30–17:00 in summer, closed off-season). You may see graffiti from the B.L.M. (Bear Liberation Movement), which, through its terrorist acts, has forced a reluctant city government to give the sad-eyed bears better living conditions. The current bears, Pedro and Tana, are 26 years old, very senior for bears. The next generation will enjoy much better conditions.

• *Behind the pits is the...*

Old Tram Depot: This depot hosts a tourist center (TI, brewery restaurant/café with terrace). Its excellent 3-SF "Bern Show," complete with an animated town model and marching Napoleonic-era soldiers, illustrates the history and wonders of

Bern (20 min, uncomfortable benches, show in English once hourly—see schedule—or ask for a printed script, daily June–Sept 9:00–18:00, March–May and Oct 10:00–16:00, shorter hours in winter).

From here, a seven-minute hike up the pathway takes you to **Restaurant Rosengarten,** which offers a grand city view and basic, reasonably priced food (see page 99).

From the Old Tram Depot, it's an easy trip on bus #12 back to the station (1.90 SF). If wandering back through town, be sure to get off into the quieter side lanes, which have a fascinating and entertaining array of shops and little eateries.

SIGHTS AND ACTIVITIES

▲▲**The Berner Swim and Marzilibad**—For something to write home about, join the local merchants, students, and carp in a

float down the Aare River. The Bernese, proud of their very clean river and their basic ruddiness, have a tradition—sort of a wet, urban *paseo*. On summer days, they hike upstream five to 30 minutes, then float back down to the excellent (and free) riverside baths and pools (Marzilibad) just below the Parliament building.

The process is easy: Hike up the paved riverside sidewalk as far as you like, then take the steps leading into the water whenever you want to "put in." As you approach Marzilibad, just stroke over to the shore to grab one of the several poles placed to help people exit the river easily. While the locals make it look easy, this can be dangerous—the current is swift. If you miss the last pole, you're history.

If a float down the river is a bit much for you, enjoy just the Marzilibad, a well-equipped public swimming pool and park with picnic spots, restaurant, lockers, wading pools, games, and more.

River Rafting—The TI organizes rafting tours by request only (usually daily June–Sept, 55 SF, minimum of 4 people). You can raft from Bern's Kirchenfeldbrücke to Worblaufen (return by train), or from Thun (near Interlaken) to Bern.

▲▲Museum of Fine Arts (Kunstmuseum)—Featuring 1,000 years of local art, this three-story museum offers a unique opportunity to see the best of Swiss artists, from romantic folk art to the Jugendstil movement. You'll find old masters in the basement, 19th-century works on the ground floor, and 20th-century stuff upstairs (7 SF, covered by BernCard and Swiss Pass, no English on the wall but pick up free English map/brochure, Tue–Sun 10:00–17:00, closed Mon, 4 blocks north of station, Holdergasse 12, tel. 031-328-0944).

▲▲Paul Klee Center (Zentrum Paul Klee)—With his wavy building mirroring the wavy landscape of the Bern countryside,

Italian architect Renzo Piano celebrates the creative spirit of the Swiss-born artist Paul Klee. Klee wasn't just a great painter, but an interdisciplinary explosion of creative energy. The center—which fosters music and theater as well as the visual arts—has a mission: to bring art to the people. For instance, a huge zone is devoted to a children's creative workshop that includes painting and a shadow theater.

The Klee collection is in the building's middle wave. This cultural center keeps about 200 of Klee's pieces on display (out of a collection of 4,000). It's the best place in the world to experience and learn about this modernist painter of lively, almost childlike art. Artistically, you can't put Klee in a box. His paintings—mostly from the 1920s and 1930s—are playful yet enigmatic. Audioguides let you enjoy Klee's favorite music as you wander through the collection. His art is full of symbolism...or maybe we just think so. He experimented in pointillism—as you'll see in the piece *Ad Parnassum*.

Insula Dulcamara (Bittersweet Island) is a good example of Klee's enigmatic hieroglyph style. It's a puzzle—he pairs opposites: man, woman; air, water. It's 1938...is that a submarine on the horizon evoking the rise of fascism? Perhaps the black figures are death, floating in an eternal spring-like landscape. Kids

love Klee, and they always teach the art snobs a thing or two with their interpretations.

Downstairs you'll find cafés, an art database, a movie about building the museum, a cozy hangout, and the children's workshop. Pick up a free English-language booklet when purchasing your ticket (16 SF, covered by BernCard and Swiss Pass, 16–20 SF includes special exhibits, Tue–Sun 10:00–17:00, Thu until 21:00, closed Mon, take bus #12 from train station to Zentrum Paul Klee stop—6/hr, stops right at the center, Monument im Fruchtland 3, www.paulkleezentrum.ch). Children's workshops are scheduled throughout the day (15 SF for 1-hour workshop at 10:00, 12:00, 14:00, or 16:00).

Other Bern Museums—Across the bridge from the Parliament building on Helvetiaplatz are several museums (Alpine, Berner History, Communication, Natural History, Rifle, and Kunsthalle contemporary art) that sound more interesting than they are (all covered by BernCard and Swiss Pass, most open Tue–Sun 10:00–17:00, closed Mon, www.museen-bern.ch). The TI produces a pamphlet explaining all the museums.

SLEEPING

These places are listed in geographical order from the train station. The first is a block south of it, and the rest are in the old town just past Bärenplatz, about a five-minute walk away. Bern is one of several Swiss and Austrian cities hosting the Euro 2008 soccer championship—it's critical to book ahead if you'll be in town on or around game days: June 9, 13, and 17.

$$$ Hotel National is well-located, with 45 fine rooms. It's a simple, old-school, hardwood-floor time warp of a place with a classic elevator. There's some street noise, and inward-facing rooms can be noisy on Friday and Saturday, so request a quiet room (S-60–85 SF, Sb-95–120 SF, D-120 SF, Db-140–160 SF, family deals, extra bed-40 SF, elevator, Internet access, Hirschengraben 24, tel. 031-381-1988, fax 031-381-6878, www.nationalbern.ch, info @nationalbern.ch).

$$$ Hotel Continental has 40 bright and comfy Nordic-flavored rooms and a cheery breakfast room with a sun terrace (Sb-145 SF, Db-195 SF, Tb-225 SF; cheaper Fri–Sun: Sb-120 SF, Db-165 SF, Tb-195 SF, elevator, save 15 SF by skipping breakfast, Zeughausgasse 27, tel. 031-329-2121, fax 031-329-2199).

$$$ Hotel Goldener Schlüssel is an old, basic, crank-'em-out hotel with 29 rooms, right in the city center (S-90 SF, Sb-118 SF, D-132 SF, Db-158 SF, Tb-205 SF, extra bed-50 SF, elevator, Rathausgasse 72, tel. 031-311-0216, fax 031-311-5688, www.goldener-schluessel.ch, info@goldener-schluessel.ch).

$ Backpackers Hotel Glocke rents the cheapest beds in the old town (beds in 4- to 6-bed dorms-31 SF, D-78 SF, includes sheets, cheaper off-season; no breakfast, but kitchen available, non-

---

Sleep Code

(1.10 SF = about $1, country code: 41)
S = Single, **D** = Double/Twin, **T** = Triple, **Q** = Quad, **b** = bathroom, **s** = shower only. Unless otherwise noted, credit cards are accepted, English is spoken, and breakfast is included.

To help you sort easily through these listings, I've divided the rooms into three categories, based on the price for a standard double room with bath:

$$$ **Higher Priced**—Most rooms 150 SF or more.
 $$ **Moderately Priced**—Most rooms between 90–150 SF.
  $ **Lower Priced**—Most rooms 90 SF or less.

---

smoking, Internet access in lobby, laundry, kitchen, reception open 8:00–11:00 & 15:00–22:00, Rathausgasse 75, tel. 031-311-3771, fax 031-311-1008, www.bernbackpackers.com, info@bernbackpackers .com).

$ Bern Youth Hostel is a big, institutional place below the Parliament building near the river. It's well-run and adult-friendly (dorm bed-37 SF, D-85 SF, includes sheets and breakfast, non-members pay 6 SF extra per night, dinner-14 SF, lockers, laundry, reception open 7:00–10:30 & 14:00–24:00, Weihergasse 4, tel. 031-311-6316, www.youthhostel.ch/bern, bern@youthhostel.ch).

EATING

Between the Station and Bärenplatz

Tibits, a self-service buffet in the train station building, offers a huge variety of vegetarian-only salads and sandwiches, plus two different hot dishes. Help yourself to a plate and pile it on. The price is by weight: An average helping will cost you about 20 SF (4 SF per 100 grams, 7 SF for soup and bread, variety of sandwiches for 7 SF, "juice of the month"-6 SF, Mon–Sat 6:30–23:30, Sun 8:00–23:00, Bahnhofplatz 10, tel. 031-312-9111).

Gourmanderie Moléson is a long, skinny, bistro-type place serving traditional Swiss dishes, fondue, *tartes flambées* (Alsatian pizzas; 25 SF), vegetarian meals, and two-course lunch deals for 25 SF. The dressy and very Swiss interior can be a bit smoky, but tables tumble out into the street (Mon–Fri 11:30–14:30 & 18:00–23:30, Sat 18:00–23:30, closed Sun, Aarbergergasse 24, tel. 031-311-4463).

Restaurant della Casa, a traditional Swiss place with Old World ambience inside and a few tables on the sidewalk outside, has daily specials scrawled on chalkboards throughout. While not cheap, it's been a neighborhood favorite for generations. This is

BERN HOTELS & RESTAURANTS

1. Hotel National
2. Hotel Continental
3. Hotel Goldener Schlüssel
4. Backpackers Hotel Glocke
5. Bern Youth Hostel
6. Tibits Cafeteria
7. Gourmanderie Moléson
8. Restaurant della Casa
9. Restaurant Vatter
10. Ristorante Luce
11. Kornhauskeller Restaurant
12. Restaurant Harmonie & Housi's Brotloube
13. Restaurant Rosengarten
14. Brewery Restaurant
15. Schwellenmätteli Restaurant
16. To Lorrainebad Pool

a cheese-free, yet traditional, Swiss restaurant (25–35-SF plates, closed Sun, between Parliament and the station at Schauplatzgasse 16, tel. 031-311-2142).

Restaurant Vatter is exclusively organic—serving mostly vegetarian, lots of Indian cuisine, and some meat dishes. It's a fresh, mod place with a terrace overlooking the lively Bärenplatz. The restaurant is above an organic produce store (25-SF plates, Mon–Sat 11:00–23:00, closed Sun, Bärenplatz 2, tel. 031-312-5171).

Ristorante Luce brings the cooking of Emilia Romagna in Italy to Bern. With a venerable dining hall and great seating on the square, it's known as a good value (hearty pastas and pizzas-20 SF, daily 11:30–14:00 & 18:30–22:30, Zeughausgasse 28, tel. 031-310-9999).

Around Kornhausplatz

Kornhauskeller, decorated with colorful mural paintings (see description on page 89), is a splurge. It's in the palatial cellar of the old granary, originally built to house the state's wine cellar. This dressy, pricey Mediterranean place offers lunch specials and a fine antipasto bar for those on a budget. Make a meal out of the 16-SF or 24-SF plate, telling the man behind the buffet exactly what you'd like (30–60 SF plates, Mon–Sat 11:45–14:30 & 18:00–24:00,

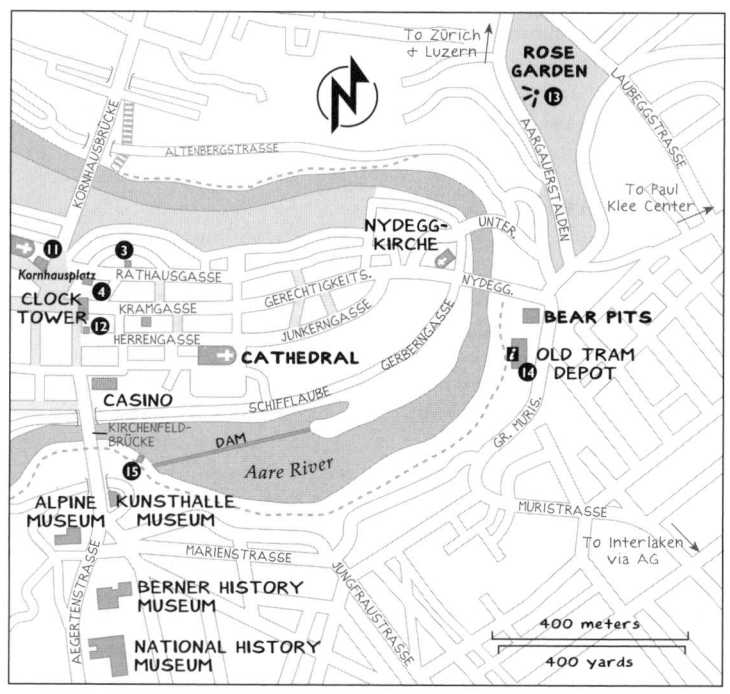

Sun 18:00–23:30, Kornhausplatz 18, tel. 031-327-7272).

Near the Cathedral

Restaurant Harmonie, owned by the Gyger family since 1915, is one of the oldest and most traditional places in town. It offers filling Swiss cuisine and is the favorite lunch spot for Swiss politicians (daily specials, 30-SF plates, closed Sat–Sun, Hotelgasse 3, tel. 031-311-3840).

Housi's Brotloube is a bakery stocked with everything you need—sandwiches, salads, fruit, drinks, and pastries—to put together a first-class picnic for the nearby Münsterplattform (Mon–Fri 6:30–18:30, Sat 6:30–13:00, closed Sun and July–Aug, next to Café Harmonie at Münstergasse 74).

Near the Bear Pits

Many finish their town walk at the bear pits and have worked up an appetite. You have two fine options here.

Restaurant Rosengarten is good for city views and a light meal, salad, or tea and cakes with local grannies (March–Oct daily 9:00–24:00, closed off-season, walk up Aargauerstalden, tel. 031-331-3206).

Brewery Restaurant offers seating in their big, bright, and

boisterous microbrewery, or on their leafy terrace overlooking the town and river. Quick and not too expensive, it's a local favorite, serving good-time food (fast and healthy 15–18-SF lunch plates, daily 11:00–24:00, in Old Tram Depot behind the bears, reserve in evening, tel. 031-368-1415).

On the Aare River

Schwellenmätteli Restaurant is a chance to join trendy locals for a meal or drink while sitting literally over the river. This mod restaurant/lounge has classy tables inside and out. At the tip of the pier is a lounge complete with sofas, mattresses, and a glass floor that lets you see the river racing underneath. The outdoor dining area and bar is open only in nice weather. The cuisine is modern Mediterranean, with some local trout (35-SF main courses, 15-SF starters, daily 9:00–24:00, 15-min riverside stroll from bear pits to Dalmaziquai 11, reservations smart for dinner, tel. 031-350-5001). The Italian restaurant across the parking lot is also good.

TRANSPORTATION CONNECTIONS

From Bern by Train to: Murten (hourly, 40 min, some transfer in Kerzers), **Lausanne** (2/hr, 70 min), **Interlaken** (2/hr, 55 min), **Luzern** (hourly, 1 hr; or 2/hr with transfer in Olten, 1.5 hrs), **Zürich** (2/hr, 1–1.25 hrs), **Fribourg** in Switzerland (2/hr, 20 min), **Freiburg** in Germany (hourly, 2 hrs, few direct, most transfer in Basel), **Zermatt** (hourly, 3.25 hrs, transfer in Brig), **Montreux** (2/hr, 1.5 hrs, transfer in Lausanne), **Lugano** (hourly, 4 hrs, transfer in Luzern, Olten, or Zürich), **Appenzell** (hourly, 3.25 hrs, transfer in Gossau), **Munich** (hourly, 5.5–6.5 hrs, 1–2 changes), **Frankfurt** (hourly, 4 hrs, half with change in Basel), **Salzburg** (hourly, 7–8 hrs, 1–4 changes), **Paris** (11/day, 5–5.5 hrs, 1 direct train in morning and 1 in evening, otherwise 1–2 changes). Train info: toll tel. 0900-300-3004 or www.rail.ch.

Route Tips for Drivers

Interlaken to Bern: From Interlaken, catch the autobahn (direction: Spiez, Thun, then Bern). Circle Bern on the autobahn, taking the fourth Bern exit, Neufeld Bern. Signs to *Zentrum* take you to Bern Bahnhof. Turn right just before the station into the Bahnhof Parkplatz (45-min meter parking outside, all-day lot inside, 2–4 SF/hr, depending on time of entry). You're just an escalator ride away from a great TI and Switzerland's capital.

Heading to Murten from Bern: From the station, drive out of Bern following signs for *Lausanne*, then follow the green signs to *Neuchâtel* and *Murten*. The autobahn ends 20 miles later in Murten.

Murten

The finest medieval ramparts in Switzerland surround the 5,000 people of Murten (or Morat, if you're speaking French). We're on the linguistic cusp of Switzerland: 25 percent of Murten speaks French; a few miles to the southwest, nearly everyone does.

Murten is a totally charming mini-Bern with lively streets, the middle one nicely arcaded with breezy outdoor cafés and elegant shops (many closed Mon). Its castle is romantically set, overlooking Lake Murten and the rolling vineyards of gentle Mont Vully in the distance. Spend a night here and have dinner with a local Vully wine, white or rosé. Murten is touristed, but seems to be enjoyed mostly by its own people.

Make time for nearby Avenches (see end of chapter). While quaint today, the town was once a powerful Roman capital—as its ruins attest.

ORIENTATION

Tourist Information

Murten's TI is just inside the city walls at the eastern end of town (opposite end from station; May–Sept Mon–Fri 9:00–12:00 & 13:00–18:00, Sat–Sun 10:00–16:30; Oct–April shorter hours and closed weekends, Französische Kirchgasse 6, tel. 026-670-5112, www.murtentourismus.ch). Get a free map and ask about sights, biking, and boat trips.

Arrival in Murten

By Train: To reach the town from the station (a 5-min walk), exit to the right, take the first left, walk up Bahnhofstrasse, then turn right through the town gate. Murten is a tiny town...a delight on foot.

By Car: You can park overnight in the old town for free (18:00–10:00). During the day, don't park inside the gates; Murten's brown-clad parking cops are infamous. Park in the lot near the castle and Co-op supermarket (5 SF/day includes in-and-out privileges, 14 SF for your entire stay if you don't move your car, 45 SF/1 week in-and-out, take ticket and pay at hotel or police station). Get the latest advice on parking from your hotelier.

Helpful Hints

Internet Access: Try **A&A Computer** (Mon–Fri 9:00–12:00 & 14:00–19:00, Sat 9:00–16:00, closed Sun, shorter hours in winter, behind train station, past Peugeot garage, at Engelhardstrasse 6, tel. 026-670-0520).

Post Office: It's across the street from the train station.

Laundry: None in town.

Local Guide: Mary Brunisholz, an American who married into this part of Switzerland, is an excellent guide with a car (150–200 SF/half-day, mobile 078-601-7040, mary.brunisholz @vtxnet.ch).

SELF-GUIDED WALK

Welcome to Murten

This introductory walk will give you the lay of the land and a lesson on the historic 15th-century Battle of Murten.

• *Start your walk just below the town's main gate at the public school, where you see a statue of the feisty local leader...*

Adrian von Bubenberg: Burgundy was the aggressive power of the day, and this Murten native stopped the power grab of the 15th century by beating Charles the Bold. Adrian von Bubenberg stood here and looked across the lake at the distant peaks of the Jura Mountains—the historic border between the Swiss and the French. (More on the battle a little later.)

The earliest Swiss clockmakers were from those Jura Mountains. Look at the **clock tower**—where's the little hand? As part of its lease, the restaurant below takes responsibility for hand-winding the clock each day, as it has since 1712. That's the Bern gate—so called because it opens up onto the road to Bern. The tiny grated window in the mighty door is a security window.

• *Rather than enter the gate, go right instead. Head along the outside of the wall, around the first turret, and look for the cannon balls.*

These cannon balls were left in the wall to remind townsfolk of their incredible victory over the Burgundians—like an Alamo with a happy ending.

• *Belly up to the lakeview terrace.*

Across the way is **Mont Vully** (mohn voo-yee)—one big vineyard and a mecca for lovers of Swiss white wine. The lowlands to the right—a rich former lakebed—are the heart of the fertile Three Lakes Region (lakes Biel, Neuchâtel, and Murten). The lush

MURTEN

To Praz,
Biel & Neuchâtel

Lake
Murten

Pantschau
Park

BOAT
DOCK

ADRIAN
VON
BUBENBERG
STATUE
WALK BEGINS

FRENCH
CHURCH

CLOCK TOWER
(BERN GATE)

TOWN
HALL

GERMAN
CHURCH

CASTLE

WALK ENDS

MUSEUM

TOWN
GATE

CATHOLIC
CHURCH

MEDIEVAL
WALLS

To pool

To Avenches

To Bern

POST

TRAIN
STATION

50 meters

50 yards

Murten

Streets: RYF, LANGMATT, BERN STR., RAFFOR, KREUZGASSE, HAUPTGASSE, RATHAUSGASSE, DEUTSCHE KIRCHG., SCHLOSSG., SCHULGASSE, LAUSANNESTRASSE, BUBENBERGSTRASSE, BAHNHOFSTRASSE, ERLACHSTRASSE, FREIBURGSTRASSE, MEYLANDSTRASSE, ALTE FREIBURGSTRASSE, VISCAULASTR., WILERWEG, PRA PURY

1 Hotel/Rest. Murtenhof & Krone
2 Hotel/Rest. Ringmauer
3 To Berger Farmhouse
4 Freiburger Falle Restaurant
5 Restaurant Anatolia
6 Restaurant Eintracht
7 Grizzly's Restaurant
8 Pizzeria Taverna Italiana
9 Bar & Blumen Pub

10 Züger Bakery
11 Co-op Supermarket
12 Cinema
13 Library
14 Internet Café
15 Simonet Weapons Shop
16 Steps to Lake
17 Access to Ramparts

farmland is called the "vegetable garden of Switzerland" for its soil, which yields more than 60 varieties of produce.

The ancient Celtic Helvetii tribe recognized the fertility of this land and settled here. The Romans likewise made this land a priority in establishing their colony of Helvetia (the origin of Switzerland's official name, Confoederatio Helvetica).

• *Check out the small **church**.*

Foreseeing a showdown with Burgundy, Adrian von Bubenberg had the town walls strengthened. As three-quarters of the town were German-speaking, they took a vote and decided to tear down the French church to get more stones. (This little church was rebuilt for the French-speaking community six years after its big one was demolished.) As the Calvinist Reformation swept through Catholic Switzerland in the early 16th century, churches like this were stripped of their rich paintings, sculptures, and stained glass. The altar became a Bible on a table, and pulpits became the focus. The emphasis was teaching the word of God. In this church, about the only exception to the "no distractions" rule are tiny stained-glass coats of arms—heraldry of the wealthy families who helped fund its construction.

• *From here, you'll walk across town. Walk past the TI, the Bern Tower, and up the lane to the library (on right, #31).*

Notice that along with being a "Bibliothek," the **library** is also a "Ludothek." This means parents can check out toys and games for their children, rather than spend their hard-earned money keeping massive places like "Toys 'R' Us" in business. Across the street, the typically Bernese little **Web Husli** shows off its old-time loom. The door is perfect for short people—if you're under five-feet five-inches, stand tall on the threshold. After a 14th-century fire burned down the wooden town, future building was limited to the characteristic yellow Jura stone (like the library). Around the corner (left) just past the town's morgue, is the public WC.

• *Continue straight ahead to the...*

German Church: Murten's German church, built in 1710, is also post–Reformation Protestant simple. As the town is on the border between two cantons (Bern and Fribourg), for 400 years its rule was shared: Every five years, it would flip between cantons. Arrangements like this didn't sit well with Napoleon, and around 1800, he made it firmly a part of nearby Fribourg.

Inside, notice the big stucco relief (center of ceiling) with two seals: the bear for Bern and the three castles for Fribourg. The Protestant passion for Bible study is also evident in this church. The pulpit was carved from a single trunk of oak in 1460. Explore the choir (circle of seats for big shots) behind the altar. Find Adrian von Bubenberg's seat. (Hint: The window above shows the war hero in red, with his victorious local yokels in their alpine red-knit hats...underdogs whupping the Burgundians.) Pull up the seat and rest on the misericord—a lazy but permissible alternative when everyone stands during a long service. Notice that the two prime seats do double duty (on the right hand of the preacher sat the leader of Bern or Fribourg—depending on who happened to be ruling that year). To computer gamers, the stained-glass depiction of the crucifixion feels proto-Tetris (c. 1926).

• *Leaving the church, hook left around the back. Finger the limestone and sandstone tombstones, quarried from Mont Vully for noble families. Then climb the creaky stairs onto the ramparts and walk about 50 yards.*

Rampart Ramble: Murten's only required sightseeing is to scramble the ramparts (free, open daily until 21:00). Survey the town. Note the uniformity of Murten. Paint your place the wrong color, and you may be instructed to redo it—at your own expense. Scanning the countless chimneys, think of the enforced conformity that comes with living in a small town (and find the one oddball). Telephone and electricity wires are all underground. Look back at the roof of the German church. A color-blindness test is built into its tiles. (If you can find the six-sided "star of David"—not a Jewish symbol in this case, but recalling the star that guided the wise men to Bethlehem on the first Christmas—you're okay.)

• *Continue to the tower. Climb the steps for a commanding town and lake view.*

With your back to the lake, look inland and imagine the action on June 22, 1476. Mighty Charles the Bold, with his 20,000 well-armed Burgundians, was camped on the hill (with the divided forest) for 10 days, laying siege to the town of 2,000. Runners were sent out from the town to gather help. A makeshift army of about 10,000 villagers gathered on the hills to the left. Just as George Washington attacked when the Redcoats were celebrating Christmas, the Swiss swooped in as the Burgundians were still hung over from a big Midsummer Night's Eve bash. The Battle of Murten was fought in pouring rain—a muddy, bloody mess. Almost all 20,000 Burgundians were slaughtered—many driven into the lake with their armor to drown (try swimming in a coat of mail). For centuries, French bones would wash ashore. Charles the (no-longer-so-) Bold barely got away on a very fast horse.

This victory demonstrated to the Swiss the advantages of *E Pluribus Unum,* and the assemblage of the many still-fiercely independent Swiss cantons into the Helvetic Confederation snowballed. In this sweet little corner, an influential battle in European history had been fought. Burgundian power ebbed, and Europe got to know a new nation...Switzerland.

• *Walk a bit farther along the wall and descend at the next tower (across from Café-Pension Ringmauer).*

The stairs lead to a fine old clock mechanism from 1816. Once powering the big clock in the City Hall tower, it spent decades in an Ikea-like to-be-assembled pile—gathering dust in an attic. An old local, recognizing a good challenge, reassembled it into perfect working order (1991). Notice how the gearbox powers three different clock faces, and how the old hand crank raises the stones that power the clock. The white face determines the clock's time, which rings on the quarter-hour.

• *Step outside the wall, where you'll see the Catholic church (1886), private gardens along the wall, and the different stages of the wall's construction.*

The first phase was built with large river stones, some arranged in a neat fishbone pattern. Later, the town ran out of money, and the next stage shows pebbles and rubble mixed with a rough concrete. And finally, when the town prospered again, they finished the wall with finely cut sandstone.

• *Walk back into town, stopping on the first corner at the fire station-turned-community-cinema.*

Local shareholders are thanked with their names on the door. Pop into the charming theater—80 plush, red seats. Notice what's playing tonight (see "Nightlife," later in this chapter). At this corner, spin slowly, admiring the town's fine shutters.

• *Then, continue a block to the...*

Main Street: In the 19th century, Murten's townsfolk used one of three water fountains on this street. Enjoy the colorful store signs as they still hang out their shingles in the traditional fashion. Bakery and *pâtisserie* competition on this street is fierce. Drop into one for the local specialties: *Nidlechueche*, a sweet, doughy cream tart (3.20 SF per slice); and *Seelander Zwetschen*, a chocolate-covered prune truffle with liqueur.

Near the top of the main street, **Simonet Weapons** sells all the latest knives by Victorinox. There's the green "stay-glow" and even a model with a memory stick for the outdoorsman with a laptop. At the top of the street (#16), Murten's oldest house has fine paintings under its eaves. There's some nice *Schmuck* (jewelry) two doors to the right.

• *Farther to the right, at the top of town, step into...*

Murten Castle: The town castle, which houses the police station in a former prison (closed to the public), shows off an impressive gun from 1882 and a fine lake view. The nearby museum is not worth your time or money, but steps lead from there down to the lake.

ACTIVITIES

Lake Activities—To get down to Murten's lazy lakefront, find the access just past the castle, or, more centrally, at Rathausstrasse 17 (a block from Hotel Murtenhof). Just past the grassy breakwater is Pantschau, a big park. The park is flanked by cheap self-service eateries (such as La Chaloupe, with salad bar and crêpes) and the Beach House (with better lakeside seating). There's mini-golf, windsurfing gear rental and instruction, an open-air summer film fest, and a fine lakeside promenade.

One-Hour Lake Murten Cruise (with Hiking Option): Boats go about six times a day through the summer (14 SF without stops, 16 SF with stopover privileges, 4/day Oct–April, call to confirm off-season, tel. 032-329-8811 or 032-729-9600, www.navig .ch; TI can help).

Consider stopping in the small town of Praz on the French-speaking shore. From there, you have two good options: You could hike through vineyards up Mont Vully—where a bench and fine lake and Alp views await—and return on the lake with your same ticket. Or you can walk from Praz back to Murten, clockwise around the lake (2 hrs, 3.80 SF for boat from Murten to Praz).

Half-Day Three Lakes Cruise: Consider sailing on all three lakes of the region on a one-way, three-hour trip (involving one train connection). Boats leave the town of Biel (an easy train ride from Murten) daily at 9:45, cruise through Lake Biel, connect with canals to lakes Neuchâtel and Murten, and stop at several small medieval villages along the way. The boat arrives in Murten at 13:00, then turns around and heads back along the same route at 14:30, arriving in Biel at 18:20 (one-way-47 SF, round-trip-94 SF but a 52-SF "day card" covers the trip, details at TI or call BSG, tel. 032-329-8811 or 032-729-9600, www.bielersee.ch). Boats make the trip twice a day in each direction, and Murten–Biel trains run once an hour (1-hour trip).

Swimming Pool—The Olympic-size public swimming pool is outside of town next to the lake, just past the castle (8 SF, daily mid-June–mid-Aug 9:00–21:00, spring and fall 9:30–19:00, closed in winter and spring).

Biking—The Three Lakes region has 100 miles of signposted bike paths (well-described in TI's brochures). Pick up a free map or buy a top-notch one. The best easy ride circles the lake and Mont Vully (through vineyards and, if you like, to the summit for a good view).

You can rent **bikes** at train-station ticket counters (23 SF/half-day, 31 SF/day, 5 SF less with Eurailpass or Swiss Pass, includes helmets, daily 6:30–23:00). Ask about being dropped off with your bike—or dropping off your bike—at another station, which opens up interesting options (7 SF extra, limited to a few stations).

NIGHTLIFE

Movies—Murten's cute little community co-op theater plays movies nightly (15 SF, Schulgasse 18). Movies are shown in their original language (capital letter indicates the soundtrack language, small letters indicate subtitles—e.g., "Efd" means "English with French and *Deutsch* subtitles").

Theater am See hosts a lakeside summer film festival with outdoor screenings of a different movie each night (early July–early Aug, details at TI).

Pubs—There are plenty of inviting pubs and nightclubs in town. The **Bar and Blumen** sells flowers by day (check out the edelweiss) and drinks with a lake view by night (next to Town Hall and Hotel Murtenhof). The main street has an Irish bar and several other nightspots. The bar just outside the Bern Tower is popular with locals.

SLEEPING

(1.10 SF = about $1, country code: 41)
This adorable town is no secret. July through mid-September (especially on weekends) is peak time—make a reservation and expect maximum prices. When price ranges are given in the hotel listings, it means that prices vary depending on the season, type of room, or view. For a youth hostel, you'll have to sleep in nearby Avenches (see page 113).

$$$ Hotel Murtenhof & Krone, a worthwhile splurge, has 57 nicely appointed rooms—each a stylish mix of old and new. The Krone section of the hotel has smaller, plainer, less-expensive rooms and a cozy, spacious lounge. This place is well-run by the Joachim family—Theodore, Jutta, and their sons Marc and Ariste (Sb-120 SF, small Db-150 SF, big Db-230 SF, Tb-215–280 SF, family rooms, in mid-Sept–May ask for a 10 percent discount with this book, elevator, Internet access, parking 18 SF/day, next to castle at Rathausgasse 1–5, tel. 026-672-9030, fax 026-672-9039, www.murtenhof.ch, info@murtenhof.ch). They have the best lakeview restaurant in town (see below).

$$ Hotel Ringmauer (German for "Ramparts") is friendly and characteristic, with a fun mix of modern decor in a traditional setting. Showers and toilets are within a dash of all 14 rooms (S-60

SF, D-110 SF, Db-120 SF, T-145 SF, Q-165 SF, attached restaurant, near town wall farthest from lake, Deutsche Kirchgasse 2, tel. 026-670-1101, fax 026-672-2083).

$ Berger Farmhouse is the choice if "Green Acres is the place" for you—and if you have a car. Consider a night in a barn (literally) at the big, traditional Berger-Aegerter family farm. Frau Berger, who speaks German and French, fills a big room with six single beds (and can add up to four more). There's no plumbing—you use a bathroom in the family building next door. The place is generally empty, so you're likely to have it all to yourself—surrounded by hay, old farm tools, and the noise of animals (May–Nov only because there's no heat, 30 SF per bed with breakfast, she'll cook dinner for 15 SF by request, family deals, includes sheets but no towels, a third of the way to Avenches, a mile or so south of Murten, on the main road just before Greng, look for the sign, Lindenweg 2, tel. 026-670-1407).

EATING

Eating in Murten is a joy. I'd stroll the main drag up one side and down the other to survey the action before making a choice. For elegance and a lake view, it's the Murtenhof. There are several good options right on the lake a 10-minute walk from the town center. Budget eaters can picnic or find a salad bar. Bakeries make good sandwiches, but they close by about 18:00.

Anything called "Seelander" or mentioning "three lakes" is typical of this Three Lakes region. Traditional restaurants serve *Egli-Filets*, the very popular perch "from the lake" (these days actually caught in Bodensee—Lake Constance in English—up by the German border). As this is the "vegetable garden of Switzerland," restaurants pride themselves on offering good veggies. You'll want a glass of wonderfully smooth and refreshing white Vully (voo-yee) wine with your meal (about 4 SF per glass).

Restaurant Murtenhof, with a covered terrace giving diners a comfortable and classy lakeside setting regardless of the weather, serves "updated Three Lakes cuisine" and several vegetarian choices. Sipping a glass of local white wine with the right travel partner, while gazing across the lake at hillside vineyards as the sun sets, is one of Europe's fine moments. Their fresh and tasty "catch of the day" (while not *Egli*) actually *is* from the lake (19 SF). To be sure you get the limited lakeside seating, call in a reservation at 026-672-9030 (salad bar, March–Nov Tue–Sun 11:00–23:00, closed Mon and Dec–Feb). The recorded sheep baaah-ing on the soundtrack adds to the place's rustic elegance.

Ringmauer Restaurant is a good bet for French cuisine and decadent desserts, offering a dressy section (40-SF plates, 78-SF five-course fixed-price meal) and a cheaper zone (30-SF plates, 17.50-SF daily special). It has fine outdoor seating on a quiet, picturesque lane, but the indoor section can be smoky—a good sign, indicating it's a local favorite. They serve top-end local wine by the glass (closed Sun evenings and Mon, Deutsche Kirchgasse 2, tel. 026-670-1101).

Fun-loving **Freiburger Falle** serves all the old *Fribourgeoise* traditions, such as meat on a hot stone (36 SF), fondue, and so on, in a characteristic cellar under the main street. You'll eat under alphorns and castle-style chandeliers (it hides under the Irish pub at Hauptgasse 43, tel. 026-672-1222, Bruno Lüscher).

Restaurant Anatolia is a Turkish place with crayon-quality menus posted everywhere and rather high prices for ethnic food. Still, it's much loved by locals for its fresh ingredients, good cooking, and charming owner, Mehmet. Eat indoors or out, with a fine main-drag view (20–25 SF, Hauptgasse 45, tel. 026-670-2868).

Restaurant Eintracht serves local cuisine from a fun menu, including old-time chef specials. If there is a down-and-dirty, horse-meat-cookin' local hangout in town, this is it (15–25-SF plates, half portions available, healthy specials, vineyard ambience or streetside seating, closed Wed, closes Sun at 18:00, Hauptgasse 19, tel. 026-670-2240).

Grizzly's Restaurant, perfect for those in need of a quick trip back home, is a playful, enthusiastic place with an enticing menu of North American delicacies. The Yukon-chic interior comes with totem poles, buckskins, and rock and roll. The outside offers the finest seats on the main street (fresh salads, trappers' spare ribs, mussels, vegetarian options, Tue–Sat 11:00–23:30, closed Sun–Mon, reservations smart, Hauptgasse 24, tel. 026-670-0787). As the menu says, "If the meal's not ready in 10 minutes, it will be in 15. If it's not on the table in 15 minutes, have another beer."

Pizza: Murten has two pizzerias. The one on the main street has better views, but locals prefer **Pizzeria Taverna Italiana** as a better value (17-SF daily specials, 20-SF pizza and pasta, 15-SF pizzas to go, daily 10:00–14:00 & 17:00–22:00, near Hotel Murtenhof at Kreuzgasse 4, tel. 026-670-2122).

Bakeries: The main street has four bakeries, all with ample charm. **Züger** (at Hauptgasse 33) has a tearoom and offers daily indoor seating and pleasant outside seats. They have delicate, local-style, open-face sandwiches and a wide variety of salads for around 16 SF (Wed–Sat and Mon 7:00–18:30, Sun 7:45–18:30, closed Tue).

Supermarket: The giant **Co-op** (with a cafeteria) towers between the train station and city center (Mon–Thu 8:00–19:00, Fri 8:00–20:00, Sat 7:30–16:00, closed Sun).

TRANSPORTATION CONNECTIONS

From Murten by Train to: Avenches (hourly, 10 min, direction: Payern), **Bern** (hourly, 40 min, some require a transfer in Kerzers), **Fribourg** in Switzerland (hourly, 30 min), **Lausanne** (hourly, 90 min, generally transfer in Fribourg), **Zürich** (2/hr, 1.75–2.25 hrs, transfer in Bern, Fribourg, or Kerzers). Train info: toll tel. 0900-300-3004 or www.rail.ch.

Route Tips for Drivers

Murten to Lake Geneva (50 miles): The autobahn from Bern to Lausanne/Lake Geneva makes everything speedy (see Lake Geneva chapter). Murten and Avenches are 10 minutes off the autobahn. Broc, Bulle, and Gruyères are within sight of each other and the autobahn. It takes about an hour to drive from Murten to Montreux. The autobahn (direction: Simplon) takes you high above Montreux (pull off at great viewpoint rest stop) and Château de Chillon. For the castle, take the first exit east of the castle (Villeneuve). Signs direct you along the lake back to the castle.

Near Murten: Avenches

Avenches, four miles south of Murten, was once Aventicum, the Roman capital of Helvetia. Today, it's a quaint little town with an ancient theater taking a bite out of it. From the town spreads a vast field of sparse Roman ruins.

With a pleasant, small-town French ambience, Avenches (ah-vahnsh) is a quieter, less expensive place to stay than Murten. Just a few minutes away by train, it also makes an easy day trip. The **TI** (Mon–Fri 8:30–12:00 & 13:30–17:30, Sat 9:30–12:30, closed Sun, tel. 026-676-9922, www.avenches.ch) and the town are a seven-minute uphill walk from the station.

Roman Avenches

Aventicum was a Roman capital, with a population of 20,000. The

Romans appreciated its strategic crossroads location, fertile land, and comfortable climate (several times voted "most livable place to retire"). While the population of today's Avenches could barely fill the well-worn ruins of their Roman amphitheater, Aventicum was once one of the largest cities of the Roman Empire. Everything sits on Roman ruins, which were nearly quarried to oblivion over several centuries; its scant remains were finally spared in the 19th century. Today, things are carefully preserved. Metal detectors must be registered here. Mothers, knowing that turning up anything ancient will bring on the archaeologists, yell at their kids, "Don't dig!" Even the benches on the main street are bits of a 2,000-year-old temple cornice.

There are five Roman sights: the amphitheater, a lone tower, a sanctuary and a theater in a field outside of town, and a museum.

The **amphitheater,** or arena, which once seated 18,000, is the largest Roman ruin in Switzerland (free, always open). While the gladiator action is no more, it's still busy with an annual opera festival and other musical events. At the top of the amphitheater (just past the museum entrance), scan the surrounding countryside. All the farmland was once a walled Roman town of about 20,000 people. The **tower** on the ridge (on left)—the only one remaining of the original 73 towers—marks where the wall once stood. In the middle, past the lone standing column of the **sanctuary,** you can see the small **theater** ruins (see below).

The **Roman museum** fills a medieval tower attached to the amphitheater in town with three fascinating floors of Roman artifacts. Good students borrow the extensive English catalog, which affords a fairly intimate look at domestic life here back then. Don't miss the glass, mosaics, and a gold bust of Marcus Aurelius (A.D. 80) found in an old Roman sewer in 1939 (4 SF, April–Sept Tue–Sun 10:00–12:00 & 13:00–17:00; Oct–March Tue–Sun 14:00–17:00; closed Mon year-round).

Perhaps the best Aventicum experience is to spend some quiet time at sunset pondering the evocative **Roman theater** (Théâtre Romaine) and **sanctuary** in the fields, a half-mile walk out of town (free, always open, tiny free car park at the site). The single column marks "Du Cigognier"—nicknamed the "stork sanctuary" (c. 1700) for the stork nest it supported. As the site was a quarry until the 19th century, almost nothing remains.

SLEEPING

(1.10 SF = about $1, country code: 41)

$$$ Hotel Couronne is an Old World, three-star place with a modern interior. It sits grandly on the main square of little Avenches, where Yves and Isabelle Faivre rent 14 charming, bright rooms (Sb-110 SF, Db-160–210 SF, Tb-210–260, higher prices are for bigger rooms, parking-15 SF/day, next to TI, tel. 026-675-5414, www.lacouronne.ch, couronneavenches@vtx.ch).

$ Friendly **Elisabeth Clement-Arnold** rents a room in her house (D-50 SF first night, then 40 SF per night, cash only, bathroom is yours alone but down the hall, often nobody home until 19:00, reserve by email, rue Centrale 5, tel. & fax 026-675-3031, eckadima@hotmail.com).

$ The Avenches **IYHF hostel,** the only hostel in the area, is a beauty. It's run by the Dhyaf family, has 4- to 10-bed rooms, and includes breakfast, a homey TV room, table tennis, a big backyard, and a very quiet setting near the Roman theater (33 SF for dorm bed in 4-bed room, 30 SF in 6- to 10-bed room, 38 SF per person for S or D and 35 SF per person for T when available, non-members pay 6 SF extra, office open 7:00–9:30 & 17:00–22:00, no curfew, 3 blocks from center at medieval *lavoir,* or laundry, Rue du Lavoir 5, tel. 026-675-2666, fax 026-675-2717, www.youthhostel .ch/avenches, avenches@youthhostel.ch). If you're on a tight budget and have a car, this place is a great option.

Avenches

GIMMELWALD
and the BERNER OBERLAND

Frolic and hike high above the stress and clouds of the real world. Take a vacation from your busy vacation. Recharge your touristic batteries high in the Alps, where distant avalanches, cowbells, the fluff of a down comforter, the whistle of marmots, and the crunchy footsteps of happy hikers are the dominant sounds. If the weather's good (and your budget's healthy), ride a cable car from the traffic-free village of Gimmelwald to a hearty breakfast at Schilthorn's 10,000-foot-elevation, revolving Piz Gloria restaurant. Linger among alpine whitecaps before riding, hiking, or paragliding down 5,000 feet to Mürren and home to Gimmelwald.

Your gateway to the rugged Berner Oberland is the grand old resort town of Interlaken. Near Interlaken is Switzerland's open-air folk museum, Ballenberg, where you can climb through traditional houses from every corner of this diverse country.

Ah, but the weather's fine and the Alps beckon. Head deep into the heart of the Alps, and ride the cable car to the stop just this side of heaven—Gimmelwald.

Planning Your Time

Rather than tackle a checklist of famous Swiss mountains and resorts, choose one region to savor: the Berner Oberland.

Interlaken is the administrative headquarters and transportation hub of this region. Use it for business—banking, post office, laundry, shopping—and as a springboard for alpine thrills.

With decent weather, explore the two areas that tower above either side of the **Lauterbrunnen Valley,** south of Interlaken: On one side is the **Jungfrau** (and beneath it, the towns of Wengen and Kleine Scheidegg), and on the other is the **Schilthorn** (overlooking the villages of Gimmelwald and Mürren). The best overnight options are the rustic hamlet of **Gimmelwald,** the resort town of **Mürren,** or (for accommodations without the expense and headache of mountain lifts) the village of **Lauterbrunnen,** on the valley floor. I've also listed some options in the resort of Wengen and a few other mountain towns. Ideally, spend three nights in the region, with a day exploring each side of the valley.

For the fastest look, consider a night in Gimmelwald, breakfast at the Schilthorn, an afternoon doing the Männlichen–Wengen hike, and an evening or night train out. What? A nature-lover not spending the night high in the Alps? Alpus interruptus.

Getting Around the Berner Oberland

For more than a century, this region has been the target of nature-worshipping pilgrims. And Swiss engineers and visionaries have made the most exciting alpine perches accessible...

By Lifts and Trains: Part of the fun—and most of the expense—here is riding the many lifts (gondolas and cable cars). Trips above Interlaken are not covered by train passes (but for most high transport, you'll get a 25 percent discount with a Eurailpass—without using a flexi-day—and a 50 percent discount with a Swiss Pass). Ask about discounts for early-morning and late-afternoon trips, youths, seniors, families, groups (assemble a party of 10 and you'll save about 25 percent), and those staying a while. Generally, round-trips are just double the one-way cost, though some high-up trains and lifts are 10–20 percent cheaper. Three popular local passes include the following:

The **Junior Card,** for families traveling with children, pays for itself in the first hour of trains and lifts (20 SF/one child, 40 SF/two or more children, lets children under 16 travel free with parents, buy at Swiss train stations).

The **Berner Oberland Pass** is a good idea for those staying a week and exploring the region extensively (224 SF, includes 3 days of unlimited travel and 4 days of half-price fares on all trains, buses, and lifts—even all the way south to Gstaad and Brig).

The **Jungfraubahnen Pass** is more limited in scope, covering six days of unlimited transportation in just the Jungfrau region, not including the ascent to the priciest perch, the Jungfraujoch (195 SF, or 145 SF with Swiss Pass).

Study the "Alpine Lifts in the Berner Oberland" map on

BERNER OBERLAND

Note: This birds-eye view looks **south**

Swiss Passes offer discounts beyond Wengen and Mürren. Other passes offer discounts beyond Interlaken.

Mönch 13,449' *Jungfrau* 13,642'

Eiger 13,026'

JUNG-FRAU-JOCH

SCHILTHORN 9,748'

GIMMEL-WALD 4,593'

TUNNEL

BIRG 8,784'

KLEINE SCHEIDEGG 6,762'

W.-ALP

MÜRREN 5,381'

GREAT HIKE

STECHEL-BERG 3,025'

NICE WALK

GRINDEL-WALD 3,393'

MÄNNLICHEN 7,317'

GRÜTSCHALP 4,879'

GRUND

To First

WENGEN 4,180'

LAUTERBRUNNEN 2,612'

BUS

ISENFLUH

SCHYNIGE PLATTE 6,454'

WILDERSWIL 1,916'

To Luzern

ISELTWALD

EAST STN.

WEST STN.

SPIEZ

To Bern

BRIENZ

Lake Brienz

INTER-LAKEN 1,860'

Lake Thun

BALLENBERG OPEN-AIR MUSEUM

page 117. Lifts generally go at least twice hourly, from about 7:00 until about 20:00 (sneak preview: www.jungfraubahn.ch). For a complete schedule of all trains, lifts, buses, and boats, pick up the regional timetable (2 SF at any station).

By Car: Lauterbrunnen, Stechelberg, Isenfluh, and Interlaken are all accessible by car. You can't drive to Gimmelwald, Mürren, Wengen, or Kleine Scheidegg, but don't let that stop you from staying up in the mountains; park the car and zip up on a lift. To catch the lift to Gimmelwald, Mürren, and the Schilthorn, park at the cable-car station in Stechelberg (2 SF/2 hrs, 6 SF/day, see page 129 for more information). To catch the train to Wengen or Kleine Scheidegg, park at the train station in Lauterbrunnen (parking: 2 SF/2 hrs, 10 SF/day).

Helpful Hints in the Berner Oberland

Weather: The local economy lives by the weather. You're wise to be in touch. Ask at your hotel or the TI for the latest. A local TV station showing live video from the famous (and most expensive-to-reach) peaks is playing just about wherever you go. For the latest weather, you can also see www.swisspanorama.com

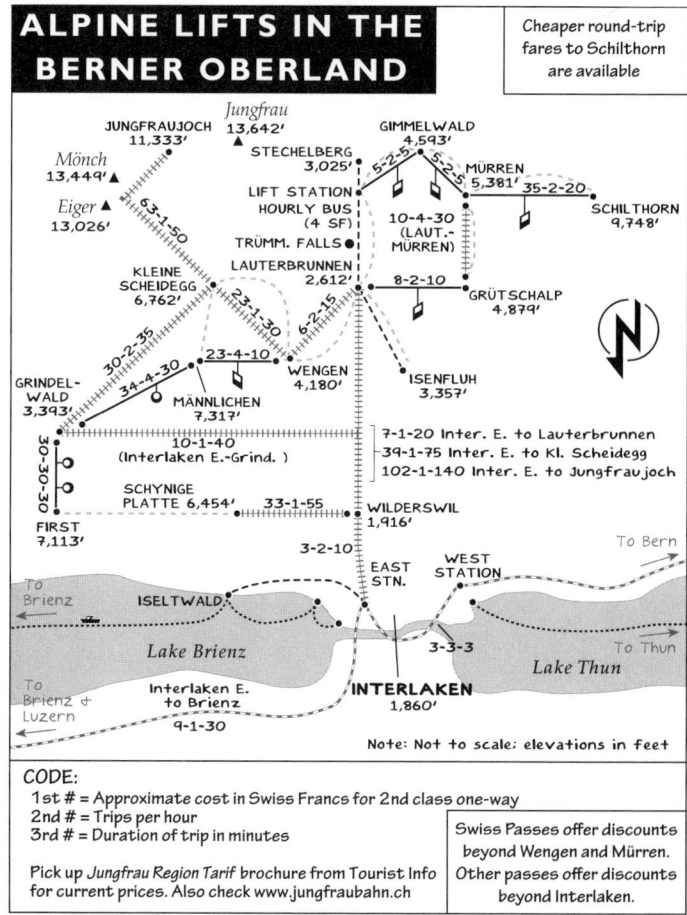

ALPINE LIFTS IN THE BERNER OBERLAND

Cheaper round-trip fares to Schilthorn are available

JUNGFRAUJOCH 11,333'
Jungfrau 13,642' ▲
Mönch 13,449' ▲
Eiger ▲ 13,026'

STECHELBERG 3,025'
LIFT STATION HOURLY BUS (4 SF)
TRÜMM. FALLS ●
LAUTERBRUNNEN 2,612'

GIMMELWALD 4,593'
MÜRREN 5,381'
SCHILTHORN 9,748'
35-2-20
5-2-5 5-2-5
10-4-30 (LAUT.-MÜRREN)

KLEINE SCHEIDEGG 6,762'
63-1-50
23-1-30
6-2-15
8-2-10
GRÜTSCHALP 4,879'

WENGEN 4,180'
ISENFLUH 3,357'

GRINDEL-WALD 3,393'
30-2-35
34-4-30
23-4-10
MÄNNLICHEN 7,317'
10-1-40 (Interlaken E.-Grind.)

7-1-20 Inter. E. to Lauterbrunnen
39-1-75 Inter. E. to Kl. Scheidegg
102-1-140 Inter. E. to Jungfraujoch

30-30-30
SCHYNIGE PLATTE 6,454'
33-1-55
WILDERSWIL 1,916'

FIRST 7,113'
3-2-10
EAST STN.
WEST STATION
To Bern

To Brienz
ISELTWALD
Lake Brienz
3-3-3
Lake Thun
To Thun

To Brienz & Luzern
Interlaken E. to Brienz
9-1-30
INTERLAKEN 1,860'

Note: Not to scale; elevations in feet

CODE:
1st # = Approximate cost in Swiss Francs for 2nd class one-way
2nd # = Trips per hour
3rd # = Duration of trip in minutes

Pick up *Jungfrau Region Tarif* brochure from Tourist Info for current prices. Also check www.jungfraubahn.ch

Swiss Passes offer discounts beyond Wengen and Mürren. Other passes offer discounts beyond Interlaken.

Berner Oberland

(entire area), www.jungfraubahn.ch (for Jungfraujoch), or www.schilthorn.ch (for Schilthorn peak).

Telephones: For efficiency, buy a phone card from a newsstand or train station ticket window. If staying in Gimmelwald, note that its sole public phone—at the cable-car station—takes only cards, not coins.

Closed Days: On Sundays and holidays (including the lesser-known religious holidays), small-town Switzerland is quiet. Hotels are open, and lifts and trains run, but many stores are closed.

Off-Season Closures: Note that at higher altitudes, many hotels, restaurants, and shops are closed between the skiing and hiking seasons: from late April until late May, and again from mid-October to early December.

Local Guidebook: For an in-depth look at the area's history, folk life, flora, fauna, and for extensive hiking information, buy Don Chmura's *Exploring the Lauterbrunnen Valley* (sold throughout the valley, 8 SF).

Visitor's Cards *(Gästekarten):* The hotels in various towns issue free visitor's cards that include measly discounts on some sights and transportation. While these cards won't save you much, you can ask at your hotel for the details.

Skiing: The Berner Oberland is a great winter-sports destination, with good snow on its higher runs, incredible variety, relatively reasonable prices, and a sense of character that's missing in many swankier resort areas. You can even schuss with the Swiss down the world's longest sledding run (9 miles long, out of Grindelwald, only open when snow's good). Three ski areas cluster around the Lauterbrunnen Valley: Mürren—Schilthorn (best for expert skiers), Kleine Scheidegg—Männlichen (busiest, best variety of runs), and Grindelwald—First (best for beginners and intermediate skiers, but lower elevation can make for iffier snowpack). Lift tickets cost around 60 SF a day, including the Sportspass Jungfrau, which covers all three areas (see www.jungfrauwinter.ch for prices and info).

Interlaken

When the 19th-century Romantics redefined mountains as something more than cold and troublesome obstacles, Interlaken became the original alpine resort. Ever since, tourists have flocked to the Alps "because they're there." Interlaken's glory days are long gone, its elegant old hotels eclipsed by the new, more swanky alpine resorts. Today, its shops are filled with chocolate bars, Swiss Army knives, and sunburned backpackers.

While European jet-setters are elsewhere, Interlaken is cashing in on a huge interest from India and the Arab world. Indians come to escape their monsoon season—especially in April and May—and to visit places they've seen in their movies (there's even a restaurant called "Bollywood" atop the Jungfraujoch). People from the hot and dry Arabian Peninsula come here just to photograph their children frolicking in the mist and fog.

ORIENTATION

Efficient Interlaken (pop. 5,500) is a good administrative and shopping center. Take care of business, give the town a quick look, and view the live TV coverage of the weather higher up (at the TI)... then head for the hills.

Tourist Information

The TI has good information on the region (May–June Mon–Fri 8:00–18:00, Sat 8:00–16:00, closed Sun; July–mid-Sept Mon–Fri 8:00–19:00, Sat 8:00–17:00, Sun 10:00–12:00 & 17:00–19:00; mid-Sept–Oct Mon–Fri 8:00–19:00, Sat 9:00–13:00, closed Sun; shorter hours Nov–April; under the 18-story skyscraper on the main street between West and East train stations, a 10-min stroll from either, Höheweg 37; tel. 033-826-5300, www.interlakentourism .ch). The *You Want It All* booklet is an almanac covering everything you need in Interlaken (except for some events, which are covered more thoroughly in the monthly entertainment guide). There's no point in buying a regional map, as good mini-versions of the map are included in various free transportation and hiking brochures. The TI organizes free walks on Mondays at 17:00 in the summer (in English with demand, call to confirm).

Arrival in Interlaken

Interlaken has two train stations: East (Ost) and West. All trains stop at both East and West stations. If heading for higher-altitude villages, get off at the East station. For hotels in Interlaken, get off at the West station. The West station also has a helpful and friendly train information desk (travel center for in-depth rail questions: Mon–Fri 9:00–12:00 & 13:30–18:30, Sat 9:00–12:00 & 13:30–17:00, closed Sun; ticket windows open daily 6:40–21:00; tel. 033-826-4750). Ask about discount passes, special fares, railpass discounts, and schedules for the scenic mountain trains. There's an exchange booth next to the ticket windows (daily 8:00–18:00). Nearby is a post office with a cluster of phone booths.

It's a pleasant 20-minute walk between the West and East stations, or there's an easy, frequent train connection (3/hr, 3.20 SF). From the East station, private trains take you deep into the mountainous Jungfrau region (see "Transportation Connections," page 129).

Helpful Hints

Laundry: Friendly Helen Schmocker's **Wäscherei** has a change machine, soap, English instructions, and a delightful riverside location (open for self-service daily 7:00–22:00—6 SF/load; open for full service Mon–Fri 8:00–12:00 & 13:30–18:00, Sat until 16:00, closed Sun, drop off in the morning and pick up that afternoon—12 SF/load; from the main street take Marktgasse over two bridges to Beatenbergstrasse 5, tel. 033-822-1566).

Bike Rental: You can rent bikes at either train station (23 SF/half-day, 31 SF/day, 5 SF less with Eurailpass or Swiss Pass, daily from 8:00, last rental at 17:00, last return at 23:00).

SELF-GUIDED WALK

Welcome to Interlaken

Most visitors use Interlaken as a springboard for high-altitude thrills (and rightly so). But the town itself has history and scenic charm and is worth a short walk. This 45-minute stroll circles from the West train station down the main drag to the big meadow, past the casino, along the river to the oldest part of town (historically a neighboring town called Unterseen), and back to the station.

• *From the West train station, walk along...*

Bahnhofstrasse: This main drag, which turns into Höheweg as it continues east, cuts straight through the town center from the West train station to the East station. The best Swiss souvenir shopping is along this Bahnhofstrasse stretch (finer shops are on the Höheweg stretch, near the fancy hotels). At the roundabout is the handy post office (with free public WCs). Just behind the post office on Marktgasse, the hardware store stocks real cowbells (both ornate and plain). At Höheweg 2, the TV in the window of the Schilthornbahn office shows the weather up top.

The 18-story **Metropole Hotel** (a.k.a. the "concrete shame of Interlaken") is by far the town's tallest building. Step right into the lobby and ride the elevator to the top for a commanding view of the "inter-laken" area, and gaze deep into the Jungfrau region to the scenic south. A meal or drink here costs no more than one back on earth. Consider sipping a drink on its outdoor view terrace (or come back tonight—it's open very late).

• *On your right is...*

Höhematte Park: This "high meadow," or Höhematte (but generally referred to simply as "the park"), marks the beginning of Interlaken's fancy hotel row. Hotels like the Victoria-Jungfrau harken back to the days when Interlaken was *the* top alpine resort (late 19th century). The first grand hotels were built here to enjoy the views of the Jungfrau in the distance. (Today, the *jung Frau*s getting the most attention are next door, at Hooters.)

The park originated as farmland of the monastery that pre-dated the town (marked today by the steeples of both the Catholic and Protestant churches—neither of any sightseeing interest). The actual **monastery site** is now home to the courthouse and county administration building. With the Reformation in 1528, the monastery was shut down, and its land was taken by the state. Later, when the land was being eyed by developers, the town's leading hotels and business families bought it and established that it would never be used for commercial buildings (a very early example of smart town planning). There was talk of building a parking lot under it, but the water table here, between the two lakes, is too high. (That's why the town cemetery is up on the hillside.) Today, this is a fine place to stroll, hang out on the park benches or at Restaurant Schuh, and watch the paragliders gracefully land.

From the park, turn left into the grounds of **Casino Kursaal,** where, at the top of each hour, dwarves ring the toadstools on the flower clock. The Kursaal, originally a kind of 19th-century fat farm, is now both a casino (passport but no tie required) and a convention center that hosts musical events and folklore shows (2–3/week in summer, fun yodeling with lots of audience participation, details at the TI).

• *Follow the path left of the Kursaal to the river (huge public swimming pool just over the river). Walk downstream under the train track and cross the pedestrian bridge, stopping in the middle to enjoy the view.*

Aare River: The Aare River is Switzerland's longest. It connects Lake Brienz and Lake Thun (with an 18-foot altitude difference—this short stretch has quite a flow). Then it tumbles out of Lake Thun, heading for Bern and ultimately into the Rhine. Its level is controlled by several sluices. In the distance, a church bell tower marks a different parish and the neighborhood of Unterseen, which shares the town's name, but in German: Like the word *Interlaken*, *Unterseen* means "between the lakes." Behind the spire is the pointy summit of the Niesen (like so many Swiss peaks, capped with a restaurant and accessible by a lift). Stroll downstream along the far side of the river to the church spire. The delightful riverside walk is lined by fine residences. Notice that your Jungfrau view now includes the Jungfraujoch observation deck (the little brown bump in the ridge just left of the peak).

• *At the next bridge, turn right to the town square lined with 17th-century houses on one side and a modern strip on the other.*

Unterseen: This was a town when Interlaken was only a monastery. The church is not worth touring. A block away, the (generally empty) **Town History Museum/Museum of Tourism** shows off classic posters, fascinating photos of the construction of the Jungfraujoch, and exhibits on folk life, crafts, and winter sports—all well-described in English (5 SF, May–mid-Oct Tue–Sun 14:00–17:00, closed Mon and mid-Oct–April, Obergasse 26).

Return to Station: From Unterseen, cross the river on Spielmatte, and you're a few minutes' walk from your starting point. On the second bridge, notice the border between the two towns, or parishes, marked by their respective heraldic emblems (each with an ibex, or wild mountain goat). A block or so later, on the left, is the Marktplatz. The river originally ran through this square. The town used to be called "Aaremühle" ("Aare mill") for the mill that was here. But in the 19th century, town fathers made a key marketing decision: Since "Aaremühle" was too difficult for English tourists to pronounce, they changed the name to "Interlaken." Judging from the throngs of tourists on the main drag, it worked.

SIGHTS AND ACTIVITIES

Near Interlaken

Boat Trips—"Interlaken" is literally "between the lakes" of Thun and Brienz. You can explore these lakes on a lazy boat trip, hopping on and off as the schedule allows (free with Swiss Pass or Eurailpass but uses a flexi-day, schedules at TI or at BLS Travel Center in West station, tel. 033-826-4760). The boats on Lake Thun (about hourly, 5-hour round-trip, 53 SF) stop at the St. Beatus Höhlen caves (30 min away, next entry) and two visit-worthy towns: Spiez and Thun. The boats on Lake Brienz (roughly every other hour, 3-hour round trip, 38 SF) stop at the super-cute village of Iseltwald and at Brienz (easy bus and train connections back to Interlaken from Brienz, near Ballenberg Open-Air Folk Museum—described on the next page).

St. Beatus Höhlen caves on Lake Thun can be visited with a one-hour guided tour (17 SF, 2/hr, April–mid-Oct daily 10:30–17:00, closed mid-Oct–March, tel. 033-841-1643, www .beatushoehlen.ch). The best excursion plan: Ride the bus from Interlaken (20-min ride, line #21—direction: Thun, departs West station at :19 past the hour); tour the caves; take the short, steep hike down to lake; and return by boat (9 SF one-way, 30 min to Interlaken, described previously).

Adventure Trips from Interlaken—For the thrill-seeker with money, several companies offer high-adrenaline trips such as rafting, canyoning (rappelling down watery gorges), bungee jumping, and paragliding. Costs range from 150 SF to 205 SF. Interlaken's two dominant companies are **Alpin Raft** (tel. 033-823-4100, www .alpinraft.com) and **Outdoor Interlaken** (tel. 033-826-7719, www .outdoor-interlaken.ch). Other companies are generally just booking agents for these two outfits. For an overview of your options, visit www.interlakenadventure.com or study the racks of brochures at most TIs and hotels (everyone's getting a cut of this lucrative industry).

Several years ago, two fatal accidents jolted the adventure-sport business in the Berner Oberland, leading to a more professional respect for the risks involved. Companies have very high standards of safety. Statistically, the most dangerous sport is mountain biking. Enjoying nature up close comes with risks. Adventure sports increase those risks dramatically. Use good judgment.

Less-Risky Adventures in and near Interlaken—Vertical Sport has a breathtaking indoor rock-climbing facility, where you can snack or enjoy a nice cup of hot chocolate while watching hotshots practice their gravity-defying skills (Tue–Sun 9:00–18:00, or until 22:00 in bad weather, closed Mon, private lessons for beginners by the hour, at the back of the park 50 yards from Hotel Savoy at

INTERLAKEN

Funicular to Harderkulm

To Brienz & Luzern

Woods

POOL

Aare River

BIG, RITZY HOTELS

EAST STATION

Private trains to Jungfrau Region

UNTERSEEN

CASINO KURSAAL

CASTLE

Höhe Matte Park

WEST STATION

POST

Höhematte Park

ALPENSTRASSE

Höhe Matte Park

TELL OPEN-AIR THEATER

Woods

200 meters

200 yards

To N18 Autobahn (Bern & Luzern)

To N18 Autobahn (Bern & Luzern) & Lauterbrunnen Valley

❶ Hotel Lötschberg, Guest House Susi's B&B & Sirinya's Thai
❷ Katy's Lodge B&B
❸ Sunny Days B&B
❹ Hotel Aarburg & Launderette
❺ Villa Margaretha
❻ Backpackers' Villa (Sonnenhof)
❼ Balmer's Herberge & Metro Bar
❽ Happy Inn Lodge
❾ Restaurant Bären

❿ Goldener Anker
⓫ Città Vecchia
⓬ Benacus Wine Bar & Rest.
⓭ Metropole Hotel & Rest.
⓮ Restaurant Schuh
⓯ Funny Farm Bar
⓰ Migros Dept. Store/ Cafeteria
⓱ Co-op Dept. Store/ Cafeteria
⓲ Town History Museum/ Museum of Tourism
⓳ Vertical Sport

Jungfraustrasse 44, tel. 033-821-2823).

Outdoor Interlaken's Seilpark offers five rope courses of varying difficulty and height in a forest, giving you a tree-top adventure through a maze of rope bridges and zip lines (37 SF, family deals, must weigh between 44 and 264 pounds; June–Aug daily 10:00–18:00; Sept–Oct Tue–Fri 13:00–18:00, Sat–Sun 10:00–18:00, closed Mon; closed Nov–May; 20-min walk out of town at Hauptstrasse 15, tel. 033-826-7719, www.outdoor-interlaken.ch).

▲▲**Swiss Open-Air Folk Museum at Ballenberg**—Across Lake Brienz from Interlaken, the Swiss Open-Air Museum of Vernacular Architecture, Country Life, and Crafts in the Berner Oberland is a rich collection of traditional and historic farmhouses from every region of the country. All the houses are carefully furnished, and many feature traditional craftspeople at work. The sprawling 50-acre park, laid out roughly as a huge Swiss map (Italian Swiss in the south, Appenzell in the east, and so on), is a natural preserve providing a wonderful setting for this culture-on-a-lazy-Susan look at Switzerland.

The Thurgau house (#621) has an interesting wattle-and-daub (half-timbered construction) display, and house #331 has a fun bread museum and farmers' shop. There's cheesemaking (near the east entry), traditional farm animals (like very furry-legged roosters, near the merry-go-round in the center), and a chocolate shop (under the restaurant on the east side).

An outdoor cafeteria with reasonable prices is inside the west entrance, and fresh bread, sausage, mountain cheese, and other goodies are on sale in several houses. Picnic tables and grills with free firewood are scattered throughout the park.

The little wooden village of Brienzwiler (near the east entrance) is a museum in itself, with a lovely pint-size church.

Cost, Hours, Information: 18 SF, half-price after 16:00, covered by Swiss Pass. A RailAway combo-ticket, available at both Interlaken stations, includes transportation to and from Ballenberg and your admission (39 SF from West station, 36 SF from East, add 13 SF to return by boat instead). The houses are open daily May–Oct 10:00–17:00, but the grounds stay open later. Craft demonstration schedules are listed just inside entry. Use the 2-SF map/guide. The more expensive picture book is a better souvenir than guide. Tel. 033-952-1030, www.ballenberg.ch.

Getting There from Interlaken: Take the train from either of Interlaken's train stations to Brienz (hourly, 30 min, 9 SF one-way from West station). From the Brienz station, catch a bus to Ballenberg (10 min, 3.20 SF one-way). Consider returning by boat (Brienz boat dock next to train station, one-way to Interlaken-21 SF).

Castles and Forts—A few impressively well-kept and welcoming old castles in the Interlaken area are worth considering for day trips by boat, bus, or car.

Thun Castle (Schloss Thun), built between 1180 and 1190 by the Dukes of Zähringen, has a five-floor historical museum offering insights into the cultural development of the region over a period of some 4,000 years. From the corner turrets of the castle, you are rewarded with a spectacular view of the city of Thun, the lake, and the Alps (7 SF, April–Oct daily 10:00–17:00, less off-season, www.schlossthun.ch).

Hünegg Castle (Schloss Hünegg) in Hilterfingen (farther along Lake Thun, toward Interlaken) contains a museum exhibiting furnished rooms from the second half of the 19th century. The castle is situated in a beautiful wooded park (8 SF, mid-May–mid-Oct Mon–Sat 14:00–17:00, Sun 11:00–17:00, closed off-season, www.schlosshuenegg.ch).

Oberhofen Castle (Schloss Oberhofen) is for those interested in gardens. Its beautifully landscaped park with exotic trees is a delight (free, mid-March–mid-Nov daily from 9:00 until dusk, closed in winter). The museum in the castle depicts domestic life in the 16th through 19th centuries, including a Turkish smoking room and a medieval chapel (7 SF, mid-May–mid-Oct Mon 14:00–17:00, Tue–Sun 11:00–17:00, closed off-season, tel. 033-243-1235).

NIGHTLIFE

Youthful Night Scenes—For counterculture with a reggae beat, check out **Funny Farm** (past Balmer's Herberge hostel, in Matten). The young frat-party dance scene rages at the **Metro Bar** at Balmer's (bomb-shelter disco bar, with cheap drinks and a friendly if loud atmosphere). And if you're into **Hooters,** you won't have a hard time finding it.

Mellower After-Dark Hangouts—The first three options are also described under "Eating": For a stylish wine bar with local yuppies, check in at the **Benacus Piazza del Vino** on the square in Unterseen. To nurse a drink with a view of the park, the outdoor tables at **Restaurant Schuh** are the place to be. The **"Top O'Met"** bar and café has great indoor and outdoor view seating with reasonable prices, 18 floors above everything else in town (in the Metropole Hotel skyscraper, open nightly until late). **Hotel Oberland** (near the post office) often has live alpine music in their restaurant/bar.

SLEEPING

I'd head for Gimmelwald, or at least Lauterbrunnen (20 min by train or car). Interlaken is not the Alps. But if you must stay...

$$$ Hotel Lötschberg, with a sun terrace and 21 wonderful rooms, is run with lots of thoughtful touches by English-speaking Susi and Fritz. This is the best real hotel value in town. Happy to dispense information, these gregarious folks pride themselves on a personal approach that sets them apart from other hotels (Sb-120 SF, Db-165 SF, big Db-185 SF, extra bed-30 SF, family deals, rates about 15 percent cheaper mid-Oct–April, closed Nov–March, elevator, coin-op Internet access, free Wi-Fi, laundry service, bike rental-25 SF/half-day; 3-min walk from West station: leaving station, turn right, after Migros at the circle go left to General-Guisan-Strasse 31; tel. 033-822-2545, fax 033-822-2579, www .lotschberg.ch, hotel@lotschberg.ch). Effervescent Fritz organizes guided adventures. He does tandem hang gliding almost every day with one of his guests (guests fly with Fritz at a discount, 140 SF,

Interlaken

Sleep Code

(1.10 SF = about $1, country code: 41)
S = Single, **D** = Double/Twin, **T** = Triple, **Q** = Quad, **b** = bathroom,
s = shower only. Unless otherwise noted, credit cards are
accepted, English is spoken, and breakfast is included.

To help you sort easily through these listings, I've divided
the rooms into three categories, based on the price for a standard double room with bath:

$$$ **Higher Priced**—Most rooms 150 SF or more.
 $$ **Moderately Priced**—Most rooms between 90–150 SF.
  $ **Lower Priced**—Most rooms 90 SF or less.

---

about 20 SF cheaper than any other deal in town).

$$ Guest House Susi's B&B is Hotel Lötschberg's no-frills,
cash-only annex, run by Fritz and Susi, offering nicely furnished,
cozy rooms (Sb-105 SF, Db-135 SF; apartment with kitchenette-115
SF/2 people, 200 SF/4–5 people—discount for 3-night stay; prices
about 20 percent cheaper mid-Oct–April, closed Nov–March,
same contact info as Hotel Lötschberg, listed first).

$$ Sunny Days B&B, a homey, nine-room place in a residential neighborhood, is run by Dave from Britain (Sb-98–110
SF, Db-110–148 SF, prices vary with size of room and view, extra
bed about 40 SF, less in winter; exit left out of West station and
take first bridge to your left, after crossing two bridges turn left
on Helvetiastrasse and go 3 blocks to #29; tel. 033-822-8343, www
.sunnydays.ch, mail@sunnydays.ch).

$$ Hotel Aarburg offers 13 plain, peaceful rooms over a res-
taurant in a beautifully located but run-down old building a 10-
minute walk from the West station (Sb-70 SF, Db-130 SF, 10 SF
more in July–Aug, next to launderette at Beatenbergstrasse 1, tel.
033-822-2615, fax 033-822-6397, hotel-aarburg@quicknet.ch).

$$ Katy's Lodge B&B is a funky old house in a quiet, handy
location. While not cozy, it rents nine basic rooms at a good price
(Db-95 SF, T-115 SF, Qb-145 SF, 6-bed room-200 SF; discount
offered with cash and this book: 5 percent off for 1 night, 10 percent off for 2 or more nights; garden, playground, 3-min walk
from West station, across from Hotel Lötschberg at Bernastrasse
7, tel. 033-821-0963, fax 033-822-7479, www.katys-lodge.ch,
katyslodge@bluewin.ch).

$ Villa Margaretha, run by English-speaking Frau Kunz-
Joerin, offers the best cheap beds in town. It's like Grandma's
big Victorian house on a residential street. Keep your room tidy,
and you'll have a friend for life (D-86 SF, T-129 SF, Q-172 SF,

the 3 rooms share one big bathroom, 2-night minimum, closed Oct–April, cash only, no breakfast served but dishes and kitchenette available, lots of rules to abide by, go up small street directly in front of West station to Aarmühlestrasse 13, tel. 033-822-1813, www.villa-margaretha.com, info@villa-margaretha.com).

$ Backpackers' Villa (Sonnenhof) Interlaken is a creative guest house run by a Methodist church group. It's fun, youthful, and great for families, without the frat-party scene of Balmer's Herberge (listed next). Travelers of any age feel comfortable here (dorm beds in 5- to 7-bed rooms with lockers and sheets-37 SF, D-98 SF, T-135 SF, Q-164 SF, 5 SF more per person for rooms with toilets and Jungfrau-view balconies, includes breakfast, kitchen, garden, movies, small game room, Internet access, laundry, bike rental, free admission to public swimming pool/spa, no curfew, open all day but reception open only 7:00–11:00 & 16:00–21:00, 10-min walk from either station, across the park from TI, Alpenstrasse 16, tel. 033-826-7171, fax 033-826-7172, www.villa .ch, mail@villa.ch).

$ Balmer's Herberge is many people's idea of backpacker heaven. This Interlaken institution comes with movies, table tennis, a cheap launderette (4 SF/load), bar, restaurant, swapping library, Internet access, tiny grocery, bike rental, excursions, a shuttle-bus service (which meets important arriving trains), and a friendly, hardworking staff. This little Nebraska, a hive of youthful fun and activities, is home for those who miss their fraternity. It can be a mob scene, especially on summer weekends (spot in 30-bed dorm-27 SF, in a 10-bed dorm-29 SF, S-43 SF, D-74 SF, T-99 SF, Q-132 SF, includes sheets and breakfast, open year-round, emailed reservations recommended 5 days in advance except for dorm beds, Hauptstrasse 23, in Matten, 15-min walk from either train station, tel. 033-822-1961, fax 033-823-3261, www.balmers.com, mail @balmers.ch).

$ Happy Inn Lodge has 15 cheap backpacker rooms above a lively, noisy restaurant a five-minute walk from the West station (dorm bed-22 SF, S-40 SF, D-80 SF, T-90–105 SF, Q-120–140 SF, breakfast-8 SF, Rosenstrasse 17, tel. 033-822-3225, fax 033-822-3268, www.happyinn.com, info@happyinn.com).

EATING

In Unterseen, the Old Town Across the River

Restaurant Bären, in a classic low-ceilinged building with cozy indoor and fine outdoor seating, is a great value for *Rösti,* fondue, raclette, fish, traditional sausage, and salads (20–25-SF plates including fondue for one, Cordon Bleu is popular, open daily, closed Mon off-season, from West station turn left on

Bahnhofstrasse and go over the river a block to Seestrasse 2, tel. 033-822-7526).

Goldener Anker is *the* local hangout—smoky, with a pool table and a few unsavory types. If you thought Interlaken was sterile, you haven't been to the "Golden Anchor." Jeannette serves and René cooks, just as they have for 25 years. This place, with its "melody rock and blues" ambience, sometimes hosts small concerts, and has launched some of Switzerland's top bands (hearty 20-SF salads, fresh vegetables, 3 courses for 20 SF, daily from 16:00, Marktgasse 57, tel. 033-822-1672).

Città Vecchia serves decent Italian with seating indoors or out, on a leafy square (15-SF pizzas, 20-SF pastas, 30-SF plates, closed Tue, on main square in Unterseen at Untere Gasse 5, tel. 033-822-1754).

Benacus Wine Bar and Restaurant is a snooty, trendy spot serving Euro-Asian modern cuisine and offering tapas with a good list of open wines (40-SF plates, closed Sun–Mon, Stadthausplatz, tel. 033-821-2020).

On or Near the Main Drag (Höheweg)

Interlaken's main drag, Höheweg, is lined with eateries. The Asian, American, and Arab group tourism cuts into the local ambience, but you do have plenty of options.

Sirinya's Thai Restaurant is run by charming Sirinya, who serves great Thai dishes and famous spring rolls at reasonable prices (17-SF plates, closed Mon, at Hotel Lötschberg—see "Sleeping," General-Guisan-Strasse 31, tel. 033-821-6535).

Metropole Hotel's "Top O'Met," capping Interlaken's 18-story aesthetic nightmare, is actually a decent café/restaurant serving traditional and modern food at down-to-earth prices. For just 5 SF, you can enjoy a glass of wine and awesome views from an indoor or outdoor table (25-SF lunch deals include 2 courses and a drink, daily 11:30–24:00, Höheweg 37, just step into the Metropole Hotel and go up the elevator as far as you can, tel. 041-210-1666).

Restaurant Schuh retains its grand-café ambience on the best real estate in town (at the corner of the park, across from Metropole Hotel and TI). The interior is a big tour-group food fight, but there's no better place to nurse a drink or coffee and watch the paragliders float into the park (live schmaltzy music, newspapers, Höheweg 56, tel. 033-822-9441).

Cheap Eats

Interlaken's two big supermarkets sell picnic supplies and also have reasonable self-service restaurants: **Migros** is across the street from the West station (Mon–Thu 8:00–18:30, Fri 8:00–21:00, Sat 7:30–17:00, closed Sun), while the **Co-op** is across the river from the West station, on your right (same hours as Migros). The only grocery store open late at night is **Co-op Pronto** (daily 6:00–22:30, 30 yards west of TI on Höheweg).

TRANSPORTATION CONNECTIONS

If you plan to arrive at Zürich Airport and want to head straight for Interlaken and the Alps, see the Zürich chapter (page 31). Note that Interlaken is connected to Luzern and Montreux (on Lake Geneva) via the Golden Pass scenic rail route (see Scenic Rail Journeys chapter).

While there are a few long-distance trains from Interlaken, you'll generally transfer in **Bern** (for Bern connections, see page 100). Train info: toll tel. 0900-300-3004 or www.rail.ch.

From Interlaken East (Ost) by Train to: Lauterbrunnen (hourly, 20 min, 7 SF each way), **Bern** (2/hr, 55 min), **Spiez** (3/hr, 20 min), **Brienz** (1–2/hr, 20 min), **Zürich** and **Zürich Airport** (hourly, 2–2.25 hrs, most direct but some with transfer in Bern, Luzern, and/or Spiez), **Luzern** (hourly, 2 hrs), **Lugano** (hourly, 5 hrs, transfer in Luzern, Zürich, or Olten), **Zermatt** (hourly, 3.5 hrs, transfer in Spiez and Brig).

From Interlaken to the Lauterbrunnen Valley

To reach the heart of the valley, drive or take the train to Lauterbrunnen (train leaves hourly from East station, 20 min). You cannot drive to Gimmelwald (park in Stechelberg and take the cable car; see below) or to Mürren, Wengen, or Kleine Scheidegg (park in Lauterbrunnen and take the cable car to Mürren or the train to Wengen/Kleine Scheidegg).

To get from Lauterbrunnen to Gimmelwald, you have two options:

1. The faster, easier way—best in bad weather or at the end of a long day with lots of luggage—is to drive or, if you don't want to rent a car, ride the postal bus from Lauterbrunnen to Stechelberg and the base of the Schilthornbahn cable-car station (bus costs 3.80 SF, hourly bus departure coordinated with arrival of train, get off at Schilthornbahn stop). With a car, it's 30 minutes from Interlaken to the Stechelberg station (parking lot: 2 SF/2 hrs, 6 SF/day).

From Stechelberg, the cable car will whisk you in five thrilling minutes up to Gimmelwald (5.40 SF, 2/hr at :25 and :55 past the hour, Gimmelwald is the first stop). Note that the Schilthornbahn is closed for servicing for a week in early May and also from mid-November through early December. During this time, you'll ride the cargo cable car directly from Stechelberg to Mürren, where a small bus shuttles you down to Gimmelwald.

Interlaken

What's What in the Berner Oberland

For such a small corner of the world, this region packs in a lot to experience. Here's a quick rundown of the place names you'll encounter.

Allmendhubelbahn (AHL-mehnd-hoo-behl-bahn): A classic old funicular from Mürren, leading to good hikes at the top (see page 145).

Ballenberg: Swiss Open-Air Folk Museum, on Lake Brienz (see page 123).

Berner Oberland: The mountainous part of the canton of Bern, sometimes referred to as the "Jungfrau region." Everything else on this list is in the Berner Oberland (also called "Bernese Oberland" in English).

Birg (beerg): Cable-car stop between Mürren and the Schilthorn, with a trail leading steeply down to Gimmelwald and more (see page 155).

Brienz (bree-ENTS): Lake on the east side of Interlaken (Brienzersee) and the namesake town on its shore.

First (feersht): Overlook point accessible by lift from Grindelwald; endpoint of hike from Schynige Platte (see page 163).

Gimmelwald (GIM-mehl-vahlt): Wonderfully rustic time-warp village overlooking the Lauterbrunnen Valley; good home-base option (see page 132).

Grindelwald (GRIN-dehl-vahlt): Expensive resort town, not to be confused with Gimmelwald.

Grütschalp (GREWTSH-alp): Station at the top of the cable car from Lauterbrunnen. It's connected by train and a trail to Mürren (see page 160).

Interlaken (IN-tehr-lah-kehn): Big town at the "entrance" to the Berner Oberland; you'll go through here to get anywhere else in this chapter (see page 118).

Jungfrau, Mönch, Eiger (YOONG-frow, munkh, EYE-gehr): Literally "Maiden, Monk, Ogre," the three major peaks of the region, from right to left (the Jungfrau's the highest, at 13,642 feet).

Jungfraubahn (YOONG-frow-bahn): Company that runs all of the trains and lifts in the area (except for the Schilthorn cable cars).

Jungfraujoch (YOONG-frow-yoke): High-altitude (11,300 feet) observation deck near the Jungfrau peak, accessible by train from Kleine Scheidegg.

Kleine Scheidegg (KLY-neh SHY-dehk): Viewpoint with breathtaking Eiger, Mönch, and Jungfrau views; has several hotels and restaurants (see page 168), plus the train station that offers pricey rides to the Jungfraujoch (page 154).

Lauterbrunnen (LOUT-ehr-broo-nehn): Small town in the middle of the Lauterbrunnen Valley. From here, a cable car goes up to Grütschalp (with connections to Mürren and Gimmelwald), the train runs up to Wengen and Kleine Scheidegg, and the postal bus goes to Stechelberg. For hotels and restaurants, see page 148.

Lauterbrunnen Valley: Valley at the heart of the Berner Oberland; most towns and activities in this chapter overlook this valley.

Männlichen (MEN-leekh-ehn): Lift station on a dramatic ridge separating the region's two valleys. Connected to Wengen and also to Grund (near Grindelwald) by lifts; also the starting point of an easy hike to Kleine Scheidegg with nonstop mountain views (see page 161).

Mürren (MEW-rehn): Pleasant resort town near Gimmelwald, midway up the Schilthorn cable-car line; a good high-mountain home base for those who find Gimmelwald too small and rustic (see page 141).

Schilthorn (SHILT-horn): The 10,000-foot peak across the Lauterbrunnen Valley from the Jungfrau, reached by cable car from Stechelberg (in the valley), Mürren, and Gimmelwald; features spectacular views and the Piz Gloria revolving restaurant made famous by James Bond (see page 152).

Schilthornbahn: Cable-car company that operates the lift on the west side of the Lauterbrunnen Valley, connecting Stechelberg (on the valley floor) with Gimmelwald, Mürren, Birg, and the Schilthorn.

Schynige Platte (SHIH-nih-geh PLAH-teh): High-altitude observation point near the entrance to Lauterbrunnen Valley, reached by funicular from Wilderswil; starting point of a long but scenic hike to First (see page 163).

Sefinen Valley (seh-FEE-nehn): Branches off the Lauterbrunnen Valley beyond Stechelberg and Gimmelwald; good for a hike (see page 157).

Stechelberg (SHTEH-khehl-behrk): At the end of the Lauterbrunnen Valley, it's the starting point of the cable car leading up to Gimmelwald, Mürren, and on to the Schilthorn (for accommodations, see page 168).

Thun (toon): Lake to the west of Interlaken (Thunersee) and its namesake town on the lake.

Trümmelbach Falls (TREW-mehl-bahkh): Striking series of waterfalls near Lauterbrunnen (see page 165).

Wengen (VAYNG-ehn): Resort town on Jungfrau side of Lauterbrunnen Valley; on the train line between Lauterbrunnen and Kleine Scheidegg (for hotels, see page 166).

Wilderswil (VIHL-dehrs-vihl): Village near entrance of the Lauterbrunnen Valley; on the train line between Interlaken and Lauterbrunnen; has funicular to Schynige Platte and trailhead to First (see page 163).

2. The more scenic route is to catch the cable car from Lauterbrunnen to Grütschalp, where a special scenic train *(Panorama Fahrt)* will roll you along the cliff to Mürren (total trip from Lauterbrunnen to Mürren: 30 min, 10 SF). From there, either walk a paved 30 minutes downhill to Gimmelwald, or walk 10 minutes across Mürren to catch the cable car down to Gimmelwald (5.40 SF).

Railpass Discounts: Beyond Interlaken, trains into the Jungfrau region are only 25 percent covered by Eurailpasses; they're free with the Swiss Pass up to Wengen or Mürren (uphill from there, Swiss Pass–holders get a 50 percent discount). You can buy your entire package of lifts for your intended hike at once, but then you don't have the flexibility to change with the weather.

Gimmelwald

Saved from developers by its "avalanche zone" classification, Gimmelwald was (before modern tourism) one of the poorest places in Switzerland. Its tradi-

tional economy was stuck in the hay, and its farmers—unable to make it in their disadvantaged trade—survived only on a trickle of visitors and on Swiss government subsidies (and working the ski lifts in the winter). For some travelers, there's little to see in the village. Others (like me) enjoy a fascinating day sitting on a bench and learning why they say, "If heaven isn't what it's cracked up to be, send me back to Gimmelwald."

Take a walk through the town. The huge, sheer cliff face that dominates your mountain views is the Schwarzmönch ("Black Monk"). The three peaks above (or behind) it are, left to right, the Eiger, Mönch, and Jungfrau. While Gimmelwald's population has dropped in the last century from 300 to about 120 residents, traditions survive. Most Gimmelwalders have one of two last names: von Allmen or Feuz. They are tough and proud. Raising hay in this rugged terrain is labor-intensive. One family harvests enough to feed only about 15 cows. But they'd have it no other way, and, unlike the absentee-landlord town of Mürren, Gimmelwald is locally owned. (When word got out that urban planners wished to develop Gimmelwald into a town of 1,000, locals pulled some strings to secure the town's bogus avalanche-zone building code. Today, unlike nearby resort towns, Gimmelwald's population is the same all year.) Those same folks are happy the masses go to

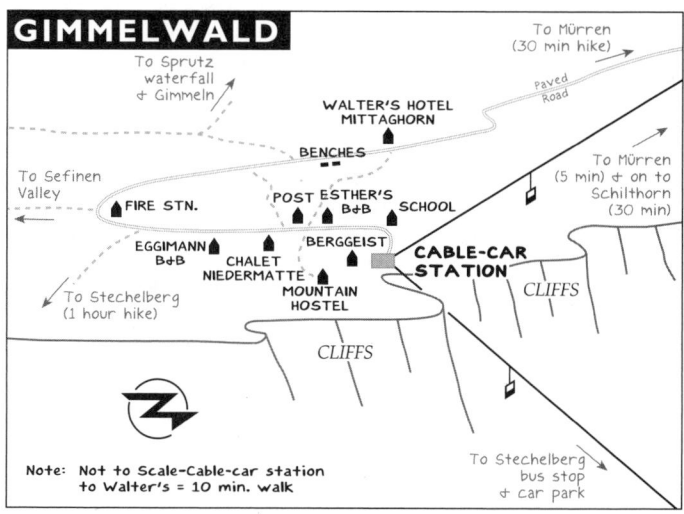

GIMMELWALD

To Mürren (30 min hike)

To Sprutz waterfall & Gimmeln

Paved Road

WALTER'S HOTEL MITTAGHORN

BENCHES

To Mürren (5 min) & on to Schilthorn (30 min)

To Sefinen Valley

FIRE STN.

POST   ESTHER'S B&B   SCHOOL

EGGIMANN B&B   CHALET NIEDERMATTE   BERGGEIST   CABLE-CAR STATION

MOUNTAIN HOSTEL

CLIFFS

To Stechelberg (1 hour hike)

CLIFFS

N

To Stechelberg bus stop & car park

Note: Not to Scale-Cable-car station to Walter's = 10 min. walk

touristy and commercialized Grindelwald, just over the Kleine Scheidegg ridge. Don't confuse Gimmelwald and Grindelwald—they couldn't be more different.

Thanks to the leadership of the village teachers (Olle and Maria) and their son (Sven), Gimmelwald now has a helpful little website (www.gimmelwald.ch). There you can check out photos of the town in different seasons, get directions for 11 of the best hikes out of town, and see all the latest on activities and rooms for rent.

SELF-GUIDED WALK

Welcome to Gimmelwald

Gimmelwald, though tiny, with one zigzag street, offers a fine look at a traditional Swiss mountain community.

• *Start this quick walking tour at the...*

Cable-Car Station: When the lift came in the 1960s, the village's back end became its front door. Gimmelwald was, and still is, a farm village. Stepping off the cable car, you see a sweet

little hut. Set on stilts to keep out mice, the hut was used for storing cheese (the rocks on the rooftop here and throughout the town are not decorative—they keep the shingles on through wild storms). Behind the cheese hut stands the village schoolhouse. In Catholic Swiss towns, the biggest building is the church. In Protestant towns,

Swiss Cow Culture

Traditional Swiss cow farmers could make more money for much easier work in another profession. In a good year, farmers produce enough cheese to break even—they support their families on government subsidies. (Throughout the Alps, governments support traditional farming as much for the tourism as for the cheese.) But these farmers have made a lifestyle choice to keep tradition alive and to live high in the mountains. Rather than lose their children to the cities, Swiss farmers have the opposite problem: Kids argue over who gets to take over the family herd.

The cows' grazing ground can range in elevation by as much as 5,000 feet throughout the year. In the summer (usually mid-June), the farmer straps elaborate ceremonial bells on his cows and takes them up to a hut at high elevations. The cows hate these big bells, which weigh upwards of 10 pounds and can cost more than 2,000 SF apiece—a proud investment for a humble farmer. When the cows arrive at their summer home, the bells are hung under the eaves.

These high-elevation summer stables are called "alps." Try to find some on a Berner Oberland tourist map (e.g., Wengernalp, Grütschalp, Schiltalp). The cows stay at the alps for about 100 days. The farmers hire a team of cheesemakers to work at each

it's the school. Gimmelwald's biggest building is the school (two teachers share one teaching position, 17 students, and a room that doubles as a chapel when the Protestant pastor makes his monthly visit). Don't let Gimmelwald's low-tech look fool you: In this school, each kid has his or her own website. In the opposite direction, just beyond the little playground, is Gimmelwald's Mountain Hostel (listed on page 139).

• *Walk up the lane 50 yards, past the town's Dalí-esque art gallery (the shower in the phone booth), to Gimmelwald's...*

"Times Square": The yellow alpine "street sign" shows where you are, the altitude (1,370 meters—that's 4,470 feet), how many hours *(Std.)* and minutes it takes to walk to nearby points, and which tracks are serious hiking paths (marked with red and white, and further indicated along the way with red and white patches of paint on stones). You're surrounded by buildings that were built as duplexes—divided vertically right down the middle to house two alp—mostly hippies, students, and city slickers eager to spend three summer months in the mountains. Each morning, the hired hands get up at 5:00 to milk the cows, take them to pasture, and make the cheese—milking the cows again when they come home in the evening. In summer, all the milk makes alp cheese (it's too difficult to get it down to the market). In the winter, with the cows at lower altitudes, the fresh milk is sold as milk.

Every alp also has a resident herd of pigs. Cheesemaking leftovers (*Molke,* whey) can damage the ecosystem if thrown out—but pigs love the stuff. (The pigs parade up with the cows, but no one notices.) Cheesemakers claim that bathing in whey improves the complexion...but maybe that's just the altitude talking.

Meanwhile, the farmers—glad to be free of their bovine responsibilities in summer—turn their attention to making hay. The average farmer has a few huts at various altitudes, each surrounded by small hay fields. The farmer follows the seasons up into the mountains, making hay and storing it above the huts. In the fall, the cows come down from the alps and spend the winter moving from hut to hut, eating the hay the farmer spent the summer preparing for them.

Throughout the year, you'll see farmers moving their herds to various elevations. If snow is in the way, farmers sometimes use tourist cable cars to move their cows. Every two months or so, Gimmelwald farmers bring together cows that aren't doing so well and herd them into the cable car to meet the butcher in the valley below.

separate families. The writing on the post office building is a folksy blessing: "Summer brings green, winter brings snow. The sun greets the day, the stars greet the night. This house will keep you warm. May God give us his blessings." The date indicates when it was built or rebuilt (1911). Gimmelwald has a strict building code. For instance, shutters can only be painted certain colors. Esther's Shop (10 yards uphill, buy things on the honor system, daily 8:00–12:00 & 17:15–19:00) has homemade and farm-raised products..

• *From this tiny intersection, we'll follow the town's main street (away from cable-car station).*

Main Street: Walk up the road. Notice the announcement board: one side for tourist news, the other for local news (e.g., deals on chainsaw sharpening, upcoming shooting competitions). Cross the street and peek into the big new barn, dated 1995. This is part of the Switzerland-wide Sleep in Straw association, which rents out barn spots to travelers when the cows are in the high country.

To the left of the door is a cow-scratcher. Swiss cows have legal rights (for example, in the winter, they must be taken out for exercise at least three times a week). This big barn is built in a modern style. Traditionally, barns were small (like those on the hillside high above) and closer to the hay. But with trucks and paved roads, hay can be moved more easily, and farm businesses need more cows to be viable. Still, even a well-run big farm hopes just to break even. The industry survives only with government subsidies (see "Swiss Cow Culture" sidebar, page 134). Small as Gimmelwald is, the postman (who sells stamps) comes daily. As you wander, notice private garden patches. Until recently, most locals grew their own vegetables—often enough to provide most of their family's needs.

• *Go just beyond the next barn. On your right is the...*

Water Fountain/Trough: This is the site of the town's historic water supply. Local kids love to bathe and wage water wars here when the cows aren't drinking from it. Detour left down a lane about 50 yards (along a wooden fence and then past pea-patch gardens) to the next trough and the oldest building in town, Husmättli, from 1658. (The town's 17th-century buildings are mostly on the road zigzagging below town.) Study the log-cabin construction. Many are built without nails. The wood was logged up the valley and cut on the water-powered village mill (also below town). Gimmelwald heats with wood, and since the wood needs to age a couple of years to burn well, it's stacked everywhere.

• *Back on the paved road, continue uphill.*

Twenty yards along, on the left, the first house has a bunch of scythes hanging above the sharpening stone. Farmers pound, rather than grind, the blade to get it razor-sharp for efficient cutting. Feel a blade...carefully.

A few steps further, notice the cute cheese hut on the right (with alpine cheese for sale). Its front is an alpine art gallery with nail shoes for flower pots. Nail shoes grip the steep, wet fields—this is critical for safety, especially if you're carrying a sharp scythe. Even today, farmers buy metal tacks and fasten them to boots. The hut is full of strong cheese—up to three years old.

Look up. In the summer, a few goats are kept here (rather than in the high alp) to provide families with fresh milk (about a half-gallon per day per goat). The farmers fence off the fields, letting the goats eat only the grass that's most difficult to harvest.

On the left (at the B&B sign) is the home of Olle and Maria, the village schoolteachers. Maria runs the Lilliput shop (the "smallest shop with the greatest gifts"—handmade delights from the town and region, just ring the bell and meet Maria). Her older children, Sven and Sara, do a booming trade in sugar-coated almonds; little sister Carina competes with cookies.

• *Fifty yards farther along is the...*

Alpenrose: At the old schoolhouse, notice the big ceremonial cowbells hanging under the uphill eave. These swing from the necks of cows during the procession from the town to the high Alps (mid-June) and back down (mid-Sept). If the cows are gone, so are the bells—hanging from similar posts under the eaves of mountain huts in the high meadows.

• *At the end of town, pause where a lane branches off to the left, leading into the dramatic...*

Sefinen Valley: All the old homes in town are made from local wood cut from the left-hand side of this valley (shady side, slow-growing, better timber).

• *A few steps ahead, the road switches back at the...*

Gimmelwald Fire Station: The *Föhnwacht Reglement* sheet, posted on the fire station building, explains rules to keep the village from burning down during the fierce dry wind of the Föhn season. During this time, there's a 24-hour fire watch, and even smoking cigarettes outdoors is forbidden. Mürren was devastated by a Föhn-caused fire in the 1920s. Because villagers in Gimmelwald—mindful of the quality of their volunteer fire department—are particularly careful with fire, the town has not had a terrible fire in its history (a rare feat among alpine villages).

Check out the other posted notices. This year's Swiss Army calendar tells reservists when and where to go (in all four official Swiss languages). Every Swiss male does a 22-week stint in the military, then a few days a year in the reserves until about age 30. The *Schiessübungen* poster details the shooting exercises required this year. In keeping with the William Tell heritage, each Swiss man does shooting practice annually for the military (or spends three days in jail).

• *Take the...*

High Road to Hotel Mittaghorn: The resort town of Mürren hovers in the distance. And high on the left, notice the hay field with terraces. These are from WWII days, when Switzerland, wanting self-sufficiency, required all farmers to grow potatoes. Today, this is a festival of alpine flowers in season (best at this altitude in May and June).

• *Our walk is over. From Hotel Mittaghorn, you can return to Gimmelwald's "Times Square" via the stepped path.*

NIGHTLIFE

Evening fun in Gimmelwald is found at the **Mountain Hostel** (offering a pool table, Internet access, lots of young Alp-aholics, and a good chance to share information on the surrounding mountains). **Walter's bar** (in Hotel Mittaghorn) is a local farmers' hangout. When they've made their hay, they come here to play.

Although they look like what some people would call hicks, they speak some English and can be fun to get to know. Sit outside (benches just below the rails, 100 yards down the lane from Walter's) and watch the sun tuck the mountaintops into bed as the moon rises over the Jungfrau. If this isn't your idea of nightlife, stay in Interlaken.

SLEEPING

(4,593 feet, 1.10 SF = about $1, country code: 41)

Gimmelwald is my home base in the Berner Oberland. To inhale the Alps and really hold them in, you'll sleep high in Gimmelwald, too. Poor but pleasantly stuck in the past, the village has only a few accommodations options—all of them quirky and memorable. Rates include a new tax, which gets you into the public swimming pool in nearby Mürren (at the Sportzentrum, described on page 142). Factor the cable-car cost (5.40 SF per ride from Stechelberg or Mürren) into your accommodation costs. The cable car goes up and down twice an hour (at :25 and :55 past the hour from Stechelberg and Mürren, and at :00 and :30 from Gimmelwald). Be warned: You'll meet a lot of my readers in this town. This is a disappointment to some; others enjoy the chance to be part of a fun extended family.

$$ Maria and Olle Eggimann rent two rooms—Gimmelwald's most comfortable—in their quirky but alpine-sleek chalet. Maria and Olle, who job-share the village's only teaching position and raise three kids of their own, offer visitors a rare and intimate peek at this community (D-130 SF, Db with kitchenette-190 SF for 2 or 3 people, optional breakfast-20 SF, cash only, guarantee your reservation in advance with a check or PayPal, last check-in at 21:00, 3-night minimum, Wi-Fi; from cable car, continue straight for 200 yards along the town's only road, B&B on left; tel. 033-855-3575, oeggimann@bluewin.ch).

$$ Esther's Guest House, overlooking the main intersection of the village, rents seven clean, basic, and comfortable rooms, three of which have private bathrooms (S-45–70 SF, big D-110–120 SF, Db-110–120 SF, big T-130–180 SF, Q-170–200 SF, family room for up to 5 people-140–230 SF, cash preferred, breakfast-15 SF, 2-night minimum, low ceilings, fine guests' kitchen, tel. 033-855-5488, fax 033-855-5492, www.esthersguest house.ch, info@esthersguesthouse.ch). Esther also rents two four-person **apartments** with kitchenettes next door (140–160 SF/2 people, 190–220 SF/4 people, extra bed-30 SF, 3-night minimum, check website for details).

$$ Hotel zum Berggeist has simple rooms and the town's only restaurant. Its terrace, overlooking the hostel, has gorgeous views across the valley (Sb-80 SF, D-138 SF, Db-150 SF, T-195 SF, Q-236, room prices include 3-course dinner, backpacker mattress in attic-25 SF, free Internet access and Wi-Fi, 50 yards from cable-car station, likely closed for renovation fall 2008—with higher prices after re-opening, tel. 033-855-1730, fax 033-845-1121, www.berggeist.ch, berggeist.gimmelwald@gmail.com, Christoph).

$ Hotel Mittaghorn, the treasure of Gimmelwald, is run by Walter Mittler, a wonderful Swiss gentleman, with the help of trusty Tim. Walter's hotel is a classic, creaky, alpine-style place with memorable beds (if the bed's too lumpy or short, consider putting the mattress on the floor, or wear socks and drape the blanket over your feet), and a million-dollar view of the Jungfrau Alps. The hotel has three rooms with private showers and four rooms that share a shower (1 SF/5 min). Walter, now in his 80s, is careful not to let his place get too hectic or big. He, Tim, and Rosemarie (who comes in to clean

up) appreciate sensitive Back Door travelers. To some, Hotel Mittaghorn is a creaky nightmare, with a kitchen that would never pass code, bumpy beds, teeny towels, and minimal plumbing, run by an eccentric old grouch. These people are better off in Mürren or Interlaken (Db-86 SF, 6-SF surcharge per person for 1-night stays, cash only, free Internet access, open April–Oct). Reserve by telephone only, then reconfirm by phone the day before your arrival (tel. 033-855-1658, www.ricksteves.com/mittaghorn). Walter usually offers his guests a simple but hearty 15-SF dinner at 19:30 (by reservation only). Hotel Mittaghorn is at the top of Gimmelwald, a five-minute climb up the steps from the village intersection.

$ Chalet Niedermatte rents three rooms in the summer just 50 yards from the cable-car station (Db-75 SF, Tb-100 SF, Qb-130 SF; kitchen, laundry, organic farm selling meats and brownies, reserve by email and then reconfirm by email 2–3 days before arrival, tel. 033-855-1662, dwalle@tcnete.ch, Liesi).

$ Mountain Hostel is a beehive of activity, as clean as its guests, cheap, and friendly. Phone ahead or book on their website. To secure one of its 50 dorm beds the same day (tough in July and August), call after 9:30 and leave your name. The hostel has low ceilings, a self-service kitchen, a mini-grocery, a free pool table, laundry, free Internet access, and healthy plumbing. It's mostly a college-age crowd; families and older travelers will probably feel more comfortable elsewhere. Petra Brunner has lined the porch with flowers. This relaxed hostel survives with the help of its guests.

Read the signs, respect Petra's rules, and leave it tidier than you found it—bus your plates and clean the kitchen. Impress fellow hostelers and Petra by volunteering to chop wood for the hot tub. The place is one of those rare spots where a congenial atmosphere spontaneously combusts as the piano plays, and spaghetti becomes communal as it cooks (25 SF per bed in 6- to 15-bed rooms, includes sheets, showers-1 SF, no breakfast, hostel membership not required, 20 yards from lift station, tel. 033-855-1704, www.mountainhostel.com, mountainhostel @tcnet.ch). Petra also makes great pizza every night.

$ Schlaf im Stroh ("Sleep in Straw") offers exactly that, in an actual stable but may close in late 2008. After the cows head for higher ground in the summer, the von Allmen family hoses out their barn and fills it with straw and budget travelers. Blankets are free, but bring your own sheet, sleep sack, or sleeping bag. No beds, no bunks, no mattresses, no kidding. Esther fluffs up your straw each night. Some city slickers can't handle the flies and manure smell. Come here for the experience...not the comfort (24 SF, 18 SF for kids ages 11–15, 10 SF for kids up to age 10, cash only, includes breakfast "barn service" and one modern bathroom and showers for up to 20 people, no kitchen or cooking allowed, open late June–mid-Oct depending on grass and snow levels, almost never full, may include manure pile outside barn door; from lift, continue straight through intersection to big modern barn marked *1995* on the right; same contact info as Esther's Guest House, previously).

EATING

The only restaurant in town is at **Hotel zum Berggeist,** serving good, hearty food indoors or out on its glorious view terrace (9–15-SF light meals, 20–30-SF all-you-can-eat main courses, homemade bread and *Wurst).* The Mountain Hostel has a decent members' kitchen and makes great pizzas in the evenings (nonguests welcome). Hotel Mittaghorn serves dinner only to its guests (15 SF).

Consider packing in a picnic meal from the larger towns. Mürren, a 30-minute hike away, has good restaurants and a grocery. If you need a few groceries and want to skip the hike to Mürren, you can buy the essentials—noodles, spaghetti sauce, and candy bars—at the Mountain Hostel's reception desk, or possibly at a kiosk by Hotel zum Berggeist. Local farmers sell their produce. Esther (at the main intersection of the village) sells the basics: cheese, sausage, bread, and Gimmelwald's best yogurt—but only until the cows go up in June (daily 8:00–20:00).

Mürren

Mürren—pleasant as an alpine resort can be—is traffic-free and filled with bakeries, cafés, souvenirs, old-timers with walking sticks, GE employees enjoying incentive trips, and Japanese tourists making movies of each other. Its chalets are prefab-rustic. With help from a "panorama train," funicular, and cable car, hiking options are endless from Mürren. Sitting on a ledge 2,000 feet above the Lauterbrunnen Valley, surrounded by a fortissimo chorus of mountains, the town has all the comforts of home (for a price) without the pretentiousness of more famous resorts.

Historic Mürren, which dates from 1384, has been overwhelmed by development. Still, it's a peaceful town. There's no full-time doctor, no police officer (they call Lauterbrunnen if there's a problem), and no resident priest or pastor. (The Protestant church—up by the TI—posts a sign showing where the region's roving pastor preaches each Sunday.) There's not even enough business to keep a bakery open year-round (Mürren's bakery is open mid-June–Sept and Dec–April)—a clear indication that this town is either lively or completely dead, depending on the season. (Holiday population: 4,000. Permanent residents: 400.) Keep an eye open for the "Milch Express," a tiny cart that delivers fresh milk and eggs to hotels and homes throughout town.

ORIENTATION

Mürren perches high on a ledge, overlooking the Lauterbrunnen Valley. You can walk from one end of town to the other in about 10 minutes.

There are two ways to get to Mürren: on the "panorama train" from Grütschalp (connects via cable car to Lauterbrunnen) or on the cable car from Stechelberg (in the valley), which stops at Gimmelwald, Mürren, and continues up to the Schilthorn. The train and cable-car stations (which both have lockers) are at opposite ends of town.

Tourist Information: Mürren's TI can help you find a room and give hiking advice (July–Sept daily 8:30–19:00, Thu until 20:45, less off-season, above the village, follow signs to *Sportzentrum*, tel. 033-856-8686, www.wengen-muerren.ch). You can change money at the TI. There's an ATM by the Co-op grocery.

Helpful Hints

R & R: The slick **Sportzentrum** (sports center) that houses the TI offers a world of indoor activities. The pool is free with the regional visitor's card given by local hotels (pool open Mon–Sat 13:00–18:45, Thu until 19:45, Sun 13:00–17:45, closed May and Nov–mid-Dec). In season, they offer squash, mini-golf, table tennis, and a fitness room.

Internet Access: Connect at the **TI** (see previous page) or **Eiger Guesthouse** (see "Sleeping," later in this chapter, daily 8:00–23:00, across from train station).

Laundry: Hotel Bellevue has a slick and modern little self-service launderette in its basement (5 SF/wash, 5 SF/dry, open 24/7).

Bike Rental: You can rent mountain bikes at **Stäger Sport** (25 SF/half-day, 35 SF/day, includes helmet, daily 9:00–18:00, closed late Oct–mid-May, in TI/Sportzentrum, tel. 033-855-2355, www.staegersport.ch). There's a bigger bike-rental place in Lauterbrunnen (Imboden Bike, described on page 150). Use caution on rough stretches.

Mürren Massage: Sabina Kulicka is very strong—and she knows how to iron out your back after a good hike (90 SF/hr, lots of options, daily 8:00–21:00, Haus Montana on lower road a few doors before Hotel Alpina, tel. 033-855-4538, mobile 079-527-0832).

Skiing: The Mürren-Schilthorn ski area is the Berner Oberland's best place for experts, especially those eager to tackle the famous, nearly 10-mile-long Inferno run. The runs on top, especially the Kanonenrohr, are quite steep and have predictably good snow; lower areas cater to all levels, but can be icier. For rental gear, try the friendly, convenient **Ed Abegglen** shop (best prices, next to recommended Chalet Fontana, tel. 033-855-1245), **Alfred's Sporthaus** (good selection and decent prices, between ski school and Sportzentrum, tel. 033-855-3030), or **Stäger Sport** (one shop in Sportzentrum and another near cable-car station, tel. 033-855-2330). For more info on skiing and snowboarding, see page 300 of the appendix.

SELF-GUIDED WALK

Welcome to Mürren

Mürren has long been a top ski resort, but a walk across town offers a glimpse into its past. This stroll takes you through town on the main drag, from the train station (where you'll arrive if coming

MÜRREN

1. Alpin Palace Hotel
2. Hotel Alpina & Edelweiss Cafeteria
3. Hotel/Rest. Bellevue & Launderette
4. Hotel/Restaurant Jungfrau
5. Hotel/Restaurant Blumental
6. Eiger Guesthouse
7. Chalet Fontana
8. Chalet Helvetia
9. Chalet Böbs
10. Stägerstübli Restaurant
11. Päsci's Snack Bar Bistro
12. Tham Chinese Restaurant
13. Co-op Grocery

Note: Not to scale—Cable-car station to train station = 10-min. walk

To Grütschalp

To Grütschalp + lift down to Lauterbrunnen

ALLMENDHUBEL

FUNICULAR

To Birg + Schilthorn

SUPPENALP

SPORT-ZENTRUM

TRAIN STATION

POST

Cliffs

CABLE-CAR STATION

LIFT FOR SUPPLIES (NOT PEOPLE)

Paved road

To Birg + Schilthorn

To Gimmeln

To Gimmelwald + Stechelberg

Cliffs

Mürren

from Lauterbrunnen) to the cable-car station, then back up to the Allmendhubel funicular station.

• *Start at the...*

Train Station: The first trains pulled into Mürren in 1891. (A circa-1911 car is permanently parked at the Grütschalp station.) A display case inside the station shows an original car from the narrow-gauge, horse-powered line that rolled fancy visitors from here into town. The current station, built in 1964, comes with impressive engineering for heavy cargo. Look out back, where a small truck can be loaded up and driven away.

• *Wander into town along the main road (take the lower, left fork).*

Stroll Under the Alpin Palace Hotel: The towering Alpin Palace Hotel was the "Grand Palace Hotel" until it burned in 1928. Its Jugendstil Hall is the finest room in Mürren. The small wooden platform on the left—looking like a suicide springboard—is the place where snow-removal trucks dump their loads over the cliff in the winter. Look back at the meadow below the station: This is a favorite grazing spot for chamois (the animals, not the rags for washing cars). Ahead, at Edelweiss Hotel, step to the far corner of the restaurant terrace for a breathtaking view stretching from the big three (Eiger, Mönch, and Jungfrau) on the left to the lonely cattle farm in the high alp on the right. Then look down.

Just past the massage parlor, Haus Montana was the spot where Kandahar ski boots were first made in 1933 (to give the necessary support to daredevils racing from the Schilthorn to the valley floor in Mürren's infamous Inferno race). Today, the still-respected Kandahar boots are made in nearby Thun.

• *Continue toward...*

"Downtown" Mürren: You'll pass the main intersection (where the small service road leads down to Gimmelwald) and the only grocery store in town (Co-op). The tiny fire barn (labeled *Feuerwehr*) has a list showing the leaders of the volunteer force and their responsibilities. The old barn behind it on the right evokes the day, not so long ago, when the town's barns housed cows. Imagine Mürren with more cows than people, rather than with more visitors than residents.

• *Reaching the far end of Mürren, you come to the...*

Cable-Car Station: The first cable car (goes directly to Stechelberg) is for cargo, garbage, and the (reputedly) longest bungee jump in the world. The other takes hikers and skiers up to the Schilthorn and down to Stechelberg via Gimmelwald.

• *Hiking back along the high road, you'll enter...*

Upper Mürren: You'll pass Mürren's two churches, the Allmendhubel funicular station, and the Sportzentrum (with swimming pool and TI).

• *Consider riding the...*

Allmendhubel Funicular: A quaint-looking but surprisingly rewarding funicular (from 1912, renovated in 1999) carries nature-lovers from Mürren to Allmendhubel, a perch offering a Jungfrau view that (while much lower) rivals the Schilthorn. At the station, notice the 1920s bobsled. The restaurants here (full- and self-service) have awesome views.

Allmendhubel is particularly good for families. At 7.40 SF one-way, it's cheaper than the Schilthorn. The restaurant overlooks a great playground. And the entertaining children's hike—with rough and thrilling, kid-friendly alpine rides along the way—departs from here. This is also the departure point for the North Face hike and walks to Grütschalp (see "Hikes," page 155).

ACTIVITIES

During ski season and the height of summer, the area offers plenty of activities. In July and August, you can enjoy folkloric evenings (Wed, at the Sportzentrum), morning tours of flowers and wildlife (Sun at 7:30, meet at Allmendhubel station, 12 SF includes funicular ride up, 90 min, led by Othmar from Hotel Bellevue—call him at 078-604-1401), and weekly yoga lessons by Denise (of Chalet Fontana). Or climb down to Gimmelwald with a guide on an iron cable course (info at Mürren TI, www.klettersteig-murren.ch). In spring and fall, Mürren is pretty dead.

NIGHTLIFE

Eiger Guesthouse is a popular sports bar-type hangout with pool tables, games, Internet stations, and a Scottish host (Alan). **Stägerstübli** is another good place to congregate. **Hotel Bellevue,** with its elegant alpine-lounge ambience, is also good for a drink. (All of these places are further described under "Sleeping" or "Eating.")

SLEEPING

(5,381 feet, 1.10 SF = about $1, country code: 41)
Prices for accommodations are often higher during the ski season. Many hotels and restaurants close in spring, roughly from Easter to early June, and may also shut down any time between late September and mid-December.

$$$ Hotel Alpina is a simple place with 24 comfortable rooms and a concrete feeling—a good thing, given its cliff-edge position (Sb-85 SF, Db-160 SF, Tb-200 SF, Qb-220 SF, most rooms with awesome Jungfrau views and balconies, prices less off-season and without a view, outside of mid-June–mid-Aug ask for a 10-SF-per-night Rick Steves discount, family rooms, homey lounge; exit left from train station, walk 2 min downhill; tel. 033-855-1361, fax 033-855-1049, www.muerren.ch/alpina, alpina @muerren.ch, Cecilia and her son Roger).

$$$ Hotel Bellevue has a homey lounge, solid woodsy furniture, a great view terrace, the hunter-themed Jägerstübli restaurant, and 17 great rooms at fair rates, all with balconies and views (Sb-110 SF, Db-190 SF; special deal with this book: Db-150 SF if staying 2 nights or more except July–Aug; Internet access, tel. 033-855-1401, fax 033-855-1490, www.muerren.ch/bellevue, bellevue-crystal@bluewin.ch, Ruth and Othmar Suter).

$$$ Hotel Jungfrau offers 29 modern and comfortable rooms (Sb-95–110 SF, Db-170–220 SF, lower prices are for no-view rooms, elevator, laundry service-15 SF, near TI/Sportzentrum, tel. 033-856-6464, fax 033-856-6465, www.hoteljungfrau.ch, mail @hoteljungfrau.ch, Anne-Marie and Andres).

$$$ Hotel Blumental has 16 older but nicely furnished rooms and a fun game/TV lounge (Sb-75–80 SF, Db-150–170 SF, 10 percent cheaper in Sept–Oct, higher prices are for July–Aug, outside of July–Aug book direct and ask for a 10 percent Rick Steves discount, attached restaurant—see "Eating," tel. 033-855-1826, fax 033-855-3686, www.muerren.ch/blumental, blumental@muerren. ch, Ralph and Heidi, fourth generation in the von Allmen family). Their modern little chalet out back rents six rooms (Db-130-160 SF, includes breakfast in the hotel).

$$ Eiger Guesthouse offers 14 good budget rooms. This is a friendly, creaky, easygoing home-away-from-home (S-60–65 SF, Sb-80–95 SF, bunk D-90 SF, bigger D-100–110 SF, Db-130–150 SF, bunk Q-160 SF; special with this book: D-80 SF with a 2-night minimum year-round—making this about the best deal going for cheap beds in July–Aug; closed Nov and for one month after Easter, across from train station, tel. 033-856-5460, fax 033-856-5461, www.eigerguesthouse.com, info@eigerguesthouse.com, well-run by Scotsman Alan and Swiss Véronique). The restaurant serves good, reasonably priced dinners (25 SF).

$ Chalet Fontana, run by charming Englishwoman Denise Fussell, is a rare budget option in Mürren, with simple, crispy-clean, and comfortable rooms (35–45 SF per person in small doubles or triples with breakfast and shared bathrooms, price varies with size of room, 5 SF cheaper without breakfast; family apartment with kitchen and bathroom-120–230 SF for up to 6 people with breakfast; cash only, closed Nov–April, across street from Stägerstübli restaurant in town center, tel. 033-855-4385, mobile 078-642-3485, chaletfontana@gmail.com). If no one's home, check at the Ed Abegglen shop next door (tel. 033-855-1245, off-season only).

$ Chalet Helvetia, run by Frau Hunziker, offers a homey, clean, two-bedroom apartment with bathroom, kitchen, separate entrance, and balcony from 40 SF per person (up to 4 people, no breakfast, 2-night minimum preferred, more expensive for 1-night stays, laundry service-10 SF/load; 200 yards below cable-car station on path to Gimmelwald, look for red *Zimmer* sign on right; tel. 033-855-4169, mobile 079-234-7867, chalet.helvetia@quicknet.ch).

$ Chalet Böbs, with terrific views, is the last house in Mürren on the road to Gimmelwald. Kitty and Albert, an alphorn player, rent three apartments: two that sleep four to five people (each with double bed, bunk bed, and twin bed) and one that sleeps two people (40 SF per person, 3-night minimum stay, kitchens, tel. 033-855-1463, mobile 078-633-6091, boebs@quicknet.ch).

EATING

Many of these restaurants are in or near my recommended hotels. Outside of summer and ski season, it can be hard to find any place that's open (ask around).

Stägerstübli is everyone's favorite Mürren diner. It's the only real restaurant not associated with a hotel. Located in the town center, this 1902 building was once a tearoom for rich tourists, while locals were limited to the room in the back—which is now the nicer area to eat. Sitting on its terrace, you know just who's out and about in town (15–30-SF lunches and dinners, 25-SF dinner specials, big portions, lovely lamb, daily 11:30–21:00, Lydia).

Päsci's Snack Bar Bistro has fun, creative, and inexpensive light meals; a good selection of salads, vegetarian dishes, coffees, teas, and pastries; and impressive views (take-out available, run by a serious chef—Päsci—and Fränzi, daily 9:00–18:00, at the Sportzentrum, overlooking the ice rink).

Tham Chinese Restaurant is a good, humble, new kid on the block, bringing spice to the local eating scene (Thai and Chinese dishes, daily until 21:30, toward the train station on the lower road, tel. 033-856-0110).

Hotel Blumental specializes in typical Swiss cuisine, but also serves fish, international, and vegetarian dishes in a stony and woody dining area (15–24-SF specials, 20-SF fondue served for one or more, 15-SF raclette, 15-SF pastas, daily from 17:00, tel. 033-855-1826; see "Sleeping," previous section).

Restaurant Hotel Jungfrau is a dressy ski lodge with a modern octagonal dining room and a fine view terrace. The salad bar (11 SF per plate or 17 SF all-you-can-eat) is always excellent, and 45 SF buys you a four-course meal (23-SF cheese fondue—minimum 2 people, veggie options, nightly from 18:00, near TI/Sportzentrum, tel. 033-856-6464; see "Sleeping," previous section).

Mürren

Edelweiss cafeteria offers self-serve lunches and restaurant dinners with the most cliff-hanging dining in town—the views are incredible (17-SF pizzas anytime, 18.50-SF hearty salads, self-service until 17:00, then full service; next to Hotel Alpina—see "Sleeping," previous section).

Hotel Bellevue's restaurant is atmospheric, with three dining zones: view terrace, elegant indoor area, and the Jägerstübli—a cozy, well-antlered hunters' room guaranteed to disgust vegetarians. This is a good bet for game, as they buy chamois and deer direct from local hunters (lamb or game-35 SF, cheaper options as low as 13 SF, mid-June–Oct daily 11:30–14:00 & 18:00–21:00, closed off-season, tel. 033-855-1401; see "Sleeping").

The **Co-op** is the only grocery store in town, with good picnic fixings and sandwiches (Mon–Fri 8:00–12:00 & 13:45–18:30, Sat until 17:00, closed Sun). Given restaurant prices, this place is a godsend for those on a tight budget.

Lauterbrunnen

Lauterbrunnen is the valley's commercial center and transportation hub. In addition to its train station (with lockers) and cable car, the one-street town is just big enough to have all the essential services (bank, post office, bike rental, launderette, and so on)—plus several hotels. It's idyllic, in spite of the busy road that slices it in two. Sitting under sheer cliffs at the base of the valley, with its waterfall spurting mightily out from the cliff (floodlit at night), Lauterbrunnen is a fine springboard for Jungfrau and Schilthorn adventures.

ORIENTATION

Tourist Information

Stop by the TI to check the weather forecast, use the Internet, or buy any regional train or lift tickets you need (June–Sept Mon–Fri 9:00–12:00 & 13:00–18:00, longer lunch break Sat–Sun; Oct–March closed Sat–Sun; exit station, turn left and go uphill to TI, near Co-op grocery; tel. 033-856-8568, www.wengen-muerren.ch).

Helpful Hints

Medical Help: Dr. Bruno Durrer, who has a clinic near the Jungfrau Hotel (look for *Arzt* sign), is good and speaks English (tel. 033-856-2626, answered 24/7).

Internet and Laundry: Two places within a block of each other in the town center compete for your coins: The **Valley Hostel** is automated (Internet access-10 SF/hr, launderette-5 SF/load, includes soap, May–Oct daily 9:00–21:00, shorter hours Nov–April, don't open dryer door until machine is finished or you'll have to pay another 5 SF to start it again, tel. 033-855-2008), while **The Booking Office** is fully staffed (Internet access-12 SF/hr, self-service laundry-10 SF/load, full-service laundry-25 SF/load, May–Oct daily 9:00–20:00, shorter hours Nov–April, also books adventure sports for 110–180 SF).

Grocery Store: The **Co-op** is on the main street (Mon–Fri 8:00–12:00 & 14:00–18:30, Sat 8:00–12:00 & 13:30–17:00, closed Sun).

Bike Rental: You can rent mountain bikes at **Imboden Bike** on the main street (25 SF/half-day, 35 SF/day; full-suspension—45 SF/half-day, 65 SF/day; daily July–Aug 9:00–20:00, Sept–June 9:00–18:30, except closed for lunch 12:00–13:00 Oct–May, tel. 033-855-2114).

New Cable Car: In 2006, the 114-year-old funicular connecting Lauterbrunnen and Grütschalp (which has a panorama train to Mürren) was closed due to shifting soil. A replacement cable car opened in late 2006, running nearly twice as fast as the old funicular. Each car carries up to 100 passengers and three tons in its cargo area below. While old-time trains are more romantic, cable cars are the economic best fix.

ACTIVITIES

Hikers' Loop from Lauterbrunnen—If you're staying in Lauterbrunnen, consider this ambitious but great day plan: Ride the cable car to Grütschalp, walk along the ridge to Mürren, take the cable car up to Schilthorn and back down to Mürren, ride the funicular up to Allmendhubel, take the North Face Walk to Gimmelwald, take the lift down to Stechelberg, bus to Trümmelbach Falls, and walk through the valley back into Lauterbrunnen. Make it more or less strenuous or time-consuming by swapping lifts and hikes (all described later in this chapter). Or rent a mountain bike and do a wheeled variation on this (parking your bike in Mürren for the Schilthorn trip).

Hang Out with Base-Jumpers—In recent years, the Lauterbrunnen Valley has become an El Dorado of base-jumping (parachuting off cliffs), and each season thrill-seekers hike to the top of a cliff, leap off—falling as long as they can (this provides the rush)—and then pull the ripcord to release a tiny parachute, hoping it will break their fall and a gust won't dash them into the mountainside.

Locals generally have little respect for the base-jumpers, whom they consider reckless. But to learn more, talk with the jumpers themselves, who congregate at the **Pub Horner,** at the uphill end of town (just under the waterfall). This is the grittiest place in Lauterbrunnen, providing cheap beds and meals for base-jumpers and the only real after-dark scene. Locals, base-jumpers, and stray tourists gather here in the pub each evening (9 rooms, 32 SF for a bunk, D-64 SF and up, cheaper apartments, no breakfast, free Wi-Fi and Internet access for customers, dancing nightly from 22:00 upstairs, tel. 033-855-1673, www.hornerpub.ch, mail@hornerpub.ch, run by Gertsch Ferdinand). Their kitchen sells cheap pastas and raclette, and puts out a nightly salad bar (8–14-SF meals).

SLEEPING

(2,612 feet, 1.10 SF = about $1, country code: 41)
$$$ Hotel Silberhorn is a big, formal, 32-room, three-star hotel that still manages to feel family-run. It has generous public spaces and an elegant-for-Lauterbrunnen restaurant just above the lift station and across from the train station. Almost every double room comes with a fine view and balcony (Db-150–160 SF, Db suite-180–190 SF, tel. 033-856-2210, www.silberhorn.com, info @silberhornl.com).

$$ Hotel Staubbach, a big, Old World place—one of the first hotels in the valley (1890)—is being lovingly restored by hard-working American Craig and his Swiss wife, Corinne. Its 30 plain, comfortable rooms are family-friendly, there's a kids' play area, and the parking is free. Many rooms have great views (S-70 SF, Ss-80 SF, Sb-100 SF, D-90 SF, Db-120 SF, figure 50 SF/person in family rooms sleeping up to 6, 10 SF extra per room for 1-night stays, 20 SF extra for balcony rooms with valley view, elevator, 4 blocks up from station on the left, tel. 033-855-5454, fax 033-855-5484, www.staubbach.com, hotel@staubbach.com). Guests can watch a DVD of my TV show on the region in the lounge.

$ Valley Hostel is practical and comfortable, offering 70 inexpensive beds for quieter travelers of all ages, with a pleasant garden and the welcoming Abegglen family: Martha, Alfred, Stefan, and Fränzi (D with bunk beds-60 SF, twin D-70 SF, beds in larger family-friendly rooms-25 SF per person, breakfast-5 SF, most rooms have no sinks, kitchen, 16-SF cheese fondue on request for guests 18:00–20:00, Internet access, Wi-Fi, coin-op laundry, 2 blocks up from train station, tel. & fax 033-855-2008, www .valleyhostel.ch, info@valleyhostel.ch).

$ Chalet im Rohr—a creaky, old, woody firetrap of a place—has oodles of character (and lots of Asian groups). It offers 50 beds

Lauterbrunnen

in big one- to four-bed rooms that share six showers (27 SF per person, no breakfast, common kitchen, cash only, closed for 4 weeks after Easter, below church on main drag, tel. & fax 033-855-2182, vonallmen.rohr@freesurf.ch, Elsbeth von Allmen-Müller).

$ Matratzenlager Stocki is rustic and humble, with the cheapest beds in town (15 SF with sheets in easygoing little 30-bed co-ed dorm with kitchen, closed Nov–Dec, across river from station, tel. 033-855-1754, Frau Graf).

$ Camping: Two campgrounds just south of town provide 15–35-SF beds (in dorms and 2-, 4-, and 6-bed bungalows, sheets-5 SF, kitchen facilities, cash only, big English-speaking tour groups). **Mountain Holiday Park-Camping Jungfrau,** romantically situated beyond Staubbach Falls, is huge and well-organized by Hans. It also has fancy cabins (26 SF per person, tel. 033-856-2010, www.camping-jungfrau.ch). **Schützenbach Retreat,** on the left just past Lauterbrunnen toward Stechelberg, is a simpler campground (tel. 033-855-1268, www.schuetzenbach.ch).

EATING

At **Hotel Restaurant Oberland,** Mark (Aussie) and Ursula (Swiss) Nolan take pride in serving tasty, good-value meals from a fun menu. It's a high-energy place with lots of tourists and no view (17-SF pizzas, 20–25-SF main courses, traditional Swiss dishes, daily 11:30–16:00 & 17:30–21:00, tel. 033-855-1241).

Hotel Restaurant Jungfrau, along the main street on the right-hand side, offers a wide range of specialties, including fondue and *Rösti,* served by a friendly staff. Their terrace has a great valley view (daily 12:00–14:00 & 18:00–21:00, tel. 033-855-3434, run by Brigitte Melliger).

Hotel Restaurant Silberhorn is the local choice for a fancy meal out. Call to reserve a view table (10-SF all-you-can-eat salad bar, 25–30-SF main courses, daily from 18:00, fine indoor and outdoor seating, above the cable-car station, tel. 033-856-2210).

More in the Berner Oberland

SIGHTS AND ACTIVITIES

Lifts and Trains

Doing at least one of the two high-altitude thrill rides described here is an essential Berner Oberland experience.

▲▲▲The Schilthorn and a 10,000-Foot Breakfast

The Schilthornbahn carries skiers, hikers, and sightseers effortlessly to the 10,000-foot summit of the Schilthorn, where the Piz Gloria station awaits, with a solar-powered revolving restaurant, shop, and panorama terrace. Linger on top. Piz Gloria has a free "touristorama" film room with a "Multi-Vision" slide show and explosive highlights from the James Bond thriller that featured the Schilthorn, *On Her Majesty's Secret Service*. (To start either of the 10-minute video clips, press the 007 or "Multi-Vision" button on the column in the middle of the room).

Watch paragliders set up, psych up, and take off, flying 45 minutes with the birds to distant Interlaken. Walk along the ridge out back. This is a great place for a photo of the mountain-climber you.

When you ascend in the cable car, take a look at the altitude meter. (The Gimmelwald–Schilthorn hike is free, if you don't mind a 5,000-foot altitude gain.) Ask at the Schilthorn station for a cable-car souvenir decal.

You can ride up to the Schilthorn and hike down, but it's tough. For information on **hikes** from lift stations along the Schilthorn cable-car line, see "Hikes," page 155. My favorite "hike" from the Schilthorn is simply along the ridge out back, to get away from the station and be all alone on top of an Alp.

Youth hostelers—not realizing that rocks may hide just under the snow—scream down the ice fields on plastic-bag sleds from the Schilthorn mountaintop. (There's an English-speaking doctor in Lauterbrunnen—see page 148.)

Cost, Hours, Information: You can ride to the Schilthorn and back from Lauterbrunnen (100 SF), Stechelberg (90 SF), Gimmelwald (80 SF), or Mürren (70 SF). Snare a 25 percent discount for early and late rides (roughly before 9:00 and after 15:30) and in spring and fall (roughly May and Oct). Travelers with a Swiss Pass (who get 50 percent off) or with a Eurailpass (25 percent discount) might as well go whenever they like, because you can't double up discounts. Lifts go twice hourly, and the ride from Gimmelwald (including two transfers) to the Schilthorn takes 30 minutes. You can park your car at the Stechelberg station (2 SF/2 hrs, 6 SF/day). For more information, including current weather conditions, see www.schilthorn.ch or call 033-826-0007.

Berner Oberland

Breakfast at 10,000 Feet: The "007 Breakfast Buffet" is huge (25 SF, 8:00–11:00, save a little money by buying combo cable-car ticket before 8:40). The restaurant also serves hot dishes all day at prices that don't rise with the altitude (around 20 SF).

▲▲▲Jungfraujoch

The literal high point of any trip to the Swiss Alps is a train ride through the Eiger to the Jungfraujoch. At 11,300 feet, it's Europe's highest train station. The ride from Kleine Scheidegg takes about an hour (sit on right side for better views), including two five-minute stops at stations actually halfway up the notorious North Face of the Eiger. You have time to look out windows and marvel at how people could climb the Eiger—and how the Swiss built this train track more than a hundred years ago. The second half of the ride takes you through a tunnel inside the Eiger (some newer train cars run multilingual videos about the history of the train line).

Once you reach the top, study the Jungfraujoch chart to see your options (many of them are weather-dependent). There's a restaurant, history exhibit, "ice palace" (a cavern with a gallery of ice statues), and a 20-minute video that plays continuously. A tunnel leads outside, where you can summer ski (33 SF for gear and lift ticket), sled (free loaner discs with a 5-SF deposit), ride in a dog sled (8 SF, mornings

only), or hike 45 minutes across the ice to Mönchsjochhütte (a mountain hut with a small restaurant). An elevator leads to the Sphinx observatory for the highest viewing point, from which you can see Aletsch Glacier—Europe's longest, at nearly 11 miles—stretch to the south. Remember that your body isn't used to such high altitudes. Signs posted at the top remind you to take it easy.

One of the best hikes in the region—from Männlichen to Kleine Scheidegg—could be combined with your trip up to the Jungfraujoch (see page 161).

Cost, Hours, Information: The first trip of the day to Jungfraujoch is discounted; ask for a Good Morning Ticket, and return from the top by noon (Nov–April you can get Good Morning rates for the first or second train and stay after noon; train runs all year; round-trip fares to Jungfraujoch: from Kleine Scheidegg-107 SF, or 83 SF for first trip of day—about 8:00; from Lauterbrunnen-157 SF, or 133 SF for first trip—about

7:00; confirm times and prices, railpass holders get a better deal than Good Morning Ticket and can't combine discounts; 25 percent discount with Eurailpass, 50 percent discount with Swiss Pass). Pick up a leaflet on the lifts at a local TI (www.jungfraubahn.ch). If it's cloudy, skip the trip; for a terse and trilingual weather forecast from the Jungfraujoch, call 033-828-7931.

Hikes

There are days of possible hikes from Gimmelwald and Mürren. Many are a fun combination of trails, mountain trains, and cable-car rides. I've listed them based on which side of the Lauterbrunnen Valley they're on: west (the Gimmelwald/Mürren/Schilthorn side) or east (the Jungfrau side).

On the Gimmelwald (West) Side of the Lauterbrunnen Valley

Hikes from the Schilthorn

Several tough trails lead down from the Schilthorn, but most visitors take the cable car round-trip simply for the views (see "Lifts and Trains," above). If you're a serious hiker, consider walking all the way down (first hike) or part of the way down (second hike) back into Gimmelwald. Don't attempt to hike down from the Schilthorn unless the trail is clear of snow. Adequate shoes and clothing (weather can change quickly) and good knees are required. (If you want to visit the Sprutz Waterfall on your way to Gimmelwald, see page 158.)

From the Top of the Schilthorn (very difficult)—To hike downhill from the Piz Gloria revolving restaurant at the peak, start at the steps to the right of the cable, which lead along a ridge between a cliff and the bowl. As you pass huge rocks and shale fields, keep an eye out for the painted rocks that mark the scant trail. Eventually, you'll hit the service road (a ski run in the winter), which is steep and not very pleasant. Passing a memorial to a woman killed by lightning in 1865, you come to the small lake called Grauseeli. Leave the gravel road and hike along the lake. From there, follow the trail (with the help of cables when necessary) to scamper along the shale in the direction of Rotstockhütte (to Gimmelwald, see next hike) or Schilttal (the valley leading directly to Mürren; follow *Mürren/Rotstockhütte* sign painted on the rock at the junction).

▲▲Birg to Gimmelwald via Brünli (moderately difficult)—Rather than doing the very long hike all the way back down into Gimmelwald, I prefer walking the easier (but still strenuous) hike from the intermediate cable-car station at Birg. This is efficiently combined with a visit to the Schilthorn (from Schilthorn summit, ride cable car halfway down, get off at Birg, and hike down from there; buy the round-trip excursion early-bird fare—which

GIMMELWALD AREA HIKES

Note: Elevation in feet

1 Birg to Gimmelwald via Brünli
2 Up Sefinen Valley to Kilchbalm
3 Gimmelwald-Tanzbodeli-Obersteinberg/Stechelberg/Gimmelwald
4 Sprutz Waterfall
5 North Face Trail from Allmendhubel
6 Allmendhubel/Mürren to Grütschalp
7 Allmendhubel to Grütschalp via Winteregg

Berner Oberland

Not to Scale

is cheaper than the Gimmelwald–Schilthorn–Birg ticket—and decide at Birg if you want to hike or ride down).

The most interesting trail from Birg to Gimmelwald is the high one via Grauseeli Lake and Wasenegg Ridge to Brünli, then down to Spielbodenalp and the Sprutz Waterfall. Warning: This trail is quite steep and slippery in places, and can take four hours. Locals take their kindergartners on this hike, but it can seem dangerous to Americans unused to alpine hikes. Do not attempt this hike in snow, which you might find at this altitude, even in the peak of summer. (Get local advice.)

From the Birg lift station, hike toward the Schilthorn, taking your first left down and passing along the left side of the little Grauseeli Lake. From the lake, a gravelly trail leads down rough switchbacks (including a stretch where the path narrows and you can hang onto a guide cable against the cliff face) until it levels out. When you see a rock painted with arrows pointing to Mürren and Rotstockhütte, follow the path to Rotstockhütte (traditional old farm with light meals and drinks, mattress loft with cheap beds), traversing the cow-grazed mountainside.

For a thrill, follow Wasenegg Ridge. It's more scary than dangerous if you're sure-footed and can handle the 50-foot-long "tightrope-with-handrail" section along an extremely narrow ledge with a thousand-foot drop. This trail gets you to Brünli with the least altitude drop. (The safer, well-signposted approach to Brünli is to drop down to Rotstockhütte, then climb back up to Brünli.) The barbed-wire fence leads to the knobby little summit, where you'll enjoy an incredible 360-degree view and a chance to sign your name on the register stored in the little wooden box.

A steep trail winds directly down from Brünli toward Gimmelwald and soon hits a bigger, easy trail. The trail bends right (just before the farm/restaurant at Spielbodenalp), leading to Sprutz. Walk under the Sprutz Waterfall, then follow a steep, wooded trail that deposits you in a meadow of flowers at the top side of Gimmelwald.

Hikes from Gimmelwald
▲Up Sefinen Valley to Kilchbalm (very easy)—An easy trail from Gimmelwald is up the Sefinen Valley (Sefinental). This is a good rainy-weather hike, as you can go as far as you like. After two hours and a gain of only 800 feet, you hit the end of the trail and Kilchbalm, a dramatic bowl of glacier fields. Note that snow can make this trail unsafe, even into the summer (ask locally for information), and there's no food or drink along the way.

From the Gimmelwald fire station, walk about 100 yards down the paved Stechelberg road. Leave it on the dirt Sefinental road, which becomes a lane, then a trail. You'll cross a raging river and pass a firing range where locals practice their marksmanship (Fri and Sat evenings; the *danger of fire* sign refers to live bullets). Follow signs to Kilchbalm into a forest, along a river, and finally to the glacier fields.

▲Gimmelwald–Tanzbodeli–Obersteinberg–Stechelberg/ Gimmelwald (more difficult, for good hikers)—This eight-hour, 11-mile hike is extremely rewarding, offering perfect peace, very few people, traditional alpine culture, and spectacular views. (There's no food or drink for five hours, so pack accordingly.) As the trail can be a bit confusing, this is best done with a good map (buy locally).

About 100 yards below the Gimmelwald firehouse, take the Sefinental dirt road (described earlier). As the dirt road switches back after about 30 minutes, take the right turn across the river and start your ascent, following signs to *Obersteinberg*. After 90 minutes of hard climbing, you have the option of a side-trip to Busenalp. This is fun if the goat and cow herder is there, as you can watch the traditional cheesemaking in action. (He appreciates a bottle of wine from hikers.) Trail markers are painted onto rocks—watch carefully. After visiting Busenalp, return to the main path.

At the *Obersteinberg 50 min/Tanzbodeli 20 min* signpost, head for Tanzbodeli ("Dancing Floor"). This is everyone's favorite alpine perch—great for a little romance, or a picnic with breathtaking views of the Obersteinberg valley. From here, you enter a natural reserve, so you're likely to see chamois and other alpine critters. From Tanzbodeli, you return to the main trail (there's no other way out) and continue

to Obersteinberg. You'll eventually hit the Mountain Hotel Obersteinberg (see "Sleeping," page 169; American expat Vickie will serve you a meal or drink).

From there, the trail leads to Hotel Tschingelhorn and back to Gimmelwald (2 hours total) or Stechelberg (bottom of Schilthorn cable car, 90 min total). About an hour later, you hit a fork in the trail and choose where you'd like your hike to end.

▲Sprutz Waterfall (moderately difficult)—The forest above Gimmelwald hides a powerful waterfall with a trail snaking behind it, offering a fun gorge experience. While the waterfall itself is not well-signed, it's on the Gimmelwald–Spielbodenalp trail. It's steep, through a forest, and can be very slippery when wet, but the actual crossing under the waterfall is just misty.

The hike up to Sprutz from Gimmelwald isn't worth the

trip in itself, but it's handy when combined with the hike down from Birg and Brünli (see above) or the North Face Trail (see next entry). As you descend on either of these two hikes, the trail down to Gimmelwald splits at Spielbodenalp—to the right for the forest and the waterfall; to the left for more meadows, the hamlet of Gimmeln, and more gracefully back into Gimmelwald.

Hikes from Mürren/Allmendhubel

▲▲North Face Trail from Allmendhubel (easy and family-friendly)—For a pleasant, mainly downhill, two-hour hike (4 miles, from 6,385 feet to 5,375 feet), ride the Allmendhubel funic-

ular up from Mürren (7.40 SF, much cheaper than Schilthorn, good restaurant at top). From there, follow the well-signed route, which loops counterclockwise around to Mürren (or cut off at Spielbodenalp, near the end, and descend into Gimmelwald via the Sprutz Waterfall). As this trail doesn't technically start at Allmendhubel, start by following signs to *Sonnenberg*. Then just follow the blue signs. You'll enjoy great views, flowery meadows, mountain huts, and a dozen information boards along the way, describing the fascinating climbing history of the great peaks around you.

Along the trail, you'll pass four farms (technically "alps," as they are only open in the summer) that serve meals and drinks. Sonnenberg was allowed to break the all-wood building code with concrete for protection against avalanches. Suppenalp is quainter. Lean against the house with a salad, soup, or sandwich and enjoy the view. Just below Suppenalp is a new little adventure park with zip lines and other kid-pleasing activities.

Notice how older huts are built into the protected side of rocks and outcroppings, in anticipation of avalanches. Above Suppenalp, Blumental ("Flower Valley") is hopping with marmots. Because hunters are not allowed near lifts, animals have learned that these are safe places to hang out—giving tourists a better chance of spotting them.

The trail leads up and over to a group of huts called Schiltalp (good food, drink, and service, and a romantic farm setting). If the poles under the eaves have bells, the cows are up here. If not, the cows are still at the lower farms. Half the cows in Gimmelwald (about 100) spend their summers here. In July, August, and September, you can watch cheese being made and have a snack or drink. Thirty years ago, each family had its own hut. Labor was cheap and available. Today, it's a communal thing, with several families sharing the expense of a single cow herder. Cow herders

Hiking in the Berner Oberland

This region is a wonderful place to hike, and I've listed my favorite excursions. The super-scenic walk from Männlichen to Kleine Scheidegg is the best of all worlds: It's both dramatic and relatively easy. The hike from Schynige Platte to First is spectacular, but much more challenging, as is the hike from the Birg cable-car station down to Gimmelwald—don't try either of these in bad weather. In case of rain, the lower hikes (North Face Trail from Allmendhubel; the walk from Mürren or Allmendhubel to Grütschalp; the Sefinen Valley hike from Gimmelwald; and the stroll along the Lauterbrunnen Valley) are better bets.

To do any serious hiking, you should invest in a real hiking map. Hikers can get specifics at the Mürren TI or from hoteliers. For a description of six diverse hikes on the west side of Lauterbrunnen, pick up the fine and free *Mürren–Schilthorn Hikes* brochure. This 3-D overview map of the Mürren mountainside makes a useful and attractive souvenir. For the other side of the valley, get the *Wandern Jungfraubahnen* brochure, which also has a handy 3-D overview map of hiking trails (both brochures free at stations, hotels, and TIs).

Once under way, don't mind the fences (although be aware that wires can be solar-powered electric); a hiker has the right of way in Switzerland. Don't forget a water bottle and some munchies. Trails are well-marked, with yellow signs listing destinations and the estimated time it'll take you to walk there. Refer to maps (within this chapter) as you read about the hikes.

Weather Concerns: Locals always seem to know the weather report (as much of their income depends on it). Clouds

are master cheesemakers and have veterinary skills, too.

From Schiltalp, the trail winds gracefully down toward Spielbodenalp. From there, you can finish the North Face Trail (continuing down and left through meadows and the hamlet of Gimmeln, then back to Mürren, with more historic signposts); or cut off right (descending steeply through a thick forest and under the dramatic Sprutz Waterfall into Gimmelwald—see Sprutz Waterfall, above, for details).

▲**Allmendhubel/Mürren to Grütschalp (fairly easy)**—For a not-too-tough, two-hour walk with great Jungfrau views, ride the funicular from Mürren to Allmendhubel (6,344 feet) and walk to Grütschalp (a drop of about 1,500 feet), where you can catch can roll in anytime, but skies are usually clearest in the morning. All over the region, TV sets are tuned to the local weather station, with real-time views from all the famous peaks. The same station airs a travelogue on the region each evening at about 21:30. You can also check the weather at www.swisspanorama.com.

Snow: In the Berner Oberland, snow can curtail your hiking plans, even in July (the Männlichen lift doesn't even open until the first week in June). Before setting out on any hike, get advice from a knowledgeable local. Well into the spring, and sometimes also in early fall, the high trails (Männlichen to Kleine Scheidegg, Schynige Platte to First, and anything from Schilthorn or Birg) are likely to be impassable.

Wildlife: As hunting is not allowed in the vicinity of any lifts, animals find comfort in places you're likely to be. Keep an eye out for chamois (called *Gemsen* here)—the sure-footed "goat antelopes" that live at the top of the treeline and go a little lower when hungry. Spotting an ibex—a wild goat with horns, scrambling along the rocky terrain—is another Berner Oberland thrill. You'll also encounter marmot, big alpine mice (like 2-pound squirrels), who get really fat each summer, planning to sleep underground for six months through the winter. These burrowing rodents are fun to watch, and if you sit still, they don't see you. You'll hear them whistle. Your best viewing place is above Allmendhubel, in the meadow above the highest hut in Blumental.

Nordic Walking: You may wonder about the Germans you'll see with their walking sticks (*Alpenstock*). This is trying to be the next craze: Nordic walking. Enthusiasts claim Nordic walking is an all-body workout, activating 90 percent of your muscles and burning a third more calories than "normal" walking, while cutting way back on the strain on your back and knees when going downhill. To do it right requires proper instruction. Sticks can be rented at some outdoor shops.

Berner Oberland

the panorama train back to Mürren. An easier version is the lower Bergweg from Allmendhubel to Grütschalp via Winteregg and its cheese farm. For a super-easy family stroll with grand views, walk from Mürren just above the train tracks either to Winteregg (40 min, restaurant, playground, train station) or through even better scenery on to Grütschalp (60 min, train station), then catch the panorama train back to Mürren.

Hikes on the Jungfrau (East) Side of the Lauterbrunnen Valley

▲▲▲**Männlichen–Kleine Scheidegg (easy and with dramatic views)**—This is my favorite easy alpine hike (2.5 miles, 1.5 hours,

900-foot altitude drop to Kleine Scheidegg). It's entertaining all the way, with glorious Jungfrau, Eiger, and Mönch views. (Remember, that's the Young Maiden being protected from the Ogre by the Monk.) Trails may be snowbound into June; ask about conditions at the lift stations or local TIs (see Jungfraujoch under "Lifts and Trains," page 154).

If the weather's good, descend from Gimmelwald bright and early to Stechelberg. From here, get to the Lauterbrunnen train station by postal bus (3.80 SF, covered by Swiss Pass, bus is synchronized to depart with the arrival of each lift) or by car (parking at the large, multistory pay lot behind the Lauterbrunnen station-2 SF/2 hrs, 10 SF/day). If hiking down from Männlichen to Wengen via Kleine Scheidegg (the complete hike described in this listing), you'll buy a ticket from Lauterbrunnen to Männlichen, then from Wengen back to Lauterbrunnen, for 32 SF. (For the shorter, basic hike, pay a bit more to return from Kleine Scheidegg.) Sit on the right side of the train for great valley and waterfall views on your way up to Wengen. In Wengen, walk across town (buy a picnic, but don't waste time here if it's sunny—you can linger after your hike) and catch the Männlichen lift to the top of the ridge high above you (lift departs every 15 min, beginning the first week of June). Note that the lift can be open even if the trail is closed; if the weather is questionable, confirm that the Männlichen-Kleine Scheidegg trail is open before ascending.

Riding the gondola from Wengen to Männlichen, you'll go over the old lift station (inundated by a 1978 avalanche that buried a good part of Wengen—notice there's no development in the "red zone" above the tennis courts). Farms are built with earthen ramps on the uphill side in anticipation of the next slide. The forest of avalanche fences near the top was built after that 1978 avalanche. As you ascend you can also survey Wengen—the bright red roofs mark new vacation condos, mostly English-owned and used only a few weeks a year.

From the top of the Wengen–Männlichen lift station, turn left and hike uphill 20 minutes to the little peak (Männlichen Gipfel, 7,500 feet) for an easy king- or queen-of-the-mountain feeling. Then enjoy an hour's walk—facing spectacular alpine panorama views—to Kleine Scheidegg for a picnic or restaurant lunch. To start the hike, leave the Wengen–Männlichen lift station to the right. Walk past the second Männlichen lift station (this one leads to Grindelwald, the touristy town in the valley to your left). Ahead of you in the distance, left to right, are the north faces of the Eiger, Mönch, and Jungfrau; in the foreground is the Tschuggen peak, and just behind it, the Lauberhorn. This hike takes you around the left (east) side of this ridge. Simply follow the signs for Kleine Scheidegg, and you'll be there in about an hour—a little more for gawkers, picnickers, and photographers. You might have to tiptoe through streams of melted snow—or some small snow banks, even well into the summer—but the path is well-marked, well-maintained, and mostly level all the way to Kleine Scheidegg.

About 35 minutes into the hike, you'll reach a bunch of benches and a shelter with incredible unobstructed views of all three peaks—the perfect picnic spot. Fifteen minutes later on the left, you'll see the first sign of civilization: Restaurant Grindelwaldblick (the best lunch stop up here, open daily, closed Dec and May, described on page 168). Hike to the restaurant's fun mountain lookout to survey the Eiger and look down on the Kleine Scheidegg action. After 10 more minutes, you'll be at the Kleine Scheidegg train station, with plenty of lesser lunch options (including Restaurant Bahnhof, described on page 168).

From Kleine Scheidegg, you can catch the train to "the top of Europe" (see Jungfraujoch information, page 154). Or head

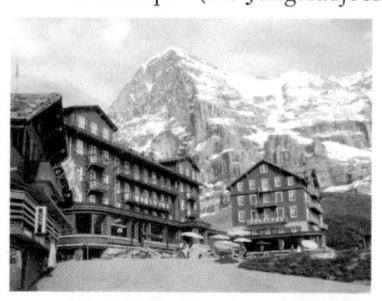

downhill, riding the train or hiking (30 gorgeous minutes to Wengernalp station, a little farther to the Allmend stop; 60 more steep minutes from there into the town of Wengen). The alpine views might be accompanied by the valley-filling mellow sound of alphorns and distant avalanches. If the weather turns bad or you run out of steam, catch the train at any of the stations along the way. After Wengernalp, the trail to Wengen is steep and, though not dangerous, requires a good set of knees. Wengen is a good shopping town. (For Wengen accommodations, see page 166.) The boring final descent from Wengen to Lauterbrunnen is knee-killer steep—catch the train.

▲▲**Schynige Platte to First (more difficult)**—The best day I've had hiking in the Berner Oberland was when I made this demanding six-hour ridge walk, with Lake Brienz on one side and all that Jungfrau beauty on the other. Start at Wilderswil train station (just above Interlaken) and catch the little train up to Schynige Platte (6,560 feet). The high point is Faulhorn (8,790 feet, with its famous mountaintop hotel). Hike to a small mini-gondola called "First" (7,110 feet), then ride down to Grindelwald and catch a train back to your starting point, Wilderswil. Or, if you

Berner Oberland

have a regional train pass (or no car but endless money), take the long, scenic return trip to Gimmelwald: From Grindelwald, take the lift up to Männlichen, do the hike to Kleine Scheidegg and Wengen (see above), then head down into Lauterbrunnen and on to Gimmelwald.

For a shorter (3-hour) ridge walk, consider the well-signposted Panoramaweg, a loop from Schynige Platte to Daub Peak.

The alpine flower park (4 SF, at the Schynige Platte station) offers a delightful stroll through several hundred alpine flowers (best in summer), including a chance to see edelweiss growing in the wild.

Lowa, a leading local manufacturer of top-end hiking boots, has a promotional booth at the Schynige Platte station that provides free loaner boots to hikers who'd like to give their boots a try. They're already broken in, but bring thick socks (or buy them there).

If hiking here, be mindful of the last lifts (which can be as early as 16:30). Climbing from First (7,113 feet) to Schynige Platte (6,454 feet) gives you a later departure down and less climbing. The TI produces a great Schynige Platte map/guide narrating the train ride up and describing various hiking options from there (available at Wilderswil station).

Mountain Biking

Mountain biking is popular and accepted, as long as you stay on the clearly marked mountain-bike paths. You can rent bikes in Mürren (Stäger Sport, see page 142) or in Lauterbrunnen (Imboden Bike, see page 150). The Lauterbrunnen shop is bigger, has a wider selection of bikes, and is likely to be open when the Mürren one isn't. On trains and cable cars, bikes require a separate ticket (costs the same as a person).

The most popular bike rides include the following:

Lauterbrunnen to Interlaken: This is a gentle downhill ride via a peaceful bike path across the river from the road (don't bike on the road itself). You can return to Lauterbrunnen by train (13 SF total for bike and you). Or rent a bike at either Interlaken station, take the train to Lauterbrunnen, and ride back.

Lauterbrunnen Valley (Between Stechelberg and Lauterbrunnen Town): This delightful, easy bike path features plenty of diversions along the way (several listed under "Rainy-Day Options," next page).

Mürren to Winteregg to Grütschalp and Back: This fairly

level route takes you through high country, with awesome mountain views.

Mürren to Winteregg to Lauterbrunnen: This scenic, paved descent takes you to the Lauterbrunnen Valley floor.

Mürren–Gimmelwald–Sefinen Valley–Stechelberg–Lauterbrunnen–Grütschalp–Mürren: This is the best ride, but it's demanding—with one very difficult stretch where you'll likely walk your bike down a steep gulley for 500 yards. You'll take the cable car from Lauterbrunnen up to Grütschalp.

Rainy-Day Options

When it rains here, locals joke that they're washing the mountains. If clouds roll in, don't despair. They can roll out just as quickly. With good rain gear and the right choice of trail, a hike in the rain can be thoroughly enjoyable, with surprise views popping out all around you as the clouds break. And there are plenty of good bad-weather options.

▲▲**Cloudy-Day Lauterbrunnen Valley Walk**—Try the easy trails and pleasant walks along the floor of the Lauterbrunnen Valley. For a smell-the-cows-and-flowers lowland walk—ideal for a cloudy day, weary body, or tight budget—follow the riverside trail from Stechelberg's Schilthornbahn station (left of river) for three basically level miles to Lauterbrunnen's Staubbach Falls, near the town church (you can reverse the route, but it's a very gradual uphill to Stechelberg). A trail was recently cut into the cliff to take visitors up "behind" Staubbach Falls (at the uphill end of Lauterbrunnen town). But the trail stops short of the actual falls, and you'll feel betrayed after making the short climb—I'd skip it.

There's a fine, paved, car-free, riverside path all the way along the valley (popular with bikers). Detour to Trümmelbach Falls (described next) en route. In this "Valley of Many Waterfalls" (literally), you'll see cone-like mounds piled against the sides of the cliffs, formed by centuries of rocks hurled by tumbling rivers.

If you're staying in Gimmelwald, try this plan: Take the lift down to Stechelberg (5 min), then walk to Lauterbrunnen, detouring to Trümmelbach Falls shortly after Stechelberg (15 min to falls, another 45 min to Lauterbrunnen). To return to Gimmelwald from Lauterbrunnen, take the cable car up to Grütschalp (10 min), then either walk to Gimmelwald (90 min) or take the panorama train to Mürren (15 min). From Mürren, it's a downhill walk (30 min) to Gimmelwald. (This loop trip can be reversed.)

▲**Trümmelbach Falls**—If all the waterfalls have you intrigued, sneak a behind-the-scenes look at the valley's most powerful, Trümmelbach Falls (11 SF, daily July–Aug 8:30–18:00, April–June and Sept–Nov 9:00–17:00, closed Dec–March, on Lauterbrunnen–Stechelberg road, take postal bus from Lauterbrunnen TI or Stechelberg cable-car station, tel. 033-855-3232, www.truemmelbach.ch). You'll ride an elevator up through the mountain and climb through several caves (wet, with lots of stairs, and—for some—claustrophobic) to see the melt from the Eiger, Mönch, and Jungfrau grinding like God's band saw through the mountain at the rate of up to 5,200 gallons a second (that's 20,000 liters—nearly double the beer consumption at Oktoberfest). The upper area is the best; if your legs ache, skip the lower falls and ride down on the elevator.

Lauterbrunnen Folk Museum (Heimat-museum)—This humble collection shows off the local folk culture and two centuries of mountaineering. You'll see lots of lace, exhibits on cheese and woodworking, and classic old photos (free with "visitor's card" if you're staying in the region, 3 SF otherwise, mid-June–mid-Oct Tue, Thu, and Sat–Sun 14:00–17:30, closed off-season, just over bridge and below church at the far end of Lauterbrunnen town, tel. 033-855-3586 or 033-855-1388).

SLEEPING AND EATING

In addition to my listings in Interlaken, Gimmelwald, Mürren, and Lauterbrunnen, consider these nearby places.

Sleeping in Wengen
(4,180 feet, 1.10 SF = about $1, country code: 41)

Wengen—a bigger, fancier Mürren on the other side of the valley—has plenty of grand hotels, many shops, tennis courts, mini-golf, and terrific views. This traffic-free resort is an easy train ride above Lauterbrunnen and halfway up to Kleine Scheidegg and Männlichen, and offers more activities for those needing distraction from the scenery. Hiking is better from Mürren and Gimmelwald.

If you're here in the winter to ski the Keine Scheidegg-Männlichen slopes, Wengen makes the best home base. Rent your gear from Molitor Sport + Mode, still run by the family of founder and famous ski racer Karl Molitor (who's now nearly 90). Even if you're not renting a thing, stop in to see the cool old photos, gear, and Karl's medals on display, which add up to a mini-ski-racing museum (on Wengen's main drag, on the left past Männlichen cable-car station, tel. 033-855-2131). Other rental shops include **Alpia Sport** (right above train station, tel. 033-855-2626) and **Central-Sport** (on the main drag, past post office, tel. 033-855-2323).

The **TI** is one block from the station: Go up to the main drag,

Berner Oberland

turn left, and look ahead on the left (daily in summer 9:00–18:00, closed Sat–Sun mid-Oct–mid-Dec, coin-op Internet access in lobby, tel. 033-855-1414, www.wengen-muerren.ch).

Sleeping Above the Train Station

$$$ **Hotel Berghaus,** in a quiet area a five-minute walk from the main street, offers 19 rooms above a fine restaurant specializing in fish (Sb-87–120 SF, Db-174–240 SF, 5 percent discount with this book and cash, elevator, Internet access; call on phone at station hotel board for free pickup, or walk up street across from Hotel Bernerhof, bear right and then left at fork, 200 yards more past church on the left; tel. 033-855-2151, fax 033-855-3820, www.wengen .com/hotel/berghaus, berghaus@wengen.com, Fontana family).

$$$ **Hotel Schönegg,** on Wengen's main drag, is a centrally located splurge, decorated with antiques and old wood (Sb-100–110 SF, Db-200–220 SF; higher July–Aug: Sb-115–125 SF, Db-230–250 SF; all rooms have balconies and great views, cozy family room with fireplace, Internet access in lobby, good restaurant with big terrace, look for big yellow hotel on main drag near TI, tel. 033-855-3422, fax 033-855-4233, www.hotel-schoenegg.ch, mail @hotel-schoenegg.ch, Herr Berthod und Frau Steiner).

Sleeping Below the Train Station

The first two listings are bright, cheery, family-friendly, and five minutes below the station: Leave the station toward the Co-op store, turn right and go under the rail bridge, bear right (paved path) at the fork, and follow the road down and around.

$$$ **Familienhotel Edelweiss** has 25 bright rooms, lots of fun public spaces, a Christian emphasis, and a jittery Chihuahua named Speedy (Sb-70–75 SF, Db-150 SF, elevator, great family rooms, TV lounge, game room, meeting room, kids' playroom, tel. 033-855-2388, fax 033-855-4288, www.edelweisswengen.ch, edelweiss@vch.ch, Bärtschi family).

$$ **Bären Hotel,** run by friendly Therese and Willy Brunner, offers 14 tidy rooms with perky, bright-orange bathrooms. Their newly redone restaurant is bright and inviting, offering garden-fresh Swiss cuisine (daily specials for 15.50 SF; Sb-70–90 SF, Db-120–130 SF, Tb-180–225 SF, pricier in winter, dinner-20 SF more, family rooms, free Internet access and Wi-Fi, tel. 033-855-1419, fax 033-855-1525, www.baeren-wengen.ch, info@baeren -wengen.ch).

$$ **Clare and Andy's Chalet (Trogihalten)** offers three rustic, low-ceilinged rooms (1-room studio: Sb-56 SF, Db-90 SF; 2-room suite: Sb/Db-106 SF, Tb-149 SF, Qb-188 SF; 4-room flat: Tb-159 SF, Qb-192 SF, 5 people-240 SF, 6 people-294 SF; breakfast-15 SF, dinner by request-35 SF, 4-night minimum preferred, prices

Berner Oberland

higher for shorter stays, cash only, all rooms with balconies; leave station and follow the street to the left until Hotel Bernerhof, then take steep downhill path for 5 min, then gravel path for 2 min; tel. & fax 033-855-1712, mobile 079-423-7813, www.chaletwengen.ch, info@chaletwengen.ch, Clare is English, Andy is Swiss).

$ Wengen Old Lodge is centrally located and offers cheap beds (30 SF per bed with sheets in a 6-bed dorm; D-90 SF, Q-140, 10 percent off with this book, 20–25 SF more per person in winter, kitchens available; walk from station toward the Co-op store, before rail bridge turn left; tel. 033-855-1573, mobile 078-745-5850, www.oldlodge.ch, info@oldlodge.ch, Angela).

Sleeping and Eating at or near Kleine Scheidegg
(6,762 feet)

Confirm price and availability before ascending. All of these places serve meals.

$$$ Hotel Bellevue des Alpes, lovingly maintaining a 1930s elegance, is a worthwhile splurge. Since the 1840s, five generations of von Allmens (subsidized by the family income from Trümmelbach Falls) have maintained this classic old alpine hotel. The hallway is like a museum, with old photos (Sb-190–220 SF, Db-310–480 SF, includes breakfast and sumptuous 5-course dinner, open only mid-June–mid-Sept, tel. 033-855-1212, fax 033-855-1294, www.scheidegg-hotels.ch, welcome@scheidegg-hotels.ch).

$$ Restaurant Bahnhof invites you to sleep face-to-face with the Eiger (dorm bed-51 SF with breakfast, 69 SF also includes dinner, D-168 SF with breakfast and dinner, in the train station building, tel. 033-828-7828, www.bahnhof-scheidegg.ch, info @bahnhof-scheidegg.ch).

$ Restaurant Grindelwaldblick, a 10-minute hike from the train station, is more charming, romantic, and remote than Restaurant Bahnhof (38 SF per bed in 8- to 20-bed rooms, includes sheets and breakfast, closed Nov and May, tel. 033-855-1374, fax 033-855-4205, www.grindelwaldblick.ch). The restaurant, with a great sun terrace and a cozy interior, sells good three-course lunches for 17 SF.

Sleeping in Stechelberg
(3,025 feet)

Stechelberg is the hamlet at the end of Lauterbrunnen Valley, at the base of the lift to Gimmelwald, Mürren, and the Schilthorn.

$$ Hotel Stechelberg, at road's end, is surrounded by waterfalls and vertical rock, with a garden terrace, good restaurant, and 20 quiet rooms—half in a creaky old building, half in a concrete, no-character new building (D-86–110 SF, Db-130, Db with balcony-168 SF, T-147 SF, Tb-186 SF, Q-180 SF, Qb-234 SF, postal bus stops here 2/hr, Wi-Fi, tel. 033-855-2921, fax 033-855-4438, www.hotel-stechelberg.ch, hotel@stechelberg.ch, Marianne and Otto).

$ The **Alpenhof,** at the top of the valley, fills a former "Nature Friends' Hut" with cheap beds. Creaking like a wooden chalet built in 1926 should, it provides a fine, inexpensive base for drivers (25 SF per bed in 2- to 6-bed rooms, breakfast-10 SF, tel. 033-855-1202, www.alpenhof-stechelberg.ch, alpenhof@stechelberg .ch, Diane and Marc).

Sleeping in Obersteinberg
(5,900 feet)
$$ Here's a wild idea: **Mountain Hotel Obersteinberg** is a working alpine farm with cheese, cows, a mule shuttling up food once a day, and an American (Vickie) who fell in love with a mountain man. It's a 2.5-hour hike from either Stechelberg or Gimmelwald. They rent 12 primitive rooms and a bunch of loft beds. There's no shower, no hot water, and only meager solar-panel electricity. Candles light up the night, and you can take a hot-water bottle to bed if necessary (S-83 SF, D-166 SF, includes linen, sheetless dorm beds-66 SF; these prices include breakfast and dinner, without meals S-37 SF, D-74 SF, dorm beds-20 SF; closed Oct–May, tel. 033-855-2033). The place is filled with locals and Germans on weekends, but it's all yours on weekdays. Why not hike there from Gimmelwald and leave the Alps a day later?

Sleeping in Isenfluh
(3,560 feet)
The yellow postal bus takes you up on a spectacular road, through a long and narrow tunnel to the tiny hamlet of Isenfluh, which is even smaller than Gimmelwald and offers better views (bus departs from Lauterbrunnen train station almost hourly at :50, 3.80 SF one-way).

$$$ **Hotel Restaurant Waldrand** has a decent restaurant (including great fresh salads) and four reasonable rooms (Db-150 SF, Tb-190 SF, cash only, includes breakfast, tel. 033-855-1227, fax 033-855-1392, www.hotel-waldrand.ch, info@hotel-waldrand.ch, Vreni and Urs Werthmüller).

ZERMATT
and the MATTERHORN

There's just something about that Matterhorn, the most recognizable mountain on the planet. Anyone who says, "You've seen one mountain, you've seen them all," hasn't laid eyes on this pointy, craggy peak. The Matterhorn seems to have a nearly mystical draw for people—it's the Stonehenge of Switzerland.

Oh, and there's a town, too. Zermatt, a little burg of 5,500 people, might well be the most touristy resort in Switzerland. While there are pockets of traditional charm, virtually everyone you meet in Zermatt earns a living one way or another from those who flock here for a peek at the peak. Aside from the stone quarries you'll pass on the way into town, tourism is Zermatt's only industry.

Be warned that Zermatt is a one-mountain town. If you have time for only one mountainous region on your trip, I'd suggest the more interesting Berner Oberland over Zermatt (for specifics, see sidebar, opposite page). Many visitors find Zermatt touristy and overrated, especially considering its inconvenient location (at the end of a long, dead-end valley in the southwest corner of the country). And if you make the long trek and find only cloudy weather, there's little else to do...other than wish for a T-shirt that reads, "I went all the way to Zermatt and didn't even see the lousy Matterhorn."

Planning Your Time

On a two-week trip in Switzerland, I'd suggest two nights and the better part of two days in Zermatt if the weather's good. (To check the weather, call the Zermatt TI at tel. 027-966-8100, www.zermatt.ch.) For efficient sightseeing, arrive or leave on the Glacier

Zermatt vs. the Berner Oberland

I've said for years that the Berner Oberland offers far more high-mountain travel thrills than the Zermatt area (see Gimmelwald and the Berner Oberland chapter). And I still stand by that—if you're going to only one alpine hideaway in Switzerland, the Berner Oberland is tops. But if you're trying to make up your mind, here are a few comparisons.

The Berner Oberland is relatively easy to reach, thanks to its more central location in the country and its good rail connections to Bern and Luzern. Zermatt is farther off the beaten track, at the end of a dead-end valley near the Italian border—and the final approach by train (from Brig) is run by a private company, not covered by your Eurailpass (though it is covered by the Swiss Pass).

Zermatt is essentially one town focused on a single mountain. The Berner Oberland is an entire alpine region, with many towns and villages to visit—from the bustling administrative center of Interlaken to the tiny, traditional village of Gimmelwald. In Zermatt, most accommodations options are in the town itself. But in the Berner Oberland, you have your choice of places to sleep—in a resort town or humble hamlet; in the valley or on a ledge overlooking the mountains.

As for sightseeing, the best part of the Berner Oberland is the Lauterbrunnen Valley, with great high-altitude attractions on both sides (the Jungfraujoch on one side, the Schilthorn on the other), plus other enjoyable lifts, towns, and hikes. Zermatt doesn't have nearly the same diversity. Budget travelers appreciate the Berner Oberland's cheaper accommodations and the discount given on mountain lifts to Eurailpass-holders (unlike in Zermatt).

Both areas are touristy, but there are more traditional tidbits of the authentic Swiss countryside in the Berner Oberland than in Zermatt. The Berner Oberland also offers a wider variety of activities than Zermatt. On a rainy day, you can poke around one of the traditional villages (like Gimmelwald) or the bigger town of Interlaken, or walk through the thundering Trümmelbach Falls.

You can tell where my heart lies. Still, if you've seen the Berner Oberland already, or if you want to sample two different mountain areas of Switzerland, Zermatt is worth a visit. And the Matterhorn is really something else—it's the reason this place is known around the world.

Zermatt

Express; it's an all-day, cross-country scenic train ride to Chur, which has good connections to Zürich and elsewhere in northeast Switzerland (see Scenic Rail Journeys chapter).

ORIENTATION

Zermatt (elevation 5,265 feet) lies at the end of the valley called Nikolaital, along the Mattervispa River in the shadow of the mighty Matterhorn (14,690 feet, "Cervino" in Italian).

The train station is at the bottom of town, a few steps from the main drag, Bahnhofstrasse. As you stand in front of the station with the tracks at your back, the heart of the village is to your right. Lifts to thrilling Matterhorn viewpoints leave from near the train station: The train up to Gornergrat is across the street and to your left, the station for the underground train/gondola/cable car to Rothorn is a few blocks ahead and to the left along the river, and the gondola/cable car station up to Klein Matterhorn is through the village to your right across the river (about three-quarters of a mile away). Details on all of these are listed below.

Zermatt brags that its streets are traffic-free. Well, not quite. Electric cars (big golf carts) buzz around the streets like four-wheeled Vespas, some with surprisingly aggressive drivers. Watch your step.

Addresses are generally not used in this small town. To find your hotel, use the map in this chapter, follow the free map from the TI, look for signs, or ask a local.

Tourist Information

Zermatt's TI is right at the train station (mid-June–Oct daily 8:30–18:00 except closed for lunch Sun 12:00–13:30; Nov–mid-June Mon–Sat 8:30–12:00 & 13:30–18:00, Sun 9:30–12:00 & 16:00–18:00; tel. 027-966-8100, www.zermatt.ch). They offer a variety of handy, free resources: an extremely detailed map that labels every building in town; a magazine with hotels and lift schedules and prices; an events brochure; and a thick, directory-type information booklet. You can also buy hiking maps here, including a detailed map for serious hikers (25.90 SF) and the good *Discovering Zermatt on Foot* hiking guide (29.50 SF).

Arrival in Zermatt

Zermatt's small train station is conveniently located in the middle of town; the TI is immediately to the right as you leave the tracks, and you'll also stumble on to a stand of Elektro-taxis right out front (see below).

Cars are not allowed in Zermatt. Drivers park in the huge lot at Täsch, a few miles before Zermatt (13.50 SF/day), then take the

ZERMATT

To Täsch & Brig

Note: Many roads in Zermatt are unmarked

TRAIN STATION

5 Hotel Bahnhof

BUSES TO LIFTS

GORNERGRAT STATION

GETWINGSTRASSE

SUNNEGGA STATION

To Rothorn

BAHNHOFSTRASSE

HOFMATTSTRASSE

12

ENGLISH CHURCH

POST

ALPINE CENTER

HINTERDORF-STRASSE

1

TRIFTWEG

8

3

MATTERHORN MUSEUM

Cemetery

CATHOLIC CHURCH

KIRCHSTRASSE

9

4 NEBEN BACH

10

OBERDORFSTRASSE

SCHLUHMATTSTRASSE

Mattervispa River

2

To Zmutt

6

To Gornergrat

7

To Klein Matterhorn Lift (Bergbahn)

B

100 meters

100 yards

Zermatt

1	Hotel Romantica	**7**	Matterhorn Hostel
2	Hotel Jägerhof	**8**	Whymper-Stube Restaurant
3	Hotel Tannenhof	**9**	Restaurant du Pont
4	Hotel Weisshorn	**10**	Pizza Roma
5	Hotel Bahnhof	**11**	Co-op Grocery
6	Youth Hostel	**12**	Migros Grocery

shuttle train into town (7.80 SF one-way, runs every 20 min until 23:00).

Getting Around Zermatt

Even though Zermatt is "traffic-free," your feet aren't your only transportation option. Two different electric **bus** lines depart across from the train station: One line goes to the Bergbahn, the lift station for Klein Matterhorn (2.50 SF, or free with lift ticket, about every 10 min), and the other goes to the hamlet perched above that station, called Winkelmatten (3.20 SF, about every 20 min). The buses are marked with their destination and make a few stops along the way before heading back to the station (when they're marked *Bahnhof*).

You can also hire your own **Elektro-taxi** (about 12 SF to anywhere in the heart of town, extra charge for luggage and rides at night, taxi stand in front of train station), or call **Taxi Zermatt** (mobile 084-811-1212).

Helpful Hints

Walking Tour: Once a week, there's a free one-hour village walking tour in English. This is a good rainy-day option (ask for the schedule at the TI).

Internet Access: You'll see coin-op Internet stations all over town. The going rate is 12 SF per hour.

Laundry: Waschsalon Doli is nice and central (20 SF to wash and dry a small load, Mon–Sat 8:30–12:00 & 14:00–19:00, closed Sun). From the station, take the first left past McDonald's and look for the sign across from the tennis courts.

Skiing: Zermatt's high elevation and variety of runs—and the chance to actually ski or snowboard from Switzerland to Italy—make it deservedly popular. Summer skiing is an option at Matterhorrn Glacier Paradise (late April–late Nov, limited area in mid-summer). A one-day lift ticket will run you about 65 SF; equipment rents for about 45 SF, and snow-wear rental adds another 30–35 SF. Ask at the TI for details.

In the winter, beginners and intermediate skiers head for Gornergrat and the Matterhorn Glacier areas; more advanced skiers prefer Schwarzsee, Rothorn, and especially Stockhorn, with its mogul-filled "freeride" runs (generally open mid-Jan–Easter). The Sunnegga area has a mix of easy and challenging runs.

Rental shops in town include Matterhorn Sport (several in town, one near Sunnegga lift, another on Bahnhofstrasse, tel. 027-967-2956), Bayard Sport + Fashion (also has several branches, including one on Bahnhofstrasse, tel. 027-966-4960), and **Dorsaz-Sport** (near Matterhorn Glacier lift, tel.

027-966-3810). See www.matterhornparadise.ch for lift-ticket prices, and page 300 of the appendix for more tips.

SIGHTS AND ACTIVITIES

In Zermatt

The town itself is short on attractions. On rainy days, the TI can only shrug, poignantly promote the Matterhorn Museum, or suggest that you go swimming in one of the big hotel pools.

Wander the Town—Zermatt is charming enough, despite its single-mindedness about catching the tourist dollar. The streets are lined with chalet after chalet. Just off the main drag, you'll spot small stands of traditional shacks set on stone stilts to keep out mice (called *mazots;* look for them around Hotel Romantica, or near the river in the Hinterdorf area). You'll also spot a handful of churches, including the big landmark Catholic church (can't miss it on Bahnhofstrasse) or the smaller English church (built for the many British mountaineers who have flocked to this region; above and behind the Matterhorn Museum).

▲▲**Matterhorn Museum**—While it's the outdoors that brings you to Zermatt, this museum is the town's best indoor activity, and it's worth a visit on a rainy day. Most of the newly spruced-up museum is underground, as it's meant to look like an archeological dig, where you can unearth the history of Zermatt and its famous mountain. Pick up the free English flier, and walk downstairs, through the reproductions of an old hotel, church, barn, and other buildings from Zermatt's past. The displays show typical furnishings, tools, and stuffed alpine fauna, as well as exhibits on the city's mountaineering history. You'll find out why Teddy Roosevelt climbed the famous peak before he was president. The reliefs of the mountain (and surrounding region) offer a helpful topographic perspective. There's a morbid room displaying artifacts found after deadly accidents and a room dedicated to July 14, 1865—the day the Matterhorn was finally conquered by a team of seven climbers. (Tragically, four of them died on the descent.) Be sure to check out the display case (near the restrooms) that holds a collection of Matterhorn memorabilia and products (10 SF, covered by Swiss Pass, audioguide-5 SF; July–Sept daily 11:00–18:00; April–June and Oct daily 14:00–18:00; Dec–March Mon–Sat 15:00–19:00, closed Sun; closed Nov; under glass dome at Kirchplatz 11, across from the big Catholic church, tel. 027-967-4100, www.matterhornmuseum.ch).

Goat Parade—A charming and unusual little event takes place each day in summer, as a small flock of local "blackneck" goats are herded through the center of town on the way to pasture (daily July–mid-Aug at around 9:00 and back home again at about 17:00). These furry goats, which are unique to the surrounding Upper Valais region, have a black head and shoulders, a white rear end, and long horns.

High-Mountain Excursions from Zermatt

You have four options for lifts up and out of Zermatt:

1. A cable-car ride to the highest lift station in Europe, **Klein Matterhorn** (not the "real" Matterhorn).

2. A side spur off the Klein Matterhorn line leading to **Schwarzsee,** with some of the closest views you'll get of the Matterhorn.

3. An underground funicular, then gondola, then cable car to **Rothorn,** with classic Matterhorn views.

4. A train up to **Gornergrat,** for good views down on a glacier.

The first trip leads to a snowy wonderland, year-round skiing slopes, and a cave carved into the ice. The other three will take you to pristine pastures with alpine lakes and Matterhorn vistas.

Pass Prices: If the weather's clear and your pockets are deep, consider springing for a **Peak Pass,** which gives you unlimited access to all of these lifts; unfortunately, the minimum length of the pass is three days, so it's a bad value for a one- or two-day visit (3 days-171 SF, 4 days-196 SF, 5 days-220 SF). The two-day **Panoramic Pass,** available only in summer, is a better deal—including Klein Matterhorn, Schwarzsee, and Rothorn (but not Gornergrat) for 133 SF. You can purchase passes at the TI or at lift stations.

Individual Tickets: Buy individual tickets directly at the lift stations. If you go after 14:30, you'll save about 20 percent on individual fares to Klein Matterhorn, Schwarzsee, or Rothorn—always ask (valid mid-June–late Sept). Eurailpass holders do not get a discount on Zermatt lifts, but Swiss Pass holders get 50 percent off. For more information, see www.matterhornparadise.ch.

For Skiers: Note that the descriptions and lift schedules in this section apply only to the summer season. If you're a skier, ask the Zermatt TI about specifics for your visit.

▲▲Klein Matterhorn (12,530 feet) and Schwarzsee (8,470 feet)

To really get your high-altitude high, zip up to the highest cable-car station in Europe, at Klein ("Little") Matterhorn. From way up here, the Matterhorn is just one of many cut-glass peaks; this is your best chance for a bird's-eye panorama of the Alps without

ZERMATT AREA

Note: Not to scale
This bird's eye view looks south

MATTERHORN
14,690'

SCHÖNBIELHÜTTE

HÖRNLIHÜTTE

Schwarzsee
8,470'

Furgg Glacier

STAFEL

To Cervinia, Italy →

ZMUTT

Klein Matterhorn
12,530'

Theodul Glacier

TROCKENER STEG

FURGG

To Trift →

FURI

Riffelsee

BERGBAHN

GORNERGRAT
10,270'

ROTENBODEN

RIFFELBERG

FINDELN-BACH

RIFFELALP

FINDELN

ZERMATT
5,265'

Monte Rosa
15,200'

Gorner Glacier

Grünsee

LEISEE

To Täsch, Visp & Brig →

SUNNEGGA

Stellisee

FLUHALP

BLAUHERD

ROTHORN
10,180'

Ober-rothorn

Findel Glacier

Zermatt

What's What in Zermatt

Bergbahn: Lift station in Zermatt for Klein Matterhorn.

Blauherd: Upper station on the Sunnegga-to-Blauherd gondola; lower station on the Blauherd-to-Rothorn cable car, with good access to hikes, including the Marmot hike.

Findelnbach: Station stop on the train from Zermatt up to Gornergrat.

Fluhalp: Small settlement known for its good restaurant, accessible by hike from the Blauherd station.

Furi: Upper station on the gondola from Zermatt; lower station on a different gondola to Schwarzsee and a cable car to Trockener Steg.

Glacier Palace: Free sight at Klein Matterhorn; a hole dug into a glacier with ice sculptures and exhibits.

Gorner Glacier: Glacier that lies between Gornergrat and Klein Matterhorn.

Gornergrat: Viewpoint (10,270 feet) between Klein Matterhorn and Rothorn. At the upper station of a train from Zermatt, it offers views of the Gorner Glacier, Matterhorn, and Monte Rosa.

Gourmetweg (Gourmet path): Hike from Sunnegga down to Zermatt via Findeln through larch forests.

Hinterdorf: Attractive old quarter of Zermatt by the river, with antique chalets and traditional *mazots* (buildings on stone stilts).

Klein Matterhorn: At 12,530 feet, the highest cable-car station in Europe, with great views of the Alps; always snow-covered.

Matterhorn: Mountain peak whose shape forms the textbook example of a "horn," which indicates that bowl-shaped valleys (cirques) were carved into the peak by several glaciers on all sides.

hiking. But note that some visitors are disappointed by this particular view because it's not the classic Matterhorn profile on all the postcard racks (for that, head to Rothorn, page 181).

You'll reach Klein Matterhorn in three parts. First, you'll take a small, six-seat gondola on a six-minute ride over pretty glacier-carved foothills to the Furi station. From Furi, you'll take a larger cable car up to Trockener Steg. (You can also take a different gondola from Furi to Schwarzsee—see page 180.) Finally, you'll board the last cable car up to Klein Matterhorn; on the left are great views down on glaciers and across to the Gornergrat train station. All the way up, you'll see plenty of ski lifts and picturesque little chalets. The area around Klein Matterhorn stays snow-covered all year long, making it a popular place for summer skiers.

Once up top, non-skiers have two sightseeing options: the

Monte Rosa: Tallest peak in Switzerland (15,200 feet).

Murmelweg (Marmot path): Hike from Blauherd down to Sunnegga through marmot habitat.

Nikolaital Valley: Deepest valley in Switzerland, with the town of Zermatt at its upper end.

Riffelalp: Station stop on the train from Zermatt up to Gornergrat.

Riffelberg: Station stop on the train from Zermatt up to Gornergrat.

Riffelsee: Lake below the Rotenboden station.

Rotenboden: Station stop on the train from Zermatt up to Gornergrat.

Rothorn: Upper station of the Blauherd-to-Rothorn cable car, offering the quintessential views of the Matterhorn.

Schwarzsee: Alpine lake at an elevation of 8,470 feet and a gondola station; the closest you can easily get to the Matterhorn.

Stafel: Village along the hike from Schwarzsee down to Furi.

Stellisee: Alpine lake along a hike from Blauherd.

Sunnegga: Upper station on the underground funicular from Zermatt and the lower station of the Sunnegga-to-Blauherd gondola; offers good access to hikes.

Trockener Steg: Upper station on the Schwarzsee-to-Trockener Steg gondola; lower station on the Trockener Steg-to-Klein Matterhorn cable car.

Winkelmatten: Cliff-hanging neighborhood above the Bergbahn lift station in Zermatt.

observation deck and the Glacier Palace. As you leave the lift, follow the hall branching to the left, and take the elevator to the **observation deck** (12,200 feet). Exit the elevator and walk another 100 steps up to stunning panoramas. On a clear day, you can see Italy and France (including Mont Blanc, Europe's highest peak).

If you follow the hall from the lift all the way to the end, you'll reach the Panorama Bar and the exit. Go outside and walk a few steps downhill to the low-profile entrance of the **Glacier Palace,** marked *Gletschergrotte* (free, daily 9:00–15:45). This place brags that it's the "highest glacial grotto in the world"—a claim

Zermatt

that makes other high-altitude glacial grottos seethe with envy. The "Palace" is basically a big hole dug into the glacier, allowing you to walk deep inside. As you wander, you'll see ice sculptures (including the Matterhorn and some flowers encased in ice) and some lackluster exhibits about glaciers, local wines, and "glacier fleas" (a.k.a. "springtails," little bugs that live up here). You can also wriggle into an actual crevasse.

Rather than going all the way to Klein Matterhorn, you could take the gondola from Furi to the alpine lake **Schwarzsee**. While a much lower elevation (8,470 feet), this area is the closest you can get to the Matterhorn (though it lacks the big-picture alpine panorama that the other lift excursions offer). You can also do this on your way back down from Klein Matterhorn (when you reach Furi, follow signs to *Schwarzsee* instead of *Zermatt*; 29 SF round-trip for just this segment from Furi to Schwarzsee and back to Furi, 19.50 SF one-way). Several popular hiking trails lead from here back down to the valley (see below).

Hikes: You won't find any hiking paths from the very top of Klein Matterhorn, since it's covered with snow year-round. The best hike on this series of lifts is at Schwarzsee. From the Schwarzsee lift station, the hike directly down to Furi is quite steep; a longer but easier and more enjoyable route is to hike down to Stafel, then on to Furi, where you can catch the gondola back to Zermatt (or continue to Zermatt on foot). Plan on the better part of a day for this excursion; easier hikes are described below.

Cost: Zermatt to Klein Matterhorn costs 85 SF round-trip (55 SF one-way); Zermatt to Schwarzsee is 44 SF round-trip (28.50 SF one-way). If you plan to do both, you'll save money by getting the Matterhorn Pass, which includes both Klein Matterhorn and Schwarzsee for 85 SF (which is like getting a trip to Schwarzsee for free). The Matterhorn Pass, sold at the lift station, is a good deal if this combo-trip is the only one you plan to do in the area; the Peak and Panoramic passes mentioned above cover this combo-trip and more.

Hours: The trip up to Klein Matterhorn is open daily year-round (generally Sept–June 8:30–16:05, July–Aug 7:00–16:20). The gondola from Furi to Schwarzsee doesn't run off-season (July–Aug 8:00–17:00, June and Sept–Oct 8:40–16:30, closed Nov–May). If the weather's iffy, confirm that the entire route (all the way to Klein Matterhorn) is open before you ascend—upper segments can close if it's too windy.

Location: The elevator to the Klein Matterhorn station is about three-quarters of a mile upriver from the train station (simply follow the river, or catch an electric bus marked *Klein Matterhorn* or *Schwarzsee* in front of the Gornergrat train station, across from the main train station).

▲▲Rothorn (10,180 feet)

While actually farther away from the famous peak than the other lifts described, Rothorn offers *the* classic Matterhorn view. When Matt Lauer wanted the best shot of the Matterhorn to broadcast on the *Today* show, he came here (and brought along some alphorn players). The passage up to Rothorn has three parts: first, an underground funicular to Sunnegga (eight cold minutes, bring a sweater), then a gondola to Blauherd, and finally, a cable car to Rothorn. All along the way are typical glacial lakes, offering a picturesque foreground for your Matterhorn photos.

Hikes: You have plenty of easy options for walking around the lakes up here. Get details at the TI before you ascend. Perhaps the best is the mostly level hike from the Blauherd station, around the Rothorn peak, past the Stellisee, to the restaurant at Fluhalp, then back again. If only the Sunnegga lift is open, it's still worthwhile to go for hiking and a great view of the Matterhorn (14.50 SF one-way). Try the 40-minute Marmot hike (Murmelweg) up to Blauherd—for a good chance of spotting these fuzzy mountain mammals—or hike from Sunnegga down to Zermatt. The Gourmetweg hike (allow 75 min) takes you through larch forests, and the path is covered with soft, fragrant pine needles.

Cost, Hours, Location: 60 SF round-trip, 39 SF one-way. You can get to Rothorn or Blauherd only between mid-June and mid-Sept (daily 8:00–16:40); the lower segment, to Sunnegga, is open longer (late May–early Oct). The whole shebang is open and ready for skiers in winter. The station for the underground funicular from Zermatt is across the river from the train station, just downstream from the Gornergrat train tracks.

▲▲Gornergrat (10,270 feet)

This viewpoint is somewhere between Klein Matterhorn and Rothorn—both geographically and in terms of your experience. A train takes you from Zermatt up to Gornergrat in about 45 minutes, with stops at other stations along the way (Findelnbach, Riffelalp, Riffelberg, and Rotenboden). On the way up, sit on the right-hand side for good Matterhorn vistas. At Gornergrat, you'll enjoy a sweeping alpine panorama with great views of the Matterhorn (though

it's not the perfect profile that you see from Rothorn). What's distinctive about Gornergrat is that it offers the best views of the Gorner Glacier that runs between it and Klein Matterhorn. It also gets you up close to the *other* big mountain in the neighborhood, which is actually taller than the

Matterhorn: Monte Rosa. This towering behemoth is the highest point in Switzerland (15,200 feet).

Hikes: The best option is to take the train from Gornergrat back to the Rotenboden station, where you can enjoy the pretty Riffelsee lake. Then walk down to the Riffelberg station and take the train back into Zermatt.

Cost, Hours, Location: 72 SF round-trip, 36 SF one-way. Two or three trains leave hourly mid-June–Sept, starting at about 8:00 and ending at 20:00 (fewer trains and shorter hours off-season, tel. 027-921-4712, www.gornergrat.ch). The Gornergrat train station is right across the street from Zermatt's train station.

Other Mountain Activities

Aside from hiking and views, adventure-seeking travelers have even more opportunities for alpine thrills near Zermatt. **Paragliding** is an expensive but unforgettable experience, best at Rothorn (about 190 SF, Air Taxi/Air Born, tel. 027-967-6744, www.paragliding-zermatt.ch). The hills above Zermatt are laced with great **mountain-bike** paths (get specifics from TI). For skiing options, see page 174.

SLEEPING

Little Zermatt has more than a hundred hotels—and all of them are expensive. This is a resort town, plain and simple, where even the budget bunks cost big bucks. I've scrutinized the options and presented you with the best deals I could find. I've listed peak summer rates (generally highest July–Aug). You'll pay less at most places in shoulder season (June and October), and more during ski season (Dec–mid-Jan). When there's a range, higher prices are for busy times, and lower prices are when it's slow (unless otherwise noted).

Sleep Code

(1.10 SF = about $1, country code: 41)
S = Single, **D** = Double/Twin, **T** = Triple, **Q** = Quad, **b** = bathroom, **s** = shower only. Unless otherwise noted, credit cards are accepted, English is spoken, and breakfast is included.

To help you sort easily through these listings, I've divided the rooms into three categories, based on the price for a standard double room with bath:

$$$ **Higher Priced**—Most rooms 150 SF or more.
$$ **Moderately Priced**—Most rooms between 110–150 SF.
$ **Lower Priced**—Most rooms 110 SF or less.

Zermatt

Many hotels close in the shoulder season (as early as mid-April). They reopen beginning in early May, but some stay on vacation until late June. Of course, several hotels are open year-round.

$$$ Hotel Romantica, a few scenic steps up from the main street, offers 15 rooms in a flower-dappled chalet surrounded by old-fashioned huts. If you like all those huts, consider sleeping in one—this hotel has converted two of them into accommodations, which cost about 200 SF. Both have tiny interiors with two stories: sitting room and modern bathroom downstairs, loft bedroom upstairs. Choose between the very low-ceilinged and rustic hut (cozy and romantic) or the hut with more modern finishes (Sb-78–85 SF, Db-150–200 SF, prices depend on demand and length of stay, tel. 027-966-2650, fax 027-966-2655, www.reconline.ch /romantica, romantica.zermatt@reconline.ch, Cremonini family).

$$$ Hotel Jägerhof has 48 homey rooms with new bathrooms and lots of charm. It's a little farther from the center, across the river toward the Klein Matterhorn lift station (Sb-86 SF, Db-172 SF, most doubles have balconies, elevator, free Internet access, fitness room, tel. 027-966-3800, fax 027-966-3808, www .hoteljaegerhofzermatt.ch/home.php, jaegerhof@zermatt.ch, Perren family).

$$ Hotel Tannenhof is a great value hiding a few steps off the main drag. Its 23 rooms are small, tight, and woody, without much character, but the location is good and the place is well-run (S-55 SF, Sb-80 SF, D-100 SF, Db-120–130 SF, T-120 SF, tel. 027-967-3188, fax 027-967-3173, www.tannenhof.zermatt.info, tannenhof @zermatt.info, Schaller family).

$$ Hotel Weisshorn offers 17 basic but comfortable rooms over a restaurant, right in the heart of town. The rooms are nothing special, but the rates are reasonable (S-61 SF, Sb-76 SF, D-106 SF, Db-134–140 SF, T-147 SF, Am Bach 6, tel. 027-967-1112, fax 027-967-3839, welcome@weisshorn-zermatt.ch).

$ Hotel Bahnhof, with 17 tidy rooms (and three dorm rooms) and some worn carpeting, could be Zermatt's best value. The basement features a relaxing lounge, dining room, and guests' kitchen. It's professionally run and conveniently located across the street from the train station (dorm bed-35 SF, S-68 SF, Sb-78 SF, D-92 SF, Db-108 SF, Qb-184 SF, no breakfast, laundry facilities, Wi-Fi, lockers, tel. 027-967-2406, fax 027-967-7216, www .hotelbahnhof.com, welcome@hotelbahnhof.com).

$ Zermatt's official **Youth Hostel** is sparkling new, looking over town from a perch high above the river. It's slick and super-modern, with key cards and bathrooms inside most rooms (or down the hall). The hostel is an especially good deal since the rates include breakfast and dinner—a real plus in expensive Zermatt (prices per person: in 8-bed room-48 SF, in 6-bed room with bathroom-53 SF, in 4-bed room without bathroom-58 SF, in 4-bed room with bathroom-61 SF, in twin D-61 SF, in D with one big bed-76 SF, in Db with one big bed-86 SF, all rates include sheets, Internet access in lobby, no age limit, no curfew, Staldenweg 5, tel. 027-967-2320, fax 027-967-5306, www.youthhostel.ch/zermatt, zermatt@youthhostel.ch). From the station, take the bus marked *Winkelmatten* to the Luchre stop (3.20 SF); the hostel is a steep hike up from there (follow the signs with the international hostel symbol).

$ Matterhorn Hostel is a more low-key, easygoing place overlooking the river. Their mission is to provide cheap beds in an expensive town, and they deliver. The floor plan is claustrophobic, with not an inch of wasted space: 10 dorm rooms with graffiti decor are upstairs; the lounge and showers are in the basement; and a tiny Internet nook (free access) is tucked under the spiral staircase (bed in 6- to 8-bed dorm-33 SF, in 4-bed room-38 SF, in 2- or 3-bed room-43 SF, 4 SF/night discount if you stay four or more nights, breakfast-7 SF, towel rental-2 SF, closed 10:00–16:00, or 11:00–16:00 in peak season, Schluhmattstrasse 32, tel. 027-968-1919, fax 027-968-1915, www.matterhornhostel.com, info @matterhornhostel.com). It's a 10-minute walk from the train station on the way to the Klein Matterhorn lift station, right on the river. Take the bus to the Bergbahn/Klein Matterhorn lift station (2.50 SF), then take the elevator up to the cable-car station and walk one block down the hill.

EATING

Zermatt's restaurants are as expensive as its hotels. If there's a cheap snack bar–type place here, I didn't find it (unless you count McDonald's). But the town has several handy bakeries and grocery stores for buying a picnic, and the streets are lined with restaurants featuring garish signs, interchangeable menus, and high prices. Simply wander down the main drag (Bahnhofstrasse) and pick the place that looks best. I ate well without breaking the bank at the two eateries listed here. They're obvious and touristy (with Japanese signs outside), but the prices and food are acceptable, and you may see locals mixed in with the out-of-towners.

Whymper-Stube, named for the first brave soul to conquer the Matterhorn, specializes in cheese dishes—that means fondue (about 25 SF per person) and raclette (8 SF per serving, two servings is enough for most). While American and Japanese tourists photograph each other eating fondue, six barstools in the corner are warmed by local regulars (kitchen open daily 12:00–14:00 & 18:00–22:00 but fondue and cold dishes are served daily 11:00–22:00, friendly staff, on Bahnhofstrasse, on the right just before the big church, tel. 027-967-2296).

Restaurant du Pont claims to be the oldest restaurant in town. Note that it doesn't claim to be the best. Its ambience—with low ceilings and Swiss folk sayings on the walls—beats the food (fondue for two-44 SF, *Rösti* for about 15 SF, daily 12:00–22:00, on Bahnhofstrasse at end of square with big Catholic church, tel. 027-967-4343).

Pizza Roma offers a good value, a friendly staff, and an escape from the worst tourist hordes. Dine in the warm, woody interior or outside on the sidewalk (12–20-SF daily specials, good 15–20-SF wood-fired pizzas, 17–20-SF pasta dishes, daily 17:00–22:30; from Bahnhofstrasse, turn right on Kirchstrasse just before the big Catholic church—it's on the right just after you cross the river; tel. 027-967-3229).

Grocery Stores: **Co-op** is across from the train station (Mon–Sat 8:15–19:00, Sun 16:00–19:00). **Migros** is across from the tennis courts on Hinterdorf Strasse (Mon–Fri 8:30–12:30 & 14:00–19:00, Sat 8:30–19:00, Sun 16:00–19:00, shorter hours in spring and fall).

TRANSPORTATION CONNECTIONS

Zermatt is at the end of the dead-end Nikolaital valley, which you can only reach on a private rail line. This train, operated by the Matterhorn Gotthard Railway (www.mgbahn.ch), connects Zermatt to Brig hourly (80 min, second-class fares: 33 SF one-way, 66 SF round-trip, covered by Swiss Pass, Eurailpass not valid or discounted). In Brig, the Matterhorn Gotthard Railway station is just across the street from the Swiss Rail station. From here, you can easily connect to destinations all over the country. If you're connecting to Lake Geneva (Lausanne or Montreux), you'll save time changing trains in Visp, which lies between Zermatt and Brig (Zermatt–Lausanne via Visp: hourly, 3 hrs total). Train info: toll tel. 0900-300-3004 or www.rail.ch.

From Brig by Train to: Bern (at least hourly, 1.5 hrs), **Zürich** (at least hourly, 2.75 hrs, some with transfer in Bern), **Lausanne** (hourly, 1.75 hrs; faster to transfer in Visp), **Interlaken** (at least hourly, 1.75 hrs, transfer in Spiez), **Luzern** (at least hourly, 3 hrs, transfer in Bern).

By Glacier Express to Eastern Switzerland: In summer, four trains depart Zermatt daily and arc scenically on high-altitude tracks over the middle of Switzerland to the east. All of these Glacier Express trains go through **Chur** (6 hrs), and some continue to **Davos** or **St. Moritz** (8 hrs total to either). In winter, there's one train per day in each direction. These trains do not require a transfer in Brig. For more details, see the Scenic Rail Journeys chapter on page 250.

APPENZELL

Welcome to cowbell country. In the moo-mellow and storybook-friendly Appenzell region, you'll find the warm, intimate side of the land of staggering, icy Alps. Savor Appenzell's cozy, small-town atmosphere.

Appenzell is Switzerland's most traditional region...and the butt of jokes because of it. Entire villages meet in town squares like Appenzell town's Landsgemeindeplatz to vote (an event featured on most postcard racks). Until 1989, the women of Appenzell couldn't vote on local issues. But lately, the region has become more progressive. In 2000, its schools were the first to make English—rather than French—the mandatory second language.

A gentle beauty blankets this region of green, rolling hills, watched over by the 8,200-foot peak of Mount Säntis. As you travel, you'll enjoy an ever-changing parade of finely carved chalets, traditional villages, and cows moaning, "Milk me." While farmers' bikini-clad daughters make hay, old ladies with scythes walk the steep roads, looking as if they just pushed the Grim Reaper down the hill. When

locals are asked about Appenzell cheese, they clench their fists as they answer, "It's the best." (It is, without any doubt, the smelliest.)

If you're here in late August or early September, there's a good chance you'll get in on (or at least have your road blocked by) the ceremonial procession of flower-bedecked cows and whistling herders in formal, traditional costumes. The festive march

---

Appenzell Card

If you stay for several days in the region, you'll receive a card from your hotel that covers all local train trips (on trains operated by Appenzeller Bahnen, as far as St. Gallen), free rides on three different cable cars, free admission to local museums, a free ride on the Kronberg luge, a discounted rate on the PubliCar shuttle service (3 SF), and more. The card is free of charge, but only if you're staying three nights or longer. Hotels and some smaller pensions offer the card; ask when you reserve.

---

down from the high pastures is a spontaneous move by the herding families, and when they finally do burst into town (a slow-motion Swiss Pamplona), locals young and old become children again, running joyously into the streets.

Planning Your Time

On a two-week trip through Switzerland, save a day for the Appenzell region. This pastoral area offers a good first look at Switzerland—but would be an anticlimax after the rugged Berner Oberland or Matterhorn. If you have only a week or less in Switzerland, skip the subtle charms of Appenzell and head instead for the high mountains.

In the Appenzell region, I prefer overnighting up on Ebenalp. But the accommodations are a little rustic for some travelers, who prefer the comfort of hotels and *Zimmer* in Appenzell town.

Getting Around Appenzell

By car, Appenzell is a breeze. Using public transportation, you can easily get to Appenzell town and Ebenalp, but connections beyond those destinations are sparse.

The center of the region is Appenzell town, connected by **train** with Wasserauen (near Ebenalp; hourly except 2/hr during rush hour, 20 min) and Herisau (same train, opposite direction, 40 min). From Herisau, bigger trains depart hourly for St. Gallen (20 min), Zürich (1.5 hrs), and Luzern (2 hrs). The Appenzell–Herisau train also stops at Urnäsch (20 min). Regional **buses** connect towns several times a day; for schedules, check with the TI or the post office.

Appenzell's shuttle service, **PubliCar,** takes passengers to locations—such as Stein—not serviced by buses (for Appenzell to Stein, figure about 8.40 SF, or 3 SF with Swiss Pass or Appenzell Card). To reserve, inquire at the TI or call 0848-553-060.

Appenzell Town

In this traditional town, kids play "barn" instead of "house," while Mom and Dad watch yodeling on TV. The town center is a painfully cute pedestrian zone that delights tourists born to shop.

ORIENTATION

Tourist Information

The TI is on the main street at Hauptgasse 4 (May–mid-Oct Mon–Fri 9:00–12:00 & 13:30–18:00, Sat–Sun 10:00–12:00 & 14:00–17:00; mid-Oct–April Mon–Fri 9:00–12:00 & 14:00–17:00, Sat–Sun 14:00–17:00; tel. 071-788-9641). For information on the greater Appenzell region, call 071-898-3300 or check out www .appenzell.ch.

Ask at the TI about the Appenzell Cattle Show (usually the first Tue in Oct).

Arrival in Appenzell Town

From the train station, take Postgasse up to Postplatz, then follow Poststrasse up to Hauptgasse, where you'll run directly into the TI. If arriving by car, park in the lot by the brewery. Walk across the bridge and veer right onto the main drag, Hauptgasse, which leads through town to Landsgemeindeplatz. You'll see a large church on your right with the TI and Appenzell Museum just past it.

Helpful Hints

Blue Monday: Appenzell's museums are closed, but hiking and biking are good any day the sun shines. Luges run every day—rain, snow, or shine.

Internet Access: Use the computers at the library on the church square (Tue–Wed 14:00–17:00, Thu 14:00–16:00, Fri 17:00–20:00, Sat 9:30–11:30, closed Sun–Mon). Hotel Säntis has a stand-up computer in its lobby (5 SF/30 min, free for guests, Landsgemeindeplatz 3).

Post Office: It's in front of the train station.

Bike Rental: Rent wheels at the train station (20 SF/half-day, 25 SF/day, return bike by 18:30). Most hotels rent bikes or can arrange a rental for you. For mountain bikes, go to the bike shop of **Elmar Neff** 20 SF/half-day, 30 SF/day, Mon–Fri 7:30–12:00 & 13:15–18:30, Sat 7:30–12:00 & 13:15–16:00, closed Sun, Hauptgasse 58, tel. 071-787-3477).

SIGHTS AND ACTIVITIES

In Appenzell Town

▲**Folk Music**—Free folk music concerts take place every Thursday (mid-June–mid-Oct) at 18:30 in City Hall, and every Wednesday at 20:00 at Hotel Hof Weissbad. You can also sometimes find live music at local restaurants—ask at the TI.

▲**Appenzell Museum**—The folk museum next to the TI provides an excellent look at the local cow culture. Ride the elevator to the sixth floor and work your way down through living rooms and displays of traditional costumes, art, and crafts (7 SF, covered by Swiss Pass, ask to borrow English handbook, April–Oct daily 10:00–12:00 & 14:00–17:00; Nov–March Tue–Sun 14:00–17:00, closed Mon).

Modern Art Museums—Appenzell has two modern/contemporary-art exhibits in great settings. Each one costs 9 SF, but a 15-SF combo-ticket gets you into both (also covered by Swiss Pass, Tue–Fri 10:00–12:00 & 14:00–17:00, Sat–Sun 11:00–17:00, closed Mon, www.museumliner.ch): **Museum Liner** is a silver-clad modern building right behind the train tracks (Unterrainstrasse 5, tel.

071-788-1800) and **Kunsthalle Ziegelhütte** is at Ziegeleistrasse 14 (tel. 071-788-1860).

Hiking

Appenzell makes a fine home base for hiking. The TI has several flyers about easy walks in the region. I've recommended two possibilities here.

Appenzell to Wasserauen—This two-hour walk, which takes you to the foot of the Ebenalp cable car (see page 195), begins near the parish church in Appenzell and leads along the creek through meadows and forests. The path is well-marked. Once you reach Wasserauen, you can take the cable car up to Ebenalp, or simply hop on the train back to Appenzell.

Barefoot Walk (Barfussweg)—This 90-minute path between Jakobsbad and Gontenbad offers a surprising and unusual experience...yes, with your shoes off. The path leads over meadows, through creeks, and on stretches of asphalted road. Two specially designed fountains along the way will refresh your feet. The path follows the philosophy of 19th-century therapist Sebastian Kneipp, who sought to treat medical conditions with water of different temperatures and pressures.

To get from Appenzell Town to the trailhead, take the train to Jakobsbad (2/hr, 8 min), do the barefoot walk to Gontenbad, and continue back to Appenzell on foot (another 45–60 min). For details on the hike, ask the TI.

Near Appenzell Town

▲**Stein**—The town of Stein has the **Appenzell Showcase Cheese Dairy** (Appenzell Schaukäserei, daily April–Oct 8:30–18:30, Nov–March 8:30–17:30, cheesemaking normally 9:00–14:00, tel. 071-368-5070, www.showcheese.ch). It's fast, free, smelly, and well-explained by the 15-minute English video and free English brochure with cheese recipes (ask for the brochure at the cheese counter). The lady at the cheese counter loves to cut it so you can sample it. The dairy also sells yogurt and cheap boxes of cold iced tea. The restaurant serves powerful cheese specialties.

Stein's great **folk moo-seum** (Appenzeller Volkskunde Museum) is next door. With old-fashioned cheesemaking demonstrations, peasant houses, fascinating embroidering machinery, cow art, and folk-craft demonstrations, this museum is fun, but not worth the 7 SF if you've seen the similar folk museum in Appenzell town (covered by Swiss Pass, Tue–Sun 10:00–17:00, closed Mon, Nov–March no demos but museum open, tel. 071-368-5056, www .appenzeller-museum-stein.ch).

Without a car, the only way to get to Stein is by PubliCar (see "Getting Around Appenzell," page 187).

APPENZELL TOWN

- ❶ Hotel Adler
- ❷ Restaurant Hotel Traube
- ❸ To Haus Lydia & Gästezimmer Koller-Rempfler
- ❹ Hotel/Restaurant Appenzell
- ❺ Restaurant Marktplatz
- ❻ Gasthaus Hof
- ❼ To Gasthaus Freudenberg
- ❽ Internet Access (Hotel Säntis)
- ❾ To Wasserauen/Ebenalp Cable Car
- ❿ To "Barefoot Walk," Kronberg Luge & Jakobsbad

▲**Urnäsch**—This appealing one-street town has Europe's cutest museum. The Appenzell Museum, on the town square, brings this region's folk customs to life. Warm and homey, it's a happy little honeycomb of Appenzeller culture. A 20-minute movie in English explains four of the major regional festivals (6 SF, covered by Swiss Pass, April–Oct daily 13:30–17:00, Nov–March open only if you call ahead, winter entry fee-20 SF for groups smaller than 4, guided tour-20 SF plus entry, good English brochure, tel. 071-364-2322).

Kronberg Luge Ride (Bobbahn)—Between Appenzell and Urnäsch, in the village of Jakobsbad, you can enjoy this bobsled ride roughly spring through fall. Each sled has seatbelts and can carry two people. Two handles at the side allow you to control the speed: push to accelerate, pull to brake. Respect the *Bremsen!*

Appenzell

signs—which suggest when to brake—and don't come too close to the sled in front of you. Since they're mounted on rails, the sleds can run in rainy or snowy weather. One ride lasts about seven minutes (9 SF per sled for adults, 6 SF per sled for kids, 81 SF/10 rides, 153 SF/20 rides, 270 SF/40 rides, multiple-ride cards shareable, daily 9:00–18:00, until 17:00 in fall, closed off-season, tel. 071-794-1289, www.kronberg.ch).

SLEEPING

Sleep in touristy Appenzell town if you want comfort—but for a rustic, high-altitude thrill, I love the low-tech, no-shower dorms at Ebenalp (see page 195). Appenzell town is small, and the hotels are central. All hotels offer the Appenzell Card (described on page 187) to guests who stay a specified number of nights. The private *Zimmer* are six blocks from the town center.

$$$ Hotel Adler, above a delicious café/bakery with the best croissants in town (daily 7:30–19:30, closed Wed Nov–June), offers two kinds of rooms: modern or traditional Appenzeller (with lamps imitating the traditional local headwear). Helpful Franz Leu, proud to be an Appenzeller, has turned the halls and traditional rooms of his hotel into a museum of regional art and culture (Sb-80–105 SF, Db-170–190 SF, suite-240–260 SF, elevator, Herr Leu can arrange bike rentals for guests, between TI and bridge on Adlerplatz, tel. 071-787-1389, fax 071-787-1365, www.adlerhotel.ch).

$$$ Restaurant Hotel Traube, two blocks from the TI, is cozy, with seven tastefully decorated rooms above a fine restaurant. The friendly Hunziker family has welcomed guests here for three generations (Sb-85–110 SF, Db-150–170 SF, Marktgasse 7, tel. 071-787-1407, fax 071-787-2419, www.hotel-traube.ch, info

---

Sleep Code

(1.10 SF = about $1, country code: 41)
S = Single, **D** = Double/Twin, **T** = Triple, **Q** = Quad, **b** = bathroom, **s** = shower only. Unless otherwise noted, credit cards are accepted, English is spoken, and breakfast is included.

To help you sort easily through these listings, I've divided the rooms into three categories, based on the price for a standard double room with bath:

$$$ **Higher Priced**—Most rooms 110 SF or more.
$$ **Moderately Priced**—Most rooms between 50–110 SF.
$ **Lower Priced**—Most rooms 50 SF or less.

@hotel-traube.ch). Don't confuse Hotel Traube ("grape" in German) with the similarly named Hotel Taube ("dove") nearby.

Zimmer: To experience a pleasant Swiss suburban neighborhood, consider the following: **$$ Haus Lydia,** a six-room, Appenzell-style home filled with tourist information and a woodsy folk atmosphere, is on the edge of town and includes a garden and a powerful mountain view. Its crisp, renovated rooms are a fine option if you have a car or don't mind a 20-minute walk from the town center (Sb-65 SF, Db-98–100 SF, great breakfast; east of town over bridge, past Mercedes-Esso station, take next right and go 600 yards, Eggerstandenstrasse 53; tel. 071-787-4233, fax 071-367-2170, www.hauslydia.ch, contact@hauslydia.ch, friendly Frau Mock-Inauen). She also rents a roomy apartment by the week (Db-82–89 SF, breakfast extra). **$$ Gästezimmer Koller-Rempfler** is a family-friendly, five-room, traditional place several blocks before Haus Lydia, a little closer to the town center (Db-90–95 SF, Tb-120 SF, cash only, Eggerstandenstrasse 9, tel. 071-787-2117, niklauskoller@hotmail.com).

EATING

The Appenzeller beer is good, famous, and about the only thing cheap in the region. Ideally, eat an early dinner up on Ebenalp at **Berggasthaus Aescher,** even if you're staying in Appenzell town (see page 197; last lift down at 19:00 July–mid Sept, 18:00 mid-May–June and mid-Sept–mid-Oct, 17:00 mid-Oct–mid-May).

In Appenzell town, many good restaurants cluster around Landsgemeindeplatz, where residents gather the last Sunday of each April to vote on local issues by show of hands. (The rest of the year, it's a parking lot.) The first four restaurants are within a block of this town square, just a few blocks up Hauptgasse from the TI (away from the bridge). All restaurants are open daily from about 8:00 to 24:00 unless otherwise noted.

Restaurant Hotel Traube offers pleasant dining indoors or out, with fresh ingredients and a wide selection of traditional Swiss and Appenzeller meals (entrées from 20 SF, Tue–Sun 9:00–24:00, closed Mon, veggie options, see "Sleeping," above).

Hotel Appenzell serves fine salads and vegetarian dishes for about 22 SF (meat dishes also available, at corner of square closest to TI, tel. 071-788-1515).

Restaurant Marktplatz is filled with locals playing cards in a traditional Appenzeller atmosphere. It prides itself on being the first non-smoking restaurant in Appenzell (closed Thu and all of Aug, on small parking lot across from Landsgemeindeplatz fountain, walk around white building with horse head, tel. 071-787-1204).

Gasthaus Hof offers a huge variety of specials, including cheese dishes that give the place an unforgettable aroma (fondue-20–24 SF, healthy salad dishes, meat "vitamin corner" meals-15–33 SF, cold meals-15–22 SF, next to Hotel Appenzell, tel. 071-787-4030, www.gasthaus-hof.ch).

Gasthaus Freudenberg has reasonably priced meals and great views over Appenzell from outdoor tables. It's a 15-minute uphill walk from the town center (healthy *Fitnessteller*-20–35 SF, veggie dishes-12–17 SF, summer grill special-20–34 SF, closed Wed and Nov; go under train station, turn right, and follow yellow signs to Freudenberg; tel. 071-787-1240).

TRANSPORTATION CONNECTIONS

From Appenzell Town by Train to: Wasserauen (near Ebenalp, described below; 1–2/hr, 20 min), **Zürich** (2/hr, 1.75 hrs with change in Gossau, 2.25 hrs with change in St. Gallen), **Chur** (hourly, 2.5 hrs, 1–3 changes), **Luzern** (2/hr, 2.75 hrs, change in Herisau or in Zürich and Gossau), **Bern** (hourly, 3.25 hrs, transfer in Gossau), **Interlaken** (hourly, 4.5 hrs, 2 transfers including Gossau or St. Gallen and Zürich or Bern), **Lausanne** (2/hr, 5 hrs, transfer in Gossau or St. Gallen), **Munich** (3/day, 4.5 hrs, transfer in St. Gallen). Train info: toll tel. 0900-300-3004 or www.rail.ch.

Route Tips For Drivers

Appenzell to Interlaken/Gimmelwald (120 miles): It's a three-hour drive from Appenzell to Ballenberg (Swiss Open-Air Folk Museum) and another hour from there to the Gimmelwald lift. Head out of Appenzell town following signs to Herisau/Wattwil. A few scenic miles out of town, in Stein, *Schaukäserei* signs direct you to the Appenzell Showcase Cheese Dairy (see page 190). From there, head for Wattwil. Drive through Ricken into the town of Rapperswil. Once you're in Rapperswil, follow the green signs to Gotthard/Zürich over the long bridge, then continue south, following signs to Einsiedeln and Gotthard. You'll go through the town of Schwyz, the historic core of Switzerland that gave its name to the country.

From Brunnen, one of the busiest, most impressive, and most expensive-to-build roads in Switzerland wings you along the Urnersee. It's dangerously scenic, so stop at the parking place after the first tunnel (on right, opposite Stoos turnoff), where you can enjoy the view and a rare Turkish toilet. Follow signs to Gotthard through Flüelen, then take the autobahn to Luzern, vanishing into a long tunnel that should make you feel a little better about your 40-SF autobahn sticker. Exit at Stans-Nord (signs to Interlaken). Go south along the Alpnachersee toward Sarnen. Continue past Sarnensee to Brienzwiler before Brienz. A sign at Brienzwiler will direct you to the Freilichtmuseum Ballenberg (Swiss Open-Air Folk Museum)/Ballenberg Ost. You can park here, but I prefer the west entrance, a few minutes down the road near Brienz.

From Brienzwiler, take the autobahn to Interlaken along the south side of Lake Brienz. Cruise through the old resort town, down Interlaken's main street. From the Interlaken East train station (Ost Bahnhof), drive past the cow pasture—with a great Eiger–Jungfrau view on your left and grand old hotels, the TI, post office, and banks on your right—to the Interlaken West train station (West Bahnhof) at the opposite end of town. If stopping in Interlaken, park there. Otherwise, follow signs to Lauterbrunnen. Gimmelwald is a 30-minute drive and a five-minute cable-car ride away (see Gimmelwald and the Berner Oberland chapter).

Side-Trip Through Liechtenstein: If you must see the tiny and touristy country of Liechtenstein, take this 30-minute detour: From Feldkirch, drive south on E77 (follow *FL* signs) and go through Schaan to Vaduz, the capital. Park near City Hall, the post office, and TI. Passports can be stamped (for 2 SF) in the TI (Mon–Fri 9:00–17:00, Sat–Sun get your stamp at the info desk behind City Hall, tel. from Switzerland 00423/232-1443). Liechtenstein's banks (open until 16:30) sell Swiss francs at uniform and acceptable rates. The prince looks down on his 4-by-15-mile country from his castle, a 20-minute hike above Vaduz (castle interior closed to the public, but there's a fine view from the grounds; catch trail from Café Berg). To leave Liechtenstein, cross the Rhine at Rotenboden, immediately enter the autobahn, drive north from Sevelen to the Oberriet exit, and check another country off your list.

Ebenalp

This cliff-hanging hut is a thin-air alternative to Appenzell town. Ride the lift from Wasserauen, five miles south of Appenzell town by road or rail line, to Ebenalp (5,380 feet). On the way up (left side), you'll get a sneak preview of Ebenalp's cave church and the cliffside boardwalk that leads to the guest house. From the top, you'll enjoy a sweeping view all the way to Lake Constance (Bodensee).

Leaving the lift, take a 12-minute hike through a prehistoric cave (slippery and dimly lit—hold the railing, and you'll soon return to daylight), past a hermit's home (a tiny museum, always open)

and the 400-year-old Wildkirchli cave church (hermit monks lived there 1658–1853), to a 170-year-old guest house built precariously into the cliff. Originally a hut housing farmers, goats, and cows, it evolved into a guest house for pilgrims coming to the monks for spiritual guidance. Today, Berggasthaus Aescher welcomes tourists, offering cheap dorm beds and hot, hearty plates of *Rösti* (see "Sleeping and Eating").

The region is a hit with hikers who make the circuit of mountain hotels. There are 24 hotels, each a day's hike apart. All originated as alpine farms. Of these, Berggasthaus Aescher is the oldest and smallest.

From Ebenalp's sunny cliffside perch, you can almost hear the cows munching on the far side of the valley. Only the paragliders, like neon jellyfish, tag your world as 21st-century. In the distance, nestled below Säntis peak, is the isolated Seealpsee ("Lake-Alp Lake"). The one-hour hike down to the lake is steep but pleasurable (take left at first fork below guest house).

Getting There: The Ebenalp lift runs at least twice hourly (18 SF up, 25 SF round-trip, half-price with Swiss Pass, July–mid-Sept 7:30–19:00, mid-May–June and mid-Sept–mid-Oct 7:30–18:00, mid-Oct–mid-May 9:00–17:00, closed for 2 weeks in both April and Nov for maintenance, free and reportedly safe parking at lift, free hiking brochure, tel. 071-799-1212, www.ebenalp.ch).

SLEEPING AND EATING

There's no reason to sleep in Appenzell town. The Ebenalp lift, across from the tiny Wasserauen train station, is a few minutes' drive or a 10-minute train ride south.

$$$ Berggasthaus Ebenalp sits atop the mountains just above the lift. Its refurbished rooms are booked long in advance for Saturdays, but are otherwise empty (4-, 6-, or 8-bed dorms with comforters-34 SF per person; D-114 SF, coin-op shower, tel. 071-799-1194, Sutter family).

$$$ Berggasthaus Seealpsee is on the idyllic alpine Seealpsee, a hike up a private road from the Wasserauen train station (loft dorm beds with sheets-33 SF, S-55 SF, Sb-65 SF, D-110 SF, Db-130 SF, showers-2 SF, tel. 071-799-1140, fax 071-799-1820, www.seealpsee.ch, berggasthaus@seealpsee.ch, Meier family).

$ Berggasthaus Aescher (see photo on page 195) promises a memorable experience. The 170-year-old house has only rainwater and no shower. Friday and Saturday nights sometimes have great live music, but are often crowded and noisy, with up to 40 people, and parties going into the wee hours. Monday through Thursday, you'll normally get a small, woody dorm to yourself. The hut is actually built into the cliff; its back wall is the rock itself. From the toilet, you can study this alpine architecture. Sip your coffee on the deck, sheltered from drips by the gnarly overhang 100 feet above. The guest book goes back to 1940, there's a fun drawer filled with an alpine percussion section, and the piano in the comfortable dining/living room was brought in by helicopter. Claudia can show you rock-climbing charts. For a strenuous 45-minute pre-dinner hike, copy the goats: Take the high trail toward the lake, circle clockwise up toward the peak and the lift, then hike down the way you originally came (dorm bed-35 SF, includes breakfast and comforter, no towels or showers available, dinner-14–22 SF, no credit cards but euros and traveler's checks accepted, closed Nov–April, 12 min by steep trail below top of lift, tel. 071-799-1142, www .aescher-ai.ch, reservations by phone only, run by Claudia and Beny Knechtle-Wyss and their five children—Bernhardt-age 24, Reto-23, Lukas-20, Lilian-19, and Dominik-17—plus 35 sheep, 20 rabbits, five chickens, three pigs, a donkey, and a dog).

LAKE GENEVA
and FRENCH SWITZERLAND

Lake Geneva, in the southwest corner of the country, is the Swiss Riviera. Separating France and Switzerland, the lake is surrounded by Alps and lined with a collage of castles, museums, spas, resort towns, and vineyards. Its crowds, therefore, are understandable. This area is so beautiful that Charlie Chaplin and Idi Amin both chose it as their second home.

French is the predominant language at Lake Geneva ("Lac Léman" in French, "Genfersee" in German). To establish a better connection with the locals, see the "French Survival Phrases" in the appendix, *s'il vous plaît*.

Skip the big, dull city of Geneva; instead, sleep in fun, breezy Lausanne. Explore the romantic Château de Chillon and stylishly syncopated Montreux. The French Swiss countryside offers up chocolates, vineyards, Gruyère cheese, and a fine folk museum.

Planning Your Time

On a quick trip, you can get a good overview of Lake Geneva's highlights in a day or less. Lausanne makes the best home base. If you're in a hurry, make a beeline for Château de Chillon. With more time, lazily float your way between Lausanne and Chillon on a scenic boat cruise, and get lost in Lausanne's old town and unique museums (the Olympics and Art Brut museums are best). If you have a car, explore some of the countryside options to the north (handiest if you're driving between here and Bern or Murten; see "French Swiss Countryside," page 217).

Getting Around Lake Geneva

Trains easily connect towns along Lake Geneva. Take the faster Direct trains if you're going between larger cities, such as Lausanne

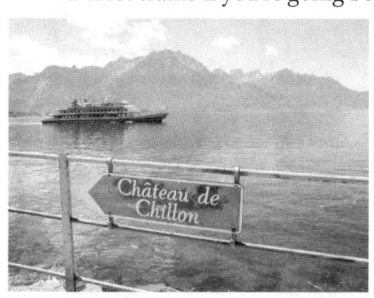

Château de Chillon

or Montreux, or the slower Régional or REV trains if you're heading for a smaller destination, such as Château de Chillon or Villeneuve (check the TV screens in the station for *Direct, Régional,* or *REV* to find the right train).

Boats carry visitors to all sights of importance. Daily boat trips (4/day in each direction May–Sept, fewer off-season) connect Lausanne with Vevey (60 min, 16.40 SF), Montreux (80 min, 21.20 SF), and Château de Chillon (90 min, 22.60 SF). Some of these boats run the whole route, making stops at several towns along the way, while others require a change in St. Gingolph, a town across the lake. Check the schedule beforehand at the TI or at the dock. First class costs about a third more and gets you passage on the deck up top, where you should scramble for the first-come, first-served chairs. You can sail free with a Eurailpass or Swiss Pass, but it uses up a travel day of a flexipass; to avoid giving up a day, you could take an afternoon cruise on the same day you arrive by train in the morning. (Tel. 0848-811-848, www.cgn.ch.)

The short cruise between Montreux and Château de Chillon is fun. The pretty town of Vevey gives you the most scenic one-hour boat ride from Lausanne and a 30-minute ride from Chillon, and makes an enjoyable destination. Evian, immediately across from Lausanne, is the French spa town famous for its mineral water. Boats go hourly (30 min, passport required) filled with people ready to enjoy its spa and tour its mineral-water facilities.

Lausanne

Lausanne is the most interesting city on the lake, proudly dubbing itself the "Olympic Capital" (it's been home to the International Olympic Committee since 1915). Amble along the serene lakefront promenade, stroll through the three-tiered, colorful old town, explore the sculptures at Olympic Park, and visit the remarkable Collection de l'Art Brut. Take a peek at the Gothic Cathedral and climb its tower for the view.

The Romans founded Lausanne on the lakefront—but with the fall of Rome and the rise of the barbarians, the first Lausanners fled for the hills, establishing today's old town. The Roman site was abandoned (scant ruins today), but in the age of tourism, the waterfront—a district called Ouchy—thrived. So the city has a design problem that goes back 1,500 years: two charming zones separated by a nondescript residential/industrial urban mess. Thankfully, the waterfront and the old town are easily linked by a steep and handy Métro line.

Lausanne has the energy and cultural sophistication of a larger city, but is home to only 125,000 people (300,000 in greater Lausanne). A progressive city government (with a mayor from the Green Party) that subsidizes art and culture, and a university with plenty of foreign students carbonate the place with a youthful spirit. That spirit shows itself in Lausanne's notoriety as a haven for inline skating and skateboarding.

ORIENTATION

The tourist's Lausanne has two parts: 1) The lakefront **Ouchy** (oo-shee), with good restaurants and the Olympics Museum; and 2) the **old town,** or *vieille ville* (vee-yay veel), with creaky Old World charm and other fine museums, directly uphill from the lake. The train station is located between the two neighborhoods, and everything's connected by the Métro funicular (undergoing renovation at least until January 2009) or the Métrobus (which takes the place of the funicular during its renovation).

Be careful to pronounce Lausanne correctly (loh-ZAHN), and don't confuse it with Luzern.

Tourist Information

Lausanne has two TIs: One is in the train station (daily 9:00–19:00), and the other is at the lakefront Ouchy Métro stop, in a blue pavilion (daily April–Sept 9:00–19:00, Oct–March 9:00–18:00, tel. 021-613-7373, www.lausanne-tourisme.ch).

At either TI, ask about **walking tours** in English (10 SF, free for students, 1.5 hrs, May–Sept Mon–Sat usually at 10:00 and 14:30, in English only if there's a guide and demand, meet in front of City Hall at Place de la Palud, call 021-321-7766 to confirm time and language). Also, check if any free **concerts** are scheduled at the cathedral.

LAUSANNE

PALAIS DE BEAULIEU

HERMITAGE

AVE. DES BERGIÈRES

COLLECTION DE L'ART BRUT

Bois de Sauvabelin

RUE DE LA BORDE

AVE. L. VULLIEMIN

R. DR. ROUX

RUE DE BUGNON

AVE. BEAULIEU

PRE DU MARCHE

AVE. VINET

R. TUNNEL

CASTLE

RUE TERREAUX

Place de la Riponne

VIEILLE

CATHEDRAL

CITY HISTORY MUSEUM

PONT CHAUD.

AVE. J. GONIN

RUE DU GRAND-PONT

R. CENTRALE

MERC.

PONT BESSIÈRES

HIGH PED. BRIDGE

FLON

VILLE

Parc Mon-Repos

R. LANG.

AVE. RUCHONNET

RUE DU PETIT-CHÊNE

Place St. François

AVE. DU THÉÂTRE

AVE. STE. LUCE

AVE. DE LA GARE

TRAIN STATION

POST

AVE. OLIVIER

BLVD.

GRANCY

Crêt de Montriond

AVE. DE LA HARPE

MONTRIOND

METRO

AVE. D'OUCHY

AVE. DE MONTCHOISI

JORDILS

OUCHY

AVE. DE L'ÉLYSÉE

To Geneva

AVE. DE RHODANIE

Parc Olympique

OLYMPICS MUSEUM & PARK

Parc du Denàntou

QUAI D'OUCHY

To Vevey & Montreux

Place du Port

N

Lake Geneva

To Geneva

To Montreux & Chateau de Chillon

To Evian, France

500 meters

500 yards

❶ Aux Bonnes Choses Bakery
❷ Migros Grocery
❸ Café du Vieil-Ouchy

Arrival in Lausanne

By Train: The train station is midway between the old town and the lakefront. This sounds inconvenient, but the Métro takes you either up to the old town or down to the lake in about two minutes, with departures every seven minutes. For most recommended hotels, take the Métro to the Lausanne-Flon stop (or, until the funicular is reopened, take the Métrobus to the Montbenon stop). Cross the street and walk on the pedestrian bridge until Rue du Grand-Pont. Cross again and you're in the old town. It seems confusing only until you do it. A **taxi** from the train station to your hotel runs about 15 SF.

By Car: Drivers headed for the old town should exit the autoroute at Lausanne Centre, following signs to *Centre* and *Riponne* (the downtown underground parking garage). If you want the lakefront, take the freeway to Ouchy (where it ends), and you'll find a big pay lot. Coming from Montreux, the smaller road (follow blue signs) leads you along the lakeshore directly into Lausanne.

Helpful Hints

Market Days: On Wednesday and Saturday mornings, produce stands fill the pedestrian streets of the old town. Saturday is flea market day on Place de la Riponne.

Internet Access: Get online at **Quanta** (daily 9:00–24:00, across street from train station and above McDonald's at Place de la Gare 4) or **Cyberland** (daily 9:00–24:00, in old town, just over pedestrian walkway at Rue du Grand-Pont 10).

Laundry: Quick-Wash is well-run and handy to the train station (Mon–Fri 7:30–20:30, Sat–Sun 9:00–20:30, self-service only, change machine, good English instructions, below train station at Boulevard de Grancy 44, at corner with Passage de Montriond, tel. 079-449-3761).

Bike Rental: Lausanne, along with Zürich and Bern, now offers free bikes. Get a bike at **Lausanne Roule,** at Place de la Riponne (April–Oct daily 7:30–21:30; from the train station, head uphill toward the huge Palais de Rumine to reach Place de la Riponne, passing the stop for buses #5, #6, and #8; leave picture ID and 20-SF deposit, mobile 076-411-8378, www.lausanneroule.ch). Lausanne Roule may move—call ahead or check their website before heading there.

You can rent a bike at Lausanne's train-station baggage office (23 SF/half-day, 31 SF/day, 5 SF less with Eurailpass or Swiss Pass, daily 8:30–19:00, reserve ahead on weekends, tel. 051-224-2162, www.rentabike.ch). Ask about dropping off the bike at a different train station (7 SF extra, limited to a few stations).

Don't use a bike in town—use it to explore the lakeside,

vineyards, and villages. It's a three-hour lakefront pedal to Montreux.

In Ouchy, **Delacombaz Sport & Action** rents bikes and inline skates, but has erratic opening times (bikes cost 10 SF first hour, then 2 SF every 15 min, next to Ouchy Métro station, tel. 079-606-2761, www.delacombaz.ch).

Late-Night Groceries: The train station has a grocery store open long hours (daily 6:00–24:00).

Getting Around Lausanne

Lausanne is steeper than it is big. A five-stop funicular Métro system connects the lakefront (stop called **Ouchy,** with boat landing) with the train station **(Gare-CFF)** and the upper part of Lausanne (*vieille ville* or *centre ville,* stop called **Lausanne-Flon**).

While the Métro is under renovation (probably at least until January 2009), a Métrobus connects the various stops as follows: From the lakeside Ouchy stop, the Métrobus heads uphill, stopping first at the Gare-CFF stop at the train station, then continuing to Montbenon, which is right behind the Lausanne-Flon Métro stop (runs every 7 min, 6:00–24:00).

Your ticket choices are 1.80 SF (good for three city bus stops or two Métrobus stops), 2.40 SF (good for 1 hour of buses and Métrobus), or 7 SF (good for 1 day of travel on buses and Métrobus, 6:00–24:00). Buy bus tickets before boarding from the TI, ticket windows, or ticket machines. Some of the older ticket machines don't give change (dropping in a big coin is a costly mistake), but the newer machines do (look for the white-and-green machines with piggy-bank stickers). Your railpass is not good on public transportation in Lausanne (except lake boats—see above).

Taxis are pricey—figure 15 SF for a short ride.

SELF-GUIDED WALK

A Stroll Through Old Lausanne

There's no way to see this town without lots of climbing. Locals are used to it (enjoy the firm legs). This self-guided stroll introduces you to Lausanne's charming old town *(vieille ville)*. It's a big counterclockwise circle, taking you from the Church of St. Francis up to the cathedral (and castle just beyond), then more or less back to the starting point. While you can begin this walk at the Church of St. Francis (skip to the "Place St-François" section), you're more likely to arrive at the Lausanne-Flon Métro station.

Rue du Grand-Pont: From the Lausanne-Flon Métro stop (or the Métrobus' Montbenon stop), walk to the high pedestrian bridge. This leads to the main thoroughfare through the city, Rue du Grand-Pont. Orient yourself from midway across

Lausanne

OLD LAUSANNE WALK

Walk

❶ Start of Old Town Walk

❷ Rue du Grand-Pont

❸ Place St-François

❹ Castle

❺ Cathedral

❻ Esplanade de la Cathedral

❼ Place de la Palud

❽ Place de la Riponne

Other

❾ Hôtel des Voyageurs

❿ Hôtel Elite

⓫ Hôtel Régina

⓬ Hôtel du Marché

⓭ To Lausanne GuestHouse & Backpacker

⓮ Café Romand

⓯ Restaurant Manora

⓰ Café du Grütli

⓱ Le Bleu Lézard

⓲ Vinothèque Nomade

⓳ Le Lyrique

⓴ Traiteur Bosphore

㉑ Launderette

㉒ Bike Rental

the pedestrian bridge (Passerelle du Flon). Below you stretches Flon—until recently, a down-and-dirty industrial zone. Now, the old warehouses are renovated and throb at night with trendy bars, restaurants, theaters, and discos. The recommended Vinothèque Nomade is immediately below (see page 213). The only reminder of the mills that once churned here is the name of the hottest dance club in town: MàD (stands for "Moulin à Danse," or "Dance at the Mill," Rue de Genève 23, tel. 021-340-6969). You'll either see a huge construction site here or a new Métro line—a super-high-tech job that will zip from Flon to the top of town (due for completion by the end of 2008).

• *Walk to where the pedestrian bridge hits the busy street. Head for the green copper spire of the Church of St. Francis (to the right). As you walk along Rue du Grand-Pont, enjoy fine views of the cathedral on your left; you'll see the Métro construction below on your right.*

Place St-François: The Church of St. Francis marks the town's center and transportation hub, with the grand post office and banks on the right. The church is Gothic, founded by Franciscans in the 13th century. But in 1536, it went Protestant—and was gutted of decorations. Later, a grand Baroque organ was installed. (Note that bus #2 goes from here to the Collection de l'Art Brut—see page 208.)

Head uphill (passing to the left of the church) up Lausanne's pedestrianized "Fifth Avenue," Rue de Bourg—home to the finest shops. When the street ends, turn left, continuing uphill and over the bridge toward the cathedral. The railing on the bridge is psychologically designed to discourage suicidal people from leaping. While Switzerland seems to have it all, mind-sets can be conservative, the orderliness can be stifling, and life here can be stressful—or even depressing (the country has one of the highest suicide rates in Western Europe). Here in Lausanne, between Christmas and New Year's, social workers are stationed on this bridge with soup and coffee to counsel and comfort the distraught people who congregate here, contemplating ending it all.

Walking toward the cathedral, you'll notice that Lausanne's old town—filled with administration buildings, offices, schools, and apartments—is subdued compared to most other European old towns, which are lively with lots of eateries.

• *Climb past the cathedral (we'll come back) and continue up the cobbled Rue Cité-Derrière to the summit of the old town, where you'll find the...*

Castle: Lausanne's castle is closed to the public, but the views are free. The statue celebrates Major Davel, a local William Tell–like hero. In 1536, the Bernese swept into this region (Canton Vaud) and took over, converting it to Protestantism and ruling it for two centuries. In 1723, Davel's heroic attempt to free his country ended in his decapitation. Only in 1798 was Napoleon able to free Vaud. In 1803, the region entered the Swiss Federation.

Walk downhill (toward the big, blocky cathedral tower). Halfway to the church on your right is the **Cantonal High School** (called "gymnasium" here). One of two great buildings from the Bernese period, this was built as a school to train a new kind of Christian leader after the Reformation. This was the first French-speaking Protestant school (c. 1590)—predating similar schools in Geneva (which, under the leadership of John Calvin, was the center of the Swiss Reformation).

• *Continue to the...*

Cathedral: This is the biggest church in Switzerland, at more than 300 feet long. Go inside (free, April–Sept Mon–Fri 7:00–19:00, Sat–Sun 8:00–19:00, Oct–March daily until 17:30; tower and welcome center open April–Sept Mon–Sat 8:30–11:45 & 13:30–18:00, Sun 14:00–18:00, Oct–March daily until 17:00).

This is an **Evangelical Reform Church,** meaning that it belongs to the tradition of early Protestant reformer John Calvin—and like its founder, it remains very strict (members aren't allowed to dance, or even to have buckles on their shoes). Iconoclasm, the removal of religious symbols, suited the Calvinists well. The once-ornate cathedral, originally dedicated to Mary, was cleared of all its statues and decorations. Its frescoes were plastered over, and its fine windows were trashed and replaced by plain ones (the colored windows were added in the 20th century).

The **pipe organ** is American-made by Fisk, a Boston company that won the commission. Locals love their organ and figure its cost (four million SF) was money well spent. They hold many free concerts here, generally on Friday evenings. Look back at its 6,700 pipes—the "stiletto in Oz" design represents the wings of angels. (The old pipes now toot in a church in Gdańsk, Poland.)

The **rose window** in the south transept has the church's only surviving 13th-century glass. The rest of the glass dates from the early 1900s. The north transept has some dreamy blue Art Nouveau scenes. Below the rose window (and just to the left) is the Mary Chapel—once the most elaborate in the church. In 1536, it was scraped clean of anything fancy or hinting of the Virgin Mary. Look at the bits of surviving original paint, and imagine the church in its colorful glory six centuries ago.

The **Painted Portal** (on the right side of the nave, the church's main entrance in the Middle Ages) may still be under renovation during your visit. It's remarkable for its painted Gothic statuary: Jesus overseeing the coronation of Mary. The panels below illustrate Mary's death and Assumption.

For a grand view of nearly the entire lake—and lots of Alps—climb the 225-step **tower** (2 SF, April–Sept Mon–Sat 8:30–11:30 & 13:30–17:30, Sun 14:00–17:30, Oct–March daily until 16:30).

As the city was originally built of wood, it burned down several times. Since the Middle Ages, a **watchman** has lived in the church's tower. His job: to watch for fires and to call out the hours. The city is made of stone today—so there's little danger of fire—and people now sport watches of their own. Nevertheless, Lausanne's night watchman, the last one of his kind in Switzerland, still calls out the hours. Each night on the hour, from 22:00 to 2:00 in the morning, he steps onto his balcony and hollers. His first announcement: "I am the watchman. I am the watchman. We just had 10 o'clock. We just had 10 o'clock."

• *Back outside, belly up to the fine viewpoint immediately in front of the cathedral.*

Esplanade de la Cathedral: On a clear day, look behind the spire of the Church of St. Francis to see the French Alps (Chamonix and Mont Blanc, over there somewhere, are just out of sight). Evian, the famous French spa town, is immediately opposite Lausanne. On the right, the soft, rolling Jura Mountains, which mark the border of France and Switzerland, stretch all the way from Lake Geneva to Germany.

• *Notice that the City History Museum is across the square from the cathedral (see "Sights and Activities," later). Now's a good time to visit. Then go from the cathedral to...*

Place de la Palud and Place de la Riponne: A covered wooden staircase (Escaliers du Marché) leads down from the cathedral. You'll pass Le Barbare ("The Barbarian"), a pub famous for its fine hot chocolate, and the recommended Café du Grütli (see "Eating," page 213). Place de la Palud (pictured on page 200) is marked by its colorful Fountain of Justice (with the blindfolded figure of Justice holding her sword and scales...commanding fairness as she stands triumphantly over kings and bishops). Imagine the neighborhood moms sending kids here to fetch water in the days before plumbing. The City Hall is the other fine Bernese building in town (1685, on right). Uphill from City Hall, Rue Madeleine leads to our last stop, the vast and modern Place de la Riponne. The Palais du Rumine (former university), overlooking the square, now houses a collection of museums (all of which you may skip).

• *Your tour is over. Now enjoy some of Lausanne's fine museums.*

SIGHTS AND ACTIVITIES

In the Old Town

▲▲**City History Museum**—Facing the cathedral, this museum traces life in Lausanne from Roman times to the present with many fascinating displays. You'll see exhibits on music (from the time of Bach), the Reformation and its roots, the cathedral before Calvin, the Bernese epoch (Protestant, 1536–1798), and the beginnings of the modern era.

The highlight for many is the 1:200-scale model of Lausanne in the 17th century (based on an engraving from 1638—see copy on wall). You're viewing the town from the perspective of the lakefront district of Ouchy, with the Church of St. Francis in the foreground. You can see river valleys that have since been obliterated by the modern city. The little water mills mark the birthplace of industrial Flon. While the city's walls are long gone, its vineyards survive. (When you enter the museum, request to hear the 18-minute recorded English commentary on the model, and they'll book you a time.) Adjacent rooms show the construction of the Grand-Pont and an interesting collection of historic photos (8 SF, covered by Swiss Pass, Tue–Thu 11:00–18:00, Fri–Sun 11:00–17:00, closed Mon except July–Aug, Place de la Cathédrale 4, tel. 021-315-4101, www.lausanne.ch/mhl).

▲▲**Collection de l'Art Brut**—This well-displayed, thought-provoking collection shows art produced by untrained artists, many labeled (and even locked up) by society as "criminal" or "insane." Read thumbnail biographies of these outsiders (posted next to their works), and then enjoy their unbridled creativity.

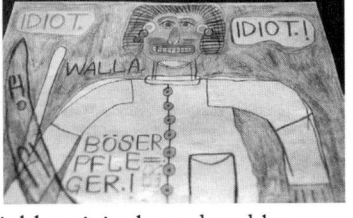

In 1945, the artist Jean Dubuffet began collecting art he called "Brut"—untrained, ignoring rules, highly original, produced by people "free from artistic culture and free from fashion tendencies." In the 1970s, he donated his huge collection to Lausanne, which now displays 30,000 works by 500 artists—loners, mavericks, fringe people, prisoners, and mental-ward patients. Dubuffet said, "The art does not lie in beds ready-made for it. It runs away when its name is called. It wants to be incognito" (8 SF, covered by Swiss Pass, Tue–Sun 11:00–18:00, closed Mon except July–Aug; bus #3 from station, direction: Bellevaux, stop: Beaulieu; or bus #2, direction: Desert, stop: Jomini; each bus stops within 100 yards of museum, Avenue des Bergières 11, tel. 021-315-2570, www.artbrut.ch).

In Ouchy, Lausanne's Waterfront

The charm of Lausanne lies on its lakefront. The handy Métro (or the replacement Métrobus) connects Ouchy with the train station and the old town every seven minutes. Within 100 yards of the Ouchy Métro stop, you'll find everything (except shopping opportunities and a sandy beach): TI, bike rental, boat dock, the start of the lakeside promenade, and a park. The place is lively from Easter through October, and dead otherwise.

A big C-shaped **weathervane** stands on the breakwater. Identify which of the four winds is blowing by lining the "C" up with semicircle cutouts in the four granite pillars (crouch). By matching the "C" with the pillar that creates a perfect "O," you learn the prevailing wind. Nearby, notice the solar-powered **Aquarel tour boats,** which run quietly, smoothly, slowly, and green (7 SF, 30-min tours, www.lausanne.ch/aquarel). Lausanne's current mayor, from the Green Party, is making environmentalism popular. Speaking of green, this city has more green space per inhabitant (300 square feet) than nearly any city in Europe.

▲▲**Olympic Park and Museum**—This beautiful park and high-tech museum celebrate the colorful history of the Olympic Games.

The expensive but excellent museum is a thrill for Olympics buffs—and plenty of fun for those of us who just watch every two years. Given the informative English descriptions and many thrilling video clips to see, plan on spending two hours here (15 SF, family-35 SF, covered by Swiss Pass, audio-guide-3 SF, May–Sept daily 9:00–18:00, Oct–April closed Mon; from Ouchy Métro stop, turn left and walk 5 min to Quai d'Ouchy 1, then ride the outdoor rolling staircase; tel. 021-621-6511, www.olympic.org). As you enter, note the time of the next six-minute introductory video—it's worth watching.

The museum celebrates Pierre de Coubertin, who in 1894 founded the International Olympic Committee and restarted the games after a 1,500-year lapse. The Olympic spirit is one of peace. Coubertin acknowledged that to ask nations to love each other was naive, but to ask them to respect one another is a realistic and worthy goal.

The ground floor traces the history of the Games, from ancient Greek artifacts to a century's worth of ceremonial torches. Upstairs are medals and highlights from each Olympiad and historic, well-described equipment used for various Olympic events (find Jesse Owens' spiky jumping shoe from 1936—a design that led to the first Adidas; Carl Lewis' shoes from L.A. in 1984; the Michael Jordan–signed basketball from the 1992 Barcelona "Dream Team"; and Cathy Freeman's shoes from the 2000 Sydney games). At the top of the museum, you'll find a lakeview terrace and swanky restaurant (healthy *plat du jour* for 19 SF).

In the basement is a 3-D theater (called "Salle Nagano"; note the posted movie times as you buy your ticket, and plan accordingly) and an extensive film archive of suspenseful moments in the history of the Games (roughly 5 min each, 450 to choose from). Your ticket includes two of these mini-documentaries—if enthralled, you can buy three more for 5 SF.

Pauper athletes can enjoy much of the complex for free. Walk through the spiraling core of the complex for a sense of the action. Then enjoy the park's Olympic flame (in front of museum), athletic monuments, and lake views (take escalator to top, ask in museum for free brochure explaining sculptures, and wander back down to lake; avoid the café in the park).

Near Lausanne: Lakeside and Vineyard Excursions on Foot or Bike

A delightful promenade stretches in both directions from the Ouchy Métro stop. The best easy **walk** is east (left as you face the lake, 75 min to Lutry). From Lutry, you can catch the train back to Lausanne (2/hr, 8 min). If you hike, bring the TI's *Discover the Terraces of Lavaux* flier (describes several hikes, including this one). The trail is marked with blue plaques explaining in English the flora, fauna, and culture you're enjoying.

Picturesque **vineyards** abound along the lake near Lausanne. My favorite plan: a 5- to 10-minute train ride to Chexbres or Grandvaux, then a walk through the villages—following the yellow signs—toward Lutry for stunning views of Lake Geneva. From Lutry, hop the train back to Lausanne (2/hr, 8 min).

The best **bike path** goes west (after sharing with cars for half a mile, the trail leaves the road and hugs the shoreline all the way to Morges). You'll pass Vidy (with its Roman ruins—just foundations, free), the headquarters of the International Olympic Committee (not open to the public), lots of sports facilities, and finally just peaceful lakefront parkland stretching to Morges (about 6 miles away, easy return by boat or train).

SLEEPING

Lausanne hotels are expensive. The only cheap doubles are at the Lausanne GuestHouse. The Régina, Voyageurs, and Marché hotels are in the old town (for the Régina and Voyageurs, take the Métro up to the Lausanne-Flon stop—or the Métrobus up to

Sleep Code

(1.10 SF = about $1, country code: 41)
S = Single, **D** = Double/Twin, **T** = Triple, **Q** = Quad, **b** = bathroom, **s** = shower only. Unless otherwise noted, credit cards are accepted, English is spoken, and breakfast is included.

To help you sort easily through these listings, I've divided the rooms into three categories, based on the price for a standard double room with bath:

$$$ **Higher Priced**—Most rooms 170 SF or more.
 $$ **Moderately Priced**—Most rooms between 100–170 SF.
  $ **Lower Priced**—Most rooms 100 SF or less.

the Montbenon stop, cross the street and walk on the pedestrian bridge, cross Rue du Grand-Pont, walk up Rue Pichard, and take the first right; for the Marché, take bus #5 from the station to Place de la Riponne, then walk 5 min up Rue Pré-du-Marché). The Elite and Lausanne GuestHouse are closer to the train station.

$$$ Hôtel Régina, on a steep pedestrian street immersed in old-town charm, is a find: 36 comfy, remodeled rooms, hospitable hosts (Michel and Dora), and a great location (Sb-138 SF, Db-178 SF, Tb-208 SF, suites-165–325 SF depending on number of people, 10 percent less Fri–Sun for stays of at least 2 nights if you mention this book when reserving, cheaper in winter, non-smoking rooms, Internet access, Rue Grand Saint-Jean 18, tel. 021-320-2441, fax 021-320-2529, www.hotel-regina.ch, info@hotel-regina.ch).

$$$ Hôtel des Voyageurs, part of the Comfort chain, has 33 predictable rooms across the street from Hôtel Régina. It lacks Régina's charm, but it's in an equally good location (Sb-140 SF, Db-185 SF, Tb-205 SF, about 10 percent cheaper July–Aug and on weekends, non-smoking rooms, elevator, Internet access, parking-15 SF/day, Rue Grand Saint-Jean 19, tel. 021-319-9111, fax 021-319-9112, www.voyageurs.ch, hotel@voyageurs.ch).

$$$ Hôtel Elite, run by the Zufferey family, is on a quiet, leafy, residential street just above the train station. Its 33 rooms are pleasant and modern (Sb-140 SF, Db-180–260 SF depending on size and view, Tb-210–265 SF, non-smoking rooms, elevator; from station, cross the street and go uphill around McDonald's, take first right to Avenue Sainte-Luce 1; tel. 021-320-2361, fax 021-320-3963, www.elite-lausanne.ch, info@elite-lausanne.ch).

$$ Hôtel du Marché, an older, funky but clean hotel with pastel-colored rooms, is a five-minute walk from Place de la Riponne in the old town (S-70 SF, Sb-100 SF, D-100 SF, Db-130

SF, Tb-155 SF, breakfast-10 SF, some non-smoking rooms, Rue Pré-du-Marché 42, tel. 021-647-9900, fax 021-646-4723, www .hoteldumarche-lausanne.ch, info@hoteldumarche-lausanne.ch).

$ Lausanne GuestHouse & Backpacker has to be one of Switzerland's best hostels. This elegant, century-old house, which offers dorm beds and private rooms, turns its back on the train tracks. All of its rooms overlook the lake on the quiet side (bunk in 4-bed dorm-37 SF, S-85 SF, Sb-94 SF, D-90 SF, Db-110 SF, no breakfast, no smoking, no curfew, reception open 7:30–12:00 & 15:00–22:00, Internet access, lockers, laundry, bike rental, kitchen, garden, parking; 5-min walk from train station: Leave out the back by track 9, go down the stairs, and turn right to Epinettes 4; tel. 021-601-8000, www.lausanne-guesthouse.ch, info@lausanne -guesthouse.ch).

EATING

In Ouchy

The lakeside Ouchy district is *the* place to relax. Immediately in front of the Métro stop is a fun zone with fountains, parks, playgrounds, promenades, and restaurants. The only good, budget eating option is a picnic with the local office gang on any of the many inviting benches or scenic lakeside perches. **Aux Bonnes Choses** is a small bakery with a heart for picnickers, offering good sandwiches, salads, pastries, and drinks to go. This is infinitely better than the lousy kiosk options in the waterfront park (daily 6:30–19:00, 5-SF salads Mon–Fri only, left as you exit Métro, Place de la Navigation 2, tel. 021-617-8857). Another good spot to shop for your picnic is the **Migros** grocery store on Avenue de Rhodanie (daily 8:00–21:45).

Café du Vieil-Ouchy, charming and reasonably priced, seems a bit out of place among all the fancy and expensive restaurants. It offers traditional Swiss cuisine, including cheese fondue and hash brown–like *Rösti* (16–22-SF entrées, Thu–Mon 11:30–14:30 & 17:30–22:00, closed Tue–Wed, Place du Port 3, tel. 021-616-2194).

In the Old Town

Café Romand is a classic Swiss brasserie—plain, smoky, and filled with natives enjoying hearty French Swiss home cooking. Local students, pensioners, and businessmen sit under old-time photos in this characteristic yet simple eatery like they own the place (20–25-SF plates, Swiss white wines by the glass and carafe—see list of what bottles are open behind bar, daily specials, closed Sun, at Place St-François 2, tel. 021-312-6375).

Restaurant Manora is part of a modern, self-service chain offering a quick and healthy series of buffet lines where you grab what looks good: hot meals, salads (4.90-SF, 7.90-SF, and 10.70-SF plates), fancy fruit juices, desserts, and so on (Mon–Sat 6:45–22:45, Sun 7:45–22:45, where Rue du Grand-Pont hits Place St-François).

Café du Grütli (named for the meadow where Switzerland was born) offers typical French Swiss cuisine near Place de la Palud. Choose from three tempting areas to eat: outside on a cozy cobbled lane; ground-floor, circa-1850, Parisian-bistro style; or upstairs, with antlers and the ambience of a 13th-century castle. As the owner's family is into hunting, you'll find game on the menu (20–30-SF plates, Mon–Fri 9:00–14:30 & 18:00–23:00, Sat 8:30–15:30 & 18:00–23:30, closed Sun, Rue de la Mercerie 4, tel. 021-312-9493).

Le Bleu Lézard has great French cuisine, a typical French atmosphere, and a trendy clientele that appreciates its candlelit, bohemian interior and fun outdoor porch (20-SF salads, good veggie options, daily 7:00–24:00, open later on weekends, smoky interior, jazz bar downstairs, Rue Enning 10, tel. 021-321-3830).

Vinothèque Nomade is primarily a wine bar, where you can choose from 40 different wines available by the glass (and many more by the bottle). To order appetizers, see their short "tapas" menu. Browse among the many bottles (take-away prices and drink-in prices marked), and take your favorite into the bistro which serves tasty and beautifully presented Mediterranean dishes (25–45-SF plates, 19-SF daily specials, strong on vegetables). Locals sip their wine and hang out on the big modern sun terrace (daily 10:00–24:00, below the pedestrian bridge, down the elevator, across from Flon Métro stop at Place de l'Europe 9; tel. 021-320-1313).

Le Lyrique is a neighborhood restaurant filled with locals enjoying their *souvlaki, keftedes,* and calamari in a warm, candlelit (but smoky) interior. The traditionally Greek dishes include vegetarian options, and the wine selection is good (18–35-SF main dishes, Mon–Sat 12:00–14:00 & 18:00–22:30, closed Sun, no English menu, Rue Beau-Séjour 29, tel. 021-312-8892).

Traiteur Bosphore is a good option for a quick and inexpensive take-away lunch or early dinner. Popular with locals who enjoy the better-than-average döner kebabs (8 SF), the place has no seating—stand at back counter or walk to the nearby Place de la Louve and find a bench (Mon–Sat 10:00–19:00, closed Sun, Rue de la Louve 7, across from Manor department store, tel. 021-311-0770).

TRANSPORTATION CONNECTIONS

From Lausanne by Train to: Montreux (4/hr, 25 min), **Château de Chillon** (2/hr, 35 min on REV train), Geneva (5/hr, 40 min), **Bern** (2/hr, 70 min), **Murten** (hourly, 90 min, change in Fribourg,

Neuchâtel, or Payerne), **Interlaken** (2/hr, 2.25 hrs, transfer in Bern; or go via Golden Pass scenic route, with transfers in Montreux and Zweisimmen—see Scenic Rail Journeys chapter on page 250), **Luzern** (hourly, 2.5 hrs; more frequent with transfer in Olten and/or Bern; or go via Golden Pass route—see Scenic Rail Journeys chapter), **Zürich** (2/hr, 2.25 hrs), **Zermatt** (hourly, 3 hrs, change in Visp—not Brig, unless connecting to Glacier Express), **Lyon** (almost hourly, 2.75–3.25 hrs, transfer in Geneva), **Chamonix** (every 2 hrs, 2.5–3 hrs, change in Martigny and/or Le Châtelard-Frontière), **Paris** (6/day, 4 hrs). Train info: toll tel. 0900-300-3004 or www.rail.ch.

For boat connections from Lausanne, see "Getting Around Lake Geneva" near the beginning of this chapter.

Château de Chillon

This medieval castle, set wistfully at the edge of Lake Geneva, is a ▲▲▲ joy. Remarkably well-preserved, it has never been damaged or destroyed—always inhabited, always maintained. The Savoy family (their seal is the skinny red cross on the towers) enlarged it to its current state in the 13th century, when this was a prime location—at a crossroads of a major trade route from England and France to Rome.

Château de Chillon (shee-yon) was the Savoys' fortress and residence, with four big halls (a major status symbol) and imprac-

tically large lakeview windows (because their powerful navy could defend against possible attack from the water). But when the Bernese invaded in 1536, the castle was conquered in just two days, and the new governor made Château de Chillon his residence (and a Counter-Reformation prison). With the help of Napoleon, the French-speaking people on Lake Geneva finally kicked out their German-speaking Bernese oppressors in 1798. The castle became—and remains—the property of the Canton of Vaud. It's been used as an armory, a warehouse, a prison, a hospital, and a tourist attraction. Rousseau's writings first drew attention to the castle, inspiring visits by Romantics such as Lord Byron and Victor Hugo, plus other notables, including Dickens, Goethe, and Hemingway.

Follow the free English brochure from one fascinating room to the next. Enjoy the castle's tingly views, dank prison, battle-scarred weapons, simple Swiss-style mobile furniture, and 700-year-old toilets (Rooms 15 and 22). Bonivard's Prison (Room 7) is named for a renegade Savoy who was tortured here for five years (lashed to the fifth column from the entrance). When the Romantic poet Lord Byron came to visit, Bonivard's story inspired him to write *The Prisoner of Chillon*, which vividly recounts a prisoner's dark and solitary life ("And mine has been the fate of those/To whom the goodly earth and air/Are bann'd, and barr'd—forbidden fare"; full text available in the gift shop). You can still see where Byron scratched his name in a column (third from entrance, covered by glass). The chapel (Room 18) uses projectors to simulate the original frescoes. Models in Room 24 explain the construction of the castle. Remember the grand views from the lakeside windows? Notice the small slits facing the road on the landside (courtyard, Room 25), which are more practical for defense. The 130-step climb to the top of the keep (Room 32) isn't worth the time or sweat. Stroll the patrol ramparts, then curl up on a windowsill to enjoy the lake.

Cost, Hours, Information: 10 SF, covered by Swiss Pass, April–Sept daily 9:00–18:00, shorter hours off-season, easy parking, tel. 021-966-8910, www.chillon.ch. Guided tours in English are usually available for individuals at 11:30 and 15:45 for an extra 6 SF (mid-June–mid-Sept).

Getting to Château de Chillon: The castle sits at the eastern tip of Lake Geneva, about 20 miles east of Lausanne (and about a mile east of Montreux).

From Lausanne, you can connect to the castle using a combination of various methods: train, bus, boat, and hike.

The twice-hourly **REV train** (direction: Villeneuve, 35 min, 10.40 SF) takes you directly to the station at Veytaux-Chillon, a 10-minute walk along the lake (ideal for picnicking) from the castle.

The faster and more frequent **Direct train** whisks you to Montreux (4/hr, 20 min, 9.80 SF), where you transfer to a bus. From the Montreux station, cross Avenue des Alpes and go down the stairs. Cross the street and find the blue bus stop on your right, where you can hop **bus #1** to Château de Chillon (3 SF, direction: Villeneuve, stop: Chillon; buy tickets from machine on board, first select the fare: A for *Adulte*, then the destination: zone 1). You can also **hike** the one mile from Montreux to Château de Chillon.

To return to Lausanne, simply reverse the directions (catch the train from the Veytaux-Chillon station back to Lausanne—trains leave hourly at :26 past the hour—or hop the bus from Château de Chillon to Montreux, direction: Vevey, stop: Escaliers de la Gare, take handy escalator up to the station and catch the train the rest of the way to Lausanne).

A slower but more scenic route is by **boat** between Château de Chillon and Montreux or Vevey, connecting to Lausanne with trains. For a longer trip, sail one-way between Château de Chillon and Lausanne (90 min). True *See*farers would prefer a round-trip (see "Getting Around Lake Geneva," page 199).

Montreux

This expensive resort has a famous jazz festival each July. The lakeside promenade takes you along parks, palm trees, *crêperies,* ice-cream stands, modern sculptures, and the Friday produce market. In the center, meet the statue of Freddie Mercury, who had strong bonds with Montreux. His band, Queen, bought the local Mountain Recording Studios in 1978.

The wonderful Montreux **TI** has tons of brochures and extensive information about the region, excursions, and a list of moderately priced rooms in the center (Mon–Fri 9:00–18:00, Sat–Sun 10:00–17:00, tel. 084-886-8484, www.montreux-vevey.com). In summer, you can take a two-hour **walking tour** of the city (10 SF, April–Sept Wed–Sat at 10:00, no tours Sun–Tue or Oct–March, meet in front of TI, call TI to confirm).

For Internet access, try **Cyberworld,** located in the Hollywood cinema complex a few blocks north of the TI (3 SF/15 min, Mon–Fri 12:00–23:00, Sat 13:00–23:00, Sun 15:00–22:00, Grand-Rue 90).

For an easy way to see several sights in the French Swiss countryside, including the town of Gruyères and the chocolate factory in Broc, take a ride from Montreux on the **Chocolate Train** (described on page 218).

If you're driving from Montreux to Lausanne, consider visiting the **Corniche de Lavaux.** This rugged, sometimes frightening Swiss Wine Road swerves through picturesque towns and the stingy vineyards that produce Lake Geneva's tasty but expensive wine. From Montreux, go west along the lake through Vevey, following blue signs to *Lausanne* along the waterfront and taking the Moudon/Chexbres exit. Be sure to explore some of the smaller roads. **Hikers** can take the boat to Cully and explore on foot from there.

SLEEPING

In and near Montreux
(1.10 SF = about $1, country code: 41)

$$$ Hôtel Splendid claims to be the oldest hotel in town, with 24 refurbished but plain rooms (some a bit musty). The bathrooms are new, and the double-paned windows keep out noise. The front rooms are more expensive, with lake views worth the extra cost (Sb-115–160 SF, Db-190–230 SF, Tb-255 SF, non-smoking, elevator, free Internet access, 5-min walk from train station, across the street from TI, above Mayfair Café at Grand-Rue 55, tel. 021-966-7979, fax 021-966-7977, www.hotel-splendid.ch, mayfaircafe @bluewin.ch).

$$ Hôtel Parc et Lac, just a few doors down from Hôtel Splendid, has seen better days, but its creaky rooms, with their worn carpets and old furnishings, have a certain charm. It also has about the cheapest beds you'll find in the town center. Rooms in front come with a nice view of the lake (most with small balconies), but also some street noise. The back rooms are cheaper and quieter, but have no view (Sb-90–130 SF, Db-150–180 SF, elevator, 5-min walk from train station, Grand-Rue 38, tel. 021-963-3738, fax 021-963-2317, parcetlac@bluewin.ch).

$ Montreux Youth Hostel is on the lake, a 10-minute stroll north of Château de Chillon (bunk in 6-bed room-32 SF, bunk in 4-bed room-35 SF, D-90 SF, nonmembers pay 6 SF extra, 14.50-SF meals available; check-in 17:00–22:00; Passage de l'Auberge 8, tel. 021-963-4934, fax 021-963-2729, www.youthhostel.ch/montreux, montreux@youthhostel.ch).

$ Backpackers Riviera Lodge, centrally located on the main square in nearby Vevey, offers cheap beds in a 19th-century townhouse on the lake. Guests receive the Riviera Card, which covers transportation and up to 50 percent off on various museums, including Château de Chillon (dorm bed-27 SF, D-88 SF, breakfast-8 SF, kitchen, Internet access, 3-min walk from station, Place du Marché 5, tel. 021-923-8040, www.rivieralodge.ch, info @rivieralodge.ch).

TRANSPORTATION CONNECTIONS

From Montreux by Train to: Lausanne (4/hr, 25 min), **Bern** (2/ hr, 1.5 hrs, transfer in Lausanne), **Geneva** (2/hr, 1 hr).

French Swiss Countryside

The sublime French Swiss countryside is sprinkled with crystal-clear lakes, tasty chocolates, smelly cheese, and sleepy cows. If you're traveling between Murten, Lausanne, and Interlaken (see map on page 218), take time for a few of the countryside's sights, tastes, and smells.

Getting Around the French Swiss Countryside

This region is ideal by car. By public transportation, it's more difficult. Cross-country **buses** use Fribourg and Bulle

FRENCH SWITZERLAND

To Fribourg & Bern

FRANCE

VALLORBE

To Avenches & Murten

To Yverdon

ROMONT

Lake Gruyères

To Paris

A1

E23

BULLE

BROC

GRUYÈRES

To Spiez & Interlaken

LAUSANNE

N1

PAL.

E27

CORNICHE DE LAVAUX

N12

MOLÉSON

MONT-BOVON

CHOCOLATE TRAIN

To Geneva

A1 E62

OUCHY

VEVEY

GOLDEN PASS TRAIN

NYON

Lake Geneva

MONTREUX

CHÂTEAU DE CHILLON

YVOIRE

EVIAN-LES-BAINS

VILLE-NEUVE

LES DIABLERETS

COL DU PILLON

N1

FRANCE

AIGLE

VILLARS

GLACIER DES DIABLERETS

TAVEYANNE

To Geneva

To Chamonix

A9

N9

To Milan & Zermatt

10 Miles

10 Kilometers

MARTIGNY

as hubs: Bulle–Gruyères (2/day, 15 min), Fribourg–Bulle (hourly, 30 min). The **train** is definitely the best bet between Bulle and Gruyères (hourly, 7 min) and is also handy between Bulle and Broc (hourly, 10 min).

For an easy all-day side-trip from Lake Geneva, consider hopping on the **Chocolate Train** in Montreux. The train carries either panoramic or old-time belle époque coaches. It leaves from Montreux at 9:35 and begins by following the same route as the Golden Pass (see Scenic Rail Journeys chapter). You'll be served coffee and a croissant while enjoying the scenic ride. At 10:45, the train stops to visit the Gruyères cheese factory (described on page 220). From there, a bus takes you up to the picturesque old town of Gruyères for a visit to the castle (included) and some time for lunch (on your own). Then the journey continues to the town of Broc, where you'll tour the Cailler Chocolate Factory (including a film and chocolate tasting; described below). The train returns to Montreux at 17:52 (88.40 SF, first class only, 28 SF reservation fee with first-class Swiss Pass, July–Aug Mon–Fri, June and Sept–Oct Mon and Wed only, departs from Montreux at 9:35, tel. 0900-245-245; from elsewhere in Europe, dial 00-41-840-245-245; from the US call 011-41-840-245-245; www.mob.ch).

Bulle

On your way to the Fribourger Alps, stop in the town of Bulle, which has a charming, distinctly French ambience. On Tuesdays, the weekly produce-and-craft market fills the center of town. The market gets bigger and more colorful in summer, when many vendors wear their traditional costumes and sell handmade crafts. The castle on the main square is closed to the public; it houses the police department.

The **TI** is located between the castle and the train station; follow the blue signs (Mon–Fri 9:00–12:00 & 13:30–18:30, Sat 9:00–12:00, closed Sun, tel. 084-842-4424, www.info-bulle.ch).

▲▲**Musée Gruèrien**—The museum, a two-minute walk through the castle grounds, is worth a visit. Somehow this unassuming little town built a refreshing, cheery folk museum that manages to teach you all about life in these parts and leave you feeling very good (6 SF, free English guidebook, Tue–Sat 10:00–12:00 & 14:00–17:00, Sun 14:00–17:00, closed Mon, tel. 026-916-1010, www.musee-gruerien.ch). When it's over, the guide reminds you, "The Golden Book of Visitors awaits your signature and comments. Don't you think this museum deserves another visit? Thank you!"

Cailler Chocolate Factory

To fight their image of being a boring "old grannies" chocolate, Cailler invited famous designers to reinvent the brand. Wonderful new chocolate creations resulted. The winner of the competition was Parisian Jean Nouvel (the architect responsible for Luzern's Culture and Conference Center). Nouvel also designed imaginative displays for the factory. Visitors wander through chocolate-dark corridors while films and slide shows explain the production and shipment of chocolate. In one room, you can taste almonds or hazelnuts, crumble a cocoa bean in the palm of your hand, and touch a block of cocoa butter. In the tasting room, friendly employees are happy to answer your questions as you sample the new creations from elegant trays (free, April–Oct Mon–Fri 9:30–16:00, closed Sat–Sun and Nov–March, groups of 4 or more should call a day in advance to reserve, located in sweet-smelling town of Broc, follow signs to *Nestlé* and *Broc Fabrique*, tel. 026-921-5151, www.cailler.ch).

▲Gruyères

This ultratouristy town, famous for its cheese, fills its fortified hilltop like a bouquet. Its ramparts are a park, and the ancient buildings serve tourists. Hotels here are expensive. The TI is at the town entrance (daily 9:30–12:15 & 13:00–17:30).

Castle—Gruyères' castle is skippable, but worth a short stop for the setting (8.50 SF, 16-SF combo-ticket includes H. R. Giger Museum, covered by Swiss Pass, daily April–Oct 9:00–18:00, Nov–March 10:00–16:30, tel. 026-921-2102, www.chateau -gruyeres.ch). If you're driving, minimize your walk by driving up to the second parking lot.

H. R. Giger Museum—This museum, a spooky, offbeat contrast to idyllic Gruyères, is dedicated to the Swiss artist who designed the monsters in the *Alien* movies. Not for the faint of heart, this museum shares those movies' dark aesthetic (12 SF, 16-SF combo-ticket includes castle, covered by Swiss Pass, April–Oct daily 10:00–18:00; Nov–March Tue–Fri 13:00–17:00, Sat–Sun 10:00–18:00, closed Mon; www.hrgigermuseum.com).

▲▲**Gruyères Fromageries**—You have two very different chee-semaking exhibits to choose from in and near Gruyères—one is old and up in the hills, and the other is new and handy. The cute cheese shop in the modern center has lunches and picnic goodies.

Ye Olde Cheesemaker: Five miles above Gruyères, a dark and smoky 17th-century farmhouse in Moléson gives a fun look at the traditional, smelly way of crafting cheese in a huge caul-dron over an open fire (3 SF, mid-May–mid-Oct daily 9:00–19:00, closed off-season, cheese actually made at 10:00 and 14:30, Place de l'Aigle 12, tel. 026-921-1044, www.fromagerie-alpage.ch, TI tel. 026-921-8500, www.moleson.ch).

New Cheese Factory: Closer and modern, the cheese-produc-tion center at the foot of Gruyères town (follow *Fromagerie* signs) opens its doors to tourists. Admission includes a sample of three varieties of Gruyère cheese and an English audioguide—punch 444 for English, then the number listed next to the displays (5 SF, daily 9:00–19:00, tel. 026-921-8400, www.lamaisondugruyere.ch).

Glacier des Diablerets

For a grand alpine trip to the tip of a 10,000-foot peak, take the three-part lift from Reusch or Col du Pillon. The trip takes about 90 minutes and costs 54 SF. Stay for lunch. From the top, you can see the Matterhorn and a bit of Mont Blanc, the Alps' highest peak. This is a good chance to do some summer skiing (normally expensive and a major headache). A lift ticket and rental skis, poles, boots, and coat cost less than 100 SF.

The base of the lift is a two-hour drive from Murten or Gimmelwald. Your best public-transportation bet is to catch an early train to Diablerets with a transfer in Aigle. Then bus to Col du Pillon (6/day) and take the cable car to the top (last departure at 16:00). For more ski information, call 024-492-0923 or check www.glacier3000.ch.

▲▲Taveyanne

This remote hamlet is a huddle of log cabins used by cowherds in the summer. Taveyanne is two miles off the main road between Col de la Croix and Villars (a small sign points down a tiny road to a jumble of huts and snoozing cows stranded at 5,000 feet). The hamlet's old bar is a restaurant, serving a tiny community of vacationers and hikers.

The town's inn is **$ Refuge de Taveyanne** (from 1882), where the Seibenthal family serves meals in a rustic setting with no electricity, low ceilings, and a huge, charred fireplace. Consider sleeping in their primitive five-mattress loft (15 SF, D-30 SF, cash only, access by a ladder outside, bathroom outside, closed Mon–Tue except July–Aug, closed Nov–April, tel. 024-498-1947). It's a fine opportunity to really get to know prize-winning cows.

LUGANO

The town of Lugano, the leading city of the Italian-speaking Swiss canton of Ticino, gives you Switzerland with an Italian accent. The town (population 53,000) sprawls luxuriously along the shores of Lake Lugano. Just a short, scenic train ride over the Alps from the German and French regions of Switzerland, Lugano has a splashy, zesty, Mediterranean ambience. It attracts vacationers from the rainy north with its sunshine, lush vegetation, inviting lake, and shopping. While many travelers come here for the fancy boutiques, others make this a base for hiking, cruising the lake, and passing lazy afternoons in its many gardens. While its mountains are not mighty, its beaches are lousy, and it can feel a little geriatric, Lugano has a unique charm that merits at least a short visit.

Planning Your Time

Lugano lies conveniently at the intersection of the William Tell Express and the Bernina Express—two of Switzerland's more scenic train rides. Blitz sightseers arrive on the William Tell one day and take off on the Bernina Express the next. If relaxing is on your itinerary, spend two nights and a full day here, arriving and departing on the scenic trains.

ORIENTATION

The old town is on Lake Lugano, which is bordered by promenades and parks. A funicular connects the old town on the lakeside with the train station above. Nearly everything in this chapter is within a five-minute walk of the base of the funicular.

Note that most people in Lugano speak Italian; you're surrounded on three sides by Italy (see "Italian Survival Phrases" in the appendix). In this corner of Switzerland, a *Strasse* (street) becomes a *Via*, and a *Platz* (square) becomes a *Piazza*.

Tourist Information

Lugano's TI faces the boat dock a couple of blocks below the funicular (Mon–Fri 9:00–19:00, Sat 9:00–18:00, Sun 10:00–18:00, shorter hours off-season, Palazzo Civico, Riva Albertolli, tel. 091-913-3232, fax 091-922-7653, www.lugano-tourism.ch). The TI offers free **walking tours** (Sun, Mon, and Thu at 9:30, 2.25 hours).

Arrival in Lugano

The train station has lockers (small locker-5 SF, big locker-7 SF, always accessible), a less convenient and pricier baggage-storage counter (7 SF, short hours), ATMs, a convenient grocery (Shop Aperto di Lugano, daily 6:00–22:00), and a room-finding service, but no real TI. The easiest way to get to the town below is by funicular (1.10 SF, free with Swiss Pass, daily 5:20–23:50, every 5 min).

Helpful Hints

Internet Access: Mondailpay, at Via Canova 9, is the only real Internet café in town (8 SF/hr, Mon–Fri 9:00–18:30, Sat 10:00–17:00, closed Sun). At **Burger King,** any meal comes with 30 minutes of free Internet access (lakefront, on Piazza R. Rezzonico).

Local Guide: Christa Branchi teaches enthusiastically about her home town (200 SF/half-day, 300 SF/day, tel. 091-606-3302, christabranchi@hotmail.com).

SELF-GUIDED WALK

Welcome to Lugano

While many might think a guided walk of resorty Lugano is absurd, there's actually some interesting history hiding out. This short stroll gets you well-oriented and covers the essentials. Start on Piazza Cioccaro, at the base of the funicular (which connects the train station with the town center).

• *Walk downhill 50 yards to the right, into...*

Via Pessina: In this tangled and colorful little corner are several small shops run by Signor Gabbani. Go in the wine shop

LUGANO CENTER

1. To Hotel International au Lac
2. Hotel San Carlo
3. Hotel/Restaurant Pestalozzi
4. Art Hotel Stella
5. Hotel & Backpackers Montarina
6. Pizzeria Tango
7. Co-op Cafeteria
8. Manora Cafeteria
9. La Tinera
10. Bottegone del Vino
11. Olympia Restaurant
12. Vanini Café
13. Sass Café
14. To Cantine di Gandria Eateries

(marked *Bottega del Vino*). Its ceiling is mossy with *boccalini* (traditional quarter-liter wine carafes, typical of the rustic grottos of Ticino).

• *Farther down, at Via Pessina 3, is...*

Grand Café al Porto: This venerable institution is both Lugano's best spot for cakes and coffee and the most historic café in town (daily 8:00–18:30). The *1803* above the fireplace is the date it opened—and also when Ticino joined the Swiss Federation. Once a convent (notice the fine *sgraffito* facade), the café evokes the 19th-century days when Giuseppe Mazzini and fellow Italian patriots would huddle here—safely over the border—planning their next move to unify Italy. Much later, as World War II wound down, US dignitary Allen Welsh Dulles met right here with Nazi and Italian representatives to organize a graceful end to the war and prevent the Germans from ruining Italy with a scorched-earth retreat. And in more carefree times, this is where Clark Gable and Sofia Loren dipped cookies in their coffee.

• *Just past Grand Café al Porto, take a left at the fountain into...*

Piazza della Riforma: This square is Lugano's living room. The city is proudly liberal, even today, as the name of its main square implies. Its progressive spirit from the days of the Risorgimento (Italian unification) survives today as Lugano

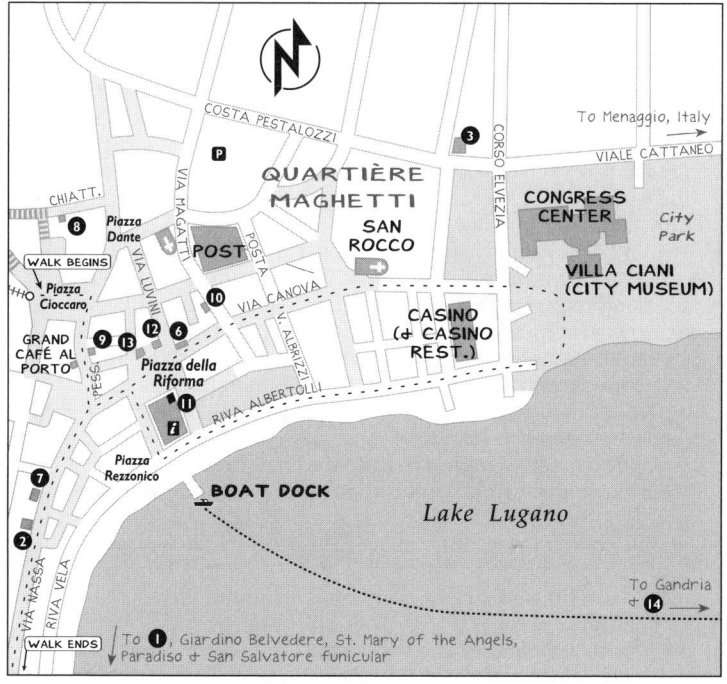

remains one of the most liberal-voting cities in Switzerland. This square—with geraniums cascading on all sides—hosts an open-air cinema, markets (Tue and Fri), and local festivals.

• *Facing City Hall, go left (past the* farmacia*) down...*

Via Canova: This road leads directly to the city park. Along the way, you pass the creamy, elegant little Church of San Rocco. Its rich frescoes celebrate the saint responsible for protecting the city against the plague. Behind that is the Quartière Maghetti, an entire city block turned into a popular mall—lots of shops and fun eateries by day and a lively, youthful bar scene after hours.

• *Via Canova dead-ends at a pink palace in the...*

City Park (Parco Civico Villa Ciani): The park's centerpiece, the Villa Ciani, houses the city museum. Sprawling from here along the lake is a lush park filled with modern art and exotic trees from around the world. Its water gate evokes the 19th century, when this was the private domain of aristocrats. The flower beds are organized to show off maximum color all year long. It's lit at night and particularly good for a late, romantic stroll (open daily 6:30–23:30).

• *From the City Park, walk back to the town center along the...*

Waterfront: The casino restaurant overlooks the lake. Ride its glass *elevatore* up and down for a fun and free view. Then continue

Lugano

The Story of Lugano

Lugano's history is tied to its strategic position: where the Italian world is pressed up against the Alps and just below the most convenient alpine passes. The Celts crossed the Alps here and left their mark. The ancient Romans were here, too—the oldest sacred building in Switzerland is an early Christian baptistery on this lake.

In 1220, when the first road over the Gotthard Pass was built, the Swiss took an interest in acquiring the Italian-speaking region of Ticino, leading to a battle for control. The nearby town of Bellinzona is named not for the Italian *bella* ("beautiful"), but for the Latin *bellum* ("war")—and this truly was a medieval war zone. Several castles in Bellinzona recall a pivotal Swiss victory in 1513. With this success, the Swiss gained a toehold in Ticino.

But the feisty region maintained its independence. In 1798, Ticino even stood up to Napoleon by creating an independent Republic of Ticino. But the people of Ticino were unable to rule themselves peacefully, and five years later (in 1803), they decided to join the Swiss Federation. With that event, the present-day borders of Switzerland were finally established.

In the 19th century, Lugano—Italian-speaking, just a short trip from Milan, yet safely over the border in Switzerland—provided a refuge and staging ground for intellectual Italian revolutionaries. They'd meet here to plan the Risorgimento, the struggle for Italian unification (c. 1840–1869). Later in the 19th century, tourism arrived and the grand lakefront hotels were built.

Today, Lugano is second among Swiss cities only to Zürich in its number of banks. It's easy for Italians and others with suitcases of hard cash—black money—to swing by and take advantage of the secret bank accounts. (Locals claim George H. W. Bush stops by about annually.) But the mentality here remains Italian. Rather than the Zürich model ("live to work"), the people of Lugano brag that they work to live.

strolling through the arcade or under the mulberry trees (a favorite of silk worms, dating from the time when silk was a local industry) until you reach the boat dock opposite the TI.

• *A block inland from the TI is Piazza della Riforma again. The first left is...*

Via Nassa: This is one of Lugano's main shopping streets. Stow your guidebook and just enjoy the wandering, window-shopping, and people-watching for several blocks. It's fun to assume that half the briefcases you pass are filled with cash. Along this gauntlet of boutiques and jewelry shops under typical Lombardi arcades, notice all the clocks. If you're trying to get away from time...this is a nightmare. At #22, the Co-op department store (closed Sun) has a good selection of Swiss chocolates (just inside the door on the left) and a handy top-floor cafeteria (lunch only, great views).

• *Follow Via Nassa until it dead-ends at the small but historic...*

Church of St. Mary of the Angels (Chiesa Santa Maria degli Angioli): This unpretentious little lakefront church, which dates from 1499, was part of a monastery (next door, described later). Inside the church, you'll find the city's best frescoes. Bernardino Luini (from Milan) painted *The Passion and Crucifixion of Christ* and *The Last Supper* in 1529. After enjoying the gentle expressions and calm beauty of his art, you'll understand why Luini is nicknamed the "Raphael of the North."

The Passion and Crucifixion of Christ, the artistic highlight of all Ticino and the finest Renaissance fresco in Switzerland, is on the wall that separates the nave from the altar area. Follow the action as the scenes from Christ's passion are played out, from Jesus being crowned with thorns (left) to the doubting apostle Thomas touching Jesus' wound after his resurrection. The central and dominating theme is the crucifixion. The work is riddled with symbolism. For instance, at the base of the cross, notice the skull and femur of Adam, as well as his rib (from which Eve was created). Worshippers saw this and remembered that without Adam and Eve's first sin, none of the terrible action in the rest of the fresco would have been necessary. Luini spent a decade working on this. Take an extremely close-up look at the fresco technique.

The altar is rich and unusual with its wooden inlay work. *The Last Supper* (back left wall) was sliced off a wall of the monks' dining hall and put on canvas to be hung here.

• *On the lakefront across from the church begins the...*

Giardino Belvedere: This delightful little garden park is an open-air modern-art museum. The building facing it was once a monastery, then the Grand Hotel Palace. This first grand hotel on the lake was radical in that it actually faced the lake. From here, survey the scene. Paradiso, the big hotel zone with its 80-foot-high fountain, is a 15-minute walk along the lakeside. From there, the San Salvatore lift zips sightseers to the summit (described next). The ridge across the lake marks the border of Italy.

ACTIVITIES

San Salvatore: Lugano's Best 360-Degree Mountaintop View

Lugano is a base from which several relatively small peaks can be conquered sweat-free by lifts. At about 3,000 feet, Lake Lugano's mountains are unimpressive compared to the mightier Alps farther north. Still, if you want the complete Lugano experience, you need to enjoy the commanding mountaintop views over the lake.

San Salvatore is the easiest and most rewarding peak. You'll begin at Paradiso (a 15-min walk from Lugano, or take bus #1 from the Lugano TI). From there, a funicular slides you from up and up (26 SF round-trip, 12-min ride, departs on the half-hour, half-price with Swiss Pass, daily June–Sept 8:30–22:30, April–May 8:30–18:30, late March and Oct–mid-Nov 8:30–17:00, closed mid-Nov–mid-March, www.montesansalvatore.ch). At the top, you'll find a self-serve cafeteria (closes at 18:00), a fancy restaurant (way overpriced, and after dark you have no views), a playground, and excellent viewpoints. From the lift, be sure to climb five more minutes to the actual summit, where you'll find a small church. Then climb to the rooftop of the church for an incredible 360-degree view.

Cruising Lake Lugano with a Stop in Gandria

Lake Lugano is made to order for a boat trip. Along with pedal boats and simple cruises from village to village, there are fancier excursions (a lunch trip, a grand tour, a shopping excursion into Italy, and an evening dinner cruise). For details, ask at the TI.

One-Hour Loop Trip: The best basic trip is the one-hour circle from Lugano. This cruise stops at several desolate restaurants and hamlets along the far side of the lake, visits Gandria (a peaceful and picturesque little fishing town with several romantic view restaurants), then returns to Lugano (20.80 SF round-trip including stopovers, or 12.60 SF for one segment, free with Swiss Pass). You can get off and hike. The far side of the lake has a trail lacing together several little grottos and hamlets (each with a boat stop) with hiking times and directions clearly marked. For information on the hike, ask the TI, your hotel, or even the guys on the boat. Carefully note when the next boat comes by and exactly where it stops (as this can be confusing).

Cantine di Gandria has two characteristic *trattorias* and wine grottos—great for a rustic meal or just a snack and a drink (note they close on different days, so at least one is sure to be open on any given day). A five-minute walk from Cantine di Gandria takes you to the **Customs Museum** (Museo Doganale) with underwhelming exhibits on customs and smuggling (free, no English but worth a 10-min visit, April–Oct daily 13:30–17:30, closed Nov–March). Boats stop alternately at Cantine di Gandria and Museo Doganale.

Gandria is the most intriguing stop. This dense cluster of fishing houses hangs over the lake with a few lazy and romantic hotels

and several inviting restaurants. **Restaurant Miralago Gandria** is immediately above the ferry dock (mediocre food, fair prices, extremely romantic setting, closed Wed, tel. 091-971-4361). You can lob bits of bread to the hungry birds, rewarding the ones who fly high circles by your lakeside table. **Locanda Gandriesi** has better cooking but is farther from the boat dock and birds. If stopping here, you can walk back to Lugano (great 45-min lakeside path before hitting the Castagnola suburb of Lugano and a boring 30-min walk along streets into town). To enjoy just the more interesting part of the walk, catch bus #1 from the Castagnola post office.

Half-Day Plan: Here's a pleasant way to spend a late afternoon and evening (confirm boat times before departing—schedules are subject to change): 15:45-Walk from Lugano to Paradiso,

16:00-Catch the boat from Paradiso to Gandria and have a drink and appetizer, or an early dinner in Gandria (at Miralago Gandria—early diners always get lakeside tables), 18:05 or 19:00-Catch the boat to Paradiso (next one not until 22:45). Once at Paradiso, walk to the San Salvatore lift, ride the lift to the summit of the mountain (best at twilight but disappointing after dark), ride back down, and walk along the lake from Paradiso back to Lugano.

SLEEPING

In Lugano's Old Town

$$$ **Hotel International au Lac** is a classic, pricey old hotel with 80 rooms and some Lake Lugano views. It's conveniently and scenically located where pedestrian-only Via Nassa hits the lake. Four generations of Schmids have maintained the early-20th-century ambience since 1906, with old photos, inviting lounges, antique furniture, and—it seems—many of their original guests (Sb-120–185 SF, Db-200–298 SF depending on size and view, Tb-290 SF, family-friendly, Internet access, terrace restaurant, fun view seats on balcony of bar, swimming pool, parking-20 SF/day, Via Nassa 68, tel. 091-922-7541, fax 091-922-7544, www.hotel-international .ch, info@hotel-international.ch).

$$ **Hotel San Carlo,** also on the pedestrian-only shopping street, but closer to the center, rents 22 small but cheerful rooms. This welcoming place is run by Anna Martina and Beppe. The flamboyant Italian-mod design within its old walls is fun and refreshing (Ss-95 SF, Sb-130 SF, Ds-145 SF, Db-170 SF, cheaper off-season, non-smoking rooms, elevator, Via Nassa 28, tel. 091-922-7107, fax 091-922-8022, sancarlo@ticino.com).

$$ **Hotel Pestalozzi,** near the city park, is plain and vaguely institutional. It offers fresh, modern rooms with a woody Nordic touch and some lake views (S-64 SF, Sb-100–106 SF, D-108 SF, Db-168 SF, lakeview Db-178 SF, elevator; good restaurant—see page 232; Piazza Indipendenza 9, tel. 091-921-4646, fax 091-922-2045, www.attuale.com/pestalozzi.html, pestalo @bluewin.ch). Though a bit of a walk from the train station funicular, this hotel is a particularly good value.

Near the Train Station

$$ **Art Hotel Stella,** a wonderful little oasis, offers 14 rooms between slick office buildings just behind the train station. Owner Antoinette Burkhard's love of modern art is evident, with statues on the patio and fun paintings throughout (Sb-110 SF, Db-170 SF, 5 percent discount with this book, some rooms have terraces, Internet access, swimming pool; exit the station at rear, follow

---

Sleep Code

(1.10 SF = about $1, country code: 41)
S = Single, **D** = Double/Twin, **T** = Triple, **Q** = Quad, **b** = bathroom,
s = shower only. Unless otherwise noted, credit cards are
accepted, English is spoken, and breakfast is included.

To help you sort easily through these listings, I've divided
the rooms into three categories, based on the price for a standard double room with bath:

$$$ **Higher Priced**—Most rooms 200 SF or more.
$$ **Moderately Priced**—Most rooms between
120–200 SF.
$ **Lower Priced**—Most rooms 120 SF or less.

---

tracks right for 50 yards, take the first left uphill, then turn left
to Via F. Borromini 5; tel. 091-966-3370, fax 091-966-6755, www
.arthotelstella.ch, info@arthotelstella.ch).

$ Hotel & Backpackers Montarina, a creaky old mansion in
a palm garden overlooking the lake, rents 24 huge antique double
rooms and 140 dorm beds (dorm bed in 5- to 16-bed room with sheets-
30 SF, S-70 SF, Sb-80 SF, D-100 SF, Db-120 SF, breakfast buffet-
12 SF, Internet access, reception open 7:30–23:00, lockers, small
kitchen, swimming pool, free parking, Via Montarina 1, tel. 091-
966-7272, fax 091-966-0017, www.montarina.ch, info@montarina
.ch). As you exit the train station at the rear, walk left along the
tracks, and you'll see the pink buildings and the big sign.

EATING

My recommended restaurants are all in the old town. Lugano is
not the best place for lakeside dining. For better value, cross the
lake to the remote little grotto restaurants, or visit the town of
Gandria (both options described on page 229). If enjoying the
wine, realize that you'll pay the same per liter for the little one-
deciliter (about 3.5 oz) glasses as you do for the big half-liter (about
17 oz) carafes—so go with the small glasses and try several different wines. Experiment. The Ticino merlot is great.

Pizzeria Tango serves Italian cuisine with Ticino influence
and a helpful waitstaff. While a few of its tables face the busy main
square, its interior and the tables facing a quiet little square on the
back may be more inviting (25-SF daily plates, 15–20-SF pizzas,
open daily until very late, Piazza della Riforma, tel. 091-922-2701).

Co-op Cafeteria, midway along the Via Nassa pedestrian
mall, has an elegant-as-cafeterias-go dining area on its top floor

with a pretty rooftop terrace (Mon–Sat 11:30–14:30, closed Sun, Via Nassa 22).

Manora is an easy self-service restaurant offering healthy food and indoor and outdoor seating. It's in the Manor supermarket on Piazza Dante Alighieri (100 yards from bottom of train station funicular; Mon–Sat 7:30–22:00, Sun 10:00–22:00).

La Tinera, beloved by locals, serves affordable, traditional Ticinese cuisine. It's tucked away in an old wine cellar, with heavy wooden furniture and a display of wine bottles and antique copper cookware (often closed in Aug, meat dishes-20–30 SF, smaller dishes-13 SF, Mon–Sat 8:30–15:00 & 17:30–23:00, closed Sun, Via dei Gorini, behind Piazza della Riforma, tel. 091-923-5219).

Restaurante Pestalozzi, close to the city park, is a stylish belle époque restaurant serving reasonably priced meals in a smoke-free and alcohol-free setting (15-SF daily specials, open daily 18:30–21:30, Piazza Indipendenza 9, tel. 091-921-4646).

Bottegone del Vino is an expensive little eatery appreciated for its fine wine. The menu is small and rustic, the wine is excellent, and the ambience is of a quality wine bar. Sitting here you feel "in the know"—but order carefully, as prices really add up (Mon–Sat until 24:00, closed Sun, a block off Piazza della Riforma at Via Magatti 3, tel. 091-922-7689).

Around Piazza della Riforma: In addition to Pizzeria Tango (described previously), several other restaurants offer decent food and great people-watching from outdoor tables on the square. Consider **Sass Café** (classy wine bar with 18-SF daily specials and 30-SF à la carte items), **Olympia** (19-SF pastas, 30-SF main dishes, below City Hall, the mayor's fave), and **Vanini Cafe** (tops for coffee and desserts; try the *marron glace*—candied chestnuts).

TRANSPORTATION CONNECTIONS

Lugano is a long detour from virtually anywhere else in Switzerland. It's best connected to other Swiss destinations by scenic trains: the **William Tell Express** (train-and-boat combination to Luzern) or the **Bernina Express** (bus-and-train combination to eastern Switzerland). The Bernina Express bus leaves for Tirano near Lugano's train station (200 yards to the left as you leave the station, see chart at station). More details about these trips are in the Scenic Rail Journeys chapter on page 250. Train info: toll tel. 0900-300-3004 or www.rail.ch.

From Lugano by Train to: Luzern (hourly, 3 hrs, half with easy change in Arth-Goldau), **Zürich** (hourly, 3 hrs, half with easy change in Arth-Goldau), **Interlaken** (hourly, 5 hrs, transfer in Luzern, Zürich, or Olten), **Bern** (hourly, 4 hrs, transfer in Luzern, Zürich, or Olten), **Milan** (hourly, 1.5 hrs).

From Lugano by Bus to St. Moritz: The Palm Express bus to St. Moritz leaves only once a day in peak season and just on weekends off-season, but it's handy if you're headed to Italy's Lake Como, because it stops in lakeside Menaggio en route (departs Lugano's train station usually at 11:40 but confirm time in advance; 50 min to Menaggio, 4 hrs to St. Moritz; daily mid-June–mid-Oct, mid-Oct–mid-June runs Sat–Mon only; www.swisspost.ch).

From Lugano to Milan's Airports: The closest major airports to Lugano are actually in Italy, near the city of Milan: Malpensa Airport and Linate Airport (www.sea-aeroportimilano.it). To reach either, first take the 1.5-hour train to Milan's Central Station. From that station, cheap and easy shuttle buses leave about every 15 minutes for both Malpensa and Linate.

PONTRESINA, SAMEDAN,
AND ST. MORITZ

High in the mountains of the canton called Graubünden, in the southeast corner of Switzerland, two valleys meet, carving out a picturesque region called the Upper Engadine ("Oberengadin" in German). This area is rich with rugged mountain scenery and colorful folk traditions, and is a handy stopover for tourists taking the scenic Bernina Express.

There may not seem to be a lot of history here, but the trained eye sees it everywhere. Celtic people inhabited this region centuries before Christ. The hillsides are still terraced, recalling the hard work that came with farming up here in ancient times. History is in the region's unique language, too: Romansh is a vulgar form of Latin that arrived here with the Etruscans, who were chased here as Rome expanded. Town names date back to various invaders. For instance, "Pontresina" comes from "Bridge of the Saracens."

The most famous town here is the glitzy ski resort of St. Moritz, but for a more authentic Back Door experience, head for Pontresina or Samedan—where workaday Swiss people go to find some high-altitude fun. In these towns, you don't find English newspapers—an indication that while there are many visitors, most are from nearby.

Planning Your Time

The three towns in this chapter—Pontresina, Samedan, and St. Moritz—form a convenient little triangle, each about 10 minutes apart by train. With a full day here and some good planning, you can sample all three and throw in a hike to boot. This area isn't worth a long detour, but it happens to link two scenic rail trips: the Bernina Express and the Glacier Express (see Scenic Rail Journeys

PONTRESINA, SAMEDAN, AND ST. MORITZ AREA

chapter). Hop off the train, set up a home base, explore—then continue on your way.

This remote region has two distinct tourist seasons: summer (June–Oct) and winter (Dec–March). Outside of these seasons, many places are closed and the area can feel dead.

Guest Card: If you're staying more than two nights here, your hotelier may give you a free "Mountain Railways Inclusive" card, which covers most transportation in the Upper Engadine region, including lifts, trains, and buses, as well as guided hikes. Not all hoteliers give it out, and of those who do, some require two-night rather than three-night stays. Ask at your hotel.

Winter Activities: If you're here in winter and want to ski some of the most famous slopes in the world, head for Corviglia, the largest ski area in the region, which offers varied terrain, mostly intermediate runs, and good snowboarding (convenient from St. Moritz, or a bus ride from Pontresina). Other areas to consider are

Corvatsch–Furtschellas (great views, bus #2 from St. Moritz or Pontresina) and Diavolezza–Lagalb (smaller, less crowded, mostly intermediate and expert runs, great for non-skiers who want views). Both cater mainly to intermediate and expert skiers. See www.bergbahnenengadin.ch for more information, and to buy lift tickets in advance. Winter isn't just about hitting the slopes, though—the area has more than 100 miles of cross-country skiing trails, great sledding, Nordic walking, and spectator sports such as polo in the snow (horses and all). Ask at the TI for information.

Pontresina

Pontresina—a popular winter and summer mountain resort with about 2,000 residents—makes a good Graubünden home base. At 6,000 feet above sea level on a wind-protected terrace overlooking the Bernina Valley, Pontresina faces southwest and enjoys plenty of sunshine. Popular trails through its larch forests offer spectacular views of the 13,000-foot Piz Bernina peak and the immense Morteratsch glacier.

Pontresina's first tourists, mostly German and British, arrived in the 1850s. For a while, it was a summer-only destination. But by the early 1900s, the Muottas Muragl railway was inaugurated, the first grand hotels were built, and tourists began showing up in winter, too.

ORIENTATION

Pontresina sits above a river overlooking its valley. Virtually everything of interest (except the train station) is along Via Maistra (may-strah), which means "Main Street" in Romansh.

Tourist Information
The TI is in the heart of town in the slick Rondo Culture and Congress Center (July–Aug Mon–Fri 8:30–18:00, Sat 8:30–12:00 & 15:00–18:00, Sun 16:00–18:00, shorter hours off-season, tel. 081-838-8300, fax 081-838-8310, www.pontresina.com).

Arrival in Pontresina
The train station lies at the foot of the town. You can take a 10-minute uphill walk to the city center, following the white signs to Pontresina. Or, easier, take bus #1 or #2 to Pontresina Post (2/hr, 2.80 SF, free with Swiss Pass, buy ticket at counter inside train station). Walking the 10 minutes from Pontresina back down to the train station on Via da Mulin offers spectacular gorge views along the way.

Graubünden

Switzerland's biggest canton, isolated by high mountain ranges, is also one of its most conservative. The name Graubünden goes back to 1395, when a group of farmers wearing gray clothes organized themselves in the "Gray League" to fight for their autonomy. This fiercely independent region didn't join the Swiss Confederation until 1803.

People in Graubünden believe the best way to control nature is to obey it. Passionate about their environment, they purify all dirty water before returning it to the rivers. Locals are currently going through the expensive process of removing canals (built to direct streams and rivers) and allowing the water to choose its own course once again. The natives love their beautiful countryside and cherish their customs—predictably voting against EU membership and other issues that might compromise Swiss neutrality and self-determination.

Graubünden has three official languages: German, Italian, and Romansh (an ancient dialect that comes directly from Latin). You'll overhear conversations where one person speaks Italian, the other replies in German, a third butts in with Romansh...and everybody understands each other. On the trains, the announcements are in German and Romansh.

Graubünden cuisine is hearty. Try *Pizokel*, a *Spätzle*-like creation of cheesy flour dumplings. In fall, you might find *Pizokel* made from chestnut flour and served with wild mushroom stew. The Graubünden's air-dried beef, *Bündnerfleisch*—very expensive and sliced paper-thin—is popular throughout Switzerland. *Capuns* are cabbage leaves stuffed with a mix of dough, leeks, bacon, onion, and air-dried beef. *Bündner Gerstensuppe* is a creamy barley and vegetable soup. For a Graubünden dessert, it's got to be *Nusstorte*, a rich walnut cake.

Helpful Hints

Internet Access: You'll find public Internet terminals at **Hotel Post** (8 SF/30 min, daily 8:00–21:00, closed in May, Via Maistra) and **Hotel Saratz** (5 SF/30 min, June–Sept open 24/7, closed Oct–May, opposite TI on Via Maistra). Most hotels offer Internet access (generally for a fee) to their guests.

Local Guide: Ulla Währer is a charming and knowledgeable guide with expertise on the whole region (100 SF/1 hour, 150 SF/2 hours, 180 SF/4 hours, 300 SF/day, tel. 081-832-1381, ulla.waehrer@freesurf.ch).

Ski Rental: Try **Gruber Sport** (on Via Maistra across from Hotel Schweizerhof, tel. 081-842-6236) or **Engadina Sport** (also on main drag at Via Maistra 40, tel. 081-842-6262).

SIGHTS AND ACTIVITIES

Church of St. Mary—Above town, next to the five-sided, 13th-century Spaniola Tower, stands this remarkable little church (limited hours, generally July–Oct Mon–Fri 15:30–17:30, closed Sat–Sun). Faded 13th-century, Byzantine-inspired frescoes survive on the west wall. The other walls and ceiling were richly decorated by an Italian workshop (1497). The bright colors are original; it's never been repainted. The frescoes depict the legend of Mary Magdalene and (above) the story of Lazarus' resurrection. Imagine this church packed with illiterate villagers five centuries ago.

Alpine Museum—This little museum is worth a quick visit. Situated in an old Engadine town house, it offers exhibits on the development of alpine mountain climbing, the regional mining industry, hunting, and local animals. About 130 of the 250 different bird species found in the Upper Engadine are shown here. Listen to the recorded songs of 60 different birds on their primitive aviary jukebox. The 20-minute slideshow is in German and makes you feel like a wimp. Still, it's interesting for its images of "the mountain experience" (5 SF, June–Oct Mon–Sat 16:00–18:00, closed Sun, Via Maistra).

Biking—Several sports stores rent bicycles, inline skates, tennis rackets, and other gear. **Fähndrich Sport** rents good mountain bikes with various suspensions (22–25 SF/half-day, 35–40 SF/day, helmets-7 SF/half-day or 10 SF/day, Mon–Fri 8:00–12:00 & 14:00–18:30, Sat until 17:00, closed Sun except July–Aug, at Hotel Allegra on Via Maistra, tel. 081-842-7155, www.faehndrich-sport .ch). **Flying Cycles,** at the Pontresina train station, rents a huge selection of mountain bikes and fun, easy-to-learn electric-powered bikes (23 SF/half-day, 31 SF/day, both rates 5 SF cheaper with Swiss Pass, helmets-8 SF, daily 6:30–19:00, tel. 081-288-5336). Riding the train to the Bernina Pass and biking nine miles back into town is just one of many fun biking options.

Bus #2 Joyride—Bus #2 runs scenically back and forth through the valley's towns and villages (2/hr, 2.80 SF). Consider it for a cheap survey of the neighborhood while connecting the three main towns. Just hop on and pay the driver or flash your Swiss Pass.

Music—Free summer classical music concerts are offered in the Tais Forest across the river, and (on rainy days) in the Rondo Center and other locations around town (daily at 11:00, mid-June–mid-Sept, confirm and get details at TI).

Swimming—The newly renovated covered public pool on Via Maistra also has a sauna (pool only-7 SF, pool and sauna-14 SF, Mon–Fri 10:00–21:00, Sat–Sun 10:00–19:00; sauna mixed-sex daily except Thu, when it's women-only).

Hiking

Pontresina is a hiker's paradise. The town boasts Switzerland's largest mountaineering school and has a good reputation for adventure sports. Shops lining Via Maistra rent all kinds of sports gear.

Upper Engadine trails come with high altitudes. Hikers should bring the appropriate gear (solid shoes, sun protection, windbreaker, hat, and water). Even in summer, with cold winds blowing down from the snow-capped mountains, it can get cold—especially on chairlifts. The sun is strong and the air is thin, so use sunscreen. Hiking trails are marked according to their difficulty. Yellow signs indicate easy hikes and walks. White-and-red signs indicate more demanding hikes, where real hiking boots are in order. Blue signs indicate alpine routes that require serious gear (these dangerous trails include rock climbing and glacier crossings).

The flowers in the Alps are protected; pick one, and you may be fined. Some meadows are also protected for haymaking. Signs ask you to stick to the trails, as trampled grass is hard to cut.

The TI has a great free brochure with a panoramic map listing the region's many hikes. Of the 80 hikes it lists and describes, consider this one first...

Pontresina to Muottas Muragl to Alp Languard—For maximum alpine thrills per calorie burned, consider this three-hour hike. It comes with grand views and takes you gradually down 1,000 feet in altitude. From Pontresina (6,000 feet), catch bus #1 or #2 (2/hr, 2.80 SF) to the Muottas Muragl funicular (19 SF one-way, 29-SF combo-ticket also covers your trip back down to Pontresina on the Alp Languard lift, see below for details).

The funicular lifts you to a lofty restaurant (8,105 feet), from where you hike over to Alp Languard (7,710 feet). Midway, there's a great soup or coffee-and-cakes stop (ask for the WC key for a fun alpine memory). Each year, a different appreciation-of-nature theme is displayed along this trail. Keep your eyes open for ibex, bighorn stags, and marmots.

At Alp Languard, a chalet serves reasonably priced traditional meals (see page 243). From Alp Languard, hike or ride the lift down to Pontresina (13 SF one-way, 20 SF round-trip, lift covered by 29-SF Muottas Muragl combo-ticket described previously, runs daily 8:30–17:30).

Other Hikes—A fun way to explore the nearby Roseg Valley and marvel at its glacier (from a distance) is to hike two hours up the valley and take the horse-drawn "omnibus" back to Pontresina (reservations required, June–Oct departures at fixed hours, 22 SF one-way, 32 SF round-trip, tel. 081-842-6057, Luigi Costa). You can also rent a private carriage (100 SF one-way, 150 SF round-trip).

Consider taking the train up to the Bernina Pass (7,000 feet), hike around for a couple of hours, then take the train back—or, to get even higher, ride the cable car from the Bernina Pass up to Diavolezza (9,930 feet, 22 SF one-way, 32 SF round-trip, 2/hr, daily 8:30–17:00).

The TI offers various guided hikes with themes, such as "Experiencing Wilderness with Marmots and Ibex" (ask at TI for price, free with Mountain Railways Inclusive guest card—see page 235, cable-car ride costs 13 SF one-way, 20 SF return, 3–4 hikes per week, reservations required). While the hikes are guided in German, some mountaineers speak English and can be hired privately through the TI.

Near Pontresina: Muottas Muragl

This impressive alpine perch (8,105 feet) overlooking Samedan is accessible by foot (from Pontresina) or by funicular. To reach the funicular, you can either take bus #1 or #2 from Pontresina, or you can catch the train between Pontresina and Samedan and get off at Punt Muragl (it's a request-only stop, press the green button, or it won't stop). The funicular dates from 1907 (19 SF one-way, 27 SF round-trip, 29-SF combo-ticket lets you go up this funicular and down the Alp Languard lift, 2/hr, daily 8:00–23:00, cheaper after 18:00).

Once up top on Muottas Muragl, you can hike, lounge around on deck chairs (10-SF rental), have a meal (self-service or pricey but good restaurant), or even spend the night. Keep an eye out for alpine animals.

Sleeping at Muottas Muragl: **$$ Alpine Hotel Muottas Muragl** offers a secluded overnight high in the Alps. When the lift takes the last tourist down, things become as peaceful as the Alps can be. Rooms are clean and simple (open June–Oct only, S-90 SF, S with view-100 SF, D-160 SF, D with view-180 SF, Q-280 SF, tel. 081-842-8232, fax 081-842-8290, www.muottasmuragl.ch, info@muottasmuragl.ch).

SHOPPING

Many sports and souvenir shops line Via Maistra. A typical product from the Upper Engadine is furniture carved from Arven pine (a.k.a. Scotch pine). The pine, special to this region, starts out light, darkens with time, and has spots where the branches used to be. Look for the tree's characteristic five-needle clusters when hiking.

Rominger Möbel, a local furniture store, makes the Arven pine furniture it sells. Its upstairs showroom is like a modern Engadine home show—walking among hand-carved beds, tables, and dressers gives you a sense of good living high in this remote corner of Switzerland (closed Sun, 5-min walk from town center on Via Maistra in the direction of Bernina Pass, tel. 081-842-6263, www.rominger.ch).

SLEEPING

$$$ Hotel Bernina, a well-run and woody three-star place, feels like high quality, from the friendly pick-up at the station to the traditionally clad waitresses who serve your breakfast coffee. Its rooms are a fine value for this area (Sb-110–135 SF, Db-210–260 SF depending on room and season, tel. 081-838-8686, fax 081-838-8687, www.hotelbernina.ch, info@hotelbernina.ch).

Pontresina

> ## Sleep Code
>
> **(1.10 SF = about $1, country code: 41)**
> **S** = Single, **D** = Double/Twin, **T** = Triple, **Q** = Quad, **b** = bathroom,
> **s** = shower only. Unless otherwise noted, credit cards are
> accepted, English is spoken, and breakfast is included.
>
> To help you sort easily through these listings, I've divided
> the rooms into three categories, based on the price for a stan-
> dard double room with bath:
>
> **$$$ Higher Priced**—Most rooms 180 SF or more.
>   **$$ Moderately Priced**—Most rooms between
>   130–180 SF.
>   **$ Lower Priced**—Most rooms 130 SF or less.
>
> Most hotels in this region have a severe cancellation policy (30
> days in advance with no penalty, but thereafter, you'll gener-
> ally have to pay for the entire period you reserved).

$$$ Chesa Mulin Hotel Garni, below the main street, offers modern, bright, and comfortable rooms, each with a painting depicting a local legend. An inviting sitting area with open fireplace and library makes bad weather tolerable. The friendly Isepponi-Schmid family takes good care of their guests (Sb-114 SF, Db-198 SF, sauna, sundeck, free Internet access, Via da Mulin 107, tel. 081-838-8200, fax 081-838-8230, www.chesa-mulin.ch, info@chesa-mulin.ch).

$$ Hotel Engadinerhof, while less cozy, can be a good value. Its 80 rooms gather around a sprawling and classic Old World lounge. The cheaper sink-only rooms ("Category A") are clean and have well-preserved furniture from the 1930s (S-65 SF, D-115 SF). "Category B" offers the same old-fashioned rooms, plus antique bathrooms (Sb-85 SF, Db-160 SF). "Category C" gets you modern rooms (Sb-95 SF, Db-180 SF; Internet access, Via Maistra, tel. 081-839-3100, fax 081-839-3200, www.engadinerhof.com, info @engadinerhof.com).

$ Youth Hostel Tolais, across the street from the train station, rents 120 beds. There's no curfew, and guests have 24-hour access (though check-in is limited to 16:00–18:30 & 19:30–22:00, checkout is 7:30–10:00; dorm bed-48–64 SF depending on season and number of beds in room, D-142 SF; price includes sheets, breakfast, and dinner; 7 SF less for breakfast only, members pay 6 SF less per day, self-serve restaurant—winter only, game and TV room, tel. 081-842-7223, fax 081-842-7031, www.youthhostel .ch/pontresina, pontresina@youthhostel.ch).

EATING

Virtually all restaurants in Pontresina are part of a hotel, apart from a few bakeries that serve reasonably priced meals. Picnickers will seek out the **Co-op** grocery, between the train station and the town center on Via da Mulin (Mon–Fri 8:00–12:15 & 14:00–18:30, Sat 8:00–17:00, closed Sun).

Café Puntschella is the local favorite for good, healthy, reasonably priced, local-style dishes, a 15-SF salad bar, and great desserts. With a no-frills diner ambience, it offers indoor and outdoor seating and an entertaining menu (Engadine specialties-20–25 SF, pastas-15 SF, salads-11–15 SF, daily 7:30–22:00, shorter hours off-season, Via da Mulin, tel. 081-838-8030).

Colani Stübli, a cozy eatery, serves regional and seasonal specialties (18 SF for local dishes such as *Krautpizokel* and *Capuns,* daily lunch special-20 SF, entrées-30–40 SF, daily 11:30–14:00 & 18:00–21:00, smaller dishes after 21:00, at Hotel Steinbock on Via Maistra, tel. 081-839-3626).

Bündnerstübli dishes up hearty, traditional meals with fish and game in a woody, Old World setting. Half portions are no problem. Consider being adventurous with the traditional appetizers, which work as main plates (fish and game-29–46 SF, vegetarian dishes-16–20 SF, *Fitnessteller*-28 SF, daily 18:00–21:30, at Hotel Rosatsch, Via Maistra 71, tel. 081-838-9800).

Elegant Five-Star Hotel Dining Rooms: Pontresina's two top hotels each have wonderful restaurants in sumptuous dining rooms. **Stüva-Bella Restaurant** is expensive and exclusive, with a flair for serving inventive and light regional and international cuisine. Their five-course fixed-price meal for 90–100-SF is a good splurge, but you'll be amazed at how well you can eat with only their 10-SF salad bar and a cheese plate (soups-12 SF, entrées-40–50 SF, June–Sept and Jan–March daily 19:00–22:30, closed April–May and Oct–Dec, in Hotel Walther on Via Maistra, tel. 081-839-3636). **Grand Hotel Kronenhof** dominates the town and has public rooms fit for a Vienna palace. It's less accommodating to anyone concerned about price, but if you've got francs to burn, its five-course fixed-price meal for 155 SF is a memorable splurge (Via Maistra, tel. 081-830-3030, www.kronenhof.com).

Eating Above Pontresina: **Alp Languard Chalet,** at the top of the lift (7,710 feet up—see page 240), serves affordable meals with unbeatable views (raclette-15 SF, daily special-18 SF, June–Oct daily 8:30–16:00, tel. 079-719-7810).

Samedan

Little Samedan (sah-MAY-den) offers the best possible peek at Upper Engadine culture and architecture. This village, which has the most traditional Engadine architecture of the three towns, is the historic capital of the valley. Romansh remains its first language.

Tourist Information: Samedan's TI is on Via Plazzet (Mon–Fri 8:00–12:00 & 13:30–18:00, Sat until 17:30, closed Sun, also closed Sat off-season, tel. 081-851-0060, www.samedan.ch).

SELF-GUIDED WALK

Samedan Town Stroll

There's little to do in Samedan other than relax and enjoy a stroll. For a short hike from the town center, walk uphill on Surtuor, following the white sign for *Kath. Kirch.*

The 13th-century, castle-like **stone tower** was the private tower of a noble family. From its wooden balcony, they'd oversee festivities in their little domain.

The next house up, at **#12,** dates from 1656. This X-shaped house is in the form of a St. Andrew's cross, made of extended roof beams. This was a popular way to bless homes here. Notice the sturdy beam ends—roofs were built to support heavy stones and snow. Houses come with Romansh names. You'll see *Chesa Juzi* (Juzi's House) and *Chesa dals 3 Frers* (House of the Three Brothers).

The **Catholic Church** (Neo-Romanesque from 1910, with a bell dating back to 1505) stands at the top of the town. From here, survey the surrounding slopes. Notice the ancient terracing from Celtic peoples. Continue uphill, passing the ski lift, and pause at the yellow benches for the gorgeous view. Samedan lies at the point where the two valleys of the Inn and Flaz Rivers merge. From here, the Inn River continues through Innsbruck before joining the Danube.

Huff and puff the thin air (you're at 6,000 feet) to the dramatically situated Protestant **Church of St. Peter.** The Romanesque bell tower (c. 1100) predates today's late Gothic church (c. 1480; now a burial church, generally closed to tourists).

Benches line the cemetery walls and offer sunny, wind-protected picnic spots. Beneath you stretches the highest-altitude

Traditional Engadine Architecture

Samedan and Pontresina both have fine old traditional houses. A short stroll in either town shows plenty of tradi-

tional elements and medieval ingenuity to stay warm in the harsh mountain weather. Walls are thick—typically two feet—for insulation. Notice how windows are like the narrow end of a funnel—originally covered with animal skin rather than glass. Bay windows gathered maximum precious light and came with built-in seats where women would sit to do handwork.

The structural essence of these grand farmhouses—even though thoroughly modernized—survives. You can still see the big lower door for animals, and the big upper door for hay and the carriage—with a smaller door built into it for people to get in and out while minimizing heat loss. People had the animals sleep below in the hope their rising body heat would warm the living space above. Proud noble family coats of arms still decorate buildings, as many local families can trace their heritage to the Middle Ages.

Look for the traditional Engadine *sgraffito* ornamentation on exterior walls. To make *sgraffito*, facades are covered with a layer of dark plaster, which is then covered with white or colored plaster. Decorations—which are much more durable than painted facades—are scratched within three hours through the wet white layer, so that the dark background appears. These rustic and crude decorations look modern, but have a long history.

airport in Europe, a favorite among gliders (launched by a yellow truck with a huge winch, rather than an airplane).

SLEEPING AND EATING

(1.10 SF = about \$1, country code: 41)

While Pontresina has more eating and sleeping options (see page 241), Samedan hoards the lion's share of this valley's Graubünden quaintness.

\$\$\$ Hotel Bernina, a grand hotel next to Hotel Post, will be closed much of 2008 for renovation (Db-200–250 SF, call first to see if they're open, tel. 081-852-1212, fax 081-852-3606, hotel -bernina@bluewin.ch).

$$ Hotel Post dates back to the days when people stopped here to warm up and change horses rather than to play golf and ski. Renting nine comfy, woody rooms, it's one of the few places with rustic character left in town (closed in May; Sb-75–85 SF, Db-150–160 SF, good restaurant, near train station, tel. 081-852-5354, fax 081-852-4692, www.poestli-samedan.ch, info@poestli-samedan.ch).

Eating: **Hotel Post Restaurant** is a characteristic old eatery run with a passion for the local culture (Noldi's specialties-22 SF, a fun tasting fixed-price meal for 30 SF, closed Sun). The **Bernina Pizzeria** next door is also a good value.

St. Moritz

The oldest—and perhaps best-known—winter resort in the world, St. Moritz has long been the winter haunt of Europe's rich and famous. Its sister city says it all: Vail.

It's said that in 1864, St. Moritz hotel pioneer Johannes Badrutt invented winter tourism in the Alps. To allay his British guests' skepticism, he offered them free accommodations if the winter weather was bad. They came and enjoyed fine weather. He liquored them up, they had fun...and they brought their friends along the next year. St. Moritz hosted the Winter Olympics in 1928 and 1948.

St. Moritz itself is little more than luxury hotels and designer boutiques, though it offers livelier nightlife than surrounding towns. For the jet set, winter is prime time in St. Moritz. Summer is quieter and popular with sporty types and nature lovers. While celebrity-spotting drops way, way off in the summer, prices are more reasonable. It's also a great time for hiking and adventure sports. Visitors enjoy inline skating, polo, golf, paragliding, horseback riding, and evening concerts. Cable cars zip you to some great mountaintops.

ORIENTATION

St. Moritz has two centers: the town (Dorf) and the spa (Bad). The Dorf is on a steep slope. The train station, at the foot of St. Moritz Dorf, is a downhill hike from the town center. St. Moritz Bad sprawls on a level plain along the lake. Along with the spa, you'll find all the sport facilities at St. Moritz Bad (covered pool, tennis courts, ice-skating hall, horseback riding facilities, and so on). Bus #3 connects Dorf, Bad, and the train station (4/hr, 2.60 SF).

Tourist Information

The TI is in the center of St. Moritz Dorf (July–Aug Mon–Fri 9:00–18:30, Sat 9:00–18:00, Sun 16:00–18:00; off-season Mon–Fri 9:00–12:00 & 14:00–18:00, Sat 9:00–12:00, closed Sun; Plaza Mauritius, tel. 081-837-3333, fax 081-837-3366, www.engadin .stmoritz.ch).

Arrival in St. Moritz

St. Moritz's train station is near the lake, just below the Dorf. Pick up a free map at the train information counter (lockers but no TI or bike rental at station). The train station café is a good budget eatery (9–17 SF, daily 7:00–21:00). To avoid the steep uphill hike from the train station to Dorf, hop on bus #3 (4/hr, 2.60 SF).

Helpful Hints

Altitude Alert: Don't forget that St. Moritz is at a high elevation (6,090 feet); you might feel dizzy and tired, and your body needs to adapt. Top athletes from all over the world come here for altitude training before the Olympics.

Shopping: The **Co-op** department store and grocery are on Plaza da Scoula and Via dal Bagn (Mon–Fri 8:00–18:30, Sat 8:00–17:00, closed Sun).

Ski Rental: Boom Sport, in St. Moritz Bad, has a knowledgable staff, good selection, and handy location (Via Tegiatscha 5, tel. 081-832-2222). In St. Moritz Dorf, there's **Scheuing Sport** (near bus stop and TI on Plaza da Scoula, tel. 081-833-3170).

SIGHTS

Segantini Museum—This museum is dedicated to the ultimate painter of alpine life. Giovanni Segantini came here to get away from the misty air of Milan. The crisp alpine atmosphere was great for capturing the bright, sharp, crystal-clear mountain light. Painting in the open air with brushstrokes that invigorated his fascinating scenes, Segantini created works reminiscent of the French Impressionists. The tiny museum, which looks like a Neo-Byzantine church, is actually based on Segantini's design of the Swiss Pavilion for the 1900 World's Fair in Paris—but made of local stone, rather than the originally intended steel. Segantini died young (at age 41, in 1899), and money ran out before this grandiose pavilion could be built. Segantini's masterpiece, the *Alpine Triptych,* was painted for the World's Fair, but also never completed. Segantini's ill-fated vision—both his pavilion and his life's major work—is now here, near where he settled in his thirties. His paintings are bursting with symbolism—life, nature, death. He lovingly carved the frames ornamented with the five-needled Arven pine (10 SF, June–Oct and Dec–April Tue–Sun 10:00–12:00 & 14:00–18:00, closed Mon, March–May, and Nov, take bus #2 to Via Somplaz 30, tel. 081-833-4454, www.segantini -museum.ch).

Engadiner Museum—The historic, domestic, and social cultures of the Engadine region are displayed in this museum. The building (from 1905) houses interiors from throughout the Engadine (such as a patrician living room, a smoky farm kitchen, and a four-poster bed), as well as an exhibit on the discovery of the spa water that put St. Moritz on the vacation map (5 SF, Mon–Fri 9:30–12:00 & 14:00–17:00, Sun 10:00–12:00, closed Sat and May, Via dal Bagn 39, take bus #3 to Via Aruons, tel. 081-833-4333).

SLEEPING

(1.10 SF = about $1, country code: 41)

$$ Youth Hostel Stille, at the boring, residential eastern end of St. Moritz Bad, offers 190 beds and all the services, activities, games, and lavish extras a top-end hostel can have (dorm bed-48 SF, D-122 SF, Db-144 SF, price includes breakfast and three-course dinner, prices about 10 SF higher in winter, members pay 6 SF less, reception open 7:00–10:00 & 16:00–22:00, 10-min walk from bus stop on Via Sela, Via Surpunt 60, tel. 081-833-3969, fax 081-833-8046, www.youthhostel.ch/st.moritz, st.moritz @youthhostel.ch).

EATING

As in Pontresina, most of St. Moritz's restaurants are in hotels. An exception is **Restaurant Engiadina,** famous for its raclette and fondues (35 SF, lunch specials around 19 SF, Mon–Sat 11:30–14:00 & 18:15–21:30, closed Sun, in center of St. Moritz Dorf at Plaza da Scuola).

Veltlinerkeller, decorated with a huge stuffed moose head, serves a variety of grilled meats and Italian specialties (lunch special-18 SF, entrées-26–30 SF, daily 9:00–14:00 & 17:00–23:00, in St. Moritz Bad at Via dal Bagn 11, tel. 081-833-4009).

Restaurant Hauser is the standard stop for local workers who know where to find the best-value meal in town (long hours daily, below Hotel Hauser at Via Traunter Plazzas 71, tel. 081-837-5050).

TRANSPORTATION CONNECTIONS

By Train: **St. Moritz, Pontresina,** and **Samedan** are all connected to each other by train (hourly, 10 min, 4.60 SF). From these towns, trains go to **Chur** (hourly, 2 hrs), **Tirano** (hourly, 2.5 hrs), and **Zürich** (hourly, 3.75 hrs, transfer in Chur). From Pontresina, you may have to change in Samedan. For details on the Bernina Express and Glacier Express, see the Scenic Rail Journeys chapter. Train info: toll tel. 0900-300-3004 or www.rail.ch.

By Bus: Bus #2 connects Pontresina, Punt Muragl, Samedan, and St. Moritz (2/hr, 2.80 SF).

St. Moritz

SCENIC RAIL JOURNEYS

Golden Pass • William Tell Express • Bernina Express •
Glacier Express

Switzerland has one of the world's best rail networks—and many of its tracks run through some of the world's best scenery. While just about any train ride in Switzerland is photogenic, four are aggressively marketed as the most spectacular: the Golden Pass, William Tell Express, Bernina Express, and Glacier Express. If you're looking for a scenic day enjoying the Alps from the window of your train, and would like to do it in one of Switzerland's unique "panorama cars" (offering huge windows that sweep halfway across the ceiling), these journeys can be great experiences. While they aren't quite as "fantastic with countless highlights" as they're advertised to be (the high lifts in ski areas like the Berner Oberland are much higher and more breathtaking), the trains are a fun way to do some sightseeing while getting from point A to point B.

This chapter provides you with all the logistical, nuts-and-bolts information you'll need to splice each of these journeys into your itinerary. I've also written a commentary on each route, describing the highlights in the direction that most travelers are likely to go. If you travel in the opposite direction, the same information still applies—just hold the book upside down.

This chapter also includes information about Chur, a town that's not really worth a visit, except that it lies at the intersection of the Bernina Express and Glacier Express routes. Chur makes for a handy pit stop or overnight if connecting these trips.

Tickets

Schedules Can Change: In this chapter, I've listed specific departure and arrival times, but these schedules are always subject to

SCENIC SWISS RAIL ROUTES

GERMANY

FRANCE

•Zürich

Luzern•

•Boat

AUSTRIA

Flüelen

Landquart

•Wassen

Chur

Inter-
laken

Davos

Spiez•

•Andermatt

Disentis

•Filisur

Lausanne

•Zweisimmen

Airolo

St. Moritz

•Gstaad

Montreux

Brig

Pontresina

Visp

Poschiavo•

•Geneva

Locarno•

•Bellinzona

Tirano

Zermatt•

Sorico

Bus

Lugano•

Menaggio

ITALY

- - - - - - Golden Pass   ———— William Tell Express

- - - - - Glacier Express   ———— Bernina Express

change—it's essential to confirm the times before you travel. Timetables for most of these trains appear on the Swiss Rail website: www.rail.ch. (Also try Germany's all-Europe rail site, http://bahn.hafas.de/bin/query.exe/en; or call the Swiss Rail info line at 0900-300-3004, 1.20 SF/min.) Any train station in Switzerland can provide you with free schedules. Each scenic rail line also operates its own website, with even more details (listed in each section, below).

Buying Tickets: Tickets and reservations for all of these scenic rail lines—including those run by private rail companies—can be purchased at any train station in Switzerland. In the US, you'll pay more (about $20 per order) to get tickets and reservations through your travel agent or at www.raileurope.com. Getting your reservations before you go also limits your flexibility, as reservations made through US agents are nonchangeable and nonrefundable—unlike reservations made at train stations in Europe.

Reservations: You can book these journeys as early as two months ahead, or as late as the day before (at any Swiss train station or on the various websites). The Glacier Express requires reservations. If you want to take the official tourist package for the William Tell Express or Bernina Express, reservations are also required. Reserve the Golden Pass only if you want a front-row VIP seat. To save money and maximize your flexibility, you can take standard (non-panoramic) trains on the Golden Pass, William

Tell Express, and Bernina Express routes without a reservation (though the bus segment of the Bernina Express requires a reservation, it's easy to purchase from the driver on the bus). These alternatives are explained in each section below.

Eurailpass and Swiss Pass: Two major types of railpasses can be useful in Switzerland: A Eurailpass (Global Pass or Selectpass that includes Switzerland) and a Swiss Pass. These railpasses cover most of your travel on the scenic rail journeys. But seat reservations always cost extra, and some trips aren't fully covered by a railpass: Even if you have a Eurailpass or Swiss Pass, you'll pay 38 SF extra for the William Tell Express package trip. However, traveling the same route on standard trains, rather than on the designated tourist trains, is fully covered by a railpass. And on the Glacier Express, two different segments of the trip are free with a Swiss Pass, but not covered by a Eurailpass (with a Eurailpass, Disentis to Brig costs 45 SF second-class; Brig to Zermatt costs 34 SF).

When booking your ticket or buying reservations, make sure the ticket agent understands what type of pass you have (if any) and exactly what trip you're taking. Confirm that you've gotten all the reservations and other tickets you need to complete your trip. While rail agents generally know what railpasses cover, sometimes they don't—leading to frustrating run-ins with conductors who insist that you've only paid for part of your trip.

Train Types

Various types of trains, with various types of cars, run these routes. Here are some key distinctions to look for:

Classes: Most trains have first- and second-class cars. In bigger train stations, a digital panel on the tracks indicates departure time, destination, and the composition of the train (that is, at which part of the platform you'll find the first- or second-class cars).

Panoramic vs. Standard Cars: All of the routes in this chapter offer special panoramic cars. On some trains—such as Golden Pass and Bernina Express—all of the cars are panoramic, so there's no need to splurge for first class. On other trains, such as Glacier Express and William Tell Express, you can choose between more expensive panoramic (first-class) and cheaper standard (second-class) cars.

Panoramic cars have huge, wrap-around windows, allowing you to see through part of the ceiling. The Golden Pass trains go one better: The driver sits in a little bubble upstairs, leaving the very fro͟ VIP seating with completely unobstructe͟ ing up. The windows in the panoramic c͟ meaning that photographs often suffer fr͟ (even with air-conditioning) can heat up on sunny da͟

Standard cars are typical train cars, featuring regular wᴉ͟ dows. With a smaller field of vision than the panoramic cars, these require a little more bobbing and weaving to enjoy the views. Aside from being cheaper, the chief advantage of the standard cars is that the windows generally can be opened, for cool air and photos without reflections. Passengers in panoramic cars are free to walk to the standard cars to open a window and snap a photo.

Standard vs. Tourist Trains: In many cases, standard trains operated by Swiss Rail run these same routes—more frequently, and usually less expensively (though you'll sacrifice things like

fancy dining cars and souvenir key chains). Because standard trains are used by local commuters, they may stop at more stations along the route than the designed-for-tourists panoramic trains. Many travelers enjoy the flexibility of following the scenic route on standard trains, enabling them to hop off and explore a village, then hop on the next standard train that comes through—without the headache of reservations (which are almost never necessary on standard trains).

Golden Pass

The exceptionally picturesque Golden Pass train route cuts a swath diagonally across the pristine center of Switzerland, connecting Zürich with Lake Geneva. Of all the rail journeys in this chapter, its central location—lacing together many of Switzerland's top sights—makes the Golden Pass the one you're most likely to take.

ORIENTATION

The Route
The Golden Pass officially runs between the cities of Zürich and Geneva, but most travelers focus on the segment between Luzern and Lake Geneva's Montreux. Better yet, hone in even more tightly—on the very best stretch, from Interlaken to Montreux.

Special panoramic cars are used between Luzern and Montreux. Because the tracks change from narrow to standard

narrow again, two train changes are required (at Inter-
Ost/East and Zweisimmen).

Route Breakdown: The entire Golden Pass route (almost 8
rs) is run by various companies and involves several train changes.
Here's the breakdown.

Zürich to Luzern: Standard trains run by Swiss Rail (2/hr,
1 hr).

Luzern to Interlaken Ost/East: Narrow-gauge panoramic
trains run by Brünig Railway (5/day, 2 hrs); also standard trains by
Swiss Rail (hourly, 2 hrs).

Interlaken Ost/East to Zweisimmen: Direct panoramic
trains run by Golden Pass (2/day, 1 hr); also standard trains run by
Swiss Rail (at least hourly, 1–1.5 hrs).

Zweisimmen to Montreux: Direct, narrow-gauge panoramic
trains run by Golden Pass (5/day, 2 hrs); also standard trains run
by Swiss Rail (9/day, 2 hrs).

Montreux to Geneva: Standard trains run by Swiss Rail
(hourly, 1 hr).

Planning Your Time: Because it connects so many knock-
out Swiss destinations (Zürich, Luzern, Interlaken, and Lake
Geneva)—and because it goes in both directions—the Golden
Pass can be spliced into your itinerary in many different ways.
I'd focus on the best stretch, using it to connect Interlaken and
Lake Geneva (3 hrs total, including the lovely 2-hr segment from
Zweisimmen to Montreux).

However you use it, check schedules along the way and plan
your layovers strategically to maximize time on the panoramic
cars. For example, if traveling from Luzern to Lake Geneva, consider taking the 8:55 panoramic train from Luzern to Interlaken
Ost/East (arriving 10:45), then wander Interlaken and have lunch
before catching the 13:25 panoramic train to Montreux (change
trains in Zweisimmen at 14:23, arrive Montreux at 16:13).
Lausanne is a little further - 25 min.

Cost and Schedule

The Golden Pass trip from Luzern to Montreux costs 67 SF second class; just the "best of" segment from Interlaken to Montreux
is 47 SF. The entire ride is covered by a Eurailpass or Swiss Pass.
Reservations, while not required, are recommended for summer
midmorning departures and the super-scenic front seats (15 SF for
front-row VIP seats, 7 SF for other seats in panoramic cars; more
details under "Seating," next page).

Special panoramic cars—some with front-row VIP seating—
depart several times each day. Standard trains run from Spiez to
Montreux every hour (2-hr trip, change trains in Zweisimmen).
These regular regional trains show you the same scenery without
the big windows.

Information: Most of the route is part of the Swiss Rail network. Special panoramic trains on the Luzern–Interlaken route are run by Brünig Railway (www.bruenig.ch). Panoramic trains on the section between Zweisimmen and Montreux are operated by MOB (Montreux–Oberland Bernois; tel. 0900-245-245 within Switzerland, from elsewhere in Europe dial 00-41-840-245-245, from the US call 011-41-840-245-245, www.mob.ch). For more on the full route, see www.goldenpass.ch. An English-language guidebook describing the route is sold on the train (12 SF).

Seating: Both standard and panoramic trains run the entire Luzern–Montreux route.

The lovely stretch from Zweisimmen to Montreux is covered by standard trains (9/day); trains with panoramic cars (2/day); and

some special "Grande Vue" trains with both typical panoramic cars and special VIP seats (3/day May–Nov, 1/day Dec–April). On these "Grande Vue" cars, the conductor drives the train from a little domed area upstairs—leaving both the front and back of the train open for passengers. The first two rows, offering VIP seats with an unobstructed view of the pristine alpine scenery coming right at you, require a supplement of 15 SF (reserve in advance, or just grab one if available and pay the conductor on the spot). The non-supplement seats just behind the supplement seats give you a bit of the grand front view (and cheapskates have been known to grab a few free minutes up front). The panoramic cars have first- and second-class seating (with panoramic ceilings in both—no need to spring for first class, unless you want VIP seats). Cars have standard seating mixed with lounge areas with sofas, tables, and a bar.

Note that on the Luzern–Interlaken section, you'll need to choose between panoramic (first class) and non-panoramic (second class) cars.

SELF-GUIDED TOUR

I've described only the best and most visually exciting portion of the Golden Pass journey, the three-hour stretch from Interlaken to Lake Geneva, focusing on the *crème de la crème*—the two hours between Zweisimmen and Montreux (described from north to south).

As you pull out of Interlaken, the train cruises along the south bank of **Lake Thun** (Thunersee). Interlaken ("between the lakes") is situated between the big lakes of Thun and Brienz. Before long, at the town of Spiez, you'll split off and head southwest to Zweisimmen.

Leaving Zweisimmen, you'll roll through **Simmental** valley, famous among American farmers for its top-end cows. Big farmhouses lie scattered in the lush meadows—an indication that the farmland is good here. The large wooden buildings are typical of Bernese farm architecture: housing the barn, sheltering the crops, and storing agricultural machines, all under one huge roof. Farming is heavily subsidized in Switzerland, and farmers form the strongest economic lobby. Trying to increase their modest income, many farmers have switched to exotic crops (like melons) or animals. These days, ostriches, yaks, bison, and highland cattle have become a common sight in the Swiss Alps.

Between Saanenmoser and Schonried, the train reaches its highest point (about 4,000 feet) and stops at the famous resort town of **Gstaad.** Although known as a favorite hangout for famous "backpackers," such as Monaco's Princess Caroline, Liz Taylor, Roger Moore, and Michael Jackson, the town does not offer many exciting sights. In winter, the modest ski slopes are not as crowded as the flashy nightspots, as most of the skiers are more into *après-*ski activities. Sipping their cocktails, they eye each other and discuss the latest trends in ski gear fashion. In summer, Gstaad hosts the Swiss Open tennis, polo, and golf tournaments, as well as music festivals. Violin virtuoso Yehudi Menuhin founded the Menuhin Festival here. While it started as an opportunity for young classical musicians to show their talent, today it's known for high-quality classical concerts.

Just south of Gstaad, you say *auf Wiedersehen* to the German-speaking part of Switzerland and *bonjour* to **French Switzerland.** The mountains are jagged. In fact, many are called *dents,* the French word for "teeth." With the change in language, you'll also see a change in culture and architecture. French-style gray stone houses are replacing half-timbered, woody, German-style chalets. The mountain airstrips—generally made for the Swiss Air Force during World War II—are used today for sightseeing flights around the Alps. The cute village of Rougemont, with its traditional chalets, is famous among the Swiss as the place where the wealthy send their girls to boarding school.

Happy **cows** spend their summers on the Alps, wandering freely and munching the fragrant herbs of these lush alpine meadows. The resulting milk is the secret ingredient for tasty Gruyère cheese. On steep hillsides here, the grass is still cut by hand. It dries in the summer sun, then is collected and stored in the barns to serve as cow salads through the winter (see "Swiss Cow Culture" sidebar in Gimmelwald chapter, page 134).

You might consider interrupting your journey in **Château**

Golden Pass

d'Oex, known for its Hot-Air Ballooning Week (last week of January). Bertrand Piccard and Brian Jones took off from here on March 1, 1999, and sailed their balloon all the way around the world. Below the train station, Le Chalet restaurant gives insight on Gruyère cheese production.

South of Château d'Oex, the valley narrows to a deep gorge. Up on the hillsides, the damage of the devastating 1999 winter storm "**Lothar**" can still be seen. Entire forests were leveled, aggravating the already precarious avalanche situation. The trees on the steep slopes stop the snow from sliding down and burying the villages. Once the trees are gone, they don't grow back. Artificial avalanche barriers need to be erected. Landslides and floods have been relatively common in recent years—an unfortunate consequence of uncontrolled deforestation and construction of vacation homes in areas that traditionally served as pastures and forestlands.

The small **lake** is dammed and used for hydroelectric power. Switzerland makes good use of its Alps for production of electricity. Although it has some nuclear power plants, 60 percent of Switzerland's energy is hydroelectric. The country exports its electricity to France and Italy.

Montbovon is the place to change trains if you're going to Bulle or Gruyères (see "French Swiss Countryside," page 217). After the first tunnel, an inscription on the barn to the right welcomes the traveler in the Gruyère region: *La Gruyère vous salue.*

The train winds its way uphill with more curves and tunnels than before. Passing through the **Jaman Tunnel,** you're engulfed in nearly two miles of darkness, then you emerge in another world—leaving the feudal Middle Ages and entering the 19th-century belle époque. At the village of Les Avants, one of Switzerland's oldest winter resorts, you catch the first glimpses of Lake Geneva sprawling deep underneath you and begin a steep descent. A series of sharp bends in tunnels takes you out of the mountains and down to lake level.

The architecture has even more of a French flair now that you've entered the "**Swiss Riviera.**" Palm trees, vines, and many sanatoriums indicate this is a warmer climate. You're surrounded by the vineyards of the Lavaux region, famous for its white wine. The view broadens to include the French Alps of Savoy across the lake, the lakeshore of the Swiss Riviera to the west, and the broad Rhône Valley to the east. As you approach Montreux—with its grand hotels—the train meanders its way intimately through private gardens.

Montreux has the only train station in Europe with three different rail gauges: regular, narrow (which you're on), and very skinny (for the Rochers de Naye train, taking sightseers to a nearby peak with views less exciting than those you've just enjoyed).

From here, it's an easy train trip to Lausanne, or a quick bus ride or about a one-mile lakefront hike to Château de Chillon (see Lake Geneva chapter).

TRANSPORTATION CONNECTIONS

From Luzern by Train to: Zürich (3/hr, 1 hr), **Zürich Airport** (2/hr, 1.25 hrs, half with change in Zürich), **Bern** (hourly, 1 hr; or 2/hr with transfer in Olten, 1.5 hrs), **Lugano** (hourly, 3 hrs, half with change in Arth-Goldau), **Chur** (hourly, 2.25 hrs, change in Thalwil).

From Interlaken by Train to: Lauterbrunnen (hourly, 20 min, 7 SF each way), **Spiez** (3/hr, 20 min), **Brienz** (2/hr, 20 min), **Bern** (2/hr, 55 min), **Zürich** and **Zürich Airport** (hourly, 2–2.25 hrs, most direct, but some with transfer in Bern, Luzern, and/or Spiez).

From Montreux by Train to: Lausanne (4/hr, 25 min), **Bern** (2/hr, 1.5 hrs, transfer in Lausanne), **Geneva** (2/hr, 1 hr).

William Tell Express

The William Tell Express figures it deserves the most famous name in Switzerland. Tell exists only in legend, but his story—being forced to shoot an apple off his son's head because he refused to bow to the Hapsburg hat—helped inspire the Swiss to rebel against their Hapsburg rulers. The train route crosses the place where the first Swiss cantons pledged "all for one and one for all," the birthplace of the Confoederatio Helvetica in 1291. The trip is half by boat and half by train from Luzern to the Italian-speaking region of Ticino (the towns of Lugano and Locarno).

Don't go out of your way to do this trip. The boat ride is low-altitude and more pastoral than thrilling, and the train ride is more interesting as a lesson in Swiss engineering than impressive for its views. (Because the train cuts through the highest mountains inside the Gotthard tunnel, it only reaches 3,600 feet above sea level.)

But if you're connecting Luzern and Italian Switzerland anyway, this route is undeniably scenic. You can book the official "William Tell Express" trip, or simply buy regular tickets with none of the hoopla. I'd save money and gain flexibility by just riding the boat and train on regular departures and skip the much-promoted tourist package. Even if you don't buy the package, you can still ride the fancy panorama train (without a seat reservation) at no extra charge.

ORIENTATION

The Route

The William Tell Express begins with a slow boat trip on Lake Luzern from the city of Luzern to Flüelen (3.5 hrs). Then a train cuts down into the Italian-speaking canton of Ticino (2 hrs). In the town of Bellinzona, you'll choose between two end points: Lugano or Locarno (I prefer Lugano).

The 3.5-hour boat trip from Luzern to Flüelen is lazy and very pretty. As the traditional steamer blows its old-time horn, you glide by idyllic lakeside resort towns and under mighty peaks. If you're in a hurry, you can get a flavor for the lake by doing a shorter round-trip cruise during your time in Luzern. Then take the train to Flüelen (1 hr from Luzern, as opposed to 3.5 hrs by boat); you'll see essentially the same scenery as the William Tell "Express" boat, but three times faster.

Whether you ride the boat or train from Luzern, in Flüelen you can join the William Tell Express panoramic train (departs Flüelen at 12:16 and 15:16). In Bellinzona, you can either transfer to a non-panoramic train to Lugano or stay on the same train to Locarno.

Another option is to skip Flüelen entirely. Standard (non-panoramic) trains make the Luzern–Lugano trip along the same route hourly in each direction (3 hrs total).

Cost and Schedule

The value of buying the official William Tell Express tourist trip (158 SF first class, 126 SF second class) is dubious. The only things that come "extra" with this pricey package are a mediocre lunch on the boat, a reserved seat on the panoramic train, a brochure about the route, and a souvenir Swiss Army–knife keychain. Travelers using a Eurailpass or Swiss Pass pay a 38-SF reservation fee to buy this official trip—but you're better off skipping the package altogether. Your railpass already covers the entire route, including the boat (but not the lunch or the seat reservation—neither of which is necessary anyway).

There are two official William Tell Express departures daily in each direction (running May–Oct only). Going north to south: The boat leaves Luzern at 9:20 and 11:25, docks in Flüelen where the panoramic train departs at 12:16 and 15:16, and arrives in Lugano at 14:46 and 17:46. Going south to north: The train departs Lugano at 10:12 and 12:12, meets the boat in Flüelen at 12:20 and 15:03, and arrives in Luzern at 15:12 and 18:25. As always, remember to confirm all times.

Information: The official William Tell Express departures are operated by the Lake Luzern Navigation Company (tel. 041-367-6767, www.lakelucerne.ch). For more information, see www.wilhelmtellexpress.ch.

Helpful Hints

Boat Ride: If you're doing the full William Tell Express route, board the boat at pier 1 across from the Luzern train station. Present your ticket and pick up your package deal, including a lunch voucher and information flyers. There's no real baggage check on the boat; travelers just stack their backpacks and suitcases in a corner.

Lunch: The official William Tell Express boat trip comes with a forgettable lunch.

Train Trip: On the official William Tell Express train from Flüelen, you'll find first class and the panoramic car way out on the platform in sector C. Yellow slips mark which seats are reserved. If you have no reservation, take any seat without a yellow marker.

Wm. Tell Exp.

SELF-GUIDED TOUR

Here's what you'll see if you're doing the entire William Tell Express route. If you're taking only the train, skip to that section.

William Tell Boat Trip

The boat trip crisscrosses **Vierwaldstättersee** (the "Lake of Four Forest Cantons"—or simply "Lake Luzern"). The trip is popular with the older generation of European tourists, who eat and drink their way through the lazy route. On a sunny day, you can sit on the deck enjoying the mountain views. Survey the boat before you settle on a seat—considering sun, shade, and wind.

After two hours, you sail into the **Canton of Uri** and the landscape gets rougher, the slopes steeper, and the villages fewer and more rustic. This is William Tell country. The legendary Swiss national hero represents the essence of the country's spirit, still felt today: the desire for independence from foreign rule. William Tell has been a popular muse: Schiller wrote a play about him based on ancient Swiss chronicles, and Rossini set the legend to music in an 1829 opera.

Swiss patriots get excited as the boat approaches **Rütli**. The meadow above is the birthplace of the Swiss Confederation. In 1291, three representatives of the founding cantons met here and swore allegiance to each other, against their oppressive Hapsburg neighbors. More than 700 years later, Switzerland is still a confederation—but now it's up to 26 cantons.

Some hikers choose to disembark at Rütli and head for the mystical meadow marked by a big Swiss flag. Then they follow the **Weg der Schweiz** ("Path of Switzerland"), a trail leading around the lake. Along the way, they contemplate stone signs representing each of the 26 cantons in the order they joined the union. The canton markers are spaced according to each canton's population (the 20-mile-long trail is designed to have exactly 5 millimeters for each Swiss citizen).

Later, the boat stops at **Tellskapelle.** This 16th-century frescoed chapel marks another legendary spot—where William Tell jumped ship on the way to prison and swam to freedom.

The last stop is **Flüelen,** where the panoramic train awaits.

William Tell Train Trip

From Flüelen, the train climbs from 1,540 feet up to 3,600 feet, at the Gotthard tunnel—the primary north–south transportation route through the Alps. You enter a classic alpine world of snowcapped mountains towering above wild valleys, with narrow gorges carved by eons of angry white water. Wooden chalets, pine forests, and lush meadows dotted with munching cows complete this image of picture-perfect Central Switzerland.

The train tracks are protected from avalanches, landslides, and waterfalls by concrete galleries. Gazing out the window, you'll see some of the greatest accomplishments of Swiss road and railroad engineering. **Wassen,** marked by its striking chapel, is the climax for trainspotters—with more trains passing per minute than just about anywhere else. First, the chapel is on your right. Then the train loops around the tiny town, and the chapel is on your left. Your train disappears into a tunnel, and when you emerge, the same chapel is still there. The train actually spirals up the slopes. (The William Tell Express package comes with a schematic map that illustrates this.)

Göschenen (where you can transfer to Andermatt and on to the Glacier Express—see page 271) is the last stop before the 9.5-mile-long **Gotthard tunnel.** After 10 minutes of rocketing through darkness, you emerge in a whole different world—a different climate, canton (Ticino, rather than Uri), and language (Italian, rather than German). Since the 13th century—long before this tunnel was built—the Gotthard Pass has been *the* major trade route over this part of the Alps, connecting northern and southern Europe. The trade continues to rumble under rather than over the

Wm. Tell Exp.

pass. These days, heavy truck traffic brings pollution and traffic jams—but little money—to Switzerland. But an ambitious new high-speed train tunnel, currently under construction, will allow shippers to transport merchandise by train and get trucks off the roads.

Welcome to **Ticino,** Switzerland's botanical garden. While the weather around Lake Luzern is often iffy, Ticino feels Mediterranean—warm and southern—making it a favorite weekend destination for the Swiss. Rather than cuckoo-clock-like chalets, the houses are now plain, square, and made of stone. Instead of conifers, the forests are full of chestnut trees. You'll see vineyards, oleander, and even palm trees. And the upcoming train stops are announced in Italian now: *"Prossima fermata...."*

While life seemed almost too good in the pristine and touristic Lake Luzern region, here in the valley of **Leventina,** the economy is tougher. Unemployment rates are high, young folks have to commute into the cities farther south for a job, houses and roads aren't as well maintained, and window boxes no longer come with so many flowers.

As you approach **Biasca,** notice a modern square building with pebble walls on your left-hand side. This is the information center for the new 30-mile-long Gotthard Base Tunnel, which will be the longest train tunnel in the world (Tue–Sun 9:00–18:00, closed Mon, tel. 091-873-0550, www.infocentro.ch). You'll see industrial buildings and factories around Biasca.

If heading to Lugano, you may need to change trains in **Bellinzona.** (The official William Tell train continues to Locarno.) The train to Lugano passes the northern tip of Lake Maggiore and goes through a quiet, lush valley lined with picturesque villages and chestnut trees. Enjoy your time in Italian Switzerland!

TRANSPORTATION CONNECTIONS

From Luzern by Train to: Zürich (3/hr, 1 hr), **Zürich Airport** (2/hr, 1.25 hrs, half with change in Zürich), **Bern** (hourly, 1 hr; or 2/hr with transfer in Olten, 1.5 hrs), **Interlaken** (hourly, 2 hrs), **Lausanne** (hourly, 2.5 hrs; more with transfer in Olten), **Appenzell** (2/hr, 2.75 hrs, change in Herisau or in Zürich and Gossau), **Chur** (hourly, 2.25 hrs, change in Thalwil).

From Lugano by Train to: Zürich (hourly, 3 hrs, half with change in Arth-Goldau), **Interlaken** (hourly, 5 hrs, transfer in Luzern, Zürich, or Olten), **Bern** (hourly, 4 hrs, transfer in Luzern, Zürich, or Olten). From Lugano, you can continue on to the **Bernina Express** (next).

Bernina Express

The Bernina Express is one of the most exciting train rides through the Swiss Alps thanks to its diversity: starting with the sunny palm-tree ambience of Lugano, getting a taste of Italy along beautiful Lake Como, climbing up and over the twisting Bernina Pass, and seeing mountain towns like Pontresina before finishing up in eastern Switzerland. The little red train with panoramic cars spirals up to 7,380 feet, passing steep mountains and cliffs, glaciers, waterfalls, and a wild, rugged landscape.

ORIENTATION

The Route
The Bernina Express combines a bus trip through Italy with a train ride up and into the mountains. The bus begins in Lugano and runs along the west side of Italy's Lake Como, eventually arriving at Tirano, where the route continues by train. From Tirano, the train crosses back into Switzerland and twists up the steep mountainside north, mastering a very steep grade on regular tracks (no cogwheels) en route to the most spectacular stretch: over the Bernina Pass. Then the train winds back down the other side, stops in mountain towns (such as Pontresina), and finally deposits you in your choice of towns: Chur, St. Moritz, or Davos.

The route can be reversed (Chur/St. Moritz/Davos to Tirano by train, then bus to Lugano). In fact, this way arguably provides an even better experience: Approaching Pontresina from the north is breathtaking, and it gets even better when the train gets to the Bernina Pass.

Planning Your Time: The trip is spectacular but long. It helps to break up the journey with an overnight or two in the Pontresina area (see Pontresina, Samedan, and St. Moritz chapter). The Bernina Express is especially enjoyable in July and August, when you can take one of the open-top yellow train cars between Tirano and St. Moritz.

If you have more time, consider taking a standard regional train along this route (rather than the official panoramic Bernina Express train). That way, you can get off as you like for hiking and exploring (see "Local Train Alternative," in "Helpful Hints").

Cost and Schedule
A one-way trip on the Bernina Express from Lugano to Chur costs 74 SF second class, 110 SF first class. If you're only going as far as Pontresina, it's cheaper (45 SF second class, 61 SF first class). The entire trip (including the bus) is covered by a Eurailpass or a Swiss

Pass, though reservations cost extra.

If you do the official Bernina Express trip, **seat reservations** are required for both the bus and the panoramic train (9 SF for train, 12 SF for bus, buy easy-to-get bus reservation from driver as you board). Remember, you can do the same stretch on a regular train without reservations (optional seat reservation-5 SF; no such option for bus).

The bus leaves daily in summer (mid-May–mid-Oct) from outside Lugano's train station at 10:00 and heads for Tirano (facing the lake with the station at your back, walk about 100 yards to the left; bus stop has yellow sign for St. Moritz and Tirano).

At 12:45, you'll arrive in Tirano. From here, trains continue north over the mountains. All trains follow the same tracks as far as Pontresina, where they fan out to three different end points: to Chur (departs Tirano 14:15, arrives Chur 18:29), to St. Moritz (departs Tirano 14:48, arrives St. Moritz 17:10), or to Davos (departs Tirano 14:31, arrives Samedan 16:44, arrives Davos 18:19). The Davos-bound train, which runs in summer only, is the only direct panoramic train from Tirano to Samedan.

If you're doing it the other way around, here are some options: From Chur, the train leaves at 8:28 and arrives in Tirano at 12:35. From St. Moritz, the train departs at 9:40, arriving in Tirano at 11:56. From Davos, the train leaves at 8:40 and reaches Tirano at 12:19. The bus from Tirano leaves at 14:25 and arrives in Lugano at 17:30. Remember to confirm all times.

In winter (mid-Oct–mid-May), the bus service stops, but the train still runs between Tirano and Chur, and Tirano and St. Moritz, but not Tirano and Davos.

Information: The Bernina Express is operated by Rhaetian Railway (tel. 081-288-6104, www.rhb.ch). You can buy an English guidebook about the Bernina Express on the train or at gift shops along the way (12 SF). A recorded English commentary plays on the train's loudspeaker. Lugano bus info: tel. 081-288-5454.

Helpful Hints

Bus Trip: The Lugano–Tirano leg of the Bernina trip (through Italy) is on a bus. Make yourself comfortable—the seats recline, and the footrests, armrests, and individual fans give you more comfort than on a standard postal bus. There are no WCs or food on the bus, so buy your snacks and drinks before boarding (a convenient spot is the Aperto shop at Lugano's train station, daily 6:00–22:00). The bus stops for a WC and snack break in Italy (accepts Swiss francs). Bags can be put under the bus. The bus trip is almost entirely through Italy.

Train Trip: Once you reach Tirano, you'll switch to a panoramic train. The train has five cars: one is first class only, with panoramic windows that don't open. The other four are regular cars (with non-panoramic windows that open); two have first- and second-class seating, two are second class only.

Topless Trains: If traveling in July or August, ask about sitting in the yellow "convertible" train cars with flip seats and no roof (they can go on the Tirano–St. Moritz tracks because there are no long tunnels). Both first- and second-class cars are panoramic and equally good.

Local Train Alternative: The train segment of the Bernina Express can be done on a standard (non-panoramic) local train. These trains stop at all stations, allowing you to hop off and walk around in the beautiful scenery. You can get off at Poschiavo for a quick visit, or at the Bernina Pass for hiking, or at Diavolezza to do a cable-car trip. Alp Grüm and Ospizio Bernina are starting points for several great hikes. Train connections are easy and quick if you're just passing through.

SELF-GUIDED TOUR

Bernina Express Bus Trip

The bus trip is more scenic than relaxing. Lakes Lugano and Como are almost fjord-like, lined with little Italian getaways. For the best views, sit on the right-hand side (seat numbers don't seem to matter).

At first, the bus takes you around Lake Lugano on narrow, windy roads, frequently honking its horn to warn oncoming traffic at tight passages. Leaving Lugano, you'll pass the town of Gandria (fun to visit from Lugano by boat—see page 229 of Lugano chapter). Shortly after Gandria, you cross the border into **Italy** (it's a non-event—bus doesn't stop, no need to show passports). You may notice a change in architecture: While the Swiss love meticulously manicured gardens and painstakingly renovated houses, the Italians take things a bit easier.

Once the bus leaves Lake Lugano, the road broadens and takes you through modern Italian villages before hitting picturesque **Lake Como** (Lago di Como). Above the town of Menaggio are your first views of the lake. The village across the lake on the right (by the funny hump of land) is the *real* Bellagio (not the Las Vegas casino). At the nearby village of Dongo, the Italian fascist dictator Mussolini was captured at the end of World War II. Tunnels occasionally disrupt your views, but you can catch glimpses of the lush lakefront. In Gravedona, the street gets narrow enough to make getting the bus through a tight squeeze. Posh private villas and gardens line the street; look for the 12th-century Romanesque Church of Santa Maria del Tiglio. From here, the trip takes you to the tiny harbor town of Domaso. This area is touristy, with plenty of campgrounds, hotels, and swimming pools.

Shortly before noon, the bus stops for 15 minutes in **Sorico,** at the northern tip of Lake Como. You'll have a chance to use the WC and buy a snack or drink at Bar Pace (Swiss francs accepted). Check out the big photograph behind the bar—George Clooney posing with the bar's proud owner on a 2002 visit. Clooney owns a grandiose villa on Lake Como.

The bus then crosses the **"Pian di Spagna"**—famous for a tense standoff between Spanish and Swiss troops during the religious wars of the Counter-Reformation. The trip continues up the fertile **Valtellina Valley,** where some of northern Italy's white wine is produced. The sunny slopes on the left side are reserved for vineyards, the right lower slopes are for woodland, and the bottom of the valley is occupied by apple plantations. This region belonged for centuries (from 1512 until Napoleon in 1797) to Switzerland's largest canton, Graubünden. While this region is Italian today, many Swiss still think of the local Veltlin wine as their own.

Tirano is our next stop. In the old town, the bus passes an impressive Renaissance church (Madonna di Tirano, on the left) before arriving at the train station at 13:00. You have time for lunch and some sightseeing before hopping on the Bernina Express train (departs at 14:15 to Chur, at 14:31 to Davos, and at 14:48 to St. Moritz). Or, to cram in more sightseeing, take an earlier departure on a regional train to gain time for a stopover in the fine town of Poschiavo (described next), and catch your Bernina Express train from there later (confirm times at the Tirano station information window).

If you're interested in the Poschiavo side-trip, see next section. Otherwise, skip ahead to "Bernina Express Train Trip, Part One."

Poschiavo

From the Poschiavo train station, walk to the main street and turn left, following the signs to *Centro* and the TI. Cross the river over the pedestrian bridge and continue left, then right, then left, following the *Information* signs. The main square, **Piazza Comunale,** is lined with Neoclassical and Neo-Gothic buildings, including an impressive Catholic church (Chiesa di San Vittore Mauro). A church stood here as early as 703, but the building has been rebuilt and renovated several times: The bell tower dates from 1202, and the Baroque front door was carved in the 1700s. Don't miss the little yellow building just before the church, with the intricate wrought-iron grills. Have a peek inside, and don't be startled by the skulls lining the walls—you're standing in front of the local ossuary.

The **TI** is located in the old Town Hall, below the 12th-century church tower. Pick up a map and the English translation for a short orientation walk: Go from the main square a block north and find the **Church of St. Ignazio.** It's ironic that this Protestant church's namesake, St. Ignatius of Loyola, was the founder of the militant Jesuit order—whose main purpose was to fight "heretic" Protestants. Notice the inscription above the central pulpit, which is fervently Protestant: *Chiesa cristiana vangelica riformata da gli errori e superstizioni umane* ("Christian evangelical church, reformed from human errors and superstitions").

Then it's back to the station...you've got a train to catch!

Bernina Express Train Trip, Part One: From Tirano to Pontresina

From Tirano, the train crosses the center of town before climbing up to **Brusio.** Here the train takes the famous circular viaduct, the only one in the world—an ingenious construction allowing the train to reach higher altitudes without the help of a cogwheel mechanism. As the train twists up, you can see the front and back cars curving in front of and behind you, riding over the viaduct.

Lay back and enjoy the most scenic part of the trip. You'll pass dark old pine forests with needle-and-moss-covered boulders.

Chestnut forests, tobacco plantations, and vineyards contribute to the lush tableau. Wildflowers along the track include bright-orange lilies and mountain azaleas. The train slaloms up the steep mountain and offers more and more views of waterfalls, steep cliffs, and the Poschiavo valley and lake far below you.

Thirty minutes after leaving Poschiavo, and before you reach the Bernina Pass, you'll spot the first glacier, **Palü Gletscher** (behind the little lake of Palüsee on the left). It lies nestled between the peak Piz Varuna (11,330 feet) on the left and the eastern summit of Piz Palü on the right (12,790 feet).

The groaning of the train is a reminder that this is the only train crossing over the Alps without a tunnel. It goes right over the summit. Ospizio Bernina—at the **Bernina Pass**—marks the highest point of this trip (7,380 feet). You'll see the White Lake (Lago Bianco), whose color comes from the snowmelt, also called "glacier milk." A watershed sign (yellow, reading *Wasserscheide*) explains that this is a European continental divide: From here, rivers flow either north (toward the Inn, Danube, and finally to the Black Sea) or south (to the Adriatic Sea via the Adda and Po Rivers).

Behind the White Lake, you can see the glaciers of **Sassal Masone** and **Piz Cambrena**. This mountain pass not only separates European drainage basins, but also cultures. In winter, when the train line was more susceptible to bad-weather closures, the remote Italian-speaking valley of Poschiavo was often cut off from Switzerland and turned itself toward its southern neighbor, the valley of Veltlin (where you were just riding the bus).

The train crosses the barren landscape and descends into the **Engadine** valley. This part of Switzerland was discovered by tourists and convalescents at the end of the 19th century. Imagine the gorgeous skiing here in the winter, which still attracts the rich and famous. After the railroad opened this secluded valley to the world, the first hotels and sanatoriums were built (the air and sunshine supposedly helped fight various diseases). Poets found their muse in the wild, romantic landscape, while painters flocked in, attracted by the quality of the light. Keep an eye out for typical Engadine architecture—small windows set in thick walls, etched *sgraffito* decorations, and carved wooden doors.

The **Montebello curve** offers you the best views over the Morteratsch glacier on the left, with the impressive peaks in the background; from left to right: the Bellavista Range (12,770 feet), Crest Agüzza (12,690 feet), and the highest peak in the canton, Mount Bernina (13,280 feet). Mount Bernina was first climbed in 1850 by a team led by rangers from the village of Schanf. Their gear consisted only of thick woolen pants, a shirt and jacket, hobnailed shoes, and a hat with a black veil to shade them from the strong sunshine.

As you continue, the tracks are lined by more and more larch trees. The milky-white waters from Lago Bianco and the Morteratsch glacier run wild in a broad riverbed alongside the tracks, as satisfied cows chew away on the meadows and waterfalls tumble down the cliffs. From the Morteratsch station, there's a fine one-hour hike to the edge of the glacier, past posts tracking the glacier's recent retreat.

Next stop: **Pontresina.** This town is a good place to break the journey (see Pontresina, Samedan, and St. Moritz chapter). Consider spending a night or two in Pontresina, exploring the quaint village of Samedan, visiting the glitzy resort of St. Moritz, and maybe doing some hiking before continuing on your way.

If you're going to **St. Moritz,** your train trip is nearly over (about 10 min after Pontresina). But on the way to **Chur** or **Davos,** there's more to see...

Bernina Express Train Trip, Part Two:
From Pontresina to Chur

Although you're leaving the glaciers behind, your trip will still lead you through magnificent mountain scenery, with steep cliffs and deep gorges.

First, you'll slide through the broad and mellow valley around Samedan, following the shortest river in Switzerland, Flazbach. On the right, look for the funicular heading up to **Muottas Muragl,** a viewpoint overlooking the valleys that come together in Samedan (for details, see page 241). This is also home to Europe's highest airport. It serves glider enthusiasts and the rich and famous who come to vacation in St. Moritz.

After Samedan, in **Bever,** the train leaves the valley and climbs to another highly spectacular leg of its journey. The section between Bever and Bergün boasts amazing engineering work. Technicians from all over the world come here to admire the diversity of spiral tunnels, looping viaducts, galleries, and bridges that span the Albula Gorge.

The train works its way up along a cheerfully splashing mountain creek, between the Arven pine and larch trees and some isolated farmhouses. The **Albula tunnel,** the highest subterranean alpine crossing in Europe, takes you up to 5,970 feet. This pass serves as another barrier between cultures and climate—the weather is often different on either side of the tunnel. Hikers can follow the tracks and read the information panels about the construction of the train line. The street along the tracks is closed in winter and considered a paradise for sledders. Every winter, 100,000 sled enthusiasts are attracted by this closed, windy road, giving them the ride of their lives on a three-mile, downhill, car-free stretch.

From **Preda,** the train loops down through five spiral tunnels and two straight tunnels, crossing nine viaducts and going under two galleries—considered the most ingenious railway line ever built. It covers almost eight miles and descends more than 1,365 feet in altitude. The village of **Bergün** will be visible three separate times as you loop around the valley. Bergün greets you with a modern public open-air swimming pool and an onion-shaped, 17th-century "Roman tower." As the train continues winding down the pretty valley, you'll often be able to see other parts of the track below or next to you. Any track you see is one you've either already been on—or will be soon...

At **Filisur,** the Bernina Express route splits again. Some trains head directly to Davos (no stops en route), while others continue to Chur. I'll continue to narrate the Chur route.

After Filisur, the Chur-bound train enters a tunnel, and an announcement reminds you to ready your camera and position yourself on the left side. Just after the tunnel, you'll cross the famous **Landwasser viaduct.** A masterpiece of engineering, its pillars were built without scaffolding. Iron towers, which formed the center of each pillar, were built first. With the help of cranes set up atop each pillar, materials were hoisted up and the brick was laid. The 425-foot-long viaduct curves elegantly in a radius of 330 feet. Below, the wild Albula River carves the dramatic gorge; above, your train's panoramic windows allow you to see the steep and rugged cliffs looming over the tracks (a particularly beautiful stretch is right after Solis). Notice how nicely the dark limestone masonry matches the surrounding landscape (it was quarried right here).

Thusis is the commercial hub of the broad and lush Domleschg valley. The trip takes you down along the Vorderrhein ("Front-Rhine") River. Notice the many fortresses, castles, towers, and ruins along the river, a reminder that taxes were levied on the traders traveling this major route between northern and southern Europe. One of Switzerland's most popular mineral waters originates in Rhäzüns. The 13th-century castle above the town now belongs to a local chemical company.

Reichenau marks the confluence of two arms of the Upper Rhine (the Vorderrhein and the Hinterrhein—"Back-Rhine"). This town became wealthy from the taxes it got from the passing merchants. The 17th-century Reichenau Castle on the Hinterrhein was once used as a school, but is now privately owned.

The train follows the Rhine at the foot of Calanda Mountain to our final stop, **Chur.** You can catch the Glacier Express (explained next) from Chur or from St. Moritz.

TRANSPORTATION CONNECTIONS

From Lugano by Train to: Luzern (hourly, 3 hrs, half with change in Arth-Goldau), **Zürich** (hourly, 3 hrs, half with change in Arth-Goldau), **Interlaken** (hourly, 5 hrs, transfer in Luzern, Zürich, or Olten), **Bern** (hourly, 4 hrs, transfer in Luzern, Zürich, or Olten).

From Pontresina to: St. Moritz (2 trains/hr, 15 min), **Samedan** (hourly trains, 6 min; 2 buses/hr, 20 min), **Zürich** (hourly trains, 3.5 hrs, transfer in Samedan and Chur), **Tirano** (hourly trains, 2.5 hrs; 3 panoramic trains per day in summer).

From Chur by Train to: Zürich (2/hr, 1.5 hrs), **Luzern** (hourly, 2.25 hrs, transfer in Thalwil), **Appenzell** (hourly, 2.5 hrs, 1–3 changes). To reach destinations in western Switzerland—such as Bern, Interlaken, or Lake Geneva—you'll transfer in Zürich (see Zürich's "Transportation Connections," page 50).

Glacier Express

This most promoted of the Swiss scenic rail routes travels between Zermatt in the southwest of Switzerland and various resort towns in eastern Switzerland (St. Moritz, Chur, and Davos). If you stay on for the whole ride, you'll spend almost eight hours crossing 291 bridges, going through 91 tunnels, and reaching an altitude of 6,670 feet.

While it's an impressive and famous journey, the Glacier Express is not necessarily the be-all and end-all of Swiss rail trips. Much of the journey is down in valleys (as opposed to along the sides of cliffs), meaning that high-altitude views are a little lacking. But the stark landscape, carved by the glaciers that gave the train its name, is striking. The trip offers a dramatic way to connect eastern Switzerland with tucked-away-in-the-mountains Zermatt (see Zermatt and the Matterhorn chapter).

ORIENTATION

The Route

The Glacier Express is a misnomer—it's hardly an express. Not only does it take its time (traveling at about 20 mph to make the full trip in almost 8 hrs), but it also makes several stops along the way. The route cuts along the southern part of Switzerland, between St. Moritz/Chur/Davos (in the east) and Zermatt (in the west). You can ride in either direction.

Planning Your Time: The most distinctive stretch of the trip is the high-mountain pass between Disentis and Brig. If you don't want to commit to the whole eight hours, you can try to connect a trip with this segment only (about 3 hrs). Remember that you can join or leave the trip whenever you like (for example, Chur in the east and Brig in the west link conveniently into Swiss rail lines to other major destinations).

Cost and Schedule

You'll pay 133 SF for second class, or 221 SF for first class, between St. Moritz and Zermatt. The entire trip is covered by the Swiss Pass (except the reservation fee, described below). But a Eurailpass covers only part of the journey; two segments are privately run and not covered by Eurail (Disentis–Brig-45 SF second class; Brig–Zermatt-34 SF; plus a 5-SF fee if you buy it on the train).

If you're riding the full length of the Glacier Express sans railpass, the cost is high enough to warrant a look at the Half-Fare Travel Card, which can quickly pay for itself (99 SF for 1 month, see page 292).

The Glacier Express recently added spiffed-up panoramic first- and second-class cars, with air-conditioning and headsets for commentary. On these new "premium" trains, the second-class panoramic seating gets extremely crowded in summer—consider splurging on first class.

In addition to your train ticket or pass, you'll have to buy a **reservation.** The panoramic trains require a reservation fee of 30 SF (same price for first or second class). If you're not starting or ending in St. Moritz, or if you're getting off along the way, you can choose a cheaper, non-panoramic train (reservation-15 SF, 10 SF off-season). But if you want to take a direct, nonstop train between St. Moritz and Zermatt, the pricier panoramic train is your only option.

From mid-May through mid-October, four trains run daily in each direction. Going from east to west, the train begins in either St. Moritz (departs at 9:17 and 10:02) or Davos (departs at 10:10); all trains stop in Chur along the way (two at 11:38 and one at 12:15). Going from west to east, the trains depart Zermatt at 8:58, 9:17, 9:58, and 10:17. All trains have panoramic cars. Off-season, frequency drops to one per day in each direction (east to west: departs St. Moritz at 9:02, stops in Chur at 11:15; west to east: departs Zermatt at 9:48). Official Glacier Express trains often stop running in fall (mid-Oct–mid-Dec) to allow for maintenance, but regular regional train service continues.

The train takes six hours to connect Zermatt and Chur, or eight hours for Zermatt to St. Moritz or Davos. Confirm all times before your trip.

Information: The Glacier Express is operated by Matterhorn Gotthard Bahn, based in Brig (Nordstrasse 20, tel. 027-927-7777, www.glacierexpress.ch or www.mgbahn.ch). There's a little recorded commentary about what you're seeing on the regular train; the headsets in the panorama cars offer more narration. For more insight, pick up a guidebook before you board, or buy the 15-SF official guide by Merian on the train.

Helpful Hints

Picking the Best Seat: I find it more enjoyable to sit facing front. For most of the trip—including the most dramatic stretch, between Disentis and Brig—it's also slightly preferable, if you're coming from the east, to sit on the left-hand side of the train (generally seat numbers ending in 1, 2, 3, and 8), which is the right-hand side if you're coming from the west (same seat numbers). Note that if you start in Zermatt with any of the seat numbers I've mentioned, you might begin your trip facing backwards; the car will soon change direction in Brig.

Luggage: You'll keep your luggage with you (they don't check it

GLACIER EXPRESS

OBERALP PASS
6,670'

ZERMATT
5,263'

ST.
MORITZ
5,824'

ANDERMATT
4,711'

DISENTIS
3,707'

REICHENAU
1,981'

BRIG
2,202'

CHUR
1,919'

7.5 HOURS   180 MILES/290 KILOMETERS   291 BRIDGES   91 TUNNELS

ELEVATIONS IN FEET

through). In second class, the luggage racks are above your seat. In panoramic class, slip it between the backs of the seats.

No-Show Bridges: Most promotional materials show the Glacier Express train venturing across ancient aqueducts and old stone bridges. It makes for picturesque publicity. But realize that you don't see these bridges from the train itself...because you're on them.

Eating on the Glacier Express: The train has a fancy restaurant car that offers lunch—handy if you're in for the full eight hours. For 38 SF, you get a salad (summer) or soup (winter), a main dish, and a dessert; 26 SF buys you just the main dish (drinks cost extra). Their trademark gizmo: a tilted wine glass. Since lunch is generally served when the train is going up a steep incline (11:00–13:30), these gimmicky glasses always get a laugh. Reservations are required for lunch (request when booking your ticket).

To save a few francs, it's fine to bring your own **picnic.** Seats in panoramic cars even come with handy tables—perfect for a grocery-store feast.

SELF-GUIDED TOUR

All Glacier Express trains—whether they begin in St. Moritz or Davos—go through Chur. I'll describe the route starting at Chur and heading toward Zermatt. (For details on most of the trip from St. Moritz to Chur, see "Bernina Express Train Trip, Part Two: From Pontresina to Chur.")

Just outside of Chur (near where the St. Moritz train line hits the Chur line), you'll be following the **Vorderrhein Gorge,** nicknamed the "Swiss Grand Canyon." It was carved by the Rhine River (though way up here in the Alps, it's a little tyke, and not navigable). After about nine miles, the train diverges from the Rhine and enters a pastoral region called Surselva, centered on the town Ilanz. This is Romansh country, where the fourth official language of Switzerland is kept alive—barely—in communities like this one. Romansh, like French and Italian, is a Romance language—but it's more directly descended from Latin than most. From this valley (Reichenau, at roughly 2,000 feet above sea level, is the lowest altitude of the route), the big climb begins.

As you approach **Disentis,** the tracks begin to twist along the edge of a canyon—making the scenery more dramatic (a taste of what's to come). You'll pull into Disentis, with its big 17th-century Benedictine Monastery looming in your window. Your car will jiggle as the cogwheel engine is attached. This new engine has gears that can lower to latch onto the cogs of an extra rail with grippable teeth. At 10 percent incline (that's 100 meters of gain per kilometer, or about 500 feet per mile), conventional train wheels start to slip. The solution: a cogwheel (a.k.a. rack-and-pinion drive).

You'll work your way up the mountain alongside the baby Rhine River. Just west of Sedrun is the staging ground for the excavation of the Gotthard Base Tunnel (which will run 30 miles under the mountain from Erstfeld to Bodio when it opens—God willing—in 2015). Just past Rueras, the track steepens and the train slows to allow its gears to latch into the cog rail. After Tschamut, the last inhabited place before Oberalp Pass, you enter

a long series of snow sheds—designed to protect the tracks (and trains) in case an avalanche strikes. You'll emerge from the sheds at **Oberalp Pass,** the literal high point of this journey (6,670 feet), and glide along the Oberalp Lake. High above you, notice the extensive network of avalanche fences—a reminder of the many generations of Swiss farmers who have learned to live on the land. The reddish streaks you might see on the snow? Believe it or not, that's sand from the Sahara Desert—caught up in high-altitude winds and carried all the way to the Swiss Alps.

As you descend from the pass, you'll travel over, then through, the modern town of **Andermatt,** home to a Swiss Army base. Deep below you is the 9.5-mile-long Gotthard Tunnel, which takes trains unscenically from Goschenen to Airolo. In this desolate terrain, notice the huge boulders embedded in the ground, deposited there by glaciers.

Soon after, you'll go through the 9.5-mile-long Furka Basis Tunnel. While it might seem like a view-killer, realize that this tunnel—finished in 1982—made it possible for the Glacier Express to continue running through the winter. Cars are allowed onto the train to ride smoothly and safely between Realp and Oberwald. This is especially handy in the winter, when the road is closed.

You'll emerge into the region of **Goms,** with more pretty villages. The village of Fiesch/Kühboden has a cable car up to Eggishorn, boasting views of all the Alps All-Stars: the Matterhorn, Mont Blanc, Eiger, Mönch, and Jungfrau.

Soon after, the train meets up with another one of Europe's great rivers, the **Rhône.** The baby Rhône, just a bubbly little mountain stream here (originating from the once-mighty Rhône glacier nearby), flows all the way to Marseille, France, and into the Mediterranean.

Finally, you'll arrive at **Brig,** an ugly industrial town with good connections to other train lines (transfer here if you're not continuing on to Zermatt). From Brig, it's 20 miles on to Zermatt and the Matterhorn, following the craggy Nikolaital Valley. Keep an eye out for vineyards—the highest in Europe. We're out of milk country and into wine country. At Stalden, a road leads up another valley to the resort of Saas-Fee. Shortly before the village of Randa, you pass a cone of rubble left by a huge avalanche that wiped out two miles of road and track here in 1991.

At **Täsch,** vast parking lots mark the end of the road for drivers. From here it's train only into the traffic-free terminus of this line, Zermatt. Think about how much the terrain has changed since you started the trip: from fertile farmlands, to tundra above the tree line, to this rough and rocky terrain.

As you continue along the valley, lined with quarries, you'll begin to get your first glimpses of the unmistakable shape of the **Matterhorn**—a fitting exclamation point marking the end of this long journey. **Zermatt**—with its bunker-like, avalanche-proof train station—lies just around the bend.

TRANSPORTATION CONNECTIONS

From Chur by Train to: Zürich (2/hr, 1.5 hrs), **Luzern** (hourly, 2.25 hrs, transfer in Thalwil), **Appenzell** (hourly, 2.5 hrs, 1–3 changes). To reach destinations in western Switzerland—such as Bern or Interlaken—you'll transfer in Zürich (see Zürich's "Transportation Connections," page 50).

From Zermatt: Zermatt is connected to the outside world via the 80-minute train ride to Brig. Brig is also a handy place to bail out of the Glacier Express route, if you're coming from the east and not going all the way to Zermatt. If you're coming from or going to Lausanne or Montreux, you'll save time changing trains in Visp, a town between Zermatt and Brig (Zermatt-Lausanne via Visp: hourly, 3 hrs).

From Brig by Train to: Bern (at least hourly, 1.5 hrs), **Lausanne** (hourly, 1.75 hrs, change in Visp), **Interlaken** (at least hourly, 1.75 hrs, transfer in Spiez), **Luzern** (at least hourly, 3 hrs, transfer in Bern), **Zürich** (at least hourly, 2.75 hrs, some with transfer in Bern).

Chur

The routes of the Glacier Express and the Bernina Express intersect in Chur—supposedly Switzerland's oldest and warmest town.

It's a handy transportation hub for these two scenic train lines and has a charming enough old town. Overall, Chur (pronounced "koor") is just a typical Swiss burg—fine for passing through, but not worth a detour. If you've got time to kill, you can wander up through the old town to two big churches (the Romanesque Cathedral and the Gothic Church of St. Martin), some remains of the medieval city wall, and the town museum (Rätisches Museum, 6 SF, no English descriptions). Follow the handy red signs pointing you to the attractions. Public WCs are next to the cathedral.

ORIENTATION

Chur fans out over the foothills from the Rhine River. The newly renovated train station is at the bottom (north end) of the town center.

Tourist Information: The TI, in the train station, offers a free town map marked with sights, hotels, restaurants, and a convenient walking-tour route, plus a free brochure with hotel listings (Mon–Fri 7:00–20:00, Sat–Sun 8:00–18:00, tel. 081-252-1818, www.churtourismus.ch).

Arrival in Chur: To get to the old town, leave the train station and walk up Bahnhofstrasse. In two blocks, you'll reach the big roundabout at Postplatz. The old town is straight ahead.

Internet Access: The **library** (Kantonsbibliothek Graubünden) offers 15 minutes online for free (thereafter 2 SF/15 min, Tue and Thu 9:00–17:45, Wed and Fri 9:00–18:45, Sat 9:00–15:45, closed Sun–Mon, Karlihofplatz, tel. 081-257-2828).

SLEEPING

(1.10 SF = about $1, country code: 41)

Sleep here only if you must, in order to connect to one of the scenic rail lines. These moderately priced places are in the old town, an easy 10- to 15-min walk from the train station.

Hotel Freieck has 37 clean, tasteful rooms with wood floors and fun, old-fashioned furniture, over a low-key café (Sb-90–130 SF, Db-150–190 SF, Tb-180–250 SF, prices depend on season—highest May–mid-Oct, Reichsgasse 44–50, tel. 081-255-1515, fax 081-255-1516, www.freieck.ch, hotel@freieck.ch, Stockmann family).

Hotel Restaurant Rebleuten, in a 500-year-old building, overlooks a quiet little square a block off Kornplatz. The eight small, rustic rooms have worn carpets but are plenty comfortable. The hotel is warmly run by the Stöhr family (Ss-70 SF, Sb-85 SF, Db-160 SF, Pfisterplatz 1, tel. 081-257-1357, fax 081-257-1358, www.rebleuten.ch, info@rebleuten.ch).

Hotel Franziskaner is charming, well-located, and features newly renovated and reasonably priced rooms (S-50 SF, Ss-75–85 SF, Db-110–160 SF, Untere Gasse 29, tel. 081-252-1261, fax 081-252-1279, www.franziskaner.biz, info@franziskaner.biz).

TRANSPORTATION CONNECTIONS

Chur is a convenient spot to catch either the Glacier Express or the Bernina Express. It also offers speedy, frequent connections to Zürich, making it an ideal junction for spicing up your trip with a scenic train.

From Chur by Train to: Zürich (2/hr, 1.5 hrs), **Luzern** (hourly, 2.25 hrs, transfer in Thalwil), **Appenzell** (hourly, 2.5 hrs, 1–3 changes). To reach destinations in western Switzerland—such as Bern, Interlaken, or Lake Geneva—you'll transfer in Zürich (see Zürich's "Transportation Connections," page 50).

APPENDIX

CONTENTS

RESOURCES

Tourist Information Offices

In the US

The Swiss national tourist office in the US is a wealth of information. Before your trip, get the comprehensive "Welcome to Switzerland" brochure and request any specifics you want (such as regional and city maps, festival schedules, and hiking information). Call 877-794-8037 or visit www.myswitzerland.com (info.usa@myswitzerland.com).

In Switzerland

The local tourist information office is your best first stop in any new city. In this book, I'll refer to a tourist information office as a **TI.** Throughout Switzerland, you'll find TIs are usually well-organized and always have an English-speaking staff. They hand out free maps of the town and have information on events, activities, and bus and train schedules. Take full advantage of their help. Try to arrive, or at least telephone, before they close.

Resources from Rick

Guidebooks and Online Updates

I've done my best to make sure that the information in this book is up-to-date—but things change. For the latest, visit www .ricksteves.com/update. Also at my website, you'll find a valuable list of reports and experiences—good and bad—from fellow travelers who have used this book (www.ricksteves.com/feedback).

This book is one of more than 30 titles in my series on European travel, which includes country guidebooks, city and regional guidebooks, and my budget-travel skills handbook, 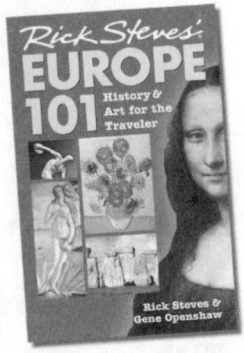 *Rick Steves' Europe Through the Back Door.* My phrase books—for German, French, Italian, Spanish, and Portuguese—are practical and budget-oriented. My other books are *Europe 101* (a crash course on art and history, newly expanded and in full color), *European Christmas* (on traditional and modern-day celebrations), and *Postcards from Europe* (a fun memoir of my travels over 25 years). For a complete list of my books, see the inside of the last page of this book.

Public Television and Radio Shows

My TV series, *Rick Steves' Europe,* covers European destinations in 70 shows, including two episodes that explore the Swiss Alps. My weekly public radio show, *Travel with Rick Steves,* features interviews with travel experts from around the world. All the TV scripts and radio shows (which are easy and free to download to an MP3 player) are at www.ricksteves.com.

Free Audiotours

If your travels take you beyond Switzerland to France or Italy, take advantage of the free, self-guided audiotours we offer of the major sights in Paris, Florence, Rome, and Venice. The audiotours, produced by Rick Steves and Gene Openshaw (the co-author of seven books in the Rick Steves series) are available through iTunes and at www.ricksteves.com. Simply download them onto your computer

Begin Your Trip at www.ricksteves.com

At our travel website, you'll find a wealth of free information on European destinations, including fresh monthly news and

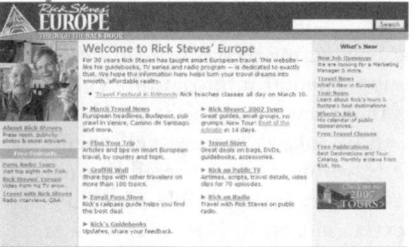

helpful tips from thousands of fellow travelers.

Our **online Travel Store** offers travel bags and accessories specially designed by Rick Steves to help you travel smarter and lighter. These include Rick's popular carry-on bags (wheeled and rucksack versions), money belts, totes, toiletries kits, adapters, other accessories, and a wide selection of guidebooks, planning maps, and DVDs.

Choosing the right **railpass** for your trip—amidst hundreds of options—can drive you nutty. We'll help you choose the best pass for your needs, plus give you a bunch of free extras.

Rick Steves' Europe Through the Back Door travel company offers **tours** with more than two dozen itineraries and 450 departures reaching the best destinations in this book... and beyond. We offer a 16-day Best of Germany, Austria, and Switzerland tour that visits the Lauterbrunnen Valley, Murten, and Lake Geneva. We also have two different Best of Europe tours, both of which make a stop in the Lauterbrunnen Valley. You'll enjoy great guides, a fun bunch of travel partners (with small groups of generally around 25), and plenty of room to spread out in a big, comfy bus. You'll find European adventures to fit every vacation length. For all the details, and to get our Tour Catalog and a free Rick Steves Tour Experience DVD (filmed on location during an actual tour), visit www.ricksteves.com or call the Tour Department at 425/608-4217.

and transfer them to your iPod or MP3 player. (Remember to bring a Y-jack and extra set of ear buds for your travel partner.)

Maps

The black-and-white maps in this book are concise, simple, and intended to help you locate recommended places and get to local TIs, where you can pick up a more in-depth map of the city or region (usually free).

Better maps are sold at newsstands and bookstores in Europe, which have a good selection, especially in touristy areas. Take a look before you buy to be sure the map has the level of detail you want. For drivers, I recommend a 1:400,000-scale map of the whole country, or even larger-scale maps of particular regions. Train travelers can usually manage fine with the freebies they get with their railpass and from the local tourist offices.

Other Guidebooks

Especially if you'll be traveling beyond my recommended destinations, you may want some supplemental information. When you consider the improvements that they'll make in your $3,000 vacation, $30 for extra maps and books is money well spent. Particularly for several people traveling by car, the additional weight and expense of a small trip library are negligible. One budget tip can save the price of an extra guidebook. Note that none of the following books are updated annually; check the publication date before you buy.

The *Lonely Planet* guide to Switzerland is thorough, well-researched, and packed with good maps and hotel recommendations for low- to moderate-budget travelers. The similar *Rough Guide to Switzerland* is written by insightful British researchers.

Students, backpackers, and nightlife-seekers should consider the highly opinionated *Let's Go: Austria and Switzerland* (by Harvard students, has the best hostel listings).

Dorling Kindersley publishes snazzy Eyewitness Guides, including one on Switzerland. While pretty to look at, these books weigh a ton and are skimpy on actual content.

The popular, skinny *Michelin Green Guide: Switzerland* is excellent, especially if you're driving. Michelin Guides are known for their city and sightseeing maps, dry but concise and helpful information on all major sights, and good cultural and historical background. English editions are sold in Europe at gas stations and tourist shops.

Recommended Books and Movies

To get in the mood for your trip, consider these books and films, which take place partly or entirely in Switzerland.

Non-Fiction: *La Place de la Concorde Suisse* (by John McPhee, in English); *Living Among the Swiss* (memoir by Michael Wells Glueck); *Why Switzerland?* (socioeconomic commentary by Jonathan Steinberg); *The White Spider* (by Heinrich Harrer, on the first Eiger ascent in the 1930s); *The Climb Up to Hell* (by Jack Olsen, on a 1957 Eiger climb); and *A Tramp Abroad* (by Mark Twain).

Fiction: *The Magic Mountain* (by Thomas Mann); *Hotel du Lac* (by Anita Brookner); *A Farewell to Arms* (by Ernest Hemingway); *Daisy Miller* (by Henry James); *The Prisoner of Chillon* (epic poem by Lord Byron); *The Night Manager* (by John le Carré); *I'm Not Stiller* (by Swiss author Max Frisch, available in English); and

Heidi (children's book by Johanna Spyri).

Films: *Three Colors: Red* (1994); *Five Days One Summer* (1982); *The Eiger Sanction* (1975); *Third Man on the Mountain* (1959); and *Heidi* (1937). In addition, the following 007 films feature scenes of James Bond skiing in Switzerland: *Goldeneye* (1995); *A View to a Kill* (1985); *The Spy Who Loved Me* (1977); *On Her Majesty's Secret Service* (1969, with scenes of the Schilthorn, in the Berner Oberland); and *Goldfinger* (1964).

MONEY MATTERS

Damage Control for Lost Cards

If you lose your credit, debit, or ATM card, you can stop people from using it by reporting the loss immediately to the respective global customer-assistance centers. Call these 24-hour US numbers collect: Visa (410/581-9994), MasterCard (636/722-7111), and American Express (623/492-8427).

At a minimum, you'll need to know the name of the financial institution that issued you the card, along with the type of card (classic, platinum, or whatever). Providing the following information will allow for a quicker cancellation of your missing card: full card number, whether you are the primary or secondary cardholder, the cardholder's name exactly as printed on the card, billing address, home phone number, circumstances of the loss or theft, and identification verification (your birth date, your mother's maiden name, or your Social Security number—memorize this, don't carry a copy). If you are the secondary cardholder, you'll also need to provide the primary cardholder's identification-verification details. You can generally receive a temporary card within two or three business days in Europe.

If you promptly report your card lost or stolen, you typically won't be responsible for any unauthorized transactions on your account, although many banks charge a liability fee of $50.

Tipping

Tipping in Switzerland isn't as automatic and generous as it is in the US, but for special service, tips are appreciated, if not expected. As in the US, the proper amount depends on your resources, tipping philosophy, and the circumstance, but some general guidelines apply.

Restaurants: Tipping is an issue only at restaurants that have table service. If you order your food at a counter, don't tip.

At restaurants that have a waitstaff, service is included, although it's common to round up the bill after a good meal (usually 5–10 percent; so for an 18.50 SF meal, pay 20 SF). Give the tip directly to your server. Rather than leaving coins on the table, the

Swiss usually pay with paper, saying how much they'd like the bill to be (for example, for an 8.10 SF meal, give a 20 SF bill and say *"Neun Franken"*—"Nine francs"—to get 11 SF change).

Taxis: To tip the cabbie, round up. For a typical ride, round up to the next franc or two on the fare (to pay a 13-SF fare, give 15 SF); for a long ride, to the nearest 10 (for a 75-SF fare, give 80 SF). If the cabbie hauls your bags and zips you to the airport to help you catch your flight, you might want to toss in a little more—but not more than 10 SF. But if you feel like you're being driven in circles or otherwise ripped off, skip the tip.

Special Services: Tour guides at public sites sometimes hold out their hands for tips after they give their spiels. If I've already paid for the tour, I don't tip extra. I don't tip at hotels, but if you do, give the porter a franc or two for carrying bags, and, at the end of your stay, leave a few francs for the maid if the room was kept clean. In general, if someone in the service industry does a super job for you, a small tip (the equivalent of a dollar) is appropriate... but not required.

When in doubt, ask: If you're not sure whether (or how much) to tip for a service, ask your hotelier or the TI; they'll fill you in on how it's done on their turf.

VAT Refunds for Shoppers

Appendix

Wrapped into the purchase price of your Swiss souvenirs is a Value Added Tax (VAT) of 7.6 percent (one of the lowest in Europe). If you spend more than 530 SF at a store that participates in the VAT refund scheme, you're entitled to get most of that tax back.

Getting your refund is usually straightforward and, if you buy a substantial amount of souvenirs, well worth the hassle. If you're lucky, the merchant will subtract the tax when you make your purchase. (This is more likely to occur if the store ships the goods to your home.) Otherwise, you'll need to:

Get the paperwork. Have the merchant completely fill out the necessary refund document, called a "cheque." You'll have to present your passport at the store.

Get your stamp at the border or airport. Process your cheque(s) at your last stop in Switzerland by the customs agent who deals with VAT refunds. It's best to keep your purchases in your carry-on for viewing, but if they're too large or dangerous (such as knives) to carry on, track down the proper customs agent to inspect them before you check your bag. To qualify, your purchased goods should be unused. If you show up at customs wearing your new Swiss sweater, officials might look the other way—or deny you a refund.

Collect your refund. You'll need to return your stamped document to the retailer or its representative. Many merchants work with a service that has offices at major airports, ports, and border crossings, such as Global Refund (www.globalrefund.com) or Premier Tax Free (www.premiertaxfree.com). These services, which extract a 4 percent fee, usually can refund your money immediately in your currency of choice or credit your card (within two billing cycles). If the retailer handles VAT refunds directly, it's up to you to contact the merchant for your refund. You can mail the documents from home, or quicker, from your point of departure (using a stamped, addressed envelope you've prepared or one that's been provided by the merchant)—and then wait. It could take months.

Customs for American Shoppers

You are allowed to take home $800 worth of items per person duty-free, once every 30 days. The next $1,000 is taxed at a flat 3 percent. After that, you pay the individual item's duty rate. You can also bring in duty-free a liter of alcohol (slightly more than a standard-size bottle of wine; you must be at least 21), 200 cigarettes, and up to 100 non-Cuban cigars. Food in cans or sealed jars is permissible as long as no meat is included. Some, but not all, types of cheese are allowed. Fresh fruits and vegetables are prohibited. Note that you'll need to carefully pack any bottles of wine and other liquid-containing items in your checked luggage, due to the three-ounce limit on liquids in carry-on baggage. To check customs rules and duty rates before you go, visit www.cbp .gov, and click on "Travel," then "Know Before You Go."

TELEPHONES, EMAIL, AND MAIL

Telephones

Smart travelers learn the phone system and use it daily to reserve or reconfirm rooms, get tourist information, reserve restaurants, confirm tour times, or phone home.

Types of Phones

You'll encounter various kinds of phones on your trip:

Swisscom **public pay phones** are easy to find. Some take only insertable phone cards (see below), some only coins, some take both, and some (marked with a yellow €) even accept euro coins.

Hotel room phones are sometimes cheap for local calls (confirm at the front desk first), but can be a rip-off for long-distance calls unless you use an international phone card (described below). But incoming calls are free, making this a cheap way for friends and family to stay in touch, provided they have a good long-distance plan for calls to Europe.

Hurdling the Language Barrier

Switzerland has four official languages: German, French, Italian, and Romansh (an obscure Romantic tongue). Most of the destinations in this book are in the German-speaking territory. No matter where you are, most young or well-educated people—especially those in larger towns and the tourist trade—speak at least some English. Still, you'll get more smiles by using the local pleasantries. See the German, French, and Italian Survival Phrases at the end of the appendix.

In German-speaking Switzerland, locals speak sing-songy *Schwyzertütsch* (Swiss German) around the house, but in schools and at work, they speak and write in the same standard German used in Germany and Austria (called "High" German, or *Hochdeutsch*—though many Swiss prefer to call it *Schriftdeutsch*, or "Written German"). The standard greeting is a hearty *Grüezi* (GROYT-see). "Thank you" is derived from French, but pronounced a little differently: *Merci* (MEHR-see). They also sometimes use the more German-like *Dunkcha* (DOON-khah).

German—like English, Dutch, Swedish, and Norwegian—is a Germanic language, making it easier on most American ears than Romance languages (such as Italian and French). German is pronounced just as it's spelled. There are a few potentially confusing vowel combinations: *ie* is pronounced "ee" (as in *Bier*, the German word for "beer"); *ei* is pronounced "aye" (as in *nein*, German for "no"), and *eu* is pronounced "oy" (as in *Deutsch*, German for "German"). Written German always capitalizes all nouns.

Give it your best shot. The locals will appreciate your efforts.

American mobile phones work in Europe if they're GSM-enabled, tri-band, or quad-band, and on a calling plan that includes international calls. They're convenient, but pricey. For example, with a T-Mobile phone, you'll pay $1 per minute for calls.

European mobile phones run about $75 (for the most basic models, but it's often easy to find phones for much less) and come without contracts. These phones are loaded with prepaid calling time that you can recharge as you use up the minutes. As long as you're not "roaming" outside the phone's home country, incoming calls are free. For more information on mobile phones, see www.ricksteves.com/plan/tips/mobilephones.htm.

Using Phone Cards

Get a phone card for your calls. Prepaid cards come in two types: insertable phone cards (usable only in pay phones) and international phone cards (usable from any phone). Either type of phone card works only in the country where it's purchased. Both are described next.

Insertable phone cards are just about the only thing that's actually cheaper in Switzerland than in other countries. Dialing direct from a Swisscom public pay phone with an insertable phone card *(Telefonkarte)* to the US costs under a dime a minute, plus a 35-cent connection charge. This is your cheapest bet for both domestic and international calls. These cards are sold at post offices and many newsstand kiosks. Simply take the phone off the hook, insert the prepaid card, wait for a dial tone, and dial away. The price of the call (local or international) is automatically deducted while you talk. Give a still-lively card to another traveler if you're leaving the country.

You can buy an **international phone card** with a scratch-to-reveal personal identification number (PIN), but in Switzerland, insertable phone cards are a much better deal. However, if you'll be traveling elsewhere in Europe, it's good to know about international phone cards, since they usually provide the cheapest way to call home (sold at kiosks and mini-marts). Because you don't have to insert them in the phone, they can also be used from hotel-room phones.

To call the US, see "Dialing Internationally," page 290.

Using Hotel-Room Phones, VoIP, or US Calling Cards

The phone in your **hotel room** is convenient (I find it handy for local calls), but expensive. While incoming calls (made by folks back home) can be the cheapest way to keep in touch, charges for *outgoing* calls, especially international ones, can be a very unpleasant surprise. Before you dial, get a clear explanation from the hotel staff of the charges, even for local and (supposedly) toll-free calls.

If your family has an inexpensive way to call Europe, either through a long-distance plan or prepaid calling card, have them call you in your hotel room. Give them a list of your hotels' phone numbers before you go. Then, as you travel, send them an email or make a quick pay-phone call to set up a time for them to give you a ring.

If you're traveling with a laptop, consider trying **VoIP (Voice over Internet Protocol).** With VoIP, two computers act as the phones, allowing for a free Internet-based call. The major providers are Skype (www.skype.com) and Google Talk (www.google.com/talk).

European Calling Chart

Just smile and dial, using this key:
AC = Area Code, LN = Local Number.

European Country	Calling long distance within...	Calling from the US or Canada to...	Calling from a European country to...
Austria	AC + LN	011 + 43 + AC (without the initial zero) + LN	00 + 43 + AC (without the initial zero) + LN
Belgium	LN	011 + 32 + LN (without initial zero)	00 + 32 + LN (without initial zero)
Bosnia-Herzegovina	AC + LN	011 + 387 + AC (without initial zero) + LN	00 + 387 + AC (without initial zero) + LN
Britain	AC + LN	011 + 44 + AC (without initial zero) + LN	00 + 44 + AC (without initial zero) + LN
Croatia	AC + LN	011 + 385 + AC (without initial zero) + LN	00 + 385 + AC (without initial zero) + LN
Czech Republic	LN	011 + 420 + LN	00 + 420 + LN
Denmark	LN	011 + 45 + LN	00 + 45 + LN
Estonia	LN	011 + 372 + LN	00 + 372 + LN
Finland	AC + LN	011 + 358 + AC (without initial zero) + LN	999 + 358 + AC (without initial zero) + LN
France	LN	011 + 33 + LN (without initial zero)	00 + 33 + LN (without initial zero)
Germany	AC + LN	011 + 49 + AC (without initial zero) + LN	00 + 49 + AC (without initial zero) + LN
Greece	LN	011 + 30 + LN	00 + 30 + LN
Hungary	06 + AC + LN	011 + 36 + AC + LN	00 + 36 + AC + LN
Ireland	AC + LN	011 + 353 + AC (without initial zero) + LN	00 + 353 + AC (without initial zero) + LN

Appendix

European Country	Calling long distance within ...	Calling from the US or Canada to ...	Calling from a European country to ...
Italy	LN	011 + 39 + LN	00 + 39 + LN
Montenegro	AC + LN	011 + 382 + AC (without initial zero) + LN	00 + 382 + AC (without initial zero) + LN
Netherlands	AC + LN	011 + 31 + AC (without initial zero) + LN	00 + 31 + AC (without initial zero) + LN
Norway	LN	011 + 47 + LN	00 + 47 + LN
Poland	LN	011 + 48 + LN (without initial zero)	00 + 48 + LN (without initial zero)
Portugal	LN	011 + 351 + LN	00 + 351 + LN
Slovakia	AC + LN	011 + 421 + AC (without initial zero) + LN	00 + 421 + AC (without initial zero) + LN
Slovenia	AC + LN	011 + 386 + AC (without initial zero) + LN	00 + 386 + AC (without initial zero) + LN
Spain	LN	011 + 34 + LN	00 + 34 + LN
Sweden	AC + LN	011 + 46 + AC (without initial zero) + LN	00 + 46 + AC (without initial zero) + LN
Switzerland	LN	011 + 41 + LN (without initial zero)	00 + 41 + LN (without initial zero)
Turkey	AC (if no initial zero is included, add one) + LN	011 + 90 + AC (without initial zero) + LN	00 + 90 + AC (without initial zero) + LN

- The instructions above apply whether you're calling a land line or mobile phone.
- The international access codes (the first numbers you dial when making an international call) are 011 if you're calling from the US or Canada, or 00 if you're calling from virtually anywhere in Europe (except Finland, where it's 999).
- To call the US or Canada from Europe, dial 00, then 1 (the country code for the US and Canada), then the area code and number. In short, 00 + 1 + AC + LN = Hi, Mom!

US Calling Cards (such as the ones offered by AT&T, MCI, or Sprint) are the worst option. You'll nearly always save a lot of money by paying with a phone card (see above).

How to Dial
Calling from the US to Europe, or vice versa, is simple—once you break the code. The European calling chart on page 288 will walk you through it.

Dialing Domestic Calls
About half of all European countries use area codes; the other half use a direct-dial system without area codes.

All phone numbers in Switzerland are 10 digits (without area codes) that can be dialed direct throughout the country. For instance, to call a recommended Swiss hotel in Gimmelwald, you'd dial the same number (tel. 033-855-1658) whether you're calling from the Gimmelwald cable-car station or from Zürich.

Dialing Internationally
If you want to make an international call, follow these three steps:

1. Dial the international access code (00 if you're calling from Europe, 011 from the US or Canada).

2. Dial the country code of the country you're calling (see chart on page 288).

3. Dial the entire phone number, keeping in mind that calling many countries requires dropping the initial zero of the phone number (see the calling chart on page 288). For example, to call the Gimmelwald hotel from the US, dial 011, 41 (Switzerland's country code), and then 33-855-1658 (the hotel's number *without* its initial 0).

To call my office in Edmonds, Washington, from anywhere in Europe, I dial 00 (Europe's international access code), 1 (the US country code), 425 (Edmonds' area code), and 771-8303.

Europeans often write their phone numbers with + at the front—it's just a placeholder for the international access code (again, that's 011 from the US or Canada, 00 from Europe).

Useful Phone Numbers
Emergencies: Dial 112.
Directory Assistance: Dial 111 for domestic numbers, dial 191 for international numbers.
Train Info: 0900-300-3004 (1.20 SF/min).
US Embassy, in Bern: Jubilaeumsstrasse 93, Mon–Fri 9:00–11:30, closed Sat–Sun, tel. 031-357-7234, http://bern.usembassy.gov.

Appendix

Email and Mail

Email: Many travelers set up a free Web-based email account with Yahoo, Microsoft (Hotmail), or Google (Gmail). Internet cafés and access points (for instance, at libraries) can be found in every city and most towns. Look for the places listed in this book, or ask the local TI, computer store, or your hotelier. Some hotels have a dedicated computer for guests' email needs—sometimes free, sometimes for a fee. Small places are accustomed to letting clients (who've asked politely) sit at their desk for a few minutes just to check their email.

Internet access for laptop users is becoming commonplace at most hotels and B&Bs. Most hotels that offer this do so for free, but some (especially fancier chain hotels) charge by the minute. You'll either access the hotel's wireless Internet (Wi-Fi, sometimes called "WLAN" in Europe), sometimes using a password provided by the hotelier; or plug your computer directly into an Internet wall socket (they can usually loan you a cable).

Mail: Even when post offices are closed, you're never too far from a yellow mailbox with an automated stamp dispenser (most train stations have one). Type in the value of stamp you want (postcard or letter to the US: 1.40 SF economy, 1.80 SF express), insert coins, and press the pound key. These machines don't give change, so if you have any amount left in the machine, print out a stamp for that amount and use it toward your next postcard.

To arrange for mail delivery, reserve a few hotels along your route in advance and give their addresses to friends. Allow 10 days for a letter to arrive. Phoning and emailing are so easy that I've dispensed with mail stops altogether.

If you need to mail items home (be warned, it's expensive), you can buy boxes and tape at most post offices.

TRANSPORTATION

By Car or Train?

Because Switzerland's train network is excellent, I recommend using public transportation here. Only a few areas—like the Appenzell region and the French Swiss countryside—are better by car. Cars are an expensive headache in the bigger cities.

Trains

Trains are generally slick, speedy, and punctual, with synchronized connections. They're also clean, roomy, and, in Switzerland, entirely non-smoking. Virtually all Swiss stations have luggage lockers. Few places in Switzerland are out of reach of the train system, though some frustrating schedules make the more out-of-the-way recommendations (such as Taveyanne in the French

Swiss countryside) not worth the time and trouble for the less determined.

Swiss trains and stations are marked "SBB CFF FFS." All those letters mean the same thing ("Swiss Federal Railways"), in three different languages: German, French, and Italian.

Schedules

Switzerland has a train info number you can dial from anywhere in the country: toll tel. 0900-300-3004 (1.20 SF/min). For Swiss timetables, visit Germany's excellent all-Europe timetable, http://bahn.hafas.de/bin/query.exe/en, or the Swiss site, www.rail .ch. At most train stations, attendants and/or machines will print out a step-by-step itinerary for you, free of charge. Major stations also have handy travel offices offering general help.

Tickets

If you're traveling without a railpass, get train tickets at the station—either at the ticket windows, or at the easy-to-use machines. Though you may see some people buying their tickets from conductors on the train (for an additional 5 SF), don't assume you can do so on all trains. If the side of the train displays a yellow-eye logo, you need to get a ticket before boarding or risk being fined 80 SF.

Swiss Railpasses

Because of high ticket prices, railpasses are a good deal in Switzerland, even for a three-day trip. But for such a little country, Switzerland has a dizzying array of train passes and deals. I've listed the most popular ones here. For the latest prices, see www .ricksteves.com/rail.

The **Swiss Pass** is the basic version, covering all trains, boats, and buses, plus admission to most Swiss museums (see page 294), and offering a 50 percent discount on most high-mountain trains and lifts. It comes in both consecutive-day and flexipass versions. Both versions completely cover the cost of any transportation for a specified number of days (but do not cover seat or overnight-train reservations).

If you're traveling with at least one other person, get the "Saver" version of the pass, which is 15 percent cheaper than individual passes. Second class (available to any age) is 33 percent cheaper than first class.

The **Half-Fare Travel Card** gives you a 50 percent discount

Legend:
- ---- Rail
- ++++ Mountain Rail
- ···· Boat
- – – – Bus

GERMANY

To Colmar
To Freiburg
To Munich

FRANCE

Schaffhausen
Konstanz
Kreuzlingen
Lindau
Bregenz
Basel
AIRPORT
St. Gallen
Olten
Zürich
Appenzell
Solothurn
Wasserauen
Feldkirch
Biel
Zug
Buchs
Vaduz
LIECHT.
Neuchâtel
Luzern
Arth-Goldau
Schwyz
Landquart
To Innsbruck
Bern
S W I T Z.
AUSTRIA
Murten
Flüelen
Chur
Arosa
Klosters
Fribourg
Inter-Laken
Disentis
Davos
Scuol
Thun
Frasne
Bulle
Spiez
Lauter-Brunnen
Jungfrau-joch
Andermatt
St. Moritz
Samedan
Lausanne
Gstaad
Airolo
Pontresina
Chillon
Montreux
Brig
AIRPORT
Visp
Locarno
Bellinzona
Tirano
Geneva
Sion
Culoz
Martigny
Saas-Fee
Domodossola
To Paris & Lyon
St. Gervais
Zermatt
Lugano
Matterhorn
Chamonix
Stresa
ITALY
MALPENSA AIRPORT
Gallarate
Chiasso

To Paris

FRANCE

Note: Not all transportation routes shown.

50 Kilometers
50 Miles

Comparing Swiss Pass Coverage

All passes that include Switzerland cover national network trains, boat trips on Swiss lakes, and many sightseeing and private rail discounts.

Here are the key routes where coverage varies:

Route or Bonus	Eurail/ Select or Two-Country Passes	Swiss Card or Transfer Ticket	Swiss Pass or Flexipass
Swiss Family Card (kids travel free)	No	Available	Available
Postal buses	No	Covered	Covered
Urban transport in 35 cities ($2/trip)	No	No	Covered
Swiss museum admissions	No	No	Covered
Brig-Disentis section of the Glacier Express scenic route ($36 2nd class, reservation extra)	No	Only if it's fastest, most direct route (from south border to south destination)	Covered
Brig-Zermatt private train to see the Matterhorn ($25 2nd class)	No	Only if it's fastest, most direct route (from south border to Zermatt)	Covered
Jungfrau Region Railways (e.g., from Interlaken: $5 to Lauterbrunnen, $8 to Grindelwald, $10 to Wengen; $160 round-trip to Jungfraujoch)	25% discount beyond Interlaken	50% discount with Swiss Card; Jungfraujoch not covered on in- and outbound round-trip	50% discount above Mürren, Grindelwald, or Wengen, except only 25% off Kl. Scheidegg-Jungfraujoch
Many high mountain lifts (e.g., Stechelberg-Schilthorn $72 round-trip/$54 off-peak)	No	50% discount with Card, not with Transfer Ticket	50% discount
Half-fare option: 50% transport discount between fully covered flexi travel days	No	50% discount with Card, not with Transfer Ticket	50% discount with flexipass
Passholder rate on international night trains	Yes	No	Yes
Overnight trains (leaving after 19:00) take only one day of flexipass	Applies	No	No
All "covered" services start use of a travel day on a flexipass, but discounts do not.			

Appendix

on all national and private trains, postal buses, lifts, and steamers (99 SF for 1 month, sold only in Switzerland). This can save you money if your Swiss travel adds up to more than $150 in point-to-point tickets. The **Swiss Card** is a variation on this, sold only in the US and at a few border stations. It includes the same 50 percent discount and adds two train rides: one ride from any point of entry (such as the German border or Zürich's airport) to any other point in Switzerland and one back from that point to any border ($187 first class, $139 second class).

Regional passes cover all travel—including trains, buses, boats, and lifts—in a particular area, such as the Berner Oberland (Berner Oberland Pass, see page 115), Zermatt area (see page 176), or Central Switzerland, around Luzern (Tell-Pass, see page 72). Buy these (in Switzerland, not the US) only if you're very focused on a single region, but note that there's usually no need to have both a regional pass and an all-Switzerland pass (or Eurailpass).

Other deals include the **Swiss Family Card,** allowing children under 16 to travel free with their parents (20 SF per child at Swiss stations, or free with Swiss train passes when requested with purchase in the US).

Eurailpasses

If you're also traveling to other countries, consider a Eurail Selectpass, which gives you up to 15 travel days (within a 2-month period, allow about $1,050) in three, four, or five adjacent countries: Choose among Switzerland, Germany, Austria, France, Italy, and other Western European countries. A 20-country Eurail Global pass is cost-effective only if you're doing a whirlwind trip of Europe (allow roughly $965 for 3 weeks). Like the Swiss Pass, these come in Saverpass versions (15 percent cheaper for two or more traveling together); unlike with the Swiss Pass, if you're over 26, you have to buy a first-class pass.

If you're combining your trip to Switzerland with travel in France, Germany, or Austria, you may want to consider a **two-country pass.**

Railpass Bonuses and Discounts

If you buy a railpass, know what extras are included—for example, boat cruises on the big Swiss lakes are covered by most railpasses. In addition, Swiss railpasses can get you free entry to many museums and discounts on many mountain lifts. Always ask. Note that while Eurailpasses include some deals in Switzerland beyond simple trains (such as on some mountain lifts), the discounts and coverage of these passes generally aren't as extensive as the Switzerland-only passes (for example, lifts in Zermatt are discounted and postal buses nationwide are free with a Swiss Pass, but both are full price with a Eurailpass).

If your railpass is a flexipass (it covers a certain number of days in a given span, rather than consecutive days), it's worth knowing when, and when not, to use up your flexi-days. Trips that are merely discounted, rather than free with the pass—most notably many mountain lifts—don't use up a day of your pass. Any time you use the pass for a free trip, however, you have to use up a day. Keep in mind that it makes sense to pay out of pocket for, say, a short boat or train ride rather than use up a valuable day of your pass for it.

Lift Lingo

The Swiss have come up with a variety of ways to conquer peaks and reach the best viewpoints and trailheads with minimum sweat. Known generically as "lifts," each of these contraptions has its own name and definition. Use the right terms, and impress your new Swiss friends.

Cogwheel Train: A train that climbs a steep incline using a gear system, which engages "teeth" in the middle of the tracks to provide traction. Also known as "rack-and-pinion train" or "rack railway."

Funicular: A car that is pulled by a cable along tracks up a particularly steep incline, often counterbalanced by a similar car going in the opposite direction (meaning you'll pass the other car exactly halfway through the ride). Funiculars, like cogwheel trains, are in contact with the ground at all times.

Cable Car: A large passenger car, suspended in the air by a cable, which travels between stations without touching the ground. A cable car holds a large number of people (sometimes dozens at a time), who generally ride standing up. When a cable car reaches a station, it comes to a full stop to allow passengers to get on and off.

Gondola: Also suspended in the air by a cable, but smaller than a cable car—generally holding fewer than 10 people, who are usually seated. Gondolas move continuously, meaning that passengers have to hop into and out of the moving cars at stations. Also, while cable-car lines usually have two big cars—one going in each direction—gondolas generally have many smaller cars strung along the same cable.

Confusingly, the "car" compartment of a cable car is sometimes referred to as a "gondola."

If you have a Swiss flexipass (rather than a Eurailpass), note that when you're *not* using a travel day, your pass gets you a 50 percent discount on all rides taken before the use of your last travel day. Unlike flexipasses for most other countries, a Swiss flexipass expires once you've used up all your travel days—even if that's well before the end of the one-month time frame noted on your pass. It can be smart to use your first travel day near the beginning of your trip, and your last travel day near (or at) the end of your trip; then you can use your flexipass throughout your entire trip for transportation discounts on the days you're not using travel days. It's confusing, but once you figure out the system, you can make it work to your advantage.

Train Notes

Scenic Rail Journeys: In addition to being convenient for transportation, many of Switzerland's trains are also breathtakingly scenic. Several trips are particularly beautiful and billed as special "theme" routes for tourists. For many visitors, these are a Swiss highlight, and I've devoted an entire chapter to them (see page 250).

Private Lines: Switzerland has some privately owned train lines. For instance, a large segment of the Glacier Express scenic journey is private. Private lines are usually covered by Swiss railpasses, but not covered by Eurailpasses (though Eurailpasses can get you discounts on certain trips). If your railpass doesn't cover an entire journey, pay for the "uncovered" portion at the station before you board the train.

Check Your Bags: If you're town- or mountain-hopping through Switzerland by train, you can lighten your load by sending your baggage ahead (drop it off at the station, pay 10 SF with ticket or railpass, 40 SF without, maximum 55 pounds). Your bag will show up within 24 hours of your arrival (usually faster) and will be held for five days (after that, you're charged 3 SF/day).

Bike 'n' Rail: Hundreds of local train stations rent bikes for about 30 SF a day and sometimes have easy "pick up here and drop off there" plans. For mixing train and bike travel, ask at stations for information booklets.

Cars

Car Rental

Research car rentals before you go. It's cheaper to arrange most car rentals from the US. Call several companies and look online to compare rates, or arrange a rental through your hometown travel agent. Two reputable companies among many are Auto Europe (www.autoeurope.com) and Europe by Car (www.europebycar .com). For the best deal, rent by the week with unlimited mileage (but for long trips, consider leasing—see below).

Expect to pay about $500 per person (based on 2 people sharing the car) for a small economy car for two weeks with unlimited mileage, including gas, parking, and insurance. I normally rent a small, inexpensive model like a Ford Fiesta. For a bigger, roomier, more powerful but still inexpensive car, move up to a Ford Focus or VW Polo. If you drop your car off early or keep it longer, you'll be credited or charged at a fair, prorated price. Always keep your receipts in case any questions arise about your billing.

Car Insurance Options

When you rent a car, you are liable for a very high deductible, sometimes equal to the entire value of the car. There are various ways you can limit your financial risk in case of an accident. You have three options: Buy Collision Damage Waiver (CDW) coverage from the car-rental company, get coverage through your credit card (free, if your card automatically includes zero-deductible coverage), or buy coverage through Travel Guard.

CDW includes a very high deductible (typically $1,000–1,500). When you pick up the car, you'll be offered the chance to "buy down" the deductible to zero (for $10–30/day; this is often called "super CDW").

If you opt instead for credit-card coverage, there's a catch. You'll technically have to decline all coverage offered by the car-rental company, which means they can place a hold on your card for the full deductible amount. In case of damage, it can be time-consuming to resolve the charges with your credit-card company. Before you decide on this option, quiz your credit-card company about how it works and ask them to explain the worst-case scenario.

Buying CDW insurance (plus "super CDW") is the easier but pricier option. Using the coverage that comes with your credit card saves money, but can involve more hassle.

Finally, you can buy CDW insurance from Travel Guard ($9/day plus a one-time $3 service fee covers you up to $35,000, $250 deductible, tel. 800-826-4919, www.travelguard.com). It's valid throughout Europe, but some car-rental companies refuse to honor it (especially in the Republic of Ireland and in Italy). Oddly, residents of Washington State aren't allowed to buy this coverage.

For more fine print about car-rental insurance, see www.ricksteves.com/cdw.

Leasing

For trips of two and a half weeks or more, consider leasing (which automatically includes CDW-type insurance with no deductible). By technically buying and then selling back the car, you save lots of money on tax and insurance. Leasing provides you a new car with unlimited mileage and a 24-hour emergency assistance program. You can lease for as little as 17 days to as long as six months. Car leases must be arranged from the US. A reliable company offering 17-day lease packages from France for about $1,050 is Europe by Car (more to pick up or drop off within Switzerland; US tel. 800-223-1516, www.europebycar.com).

Driving

You can get anywhere quickly on Switzerland's fine road system,

DRIVING: DISTANCE AND TIME

To Freiburg

GERMANY

To Colmar

To Füssen

m=miles
h=hours

45m-.75h

Basel

95m
1.5h

55m-1h

Zürich

140m-2.75h

40m-2.25h

Appenzell

115m-2.5h

FRANCE

120m-2h

60m-1h

70m-1h

60m-1h

75m-1h

35m-.75h

60m1.25h

To Innsbruck

AUSTRIA

To
Beaune

20m-.5h

Murten

Bern

Luzern

70m-1h

80m

2h

85m-1.5h

75m-1.25h

Chur

40m-1h

35m-.25h

45m-1h

130m-2.75h

60m-1.75h

135m-2.75h

60m-1h

55m-1h

Interlaken

100m
2.75h

To
Bolzano

Lausanne

15m-.5h

90m

1.5h

10m-.25h

Lauter-
brunnen

130m-4.75h

Pontresina

35m-.75h

Montreux

85m-2h

105m

95m-3h

1.75h

85m-2.5h

40m-.25h

80m
3h

Geneva

Täsch

120m-3.5h

75m-2.25h

Tirano

80m-1.5h

50m-1h

Zermatt

Lugano

20m-.5h

85m-1.75h

Chamonix

Note: Drivers must
park in Täsch to
get to Zermatt

50m-1h

100m-2h

To Lyon

Como

FRANCE

Milan

ITALY

Note: Your times may vary based on
traffic, construction, and road conditions

the world's most expensive per mile to build. Drivers pay a one-time, 40-SF fee for a permit to use Swiss autobahns—check to see if your rental car already has one (if not, buy it at the border, gas station, or car rental agency). Anyone caught driving on a Swiss autobahn without this tax sticker is likely to be stopped and fined. Seat belts are required, and two beers under those belts are enough to land you in jail.

For driving in Switzerland, your US driver's license is all that you need. If you're also planning to drive in Austria or Italy, you'll need to get an International Driving Permit (at your local AAA office or online at www.aaa.com—costs $15 plus 2 passport-type photo-booth photos).

Use good local maps and study them before each drive. Learn which exits you need to look out for, which major cities you'll travel toward, where the ruined castles lurk, and so on.

Know the universal road signs (shown in this chapter and explained in charts in most road atlases and at service stations). *Dreieck* (literally, "three corners") means a Y in the road; *Autobahnkreuz* is an intersection. Exits are spaced about 20 miles apart and often have a gas station (*bleifrei* means unleaded), a restaurant, a mini-mart, and sometimes a tourist information desk. Exits and intersections refer to the next major city or the nearest small town. Look at your map and anticipate which town names to watch out for. Know what you're looking for—miss it, and you're long autobahn-gone. When navigating, you'll see *nord*, *süd*, *ost*, *west*, or *mitte*.

To get to the center of a city, follow signs for *Zentrum* or *Stadtmitte*. Ring roads go around a city. For parking, you can pick up the "cardboard clock" (*Parkscheibe*, available free at gas stations, police stations, and *Tabak* shops) and display your arrival time on the clock and put it on the dashboard, so parking attendants can see you've been there less than the posted maximum stay.

Cheap Flights

While trains are usually the best way to connect places that are close together, if your trip extends beyond Switzerland, you may save time and money by flying.

One of the best websites for comparing inexpensive flights is www.skyscanner.net. Other comparison search engines include www.kayak.com, www.mobissimo.com, www.sidestep.com, and www.wegolo.com.

Well-known cheapo airlines in Europe include easyJet (www .easeyjet.com), RyanAir (www.ryanair.com), and BMI Baby (www.bmibaby.com). Those based in Switzerland are Flybaboo (www.flybaboo.com) and Helvetic (www.helvetic.com).

Be aware of the potential drawbacks of flying on the cheap: nonrefundable and nonchangeable tickets, rigid baggage restrictions (and fees if you have more than what's officially allowed), use of airports far outside town, tight schedules that can mean more delays, little in the way of customer assistance if problems arise, and, of course, no frills. To avoid unpleasant surprises, read the small print—especially baggage policies—before you book.

WINTER SPORTS IN SWITZERLAND

One of my favorite Swiss memories happened one winter night on the snowy slopes of the Berner Oberland. My friend Walter (who runs Hotel Mittaghorn, see page 139) and I, warmed by hot chocolate laced with schnapps, decided to go sledding between mountain-high villages. We strapped flashlights to our heads, miner-style, and zoomed through the crisp, moonlit night.

That said, this is a summertime book. I've included plenty of tips on hiking, while mostly ignoring the winter-sports scene. But winter activities are an important part of the Swiss culture (and tourist industry). Here are the basics.

Just a century ago, clever entrepreneurs in the Swiss Alps realized that skiing (which began as a method of wintertime transportation in Scandinavia 4,000 years ago) could be a profitable extension of their resorts' spring and summer seasons. Telemark (cross-country) skiing came first, then alpine (downhill) skiing, and more recently, snowboarding. Generations of Swiss skiers have honed their skills on these slopes. Big names include Erica Hess, Vreni Schneider, Maria Walliser, and Karl Molitor (who currently runs a ski rental shop in Wengen in the Berner Oberland).

You don't have to be a skier or snowboarder to enjoy Switzerland in the winter. Ski resorts offer plenty of other activities, including snowshoeing, sledding, ice skating...and shopping. Or just ride up a lift, rent a chair in the sun, and warm up with a glass of *Pflümli* (plum liqueur).

The winter-sports season begins in early December and runs through Easter. Peak time hits at Christmas and New Year's—during this period, hotel prices in resort towns surpass summer highs.

While Switzerland's resorts vary greatly, they share a rich ski culture, an astounding variety of terrain, relatively mild temperatures (compared to many American destinations), and a lively après-ski scene. For those who can afford them, the best winter activities are in the Berner Oberland (Mürren, Wengen, Grindelwald, and Gstaad); the southern canton of Valais (Zermatt, Saas-Fee, Crans-Montana, and Verbier); and the eastern canton of Graubünden (St. Moritz, Davos, Klosters, and Arosa).

The **Berner Oberland** offers the ultimate variety in terrain and character, as well as great sledding and stellar views (see Gimmelwald and the Berner Oberland chapter). The cliff-hanging town of Mürren is relatively uncrowded, and a good home base for expert skiers in winter, with the 10,000-foot Schilthorn peak as the backbone of its ski area. Across the valley, Wengen offers skiing for all skill levels, fine accommodations, and shopping, with a complex lift system connecting it to Kleine Scheidegg, Männlichen, and Grindelwald. Grindelwald, a little closer to Interlaken, is a little pricier, but has the world's longest sled run, and easy access to more than 100 miles of downhill runs, including the area's best range of beginners' runs (www.grindelwald.com).

The canton of **Valais** ("valley") is known for its excellent wine-making along the banks of the Rhône, but it's also a popular skiing destination. Connected to Italy by several high-mountain passes, Valais is home to Switzerland's best-known sight: the Matterhorn (see Zermatt and the Matterhorn chapter). The area around the Matterhorn, including the villages of Zermatt and Saas-Fee, enjoy a high elevation and good skiing.

The **Graubündener Alps** contain 14 different passes. St. Moritz, situated in the Upper Engadine valley, is so well-known that it's a registered trademark (see Pontresina, Samedan, and St. Moritz chapter). This resort town offers designer boutiques, luxury accommodations, a natural mineral-spring spa...oh, and ski slopes, too. In addition to skiing, winter visitors to St. Moritz play polo and cricket on snow, go bobsledding on natural ice, or try *Skikjöring*—skiing pulled by riderless horses.

Tips: Expect to spend 50–70 SF a day on lift tickets. Prices may get cheaper in the off-peak season (before mid-Dec and after Easter), for multiple-day passes, for Swiss Pass holders, and for seniors, teenagers, and kids (exact age cut-offs vary). Most ski areas offer half-day afternoon passes.

Rental prices are a bit higher than what you'd find in the US. Depending on the fanciness of the gear, you'll pay 40–70 SF for skiing or snowboarding equipment. If you haven't packed ski wear, you'll pay about 40 SF for ski pants, a jacket, and gloves.

Many rental shops in Switzerland belong to the Intersport rental network (www.intersportrent.ch), which sets fairly high standards for its member shops. Shops outside this network can be cheaper, but Intersport shops are generally a safe bet and offer a useful bonus: You can often pick up rental gear at one ski area and drop it at another in the region for no charge (an especially handy option in the Berner Oberland).

Always ask your hotelier if they've arranged any special rental deals through local shops. Rental prices don't vary much (since so many shops are part of the Intersport network), so choose a shop that's close to your hotel or convenient for getting up the mountain.

Swiss ski resorts are deservedly popular, and slopes can get crowded. Peak crowd times are Christmas, New Year's, mid-February to mid-March (when European school holidays hit), and Easter. The Berner Oberland also fills up in mid-January for world-class racing. Start skiing as soon as slopes open—the hordes don't usually arrive until 10:00 or later. This is especially true in swankier resorts, where well-heeled tourists enjoy long nights and short ski days.

For in-depth information on the winter scene, see *Where to Ski and Snowboard Worldwide: The Reuters Guide, Leocha's Ski Snowboard Europe, The Great Skiing & Snowboarding Guide* (Cadogan Guides), and Lonely Planet's Switzerland guidebook.

HOLIDAYS AND FESTIVALS

This is a partial list of holidays and festivals. For more information, contact the Swiss national tourist office (US tel. 877-794-8037, www.myswitzerland.com, info.usa@myswitzerland.com).

Jan 1	New Year's Day
Jan 2	Berchtoldstag (St. Berchtold Day), Harder Potschete (parade), Interlaken
Jan 6	Epiphany (closings)
Mid-Jan	Lauberhorn ski race, Wengen; Inferno ski race, Mürren
Feb	Fasnacht (Carnival), especially celebrated in Luzern, Zürich, and Bern
March 19	Josefstag (St. Joseph's Day)
March–May	International Jazz Festival (www.jazzfestivalbern.ch), Bern
Late March	International Easter Music Festival (1 week, www.lucernefestival.ch), Luzern
Good Friday	(April 10 in 2009)
Easter Monday	(April 13 in 2009)
April 15–16	Sechseläuten (Spring Festival, 2 days, www.sechselaeuten.ch), Zürich
Last Sun in April	Open-Air Parliament (public selection of delegates), Appenzell
May 1	Labor Day
Ascension	(May 1 in 2008, May 21 in 2009)
Pfingstmontag	(Whitmonday, May 12 in 2008, June 1 in 2009)
Frohleichnam	(Corpus Christi, May 22 in 2008, June 11 in 2009)
Early June	Berner Tanztage (dance festival, www.tanztage.ch), Bern
Mid-June–Early July	Zürich Festival (3 weeks, www.zuercher-festspiele.ch)
Late June–early Sept	William Tell Performance (open-air theater, www.tellspiele.ch), Interlaken
Early July	Estival Jazz (free open-air festival, www.estivaljazz.ch), Lugano
Early July	City Festival (www.festivalcite.ch), Lausanne
Mid-July	Montreux International Jazz Festival (2 weeks, www.montreuxjazz.com)
Mid-July	Gurten Open-Air Rock Festival (4 days, www.gurtenfestival.ch), Bern

Appendix

Aug 1	Swiss National Day (parades and fireworks)
Early Aug	Street Parade (city-wide rave, 1 day, www.streetparade.ch), Zürich
Aug 15	Assumption of Mary
Mid-Aug–Mid-Sept	Luzern Festival (4 weeks, classical, www.lucernefestival.ch)
Oct	Festa d'Autunno (food and wine festival, 3 days), Lugano
Nov 1	All Saints' Day
Mid-Nov	Luzern Music Festival (piano, 1 week, www.lucernefestival.ch)
Late Nov	Traditional Onion Market Fair (1 day), Bern
Dec	Christmas fairs
Dec 6	St. Nicholas Day
Dec 8	Immaculate Conception
Dec 25	Christmas
Dec 26	St. Stephen's Day

CONVERSIONS AND CLIMATE

Numbers and Stumblers

- Europeans write a few of their numbers differently than we do. 1 = 1, 4 = 4, 7 = 7.
- In Europe, dates appear as day/month/year, so Christmas is 25/12/09.
- Commas are decimal points and decimals commas. A dollar and a half is 1,50, and there are 5.280 feet in a mile.
- When counting with fingers, start with your thumb. If you hold up your first finger to request one item, you'll probably get two.
- What Americans call the second floor of a building is the first floor in Europe.
- On escalators and moving sidewalks, Europeans keep the left "lane" open for passing. Keep to the right.

Metric Conversions (approximate)

1 foot = 0.3 meter	1 square yard = 0.8 square meter
1 yard = 0.9 meter	1 square mile = 2.6 square kilometers
1 mile = 1.6 kilometers	1 ounce = 28 grams
1 centimeter = 0.4 inch	1 quart = 0.95 liter
1 meter = 39.4 inches	1 kilogram = 2.2 pounds
1 kilometer = 0.62 mile	32°F = 0°C

Climate

The first line is the average daily high; the second line, the average daily low. The third line shows the average number of days without rain. For more detailed weather statistics for destinations in this book (as well as the rest of the world), check www.worldclimate .com.

J	F	M	A	M	J	J	A	S	O	N	D
Bern											
38°	42°	51°	59°	66°	73°	77°	76°	69°	58°	47°	40°
29°	30°	36°	42°	49°	55°	58°	58°	53°	44°	37°	31°
20	19	22	21	20	19	22	20	20	21	19	21

Temperature Conversion: Fahrenheit and Celsius

Europe takes its temperature using the Celsius scale, while we opt for Fahrenheit. For a rough conversion from Celsius to Fahrenheit, double the number and add 30. For weather, remember that 28°C is 82°F—perfect. For health, 37°C is just right.

Essential Packing Checklist

Whether you're traveling for five days or five weeks, here's what you'll need to bring. Remember to pack light to enjoy the sweet freedom of true mobility. Happy travels!

- ❑ 5 shirts
- ❑ 1 sweater or lightweight fleece jacket
- ❑ 2 pairs pants
- ❑ 1 pair shorts
- ❑ 1 swimsuit (women only—men can use shorts)
- ❑ 5 pairs underwear and socks
- ❑ 1 pair shoes
- ❑ 1 rainproof jacket
- ❑ Tie or scarf
- ❑ Money belt
- ❑ Money—your mix of:
  - ❑ Debit card for ATM withdrawals
  - ❑ Credit card
  - ❑ Hard cash in US dollars
- ❑ Documents (and backup photocopies)
- ❑ Passport
- ❑ Airplane ticket
- ❑ Driver's license
- ❑ Student ID and hostel card
- ❑ Railpass/car-rental voucher
- ❑ Insurance details
- ❑ Daypack
- ❑ Sealable plastic baggies
- ❑ Camera and related gear
- ❑ Empty water bottle
- ❑ Wristwatch and alarm clock
- ❑ Earplugs
- ❑ First-aid kit
- ❑ Medicine (labeled)
- ❑ Extra glasses/contacts and prescriptions
- ❑ Sunscreen and sunglasses
- ❑ Toiletries kit
- ❑ Soap
- ❑ Laundry soap (if liquid and carry-on, limit to 3 oz.)
- ❑ Clothesline
- ❑ Small towel
- ❑ Sewing kit
- ❑ Travel information
- ❑ Necessary map(s)
- ❑ Address list (email and mailing addresses)
- ❑ Postcards and photos from home
- ❑ Notepad and pen
- ❑ Journal

Appendix

Hotel Reservation

To: _____   _____
           hotel   *email or fax*

From:_____   _____
           name   *email or fax*

Today's date: _____ /_____ /_____
                  day   *month*   *year*

Dear Hotel _____ ,
Please make this reservation for me:

Name: _____

Total # of people: _____   # of rooms: _____   # of nights: _____

Arriving: _____ /_____ /_____   My time of arrival (24-hr clock): _____
              day *month* *year*   (I will telephone if I will be late)

Departing: ____ /____ /____
               day *month* *year*

Room(s): Single____ Double ____ Twin ____ Triple ____ Quad____

With: Toilet _____ Shower _____ Bath _____ Sink only____

Special needs: View____ Quiet____ Cheapest ____ Ground Floor____

Please email or fax confirmation of my reservation, along with the type of room reserved and the price. Please also inform me of your cancellation policy. After I hear from you, I will quickly send my credit-card information as a deposit to hold the room. Thank you.

_____
Name

_____
Address

_____
City   **State**   **Zip Code**   **Country**

Appendix

Before hoteliers can make your reservation, they want to know the information listed above. You can use this form as the basis for your email, or you can photocopy this page, fill in the information, and send it as a fax (also available online at www.ricksteves.com/reservation).

German Survival Phrases for Switzerland

When using the phonetics, pronounce ī as the long I sound in "light."

Hello.	**Grüetzi.**	**groyt**-see
Do you speak English?	**Sprechen Sie Englisch?**	**shprehkh**-ehn zee **ehng**-lish
Yes. / No.	**Ja. / Nein.**	yah / nīn
I (don't) understand.	**Ich verstehe (nicht).**	ikh fehr-**shtay**-heh (nikht)
Please.	**Bitte.**	**bit**-teh
Thank you.	**Merci.**	**mehr**-see
I'm sorry.	**Es tut mir leid.**	ehs toot meer līt
Excuse me.	**Entschuldigung.**	ehnt-**shool**-dig-oong
(No) problem.	**(Kein) Problem.**	(kīn) proh-**blaym**
(Very) good.	**(Sehr) gut.**	(zehr) goot
Goodbye.	**Ciao.**	chow
one / two	**eins / zwei**	īns / tsvī
three / four	**drei / vier**	drī / feer
five / six	**fünf / sechs**	fewnf / zehkhs
seven / eight	**sieben / acht**	**zee**-behn / ahkht
nine / ten	**neun / zehn**	noyn / tsayn
How much is it?	**Wieviel kostet das?**	**vee**-feel **kohs**-teht dahs
Write it?	**Schreiben?**	**shrī**-behn
Is it free?	**Ist es umsonst?**	ist ehs oom-**zohnst**
Included?	**Inklusive?**	in-kloo-**zee**-veh
Where can I buy / find...?	**Wo kann ich kaufen / finden...?**	voh kahn ikh **kow**-fehn / **fin**-dehn
I'd like /	**Ich hätte gern /**	ikh **heh**-teh gehrn /
We'd like...	**Wir hätten gern...**	veer **heh**-tehn gehrn
...a room.	**...ein Zimmer.**	īn **tsim**-mer
...a ticket to ___.	**...eine Fahrkarte nach ___.**	ī-neh **far**-kar-teh nahkh
Is it possible?	**Ist es möglich?**	ist ehs **mur**-glikh
Where is...?	**Wo ist...?**	voh ist
...the train station	**...der Bahnhof**	dehr **bahn**-hohf
...the bus station	**...der Busbahnhof**	dehr **boos**-bahn-hohf
...tourist information office	**...das Touristeninformationsbüro**	dahs too-**ris**-tehn-in-for-maht-see-**ohns**-bew-roh
...toilet	**...die Toilette**	dee toh-**leh**-teh
men	**Herren**	**hehr**-rehn
women	**Damen**	**dah**-mehn
left / right	**links / rechts**	links / rehkhts
straight	**geradeaus**	geh-**rah**-deh-**ows**
When is this open / closed?	**Um wieviel Uhr ist hier geöffnet / geschlossen?**	oom **vee**-feel oor ist heer geh-**urf**-neht / geh-**shloh**-sehn
At what time?	**Um wieviel Uhr?**	oom **vee**-feel oor
Just a moment.	**Moment.**	moh-**mehnt**
now / soon / later	**jetzt / bald / später**	yehtst / bahld / **shpay**-ter
today / tomorrow	**heute / morgen**	**hoy**-teh / **mor**-gehn

In the Restaurant

I'd like / We'd like...	Ich hätte gern / Wir hätten gern...	ikh heh-teh gehrn / veer heh-tehn gehrn
...a reservation for...	...eine Reservierung für...	ī-neh reh-zer-feer-oong fewr
...a table for one / two.	...einen Tisch für ein / zwei.	ī-nehn tish fewr īn / tsvī
Non-smoking.	Nichtraucher.	nikht-rowkh-er
Is this seat free?	Ist hier frei?	ist heer frī
Menu (in English), please.	Speisekarte (in Englisch), bitte.	shpī-zeh-kar-teh (in ehng-lish) bit-teh
service (not) included	Trinkgeld (nicht) inklusive	trink-gehlt (nikht) in-kloo-zee-veh
cover charge	Eintritt	īn-trit
to go	zum Mitnehmen	tsoom mit-nay-mehn
with / without	mit / ohne	mit / oh-neh
and / or	und / oder	oont / oh-der
menu (of the day)	(Tages-) Karte	(tah-gehs-) kar-teh
set meal for tourists	Touristenmenü	too-ris-tehn-meh-new
specialty of the house	Spezialität des Hauses	shpayt-see-ah-lee-tayt dehs how-zehs
daily special	Tageshit	tah-gehs-hit
appetizers	Vorspeise	for-shpī-zeh
bread	Brot	broht
cheese	Käse	kay-zeh
sandwich	Sandwich	zahnd-vich
soup	Suppe	zup-peh
salad	Salat	zah-laht
meat	Fleisch	flīsh
poultry	Geflügel	geh-flew-gehl
fish	Fisch	fish
seafood	Meeresfrüchte	meh-rehs-frewkh-teh
fruit	Obst	ohpst
vegetables	Gemüse	geh-mew-zeh
dessert	Nachspeise	nahkh-shpī-zeh
mineral water	Mineralwasser	min-eh-rahl-vah-ser
tap water	Leitungswasser	lī-toongs-vah-ser
milk	Milch	milkh
(orange) juice	(Orangen-) Saft	(oh-rahn-zhehn-) zahft
coffee	Kaffee	kah-fay
tea	Tee	tay
wine	Wein	vīn
red / white	rot / weiß	roht / vīs
glass / bottle	Glas / Flasche	glahs / flah-sheh
beer	Bier	beer
Cheers!	Prost!	prohst
More. / Another.	Mehr. / Noch ein.	mehr / nohkh īn
The same.	Das gleiche.	dahs glīkh-eh
Bill, please.	Rechnung, bitte.	rehkh-noong bit-teh
tip	Trinkgeld	trink-gehlt
Delicious!	Lecker!	lehk-er

For more user-friendly German phrases, check out *Rick Steves' German Phrase Book and Dictionary* or *Rick Steves' French, Italian & German Phrase Book.*

French Survival Phrases

When using the phonetics, try to nasalize the n̲ sound.

Good day.	**Bonjour.**	bohn̲-zhoor
Mrs. / Mr.	**Madame / Monsieur**	mah-dahm / muhs-yur
Do you speak English?	**Parlez-vous anglais?**	par-lay-voo ahn̲-glay
Yes. / No.	**Oui. / Non.**	wee / nohn̲
I understand.	**Je comprends.**	zhuh kohn̲-prahn̲
I don't understand.	**Je ne comprends pas.**	zhuh nuh kohn̲-prahn̲ pah
Please.	**S'il vous plaît.**	see voo play
Thank you.	**Merci.**	mehr-see
I'm sorry.	**Désolé.**	day-zoh-lay
Excuse me.	**Pardon.**	par-dohn̲
(No) problem.	**(Pas de) problème.**	(pah duh) proh-blehm
It's good.	**C'est bon.**	say bohn̲
Goodbye.	**Au revoir.**	oh vwahr
one / two	**un / deux**	uhn̲ / duh
three / four	**trois / quatre**	twah / kah-truh
five / six	**cinq / six**	san̲k / sees
seven / eight	**sept / huit**	seht / weet
nine / ten	**neuf / dix**	nuhf / dees
How much is it?	**Combien?**	kohn̲-bee-an̲
Write it?	**Ecrivez?**	ay-kree-vay
Is it free?	**C'est gratuit?**	say grah-twee
Included?	**Inclus?**	an̲-klew
Where can I buy / find...?	**Où puis-je acheter / trouver...?**	oo pwee-zhuh ah-shuh-tay / troo-vay
I'd like / We'd like...	**Je voudrais / Nous voudrions...**	zhuh voo-dray / noo voo-dree-ohn̲
...a room.	**...une chambre.**	ewn shahn̲-bruh
...a ticket to ___.	**...un billet pour ___.**	uhn̲ bee-yay poor
Is it possible?	**C'est possible?**	say poh-see-bluh
Where is...?	**Où est...?**	oo ay
...the train station	**...la gare**	lah gar
...the bus station	**...la gare routière**	lah gar root-yehr
...tourist information	**...l'office du tourisme**	loh-fees dew too-reez-muh
Where are the toilets?	**Où sont les toilettes?**	oo sohn̲ lay twah-leht
men	**hommes**	ohm
women	**dames**	dahm
left / right	**à gauche / à droite**	ah gohsh / ah dwaht
straight	**tout droit**	too dwah
When does this open / close?	**Ça ouvre / ferme à quelle heure?**	sah oo-vruh / fehrm ah kehl ur
At what time?	**À quelle heure?**	ah kehl ur
Just a moment.	**Un moment.**	uhn̲ moh-mahn̲
now / soon / later	**maintenant / bientôt / plus tard**	man̲-tuh-nahn̲ / bee-an̲-toh / plew tar
today / tomorrow	**aujourd'hui / demain**	oh-zhoor-dwee / duh-man̲

Appendix

In the Restaurant

I'd like / We'd like...	**Je voudrais / Nous voudrions...**	zhuh voo-dray / noo voo-dree-oh<u>n</u>
...to reserve...	**...réserver...**	ray-zehr-vay
...a table for one / two.	**...une table pour un / deux.**	ewn tah-bluh poor uh<u>n</u> / duh
Non-smoking.	**Non fumeur.**	noh<u>n</u> few-mur
Is this seat free?	**C'est libre?**	say lee-bruh
The menu (in English), please.	**La carte (en anglais), s'il vous plaît.**	lah kart (ah<u>n</u> ah<u>n</u>-glay) see voo play
service (not) included	**service (non) compris**	sehr-vees (noh<u>n</u>) koh<u>n</u>-pree
to go	**à emporter**	ah ah<u>n</u>-por-tay
with / without	**avec / sans**	ah-vehk / sah<u>n</u>
and / or	**et / ou**	ay / oo
special of the day	**plat du jour**	plah dew zhoor
specialty of the house	**spécialité de la maison**	spay-see-ah-lee-tay duh lah may-zoh<u>n</u>
appetizers	**hors-d'oeuvre**	or-duh-vruh
first course (soup, salad)	**entrée**	ah<u>n</u>-tray
main course (meat, fish)	**plat principal**	plah pra<u>n</u>-see-pahl
bread	**pain**	pa<u>n</u>
cheese	**fromage**	froh-mahzh
sandwich	**sandwich**	sah<u>n</u>d-weech
soup	**soupe**	soop
salad	**salade**	sah-lahd
meat	**viande**	vee-ah<u>n</u>d
chicken	**poulet**	poo-lay
fish	**poisson**	pwah-soh<u>n</u>
seafood	**fruits de mer**	frwee duh mehr
fruit	**fruit**	frwee
vegetables	**légumes**	lay-gewm
dessert	**dessert**	duh-sehr
mineral water	**eau minérale**	oh mee-nay-rahl
tap water	**l'eau du robinet**	loh dew roh-bee-nay
milk	**lait**	lay
(orange) juice	**jus (d'orange)**	zhew (doh-rah<u>n</u>zh)
coffee	**café**	kah-fay
tea	**thé**	tay
wine	**vin**	va<u>n</u>
red / white	**rouge / blanc**	roozh / blah<u>n</u>
glass / bottle	**verre / bouteille**	vehr / boo-teh-ee
beer	**bière**	bee-ehr
Cheers!	**Santé!**	sah<u>n</u>-tay
More. / Another.	**Plus. / Un autre.**	plew / uh<u>n</u> oh-truh
The same.	**La même chose.**	lah mehm shohz
The bill, please.	**L'addition, s'il vous plaît.**	lah-dee-see-oh<u>n</u> see voo play
tip	**pourboire**	poor-bwar
Delicious!	**Délicieux!**	day-lee-see-uh

For more user-friendly French phrases, check out *Rick Steves' French Phrase Book and Dictionary* or *Rick Steves' French, Italian & German Phrase Book*.

Italian Survival Phrases

Good day.	**Buon giorno.**	bwohn JOR-noh
Do you speak English?	**Parla inglese?**	PAR-lah een-GLAY-zay
Yes. / No.	**Si. / No.**	see / noh
I (don't) understand.	**(Non) capisco.**	(nohn) kah-PEES-koh
Please.	**Per favore.**	pehr fah-VOH-ray
Thank you.	**Grazie.**	GRAHT-seeay
I'm sorry.	**Mi dispiace.**	mee dee-speeAH-chay
Excuse me.	**Mi scusi.**	mee SKOO-zee
(No) problem.	**(Non) c'è un problema.**	(nohn) cheh oon proh-BLAY-mah
Good.	**Va bene.**	vah BEHN-ay
Goodbye.	**Arrivederci.**	ah-ree-vay-DEHR-chee
one / two	**uno / due**	OO-noh / DOO-ay
three / four	**tre / quattro**	tray / KWAH-troh
five / six	**cinque / sei**	CHEENG-kway / SEHee
seven / eight	**sette / otto**	SEHT-tay / OT-toh
nine / ten	**nove / dieci**	NOV-ay / deeAY-chee
How much is it?	**Quanto costa?**	KWAHN-toh KOS-tah
Write it?	**Me lo scrive?**	may loh SKREE-vay
Is it free?	**È gratis?**	eh GRAH-tees
Is it included?	**È incluso?**	eh een-KLOO-zoh
Where can I buy / find...?	**Dove posso comprare / trovare...?**	DOH-vay POS-soh kohm-PRAH-ray / troh-VAH-ray
I'd like / We'd like...	**Vorrei / Vorremmo...**	vor-REHee / vor-RAY-moh
...a room.	**...una camera.**	OO-nah KAH-meh-rah
...a ticket to ___.	**...un biglietto per ___.**	oon beel-YEHT-toh pehr
Is it possible?	**È possibile?**	eh poh-SEE-bee-lay
Where is...?	**Dov'è...?**	DOH-veh
...the train station	**...la stazione**	lah staht-seeOH-nay
...the bus station	**...la stazione degli autobus**	lah staht-seeOH-nay DAYL-yee OW-toh-boos
...tourist information	**...informazioni per turisti**	een-for-maht-seeOH-nee pehr too-REE-stee
...the toilet	**...la toilette**	lah twah-LEHT-tay
men	**uomini, signori**	WOH-mee-nee, seen-YOH-ree
women	**donne, signore**	DON-nay, seen-YOH-ray
left / right	**sinistra / destra**	see-NEE-strah / DEHS-trah
straight	**sempre diritto**	SEHM-pray dee-REE-toh
When do you open / close?	**A che ora aprite / chiudete?**	ah kay OH-rah ah-PREE-tay / keeoo-DAY-tay
At what time?	**A che ora?**	ah kay OH-rah
Just a moment.	**Un momento.**	oon moh-MAYN-toh
now / soon / later	**adesso / presto / tardi**	ah-DEHS-soh / PREHS-toh / TAR-dee
today / tomorrow	**oggi / domani**	OH-jee / doh-MAH-nee

In the Restaurant

I'd like...	Vorrei...	vor-REHee
We'd like...	Vorremmo...	vor-RAY-moh
...to reserve...	...prenotare...	pray-noh-TAH-ray
...a table for one / two.	...un tavolo per uno / due.	oon TAH-voh-loh pehr OO-noh / DOO-ay
Non-smoking.	Non fumare.	nohn foo-MAH-ray
Is this seat free?	È libero questo posto?	eh LEE-bay-roh KWEHS-toh POH-stoh
The menu (in English), please.	Il menù (in inglese), per favore.	eel may-NOO (een een-GLAY-zay) pehr fah-VOH-ray
service (not) included	servizio (non) incluso	sehr-VEET-seeoh (nohn) een-KLOO-zoh
cover charge	pane e coperto	PAH-nay ay koh-PEHR-toh
to go	da portar via	dah POR-tar VEE-ah
with / without	con / senza	kohn / SEHN-sah
and / or	e / o	ay / oh
menu (of the day)	menù (del giorno)	may-NOO (dayl JOR-noh)
specialty of the house	specialità della casa	spay-chah-lee-TAH DEHL-lah KAH-zah
first course (pasta, soup)	primo piatto	PREE-moh peeAH-toh
main course (meat, fish)	secondo piatto	say-KOHN-doh peeAH-toh
side dishes	contorni	kohn-TOR-nee
bread	pane	PAH-nay
cheese	formaggio	for-MAH-joh
sandwich	panino	pah-NEE-noh
soup	minestra, zuppa	mee-NEHS-trah, TSOO-pah
salad	insalata	een-sah-LAH-tah
meat	carne	KAR-nay
chicken	pollo	POH-loh
fish	pesce	PEH-shay
seafood	frutti di mare	FROO-tee dee MAH-ray
fruit / vegetables	frutta / legumi	FROO-tah / lay-GOO-mee
dessert	dolci	DOHL-chee
tap water	acqua del rubinetto	AH-kwah dayl roo-bee-NAY-toh
mineral water	acqua minerale	AH-kwah mee-nay-RAH-lay
milk	latte	LAH-tay
(orange) juice	succo (d'arancia)	SOO-koh (dah-RAHN-chah)
coffee / tea	caffè / tè	kah-FEH / teh
wine	vino	VEE-noh
red / white	rosso / bianco	ROH-soh / beeAHN-koh
glass / bottle	bicchiere / bottiglia	bee-keeAY-ray / boh-TEEL-yah
beer	birra	BEE-rah
Cheers!	Cin cin!	cheen cheen
More. / Another.	Ancora un po.' / Un altro.	ahn-KOH-rah oon poh / oon AHL-troh
The same.	Lo stesso.	loh STEHS-soh
The bill, please.	Il conto, per favore.	eel KOHN-toh pehr fah-VOH-ray
tip	mancia	MAHN-chah
Delicious!	Delizioso!	day-leet-seeOH-zoh

For hundreds more pages of survival phrases for your trip to Italy, check out *Rick Steves' Italian Phrase Book & Dictionary* or *Rick Steves' French, Italian, and German Phrase Book.*

INDEX

Travel smart...carry on!

The latest generation of Rick Steves' carry-on travel bags is easily the best—benefiting from two decades of on-the-road attention to what really matters: maximum quality and strength; practical, flexible features; and no unnecessary frills. You won't find a better value anywhere!

Rick Steves' Convertible Carry-On $99.95

Our roomy, versatile 9" x 21" x 14" carry-on has a large 2600 cubic-inch main compartment, plus four outside pockets (small, medium and huge) that are perfect for often-used items. Wish you had even more room to bring home souvenirs? Pull open the full-perimeter expando-zipper and its capacity jumps from 2600 to 3000 cubic inches. When you want to use it as a suitcase or check it as luggage (required when "expanded"), the straps and belt hide away in a zippered compartment in the back. It weighs just 3 lbs.

Rick Steves' Classic Back Door Bag $79.95

This ultra-light (1½ lbs.) version of our Convertible Carry-On features the same 9" x 21" x 14" dimensions and hideaway straps, but does not include a waistbelt or expandability. This is the bag that Rick lives out of for three months a year!

Rick Steves' 21" Roll-Aboard $139.95

Our sturdy 21" Roll-Aboard is rucksack-soft in front, but the rest is lined with a hard ABS-lexan shell to give maximum protection to your belongings. We've spared no expense on moving parts, splurging on an extra-long button-release handle and big, tough inline skate wheels for easy rolling on rough surfaces. It features the same 9" x 21" x 14" carry-on dimensions, pocket configuration and expandability as our Convertible Carry-On—and at 7 lbs. it's the lightest roll-aboard in its class.

Prices and features are subject to change.

For great deals on a wide selection of travel goodies, begin your next trip at the Rick Steves Travel Store!

Visit the Rick Steves Travel Store at
www.ricksteves.com

FREE-SPIRITED TOURS FROM

Rick Steves

Small Groups
Great Guides
No Grumps

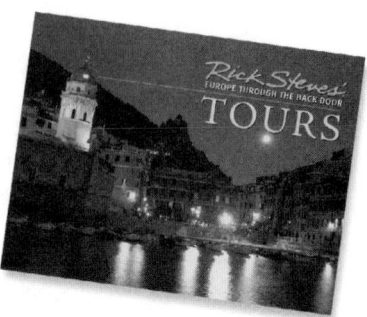

**Best of Europe ■ Family Europe
Italy ■ Village Italy ■ South Italy
Sicily ■ France ■ Eastern Europe
Adriatic ■ Prague ■ Scotland
Britain ■ Ireland ■ Scandinavia
Germany-Austria-Switzerland ■ Spain ■ Turkey ■ Greece
London-Paris ■ Paris ■ Rome ■ Venice-Florence-Rome…and more!**

Looking for a one, two, or three-week tour that's run in the Rick Steves style? Check out Rick Steves' educational, experiential tours of Europe.

Rick's tours are an excellent value compared to "mainstream" tours. Here's a taste of what you'll get…

- **Small groups:** With just 24-28 travelers, you'll go where typical groups of 40-50 can only dream.

- **Big buses:** You'll travel in a full-size 40-50 seat bus, with plenty of empty seats for you to spread out and be comfortable.

- **Great guides:** Our guides are hand-picked by Rick Steves for their wealth of knowledge and giddy enthusiasm for Europe.

- **No tips or kickbacks:** To keep your guide and driver 100% focused on giving you the best travel experience, we pay them well—and prohibit them from accepting tips and merchant kickbacks.

- **All sightseeing:** Your tour price includes all group sightseeing, with no hidden extra charges.

- **Central hotels:** You'll stay in Rick's favorite small, characteristic, locally-run hotels in the center of each city, within walking distance of the sights you came to see.

- **Visit www.ricksteves.com:** You'll find all our latest itineraries, dates and prices, be able to reserve online, and request a free copy of our Rick Steves Tour Experience DVD!

Start your trip at
www.ricksteves.com

Rick Steves' website is packed with over 3,000 pages of timely travel information. It's also your gateway to getting FREE monthly travel news from Rick—and more!

Free Monthly Travel News

Fresh articles on Europe's most interesting destinations and happenings. Rick will even send you an email every month (often direct from Europe) with his latest discoveries!

Timely Travel Tips

Rick Steves' best money-and-stress-saving tips on trip planning, packing, transportation, hotels, health, safety, finances, hurdling the language barrier…and more.

Travelers' Graffiti Wall

Candid advice and opinions from thousands of travelers on everything listed above, plus whatever topics are hot at the moment (discount flights, politics, nude beaches, scams…you name it).

Rick's Guide to Eurail Passes

The clearest, most comprehensive guide to the confusing array of railpass options out there, and how to choo-choose the railpass that best fits your itinerary and budget.

Great Gear at Our Travel Store

In the past year alone, more than 50,000 travelers have enjoyed great online deals on Rick's guidebooks, maps, DVDs—and his custom-designed carry-on bags, day packs, and light-packing accessories.

Rick Steves Tours

This year, 12,000 lucky travelers will explore Europe on a Rick Steves tour. Learn about our 28 different one- to three-week itineraries, read uncensored feedback from our tour alums, and get our free Tour Experience DVD.

Rick on TV, Radio and Podcasts

Read the scripts from the popular Rick Steves' Europe TV series, and listen to or download your choice of over 100 hours of our Travel with Rick Steves radio show.

Respect for Your Privacy

Whether you buy something from us or subscribe to Rick's monthly Travel News emails, we'll never share your name or email address with anyone else. You won't be spammed!

Have fun raising your Travel I.Q. at
www.ricksteves.com

Rick Steves

More *Savvy*. More *Surprising*. More *Fun*.

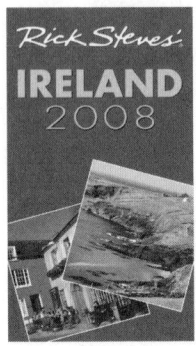

COUNTRY GUIDES

Croatia & Slovenia
England
France
Germany & Austria
Great Britain
Ireland
Italy
Portugal
Scandinavia
Spain
Switzerland

CITY GUIDES

Amsterdam, Bruges & Brussels
Florence & Tuscany
Istanbul
London
Paris
Prague & The Czech Republic
Provence & The French Riviera
Rome
Venice

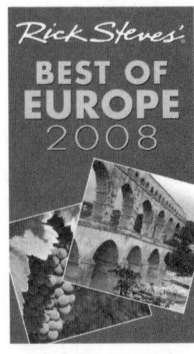

BEST OF GUIDES

Eastern Europe
Best of Europe

As the #1 authority on European travel, Rick gives you inside information on what to visit, where to stay, and how to get there—economically and hassle-free.

www.ricksteves.com

PHRASE BOOKS & DICTIONARIES

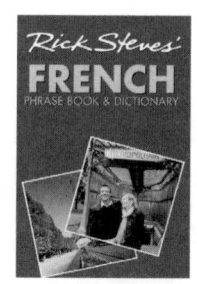

French
French, Italian & German
German
Italian
Portuguese
Spanish

MORE EUROPE FROM RICK STEVES

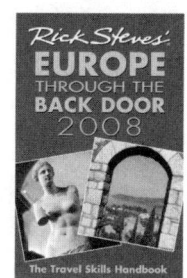

Europe 101
Europe Through the Back Door
Postcards from Europe

RICK STEVES' EUROPE DVDs

All 70 Shows 2000–2007
Britain
Eastern Europe
France & Benelux

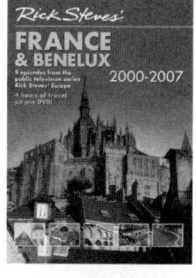

Germany, The Swiss Alps & Travel Skills
Ireland
Italy
Spain & Portugal

PLANNING MAPS

Britain & Ireland
Europe
France

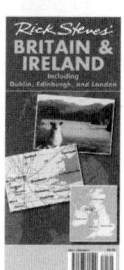

Germany, Austria & Switzerland
Italy
Spain & Portugal

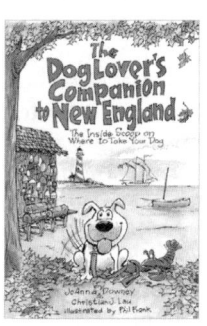

CREDITS

To help update this book, Rick relied on…

Researcher

Rich Earl

Rich loves all things Swiss, except the stinky cheese. When he's not yodeling from mountain tops, eating Swiss chocolate, and searching for the best *Rösti,* he's exploring the rest of Europe, assisting on Rick Steves' tours, or working in the Rail and Consulting departments at Europe through the Back Door.

Contributor

Gene Openshaw

Gene is the co-author of seven Rick Steves books. For this book, he wrote material on art, history, and contemporary culture. When he's not traveling, Gene enjoys composing music, recovering from his 1973 trip to Europe with Rick, and living everyday life with his daughter.

IMAGES

Location	Photographer
Front color matter: Gimmelwald	Dominic Bonucelli
Front color matter: Lauterbrunnen Valley	David C. Hoerlein
Zürich: View of Zürich from Limmat River	Cameron Hewitt
Luzern and Central Switzerland: Chapel Bridge	Cameron Hewitt
Bern and Murten: Bern Overview	Rick Steves
Gimmelwald and the Berner Oberland: Gimmelwald	Dominic Bonucelli
Zermatt and the Matterhorn: The Matterhorn	Susana Minich
Appenzell: Traditional Appenzell Gables	David C. Hoerlein
Lake Geneva and French Switzerland: Château Chillon	Cameron Hewitt
Lugano: Lake Lugano	Rick Steves
Pontresina, Samedan, and St. Moritz: Pontresina	Susana Minich
Scenic Rail Journeys: Bernina Express	Rick Steves

Rick Steves' Guidebook Series

Country Guides

Rick Steves' Best of Europe
Rick Steves' Croatia & Slovenia
Rick Steves' Eastern Europe
Rick Steves' England
Rick Steves' France
Rick Steves' Germany & Austria
Rick Steves' Great Britain
Rick Steves' Ireland
Rick Steves' Italy
Rick Steves' Portugal
Rick Steves' Scandinavia
Rick Steves' Spain
Rick Steves' Switzerland

City and Regional Guides

Rick Steves' Amsterdam, Bruges & Brussels
Rick Steves' Florence & Tuscany
Rick Steves' Istanbul
Rick Steves' London
Rick Steves' Paris
Rick Steves' Prague & the Czech Republic
Rick Steves' Provence & the French Riviera
Rick Steves' Rome
Rick Steves' Venice

Rick Steves' Phrase Books

French
German
Italian
Spanish
Portuguese
French/Italian/German

Other Books

Rick Steves' Europe Through the Back Door
Rick Steves' Europe 101: History and Art for the Traveler
Rick Steves' Postcards from Europe
Rick Steves' European Christmas

(Avalon Travel)

Avalon Travel
a member of the Perseus Books Group
1700 Fourth Street
Berkeley, CA 94710, USA

Printed in the United States of America by Worzalla
Second printing October 2008
ISBN (10) 1-56691-969-X
ISBN (13) 978-1-56691-969-2
ISSN 1552-1818

Thanks to Cameron Hewitt for writing the original information on Luzern, Zermatt, and
the Glacier Express. And thank you to my wife, Anne, for her support.

For the latest on Rick's lectures, guidebooks, tours, public radio show, and public television
series, contact Europe Through the Back Door, Box 2009, Edmonds, WA 98020, tel.
425/771-8303, fax 425/771-0833, www.ricksteves.com, rick@ricksteves.com.

Europe Through the Back Door Managing Editor: Risa Laib
ETBD Editors: Gretchen Strauch, Cameron Hewitt (Senior Editor)
Avalon Travel Senior Editor & Series Manager: Madhu Prasher
Avalon Travel Project Editor: Kelly Lydick
Avalon Travel Editorial Assistant: Jamie Andrade
Copy Editor: Judith Brown
Proofreader: Janet Walden
Indexer: Claire Splan
Research Assistance: Rich Earl, Aaron Harting
Production & Typesetting: McGuire Barber Design
Cover Design: Kari Gim, Laura Mazer
Cover Art Manager: Laura VanDeventer
Maps & Graphics: David C. Hoerlein, Lauren Mills, Laura VanDeventer, Barb Geisler,
  Mike Morgenfeld, Chris Marciewicz, Brice Ticen, Lohnes and Wright, Albert Angulo,
  Hank Evans
Photography: Cameron Hewitt, David C. Hoerlein, Rick Steves, Susana Minich, Dominic
  Bonucelli
Front cover photo: © Dominic Bonuccelli
Front matter color photos: p. i, Gimmelwald © Dominic Bonuccelli; p. iv, Lauterbrunnen
  Valley © David C. Hoerlein